Urban Sociology in Canada

Urban Sociology in Canada

PETER McGAHAN
Department of Sociology
University of New Brunswick, Fredericton

Butterworths
Toronto

Urban Sociology in Canada
© 1982 Butterworth & Co. (Canada) Ltd.

Printed and bound in Canada
54321   123456789/8

Canadian Cataloguing in Publication Data

McGahan, Peter.
Urban Sociology in Canada

Bibliography: p. 349
Includes index.
ISBN 0-409-84819-0

1. Sociology, Urban.   2. Urbanization – Canada.
3. City and town life – Canada.   I. Title.

HT127.M32   307.7'6'0971   C82-094201-4

The Butterworth Group of Companies

Canada:
Butterworth & Co. (Canada) Ltd., Toronto and Vancouver

United Kingdom:
Butterworth & Co. (Publishers) Ltd., London

Australia:
Butterworths Pty. Ltd., Sydney

New Zealand:
Butterworths of New Zealand Ltd., Wellington

South Africa:
Butterworth & Co. (South Africa) Ltd., Durban

United States:
Butterworth (Publishers) Inc., Boston
Butterworth (Legal Publishers) Inc., Seattle
Mason Publishing Company, St. Paul

Contents

v

Acknowledgments

Before archaeology had become a well-established profession, a handful of men from a variety of backgrounds explored the remains of Mayan settlements and cities in southern Mexico, Guatemala, and Honduras. Antonio del Rio, John Lloyd Stephens, Edward H. Thompson, and their fellow pioneers in the late eighteenth through the twentieth centuries sought to explain and describe the structure of Palenque, Copan, Tzak Pokoma, and other centres of this remarkable civilization. Their methods of investigation were often inadequate, the importance of objectivity and careful analysis of the evidence often ignored; yet they showed a deep sensitivity to the achievements of the Mayans. As they cleared the ruins of vegetation, as they sketched the myriad decorations, as they measured the scale of these sites, they were struck with a sense of wonder at the complexity and richness of such ancient cities.

Even a casual survey of their reports easily reawakens that sense among us as well. Although they are closer at hand and so all-embracing, Canadian urban communities in their structure, diversity, and pattern of change are as "wondrous"—as deserving of our sense of wonder—as are the Mayan remains in the tropical forests of Mesoamerica. Just as more systematic archaeological research on these ruins has evolved from that initial sentiment, so too does urban sociology attempt to cultivate the sense of wonder and direct it in the quest for a richer understanding of the urban phenomenon. This text seeks to review some of the fruits of that quest.

I am deeply indebted to many teachers, colleagues, and students for having stimulated, cultivated, and sustained my own sense of wonder at the structure of urban society. Dr. Mary G. Powers of Fordham University introduced me to urban sociology a number of years ago. Continued contact with Douglas Pullman, Noel Iverson, Nels Anderson, and the other members of my department at the University of New Brunswick has been a source of deep intellectual satisfaction to me. I have learned much, as well, from the countless opportunities I have had over the years to introduce both undergraduate and graduate students to the challenging tasks involved in understanding urban processes. I appreciate greatly Roy Bowles' criticisms of this work. His comments were most constructive. I am grateful for the assistance of the staff of Butterworth and Co. (Canada). Kathy Johnson rendered indispensable aid in the editing of the manuscript. Most important of all Beth McGahan has cheerfully endured the sacrifices we both have made during the preparation of this text; in her case, "acknowledgment" is indeed an inadequate term.

ix

Introduction

THE URBAN TRANSFORMATION

In strictly demographic terms *urbanization* represents a process of population concentration involving "the multiplication of points of concentration and the increase in size of individual concentrations" (Tisdale, 1942: 311). Cities and smaller urban centres are products of such a process. Prior to the nineteenth century, the process of urban development was sporadic. What has been termed the "first urban revolution" occurred between 6000 and 5000 B.C. in the areas around the Nile, the Tigris-Euphrates, and the Indus. A fascinating experiment in community structure transformed a series of relatively isolated agricultural villages into more extensive trade centres. Improvements in methods of irrigation, cultivation, and transportation promoted the rise of cities by permitting a surplus of food to be collected to support the urban residents. A centralized social and economic organization evolved to exploit that surplus without challenge. This encouraged internal specialization of manufacture and craft. Exchange relations between centres also solidified (Childe, 1951; Sjoberg, 1973).

Early cities, however, were limited in size. The primitive state of medicine and industry, the labour-intensive character of agriculture, and the rigid social stratification prohibited any sustained process of urban growth such as we have witnessed in the past century. This first urban revolution gave man some experience with a relatively dense pattern of settlement, but it did not give him urbanization in today's sense of a high proportion of population concentrated in cities.

Although large urban complexes such as Rome and Constantinople existed in earlier centuries, it was not until the 1800s that urban growth emerged as a significant process of social change in the Western world. It accompanied, and was stimulated by, the Industrial Revolution. Economic opportunities created by the expansion of the factory systems within cities generated vast rural-urban migration streams (Weber, 1963 ed.: 213). Advances in sanitation, medicine, industrialized agriculture, and more complex systems of transportation and communication permitted the support of an increasingly concentrated population.

The demographic dimensions of this transformation are truly staggering. For example, in 1800 less than 3 percent of the world's population lived in

1

cities of 20,000 or more; by the mid-twentieth century that proportion had risen to 20 percent—a much faster rate of increase than at any previous time in history. Similarly, only fifty cities with populations of 100,000 or more existed in 1800; by 1950 that number had grown to 900, and it has increased ever since (Davis, 1955).

By 1970 the world's population stood at approximately 3.6 billion, of which 39 percent were urban residents. Indeed, almost one-fourth lived in cities of 100,000 or more, and approximately one-third in places of 20,000 or more. The size of place in which the "average person" (taken in the demographic sense) in the world in 1970 lived was over 600,000 (Davis, 1972). The period 1950-1970 was one of rapid urban population growth:

Between 1950 and 1970 nearly 700 million were added to the earth's urban inhabitants. This was almost equal to the total in 1950; in other words, the 1950-1970 rate of increase is such that it doubles the earth's urban population every 20.3 years. If that rate is continued, the population classified as urban will equal the present *total* population of the world in 29 years (Davis, 1972: 54-55).

More dramatically, if this trend is not slowed, the world will be 100 percent urban by the year 2031, at which point the vast majority of people will be living in cities of 100,000 or more (Davis, 1972: 47-49).

The movement toward large urban scale is unmistakable. The proportion of the world's population living in cities of 1,000,000 or more doubled between 1950 and 1970. Similarly, the average size of urban place has been consistently increasing. Researchers predict that by the end of this century the number of cities of 100,000 or more will have doubled. The year 2000 will see at least three cities with populations of more than 64 million. The remaining decades of this century will show a 1700 percent increase in the number of cities in the 12,800,000+ size category. In 1950 only a small proportion (3.2 percent) of the world's total population lived in cities of 2.6 million or more; by the year

Table 1:   Proportion Urban in Continental Areas of the World:
            1950, 1960, and 1970

	1950	1960	1970
Australia-New Zealand	70.0	77.7	84.3
Northern America	63.8	69.7	75.1
Europe	53.4	58.1	63.0
U.S.S.R	42.5	50.1	62.3
Latin America	40.3	47.5	54.4
Asia	15.4	20.4	25.4
Africa	13.8	17.7	21.8
Oceania	4.9	6.0	7.8

Adapted from Davis, 1972.

2000 this proportion will have increased to one-fifth. In short, "One should not speak simply of the 'urbanization' of the world's population. One should speak, instead, of the 'metropolitanization' of the population" (Davis, 1972: 159).

Despite this worldwide trend, there are still some striking differences among regions and nations (see Table 1). Levels of urbanization are highest in Australia, New Zealand, and North America, and lowest in the under-developed countries of Asia and Africa. These discrepancies, however, mask the much higher rates of urban increase which the latter continents have been experiencing in recent decades (Hauser, 1957; Davis, 1972). The urban transformation is becoming truly a universal process.

THE CANADIAN URBAN TRANSFORMATION

Canada, like her neighbour to the south, has certainly been one of the leading participants in this urban evolution, having achieved in the years after World War II the highest rate of urban growth of any Western industrial society (Gertley and Crowley, 1977: 41; Ray, 1976: 24). In 1971 three-fourths (76.1 percent) of her population resided in urban areas; only a very small proportion (6 percent) lived on farms (Statistics Canada, 1971). The magnitude of this population redistribution can be best appreciated when it is recalled that in 1871 Canada was almost entirely a rural society—80 percent of her population lived outside urban centres (Kalback and McVey, 1971: 70). Her current level of urbanization parallels that found in the U.S. Canada, however, contains proportionately more people in areas of 100,000 or more, and has achieved a more rapid rate of increase in this concentration over the past several decades (Stone, 1967: 16).

THE CENSUS DEFINITION OF "URBAN"

Prior to 1951 the Canadian census definition of urban was restricted to the legal municipal status of incorporation. "With the rapid growth of suburbs, i.e., built-up areas outside a city's boundaries but still an integral part of the city, legal status alone became an inadequate criterion. Population density, i.e., population per square mile, became an increasingly important component of the urban classification" (Kralt, 1976: 3).

In the 1971 census an urban resident was defined as one who lived in either:

1. incorporated cities, towns, or villages with a population of 1,000 or over;

2. unincorporated places of 1,000 or more having a population density of at least 1,000 per square mile;

3. the built-up fringes of (1) and (2) having a minimum population of at least 1,000 and a population density of at least 1,000 per square mile.

In 1931 and 1941 Canadian metropolitan areas were categorized as "Greater Cities of Canada." This label was changed in 1951 to "Census Metropolitan Areas." In the 1971 census metropolitan areas were delimited according to the following criteria:

1. a principal city that had at least 50,000 inhabitants;

2. an urbanized core with a density of at least 1,000 population per square mile;

3. a labour force outside the central city of which at least 70 percent were engaged in non-agricultural activities;

4. a total population of at least 100,000. If the population of the total metropolitan area was less than 100,000 it was classified not as a Census Metropolitan Area (CMA) but rather as a Census Agglomeration (CA) (Kralt, 1976: 12, 29).

Although important urban centres existed in Canada in the early nineteenth century, only in the 1890s and subsequent decades did the level of urbanization begin to rise significantly (see Figure 1). During the governments of Laurier and Borden, Canada abandoned its position as primarily a rural-agricultural society through the mass immigration, wheat production, and industrial expansion which characterized this most critical period in its history (Brown and Cook, 1974). As the manufacturing and tertiary sectors of the economy increasingly developed, the degree of urban concentration continued to intensify. One important reflection of this is the current dominance of the metropolitan community. Today there are twenty-three metropolitan areas, within which live more than half (55.1 percent in 1971) of the nation's total population—thus reflecting, as we have just seen, a worldwide trend. Three of these areas (Montreal, Toronto, and Vancouver) each contain more than one million residents (Canada Year Book, 1973: 211; Hill, 1976: 4). In general, although small urban complexes are more numerous than larger ones, the latter are attracting an increasingly greater proportion of the total population (Stone, 1967: 77). (See Table 2.) This again reflects centralization of employment opportunities, improvements in transportation and communication facilities, and the general decline in the viability of the rural economy.

Table 2 reveals that in 1971 more than 4 million Canadians lived in urban centres each with a population of less than 30,000. Many of these are single-industry communities (Lucas, 1971). Although physically isolated from large metropolitan centres, their resource extraction functions link them closely to the national economy and the national urban system. There are today more than 800 such communities, containing one-fourth of the total non-metropolitan population (Ray and Roberge, 1981: 16).

Figure 1: Per Cent of Urban Population of Canada and Provinces, 1851-1971

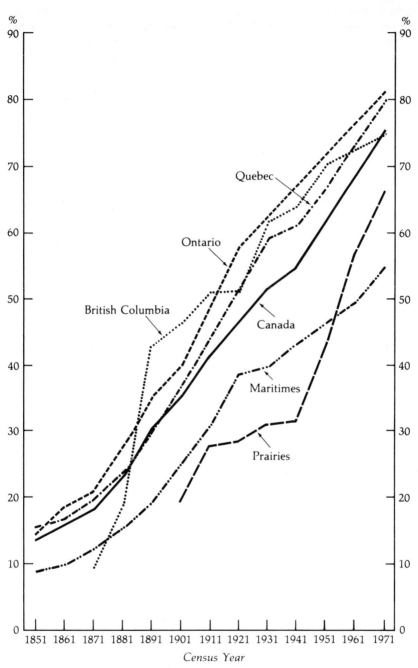

Census Year

From Stone and Siggner, 1974.

Despite its overall high national level, one important characteristic of Canadian urbanization is its regional variation, reflecting in part differences between the provinces in economic development (see Table 3). Approximately four-fifths of the populations of Ontario and Quebec were recorded as urban in 1971, followed by about three-fourths of those of British Columbia and Alberta. Most of the other provinces showed much lower proportions urban (Canada Year Book, 1973: 211; Kralt, 1976: 9-10, 12). Such regional differences appeared in past decades as well. Since 1881 Ontario, Quebec, and British Columbia consistently maintained the highest levels of urban concentration.

Table 2:   Distribution of Population in Urban Areas of 1,000 Persons and Over, by Size of Urban Centres, by Census Years Since 1871

Census year		1,000-4,999	5,000-29,999	30,000-99,999	100,000 and over[1]	Total urban
1971	N	1,640,745	2,593,280	1,930,590	10,246,170	16,410,785
	%	10.0	15.8	11.8	62.4	100.0
1961	N	1,595,070	1,641,406	1,646,703	8,400,859	13,971,937
	%	11.5	12.7	11.8	64.0	100.0
1951	N	1,166,584	1,198,365	1,230,731	5,221,957	8,817,637
	%	13.2	13.6	14.0	59.2	100.0
1941	N	909,728	1,370,375	928,367	2,645,133	5,853,603
	%	15.5	23.4	15.9	45.2	100.0
1931	N	430,742	1,305,304	696,680	2,328,175	5,160,901
	%	16.1	25.3	13.5	45.1	100.0
1921	N	764,836	1,057,965	495,566	1,658,697	3,977,064
	%	19.1	26.6	12.5	41.8	100.0
1911	N	655,097	782,771	488,748	1,080,960	3,007,576
	%	21.8	26.0	16.3	35.9	100.0
1901	N	545,037	503,187	343,266	475,770	1,867,260
	%	29.2	26.9	18.4	25.5	100.0
1891[2]	N	427,310	390,670	224,760	397,865	1,440,605
	%	29.7	27.1	15.6	27.6	100.0
1881[2]	N	[3]	298,371	220,922	140,747	[3]
	%	—	—	—	—	—
1871[2]	N	[3]	228,354	115,791	107,225	[3]
	%	—	—	—	—	—

1. Includes Census Metropolitan Areas since 1951; the incorporated places included in the CMA total do not show in the preceding three columns for 1951 and 1961.
2. Yukon and the Northwest Territories excluded.
3. Centres of 1,000-4,999 estimated: 1881, 316,000; 1871, 196,000.

Sources: 1971 Census of Canada; 1961 Census of Canada; Urquhart and Buckley, *Historical Statistics*, Series A20-24.

Table 3: Percent of Population Urban, Canada and Provinces, 1851-1971

	1851	1861	1871	1881	1891	1901	1911	1921	1931	1941	1951	1961	1971
Canada (excl. Newfoundland)	13.1	15.8	18.3	23.3	29.8	34.9	41.8	47.4	52.5	55.7	62.9	70.2	76.6
Canada (incl. Newfoundland)	—	—	—	—	—	—	—	—	—	—	62.4	69.7	76.1
Newfoundland	—	—	—	—	—	—	—	—	—	—	43.3	50.7	57.2
Prince Edward Island	—	9.3	9.4	10.5	13.1	14.5	16.0	18.8	19.5	22.1	25.1	32.4	38.3
Nova Scotia	7.5	7.6	8.3	14.7	19.4	27.7	36.7	44.8	46.6	52.0	54.5	54.3	56.7
New Brunswick	14.0	13.1	17.6	17.6	19.9	23.1	26.7	35.2	35.4	38.7	42.8	46.5	56.9
Quebec	14.9	16.6	19.9	23.8	28.6	36.1	44.5	51.8	59.5	61.2	66.8	74.3	80.6
Ontario	14.0	18.5	20.6	27.1	35.0	40.3	49.5	58.8	63.1	67.5	72.5	77.3	82.4
Manitoba	—	—	—	14.9	23.3	24.9	39.3	41.5	45.2	45.7	56.0	63.9	69.5
Saskatchewan	—	—	—	—	—	6.1	16.1	16.8	20.3	21.3	30.4	43.0	53.0
Alberta	—	—	—	—	—	16.2	29.4	30.7	31.8	31.9	47.6	63.3	73.5
British Columbia	—	—	9.0	18.3	42.6	46.4	50.9	50.9	62.3	64.0	68.6	72.6	75.7

From D. Michael Ray, ed., *Canadian Urban Trends* Vol. I © Ministry of Supply and Services Canada, 1976. Reprinted by permission of Copp Clark Pitman, Publishers.

The gap between them and the Prairies has, however, narrowed in recent years as the latter experienced greater industrialization:

> . . . particularly in Alberta where increases in business activity to service the burgeoning oil and natural gas industry stimulated urban areas during the 1950s and the 1960s. By 1911, the proportion of Alberta's population residing in urban areas approached that of British Columbia, while in Saskatchewan once the most rural of Canada's provinces, more than half of the people lived in a city or town (Gertler and Crowley, 1977: 47).

In contrast, that gap has widened with respect to the Maritimes (Stone, 1967: 37). That area, unlike other regions of the country, actually showed some increase between 1961 and 1971 in the proportion of the urban population concentrated in the smallest centres (1,000-9,999) (Kralt, 1976).

Despite these variations, at least half the population in all provinces except Prince Edward Island and the Northwest Territories now reside in urban areas, thus validating Canada's status as an urban nation. No doubt in the decades to come this pattern of concentration will continue.

This is not, however, to deny the continued presence of relatively large numbers of people in smaller communities, reflecting partly the importance of Canadian resource economies.

URBAN SOCIOLOGY AS A FIELD OF STUDY

The development of urbanization as a dominant process of both demographic and social change represents one fundamental aspect of the modern age. Urban sociology attempts systematically to describe and analyze this phenomenon. It is therefore of central importance in achieving a more complete understanding of contemporary societies.

Character of the Field

Throughout the history of its development urban sociology has manifested several interesting characteristics:

Eclecticism. More than twenty years ago Noel Gist (1957) underlined the eclectic character of urban sociology. One still finds a variety of theoretical perspectives, methodologies, and research interests represented among those examining urbanization and urban structure. While interpenetration of varying concerns and interpretations stimulates fascinating comparisons, it renders the overall integration of the field difficult to achieve.

Lack of distinctiveness. This eclecticism is rooted in a more fundamental difficulty. Urban sociology suffers from something of an "identity crisis." The field lacks clearly definable boundaries. In a society that has achieved only a low level of urbanization, the study of the city has an identifiable focus—with attention given to rural-urban comparisons and to the role of the city as a transformer of "ruralities" (or rural social and cultural attributes). In a highly urban society, however, urban sociology merges with general sociology, and its specific interests are included within other sociological specialties (Gutman and Popenoe, 1970). Consequently, as an increasing number of societies experience structural and demographic transformation, the distinctions between urban and general sociology are less obvious. Attempts are made to avoid this by redefining urban sociology in a restricted fashion. For example, in a recent text Thomlinson (1969: vii) proposed that urban *ecology* should be the only remaining "legitimate intellectual rationale for the continuance of urban sociology as a distinct field." Not uncommonly, urban researchers avoid confronting this issue directly, and, instead, concentrate on developing sets of theoretically integrated propositions within the particular area they are working—a strategy which often takes them into the realm of various specialties of sociology. The eclectic character of the field is thus reinforced.

Despite these features it is possible to organize the different concerns and areas of interest within urban sociology.

Aims and Organization of Urban Sociology

When a tourist travels to a foreign land, he frequently relies on a guide book. It contains descriptions of interesting and unusual existing sites; more mundane and abstruse features are omitted in response to his limited time and sense of immediate relevance.

An introductory text is not unlike such a guide. It too isolates some of the more significant areas of interest in a particular field and, by definition, must necessarily be selective and relatively restricted in scope. Its goal is simply to establish the means through which a "tour" of the academic discipline can be conducted. It will undoubtedly reflect the interests and biases of the organizer. Certain issues, which from another perspective may be defined as highly critical, become de-emphasized or perhaps totally ignored. The ultimate judgment of the appropriateness of such a selective "tour," it is clear, must be determined by how successful the whole journey is both in arousing some critical understanding of the strengths and weaknesses of the particular field, and in directing more intense study to specific areas.

That "tour" of urban sociology which this text will provide derives directly from the conception of the city as a socio-spatial system. The aim of urban sociology is to analyze the evolution and structure of the urban community as a socio-spatial system. As the following chart indicates, this task involves the analysis of the city's social and ecological organization from both a *dynamic* and *structural* perspective. The dynamic focus lays stress on the process of creation of the socio-spatial system; the structural emphasizes the regularized patterns within the resultant socio-spatial order.

In terms of urban social organization considered dynamically, urban sociology analyzes the process of entrance to the urban system. This includes the study of rural-urban migration and urban immigration—the preconditions for, and social consequences of, this mobility among groups, families, and individuals. This concern of urban sociology is of urbanization as an assimilation process. Structurally, the study of urban social organization entails investigation of the fate of the local community and neighbourhood in the urban system as well as the shape its social institutions—such as kinship and political units—assume. This focus can also be defined as the study of "urbanism"—of the social life found within cities.

CONCERNS AND AREAS OF URBAN SOCIOLOGY AS A FIELD OF STUDY

	Social organization	Ecological organization
Dynamic focus	Process of entrance to the urban system (urbanization as an assimilation process)	Growth of cities and concentration of population in cities (urbanization as a demographic and organizational process)
Structural focus	Fate of local community and social institutions in the urban system (urbanism)	Interrelation between urban communities to form a wider system; Internal spatial distribution of population and land use types

---

An equally important branch of urban sociology is the investigation of urban ecological organization. From a dynamic perspective this involves analysis of the growth of cities and of the increasing concentration of the population in urban communities. As we have noted earlier, this study is of urbanization considered as a demographic and organizational process. On a less general level, attention is also given to the factors promoting development of specific types of population centres, ranging from the one-industry town to the megalopolis. The structural analysis of ecological organization entails study of the interrelation between urban communities to form a wider system, such as occurs with the emergence of a metropolitan region and a national system of cities. Within each city, the structural focus also examines the patterns of spatial distribution of population and land-use types. The concern here, for example, is with residential segregation among social classes and ethnic groups.

Two additional points must be emphasized with respect to this "charting" of the field of urban sociology. First, this discipline studies the urban community as an integrated socio-spatial system. That is, a primary task is to examine the interrelation of the city's social and ecological organization—how social and spatial structures reflect and influence each other. Second, the history of the North American city in the twentieth century is one of increasing governmental intervention in urban processes. Urban sociology seeks to describe and explain the social and ecological consequences of such a trend. Administrative efforts to shape the social and spatial structures of cities through formal planning techniques and programs represent a central characteristic of contemporary urban life which urban sociologists have not ignored.

Following a review of the classical theoretical foundations of urban sociology in Part One, this text will examine each of the above divisions as they have developed within the Canadian urban scene. In short, we shall explore the nature of the Canadian urban community as a socio-spatial system.

A central goal of this text is to avoid defining urban sociology in a restricted fashion. Rather than diminish the eclectic character of the field, it seeks to give at least partial recognition to the variety of theoretical strategies and to analysis of a diversity of research problems. Any sense of what urban sociology is about can only be gained by selectively tracing through the fruits of such variety.

Part One

The Classical Foundations of Urban Sociology

The contemporary study of the urban community as a socio-spatial system has been shaped greatly by two fundamental perspectives which represent the classical foundations of urban sociology. In the following two chapters we shall briefly review the development of the classical urban typological and ecological frameworks. This will provide us with a general background to the study of urban sociology as well as an introduction to the concepts and research foci of this discipline.

Chapter 1

The Classical
Typological Perspective

A fundamental paradigm or explanatory framework which exercised great influence in the study of the city was the typological perspective (Bernard, 1973). It attempted to grasp the nature of urban social organization by contrasting it with the non-urban. It assumed that the urban is qualitatively distinct from the non-urban. In short, the urban and non-urban represent distinct social types.

This perspective was initially developed by European social theorists such as Toennies, Durkheim, and Simmel in their efforts to articulate the dramatic changes they witnessed occurring in late nineteenth- and early twentieth-century Western industrial society. Their urban theories profoundly influenced the "Chicago School" of urban sociology which emerged in the 1920s and 1930s. Louis Wirth's conception of urbanism as a way of life reflected that influence, as did Redfield's elaboration of the folk-urban typology and subsequent efforts by others to demonstrate empirically rural-urban differences.

In this chapter we shall examine each of these manifestations of the typological perspective. Although contemporary urban scholars have abandoned this framework in their study of particular aspects of urban social structure, it still frequently affects the way we think about cities and their social order.

EUROPEAN THEORISTS

The movement from agrarian-based societies to modern industrial-urban societies represented a dramatic transformation whose effects were both staggering and confusing (Hobsbawm, 1975). The newly emerging system was an awesome and complex creation whose nature and implications a variety of European social theorists sought to explain (Berry, 1973; Abu-Laban, 1974). Although from diverse intellectual backgrounds, they agreed "that European social life was changing in a common direction" and "that the changes of the industrial and democratic revolutions meant the rapid disappearance of one kind of human association and its replacement by another" (Gusfield, 1975: 4-5). The use of types as analytical devices to codify such changes was an essential part of their theories of social evolution.

15

Toennies and the City as Gesellschaft

Lenski (1963: 9) has observed: "In large measure all of the modern theories of urbanism are derived from the pioneering work of Ferdinand Toennies, entitled *Gemeinschaft und Gesellschaft*." Toennies believed that urbanization involves the emergence of a unique way of life, reflected in both the types of associations and patterns of interaction as well as in the character of the central institutions. Much subsequent research on the nature of urban social organization has attempted to apply, elaborate, or criticize his typology.

Toennies developed the analytical concepts of "Gemeinschaft" and "Gesellschaft" from his observations of the structural transformations that had occurred in European society—from a rural-agricultural to an urban-industrial complex. He converted these observations into a twofold typology, which he believed could be employed on a general level to analyze "any society, past or present, European or non-European" (Nisbet, 1966: 74). Believing that all social life is the product of human will, he derived the two types from the basic forms of volition. Natural will (liking, habit, or memory) forms the basis for Gemeinschaft groups. Rational will (careful deliberation and evaluation of the best means to achieve some particular end) forms the basis for Gesellschaft relationships. "Gemeinschaft" refers to a natural unity, a "living organism," involving an underlying consensus or mutual understanding, based on kinship, common locality of residence, or friendship. The relationship exists for its own sake and cannot be arbitrarily terminated. In contrast, "Gesellschaft" refers to a mechanical aggregate and artifact, transitory and superficial (Toennies, 1963 ed.: 35). Associations based on contract and exchange emerge out of competitive struggles. Contract legitimizes and stabilizes the exchange of goods and services and increases the rational evaluation of such relationships, but it means the disappearance of the "brotherly spirit of give and take" which characterizes Gemeinschaft.

The purest form of Gesellschaft for Toennies is the industrial urban community which has become increasingly dominant with the growth of capitalism. The institutions of the city clearly express this trend. Science replaces religion. Instead of traditional customs and mores appropriate for agricultural villages, there now exist formalized laws of contract. The industrially-based trade economy causes the demise of a general household economy. More impersonal forms of social organization reduce the centrality of the family. Where formerly folkways and customs had served as key pillars of social control in the rural community, now convention and public opinion fulfil this function in the metropolis.

Toennies treated natural will/rational will and Gemeinschaft/Gesellschaft as dichotomies that are "polar realities" rather than separate points on an underlying continuum (Abu-Laban, 1974: 29). As a result, the eventual demise of Gemeinschaft in the course of social evolution is inevitable since the two polar realities cannot coexist on a permanent basis. Toennies' types represent not only scientific concepts but also "mythic images"—that is, labels used to assess social change (Gusfield, 1975: 2) Toennies clearly romanticized the past and viewed the emergence of Gesellschaft as the loss of a superior traditional social order. Despite this bias his attempt to characterize the nature of urban society as a whole helped establish the typological framework as an influential theoretical framework.

Durkheim and the Division of Labour

Like Toennies, Durkheim analyzed the structural changes accompanying modernization. In two important works, *The Division of Labour* and *Professional Ethics and Civic Morals*, he sought to grasp the social and moral consequences of industrialization and urbanization.

Paralleling the approach of other evolutionary theorists, Durkheim contrasted two forms of integration. "Mechanical solidarity" refers to social links derived from likenesses and strongly defined collective conscience, "the totality of beliefs and sentiments common to average citizens" (Durkheim, 1964 ed.: 79). The individual is directly bound to society and totally absorbed in it. Having no free choice of his own, his relationship can be appropriately termed "mechanical." Mechanical solidarity unites an association of clans, or similar segments, into a federation controlled by "repressive law," such that any deviance from common norms causes the whole society to react against the individual.

In contrast, "organic solidarity" develops through interdependence of specialized groups in society (Durkheim, 1964 ed.: 182). This mutual interdependence of social "organs" presupposes individual differences, occupational specialization, and reduced relevance of norms applicable to the whole society. "Restitutive" or contract law regulating the exchange of goods or services and obligations assumes increasing importance. Durkheim saw this change as a mode of reorganization not disorganization.

In its normal form, the division of labour is an adequate form of integration, and the resultant society is as natural as one based on a strong collective conscience. Durkheim criticized Toennies for attributing an artificiality and absence of a true collective life to the Gesellschaft form of organization (Aldous, 1972). It is an "organic" form of social order in which norms establish harmony between specialized functions and regulate contract and exchange.

Recognizing circumstances departing from this ideal, Durkheim observed the inadequacy of normative controls in modern economic institutions, a state of "anomy" or normlessness—as occurs in strikes (Durkheim, 1958 ed.: 2). Moreover, he pointed out that with the development of the division of labour, not only do the collective sentiments become more rational and abstract, but especially in the city, the authority of tradition which forms their base loses its strength. The old are not present as representatives of that community of beliefs. Disruption of kinship ties through migration to urban centres insures the decline of traditional social controls there—an observation that reappeared in the work of many early urban sociologists.

Durkheim observed that the industrial-urban community failed to develop adequate normative controls to achieve solidarity. He attributed this to the absence of viable occupational associations with regulations governing their activities in the way the guild system developed mutual controls in the Middle Ages:

> What we especially see in the occupation group is a moral power capable of containing individual egos, of maintaining a spirited sentiment of common solidarity in the consciousness of all the workers, of preventing the law of the strongest from being brutally applied to industrial and commercial relations (Durkheim, 1958 ed.: 10).

Such groups would provide a mediating function between the individual and the state, and also regulate the specialized activities created by the division of labour.

Durkheim's analysis is significant for several reasons. It demonstrates a concern for the basis of social integration in the industrial-urban community. More than in Toennies' work, we see a profound understanding of how the newly evolved division of labour can produce cohesion if the proper conditions are met. In addition, Durkheim focuses on the problems involved in achieving this new form of integration and how these problems can be resolved.

Simmel and the Social Psychology of Urbanism

Whereas Durkheim had examined the new basis of integration in the emerging industrial-urban community, Simmel introduced an important complementary area of study. In his relatively brief essay, "The Metropolis and Mental Life," Simmel considered the social psychological adjustments that urban residents make to the kind of community in which they live. He explored the "inner meaning" of urban life and the notion of urbanism as a distinctive mode of existence.

The general problem for Simmel was how the individual in the metropolis is able to maintain his autonomy and independence in view of the size, density, and general demands of such a community. He noted, for example, that the city is characterized by a tremendous "intensification of nervous stimulation" (Simmel, 1950 ed.: 410). Urbanites are constantly bombarded with contrasting impressions that heighten consciousness. Simmel proposed that the dominance of the intellect in urban man serves to protect him from the onslaught of these stimuli. The emotions are subordinated and a certain insensitivity to individual impressions is developed.

An additional feature of the modern metropolis reinforces this character trait. That is the dominance of a money economy. Those contract and exchange relationships which Toennies saw as the essence of Gesellschaft necessitate a rational evaluation of people and things, and a de-emphasis of emotional attachment to individuals. Intellectuality is therefore a product of the dominance of this type of economic system in the city.

In short, Simmel emphasized the social psychological consequences of the division of labour in the industrial-urban community. His portrait of urban man not only complements Durkheim's macroanalysis, but also "bears startling similarities to Toennies' 'Gesellschaft personality' " (Abu-Laban, 1974: 82). The overall coordination of the city requires, he argued, "punctuality, calculability, exactness" and the exclusion of the irrational. The subjective attitudes and social relationships of urban residents reflect those traits. A unique "metropolitan style of life" therefore exists, consisting of a blasé attitude toward new experiences and an underlying sense of reserve and impersonality. This style of life also serves as a model of protection against the potential demands of the vast array of people living in the city. It represents an instrument of self-preservation.

One additional characteristic of urban man is his "cosmopolitanism," that is, an orientation which extends beyond the limits of the city. As the metropolis possesses relationships which extend to the national and international levels, so too its residents reflect this expansion in their interests, values, and patterns of association. This, in addition, demonstrates that loosening of social control which Simmel believed accompanies the growth of communities. As their size increases, the place for individual freedom becomes wider, and the desire for fulfilment as unique beings intensifies.

In general, Simmel's essay, though impressionistic, is important because it attempts both to delineate the contents of a distinctive urban way of life and attribute them to specific structural features of the city. Reflecting a typological framework, Simmel contrasts the metropolitan style of life with the non-urban. He does not fully explore variations within the former.

European Theorists: Summary

These European social theorists who attempted to articulate the implications of urbanization through the use of the typological framework demonstrated several common concerns and assumptions:

1. An attempt to grasp the nature of the urban order as a total social system through construction of types.

2. Assumption of a unidirectional path from the rural to the urban, reflecting their conception of social evolution.

3. Concern for the integration and stability of the newly-emerging industrial-urban social order. The division of labour was seen as weakening traditional "communal solidarities" (Wellman, 1978) such as those based on kinship and common residence, without providing equally strong alternatives for social integration.

4. Hence, there was a tendency to view the rural-traditional social order as superior, although this was less true for Durkheim.

5. There was a failure generally to perceive how urban life can vary cross-culturally. Construction of an urban type minimized possible variations in urban social relationships and traits from one cultural setting to another. This again, however, was less true for Durkheim (Abu-Laban, 1974: 65).

Such concerns and assumptions influenced subsequent efforts to elaborate the typological framework—in particular, that of the Chicago School.

THE CHICAGO SCHOOL

During the 1920s and 1930s a group of scholars led by Robert Park at the University of Chicago sought to systematize the insights of the European theorists and thus establish a more rigorous investigation of the contemporary urban community. The tremendous growth of Chicago—the city with which they were most familiar—during the first decades of the twentieth century stimulated interest in such a study. The rapid influx of immigrants, as well as the increasing expansion of the metropolitan area, had precipitated the emergence of a type of community the understanding of which was critical for grasping the structural transformations that modern civilization was undergoing.

One of the most important contributions of Park (Park and Burgess, 1970 ed.: 44) to general sociology and to the study of the city was his emphasis on the need for empirical research to revivify social theories as objectively as possible. He believed a priori deductions of social philosophy had inhibited the development of a true social science. This orientation informed all the work of the Chicago School, as it represented the stimulus for the many detailed studies initiated by Park's students.

This empirical perspective promoted Park's view of the city as a "social laboratory," in which institutions and patterns of association are to be examined without prejudgment. Careful observation of the varied aspects of urban life are to form the foundation of generalizations about its structure. This empiricism constituted a basis for the development of an area of study termed human ecology, which formed a second central perspective in classical urban sociology (to be discussed in the next chapter).

Park argued, as had Toennies and Durkheim, that the underlying interdependence reflected in the high levels of specialization within the urban community promotes a new form of solidarity—one "based not on sentiment and habit, but on community of interests" (Park, 1967 ed.: 16). Like his predecessors, however, Park displayed concern for the disintegrating influences of city life and the problems in maintaining social control. Those conditions which make urban growth possible also encourage a breakdown in primary group relations:

Transportation and communication have effected what I have called the "mobilization of the individual man." They have multiplied the opportunities of the individual man for contact and for association with his fellows, but they have made these contacts and associations more transitory and less stable (Park, 1967 ed.: 40).

Again reflecting the assumptions of the European theorists, he noted the decline of the neighbourhood as a socially significant unit, in addition to the weakening of the family as an important reference group. The perceived prevalence of urban crime and vice reflected the breakdown of these traditional sources of control. In addition, he observed that the potential for mass behaviour intensifies among urban residents as a consequence of heightened "mobility" and freedom from primary group restraints. The city, therefore, exists as a "laboratory for the investigation of collective behaviour"—for the study of its evolution and predominance in the urban community. Park believed there are many typical features, which, if thoroughly explored, would lead to the development of important generalizations about urban organization.

Urbanism as a Way of Life

Louis Wirth, a central figure in the Chicago School, also sought to define the typical aspects of the urban community. He went further than Park in attempting to determine more precisely the origins and nature of those forms of social organization unique to this type of collectivity. Wirth took many of the insights and generalizations of Toennies, Durkheim, and Simmel (Fischer, 1972), and, with the results of his own study, endeavoured to lay the foundations for a formal theory of urbanism, thus systematizing more explicitly the typological framework.

A first step in the development of this theory was a clear definition of the concept of "city." Following Max Weber (1958 ed.), Wirth argued against such a definition in terms of size alone. The social characteristics of a city occur at a number of different size levels. Relying on a view of the urban community as merely a physical entity is also inadequate, as the characteristics of urbanism often appear beyond the legal boundaries of the city. Nor is density by itself a precise criterion. It represents too arbitrary a basis for distinguishing between rural and urban communities. Wirth proposed that the most appropriate definition of the city—one which would permit identification of the unique characteristics of urbanism—is that of a complex of such factors, that is, "as a relatively large, dense, and permanent settlement of socially heterogeneous individuals" (Wirth, 1964 ed.: 66). He added heterogeneity because migration to the city of a vast variety of people stimulates urban growth. The task of the sociologist is, then, to determine those social traits that correlate with such a settlement. Only then can one distinguish the unique features of urbanism from rural forms of social organization—regardless of the specific historical or cultural context in which the city exists.

Wirth sought to attain this goal by establishing a loose set of propositions (Morris, 1968: 16-19) derived from the essential characteristics of the city. Taking size, density, and heterogeneity, he suggested the types of social relationships and patterns of behaviour that each of these determine (Fischer, 1972: 191f.). For example, he argued that the large population of the city promotes a wide range of individual differences. This, in turn, facilitates patterns of residential segregation in terms of language, ethnicity, and class. Such diversity necessitates reliance on formal mechanisms of social control as the traditional ties of a small village are no longer adequate. The city's size and density also influence the development of impersonal, segmental, and superficial relationships between urban residents. As Simmel had argued, these form a defensive mechanism against the potentially overwhelming impositions of the numerous persons with whom some form of contact is possible. Membership in groups is also tenuous and specialized. Exposure to a wide variety of outlets promotes a certain sense of distance from any single association. An underlying cosmopolitanism emerges. Mutual exploitation— regulated to some extent—along with a relativistic orientation toward belief systems, a general pattern of social distance, and the dominance of depersonalization and mass appeals are all products of the heightened mobility, individual variety, and social instability characteristic of large, dense, heterogeneous settlements. Wirth argued that on the basis of these three characteristics it is possible to account for all unique features of urban life. The more a particular settlement increases in size, density, and heterogeneity, the more fully it manifests these features of urbanism.

In summary, Wirth's theory is significant because, consistent with European typological theories, it synthesized two lines of thought:

> . . . a sociological one, quite Durkheimian; and a social-psychological one derived from Simmel. First, on the structural level, population size, density, and heterogeneity . . . lead sequentially to structural differentiation, formalization of institutions, and anomie. Second, on the individual level, urbanism (in the demographic sense) leads to high levels of nervous stimulation, psychological overload, and adaptation in the form of social isolation (Fischer, 1972: 189).

During the several decades since Wirth's essay first appeared in 1938, students of the city have attempted to determine the extent to which his generalizations are applicable to a wide variety of historical and cultural contexts, or are instead appropriate only for the particular type of industrial-urban community prevalent at the time he was writing. His depiction of urbanism as a type of social order clearly summarized the framework employed by Park (1952), Zorbaugh (1929), Thrasher (1963 ed.) and others associated with the Chicago School.

THE FOLK-URBAN TYPOLOGY

Paralleling Wirth's efforts and sharing many of the assumptions of the Chicago School, Robert Redfield attempted to refine the typological perspective through his formulation of the folk-urban typology.

Redfield elaborated this conceptual scheme through research in Tepoztlan (1930) and in the Yucatan (1941), both in Mexico. From these he derived an understanding of the process of urbanization as a form of cultural change and a grasp of the possible variations in community structure.

Like other villages throughout the Mexican hinterland, Tepoztlan represented a community caught in "mid-stream"—in a process of movement culturally from primitive tribe to modern city. To understand fully the nature of this transformation a comparative study was necessary. Redfield focused on the Yucatan peninsula.

In the northwest section of the state, in the single dominant urban centre—Merida—the more modern Spanish patterns held sway. Moving southeastward into the hinterland, communities increasingly incorporated Mayan and traditional models. In short, there appeared to be a cultural gradient along which communities could be arrayed according to the extent of their "modernization." Redfield compared four communities located at diverse points along this continuum: Merida—the political and economic centre of the region, where manufacturing, trade, and commerce were the chief economic activities; Dzitas—a trading centre with approximately 1200 residents and railway connections to the metropolis; Chan Kom—a village of 250, located a day's walk from the railroad and much more of an agricultural community than Dzitas; and Tusik—hidden away in the bush, with little more than a hundred inhabitants, and almost completely self-sufficient. These communities differed systematically in degree of homogeneity and isolation, with Merida and Tusik presenting the sharpest contrasts. They also varied in terms of stratification systems, kinship patterns, economic structures, and religious systems. Overall, Redfield found that cultural disorganization, secularization, and individualization increased moving from Tusik through to Merida. Whereas in the most isolated village the traditional Mayan institutions still dominated, in Merida the ancient Indian heritage had almost disappeared only to be replaced by a wider range of views of life. The farther removed a community was from Tusik, the less significance religion had in everyday life, and the greater the individual's autonomy. Redfield proposed that these patterns expressed a "natural" association among five variables: when homogeneity and isolation declined, religion, collectivism, and cultural organization likewise eroded. Tepoztlan had represented a community at an intermediate stage in this process of transformation. Indeed, paralleling the views of the European social theorists, Redfield saw the entire history of modern urban civilization in these terms.

Construction of the Ideal Type

Generalizing from these findings which supported the assertions of the Chicago School, Redfield (1947) constructed an "ideal type" of folk society which would serve as a basis for comparison of existing societies. Societies could be "arranged in an order of degree of resemblance to it." Incorporating many of the attributes found in Tusik, the ideal type consists of an isolated community in which there are intimate, familial-like relationships, and a strong sense of belonging among the residents. The society has minimal internal specialization, little commercial activity, and is relatively self-sufficient. Religion and a sacred view of life form the basis of its intense coherence and traditionalism. Such a society is morally and qualitatively distinct from the urban, which incorporates the opposites of these features.

The construction of this ideal type was the culmination of Redfield's empirical research in Tepoztlan and Yucatan. He proposed it as a means of capturing the essential differences between the urban and the non-urban, and as a basis for understanding the process of transformation from simple to more complex social structures. Subsequently, in response to a variety of criticisms Redfield (1953: 224) emphasized that what he had proposed in the ideal type was no more than an analytical tool, and not a description of actual societies. Its heuristic value lay in the kinds of questions it raised, not in those it answered. It stresses the need to analyze those situations where the hypothesized correlation between the central features of the folk or urban does *not* appear.

Criticisms of the Folk-Urban Typology

Various critical tests (e.g., Tax, 1939; Tax, 1941; Passin and Bennett, 1943; Gross, 1948; Freeman and Winch, 1957; Miner, 1953; Miner, 1966 ed.) of this conceptual scheme emerged to determine more precisely what its limitations are. Perhaps one of the most persuasive assessments was that of Oscar Lewis (1963 ed.) in his re-study of Tepoztlan. Seventeen years after Redfield had conducted his field work there, Lewis returned to investigate what changes had occurred during the intervening period. What emerged was a fuller understanding of the biases inherent in Redfield's work. Lewis showed how the community's history revealed more instances of internal conflict and individualization than Redfield had indicated. He also criticized Redfield's failure to consider Tepoztlan in its historical and cultural setting (see Beals, 1951b). In his haste to generalize about processes involved in the transformation of the folk societies into urban societies, he had neglected to consider whether there were unique factors in this context that affected the generalizability of the findings. The same criticism could be directed at Redfield's study of the Yucatan.

Lewis reasoned that these weaknesses in Redfield's study were due ultimately to the inadequacies of the folk-urban model itself. He suggested that this is *not* a useful conceptual tool for several reasons (Lewis, 1963, ed.: 432f.):

1. It emphasizes the city as the most important source of change. Redfield interpreted the transformation of rural communities as due solely to increasing contacts with urban centres, possibly neglecting other sources. Many cases of transformation represent not greater urbanization, but simple internal expansion of a rural culture.

2. Reiterating a conclusion reached by Tax (1939; 1941) in his research in Guatemala, Lewis asserted that what Redfield had proposed as a set of correlated factors (viz., on the folk side, homogeneity, isolation, sacredness, collectivism, and cultural organization) represents instead a *hypothesized* interconnection, the validity of which must yet be established. Lewis, indeed, showed how in Tepoztlan during the seventeen years since Redfield's study familial solidarity did not decline despite increasing urban influences.

3. What Lewis particularly objected to in the folk-urban typology was its global character. It tends to minimize the wide variations among primitive peoples as well as to overlook the substantial differences among urban communities. This simplification results from a concern for only the formal aspects of culture.

4. Finally, Lewis argued that many of the scheme's weaknesses derive from a fundamental anti-urban bias. The emphasis on order and harmony reflects a belief in the inherent superiority of the folk order. Manifesting the influence of European social theory, Redfield appeared unduly concerned with the disorganizing aspects of urbanization.

Recognition of the potential value of the typological mode of analysis stimulated efforts to establish alternatives to Redfield's model (e.g., Becker, 1950; Loomis and Beegle, 1950; Odum, 1953; Foster, 1953; Voget, 1954), and thus provide greater recognition to the full spectrum of types of social systems. To illustrate, Sjoberg (1952; 1960) argued for the maintenance of the concept of folk society as Redfield has used it, but pointed to the need to distinguish a "feudal" type. Whereas both are based on sacred-value orientations, the latter is structurally more complex, reflecting a higher level of technology. Animate sources of energy are more fully developed in the feudal type. This permits the production of an adequate food surplus to support some population concentration. Pre-industrial urban centres arise. Unlike in the folk society, a rigid class structure emerges in which a small elite, residing primarily in the cities, dominates the much larger population of peasants, and, with the support of the sacred traditions, is able to extract that surplus for its own ends.

Sjoberg emphasized the need not only to distinguish the feudal society as a whole from the folk order, but also to examine how the pre-industrial city within the former differs from the modern urban-industrial centre. In his own work (1960), he demonstrated how many of the traits that Redfield had attributed to the urban community are actually not fully applicable to that in the feudal order. Secularization and disorganization, for example, are much less in evidence than would be predicted using Redfield's scheme. Responding to criticisms of that scheme, Sjoberg proposed that formulating the typological framework in terms of three distinct social orders—folk, feudal, and industrial—would permit a greater understanding of how urban social structures within the latter two could differ (see also McGee, 1971).

THE RURAL-URBAN CONTINUUM

A final formulation of the classical typological perspective, closely paralleling the folk-urban scheme, was the systematic investigation of rural-urban differences. Again, a fundamental assumption of this research was that the nature of urban social organization can only be grasped by analyzing how it contrasts with the non-urban. Departing from Redfield's model, however, this approach relied less on the use of ideal types, and instead emphasized empirical placement of communities on an underlying continuum.

An early example of this approach was the analysis of Sorokin and Zimmerman (1969 ed.). Like Wirth, they dismissed size or density as a possible single distinguishing feature of urban or rural communities. They argued that sets of empirical traits must be discerned, which are logically and functionally correlated. Since these are empirical characteristics of communities, the transition from a rural to an urban order is "not abrupt but gradual." A continuum approach, therefore, is more appropriate than a simplistic dichotomy.

Sorokin and Zimmerman (1969 ed.) delineated nine orders of differences between the rural and urban (see Figure 2). They proposed that the most fundamental difference is in the occupational trait. Many of the other elements directly derive from it. Farmers are closely tied to the land, which discourages the mobility characteristic of the city. Since they themselves are recruited from the rural population, they are much less heterogeneous both ethnically and in class origins than are urban residents. As the process of urbanization progresses these differences become less intense. The significance of this trend, however, is that a clear division between the rural and urban is not now as prominent as once was thought. It does not mean, on the contrary, that these traits had incorrectly differentiated initially the country from the city.

Criticisms of the Rural-Urban Continuum

A variety of attempts to apply this perspective subsequently appeared (e.g., Goldkind, 1961; Yuan, 1964). Some of this research tended to validate in a more rigorous fashion that continuum which Redfield's study of Yucatan had suggested. However, just as Redfield's typological scheme became the object of much criticism, so too did the rural-urban continuum, for both theoretical and empirical reasons.

A major concern was the extent to which those traits categorized as urban are necessarily so, whether indeed they might also be present in more rural communities. In short, does the continuum in fact array social systems in an orderly manner?

Figure 2: Sorokin and Zimmerman's Nine Orders of Differences Between the Rural and the Urban

Trait	Rural	Urban
Occupation	Agricultural	Non-agricultural
Environment	Elementary	Artificial
Size	Small	Large
Density	Low	High
Socio-psychical characteristics (nativity, class, culture)	Homogeneous	Heterogeneous
Social mobility (vertical and horizontal)	Low	High
Direction of migration	Strong currents from country to city	Weak currents from city to country
Social stratification	Low levels of specialization, differentiation, and span	High levels of specialization, differentiation, and span
Social interaction	(1) Quantitatively few social contacts (2) Spatially narrow area of contact system (3) Primary relations more dominant proportionately (4) Personal relations more central (5) Permanent, strong, durable relations more pronounced (6) Social network less complex, differentiated, and standardized	(1) Quantitatively many social contacts (2) Spatially wide area of contact system (3) Primary relations less dominant (4) Personal relations less central (5) Casual, superficial, short-lived relations more pronounced (6) Social network more complex, differentiated, and standardized

Source: Sorokin and Zimmerman (1969 ed.)

Reiss (1955) argued that such traits as creativity, non-agricultural pursuits, and complexity of division of labour—frequently viewed as distinctively urban—can also exist in rural contexts. Social heterogeneity, mobility, and participation in formal organizations represent the products of conditions independent of the size and density of settlements (see Young and Young, 1962). He suggested that much more comparative research needed to be done on the nature of these conditions before we can accept any trait as typically urban. No firm evidence had as yet demonstrated the unique character of the city as a social system. Support for this negative assessment came from Duncan's (1957) findings in the U.S. that showed inconsistent variations in the distribution of demographic, socioeconomic and family characteristics among a number of communities, ranging from the rural farm settlement to the metropolis. This suggested that the rural-urban continuum represents a premature and over-simplified conceptualization of intercommunity variation. It is an inadequate basis for delineating the nature of urban social organization.

Reviewing the numerous applications of this perspective, Dewey (1960) found a fundamental lack of consensus in the kinds of traits used to identify "rural" and "urban." Forty different attributes appear as discriminating criteria, with only heterogeneity employed in the majority of cases. One important reason for this disagreement is the inclusion not only of elements which are the consequences of size and density, but also of those due to unique cultural conditions. As a result, the rural-urban continuum gains a greater analytical importance than it deserves.

In an article he was preparing before his death, Louis Wirth (1964 ed.: 223) emphasized again the theoretical function of the rural-urban continuum, as Redfield had done regarding his scheme:

> To set up ideal typical polar concepts such as I have done, and many others before me have done, does not prove that city and country are fundamentally and necessarily different. It does not justify mistaking the hypothetical character-istics attributed to the urban and the rural modes of life for established fact, as has so often been done. Rather it suggests certain hypotheses to be tested in the light of empirical evidence which we must assiduously gather.

The varied criticisms and modifications of this framework (see Spaulding, 1951; Friedman, 1961; Sjoberg, 1964) were attempts to respond constructively to this heuristic function.

THE CLASSICAL TYPOLOGICAL PERSPECTIVE: CONCLUSION

The classical typological perspective represented an initial effort to examine systematically the nature of urban social organization by contrasting it with other forms of community structure. In this chapter we briefly reviewed the origins of this perspective in European social theory. Louis Wirth, representing the Chicago School, sought to systematize this framework by delineating how the demographic characteristics of size, density, and heterogeneity contribute to the evolution of a uniquely urban social system. The folk-urban scheme and rural-urban continuum likewise were efforts to refine empirically the typological contrasts of Toennies and Durkheim.

This perspective in time engendered a good deal of discomfort with the entire approach. A common complaint was that it painted too broad a picture of the variations in community structure. The inherent complexity of the city belied such global characterizations. Hauser (1965: 509), for one, observed:

Although my major quarrel with the folk-urban and urban-rural dichotomies lies with the way in which they have seeped into the literature and have become accepted as generalizations based on research, rather than their utility as ideal-type constructs, I have come to feel that even in the latter role they perhaps may have outlived their usefulness.

The city as a social system contains more varied patterns than the typological schemes reflected. These tended to classify rather than explain urban social reality. In subsequent chapters we shall examine how contemporary research seeks to refine the generalizations derived from the typological framework.

Chapter 2

The Classical
Ecological Perspective

The second central paradigm in classical urban sociology was the ecological perspective. This complemented the typological framework in that it was concerned less with social structure of the city *per se*. Rather, the ecological perspective focused on the spatial reflections of that structure—that is, on patterns of urban growth as well as the spatial distribution within cities of population and land-use types. Although this approach was anticipated in the writings of a variety of social commentators and scholars in the late nineteenth century, it was more explicitly defined by the Chicago School. Just as the typological perspective encountered severe criticism, however, so too were the biases and ambiguities of the ecological perspective identified.

ANTECEDENTS

Analyses of the emerging industrial-urban system included a number of insights, though unsystematic, regarding the nature of ecological structure. Engels (1968 ed.), for example, saw how the spatial arrangement of cities such as mid-1800s Manchester reflected their class structures. In turn, residential segregation (particularly of the workers in industrial towns) promoted class consciousness (see Briggs, 1963; Marcus, 1974; Lansbury, 1974). Similarly, Booth's (1970 ed.) seventeen-year survey of the poor in London, begun in 1886, documented regularities in the spatial distribution of social classes as well as of industrial and economic enterprises. Anticipating the Chicago School, Booth recognized the tendency of the city to grow outward from the centre leading to changing class composition of neighbourhoods, or "residential succession." He saw too the relationship between increasing separation of work and residence and the evolution of a more efficient transportation system in the industrial metropolis (Pfautz, 1967).

Aside from these empirical insights, there were nascent ecological theories, subsequently refined by contemporary scholars. Most influential here was Durkheim's conception (1964 ed.) of the division of labour as a means of survival for an increasing and concentrated population. He saw clearly that urbanization heightens an organizational transformation in which specialization and differentiation evolve as modes of adaptation to the environment. One central factor affecting this process is the nature of the transportation system. Complementing Durkheim's analysis, Charles Horton Cooley (1969 ed.), better known, perhaps, for his contributions to social psychology and to the study of the socialization process, showed the importance of transportation for understanding the location of cities. "Population and wealth," he asserted, "tend to collect whenever there is a break in transportation" (Cooley, 1969 ed.: 76-78). He too saw how efficient transportation systems promote an extensive territorial division of labour among urban communities and within each encourage more widespread distribution of population and commerce.

These were useful insights into the nature of urban growth and spatial patterning. However, it was with the Chicago School that the ecological perspective emerged as a basic framework in urban sociology.

THE CHICAGO SCHOOL

In the previous chapter we reviewed briefly the contribution of the Chicago School to the typological paradigm. Of equal importance was their development of human ecology. Park (1961 ed.) was the first to delineate formally the aims, major concepts, and relations to sociology of this discipline. His conception of human ecology derived from an understanding of the organization of society. On the *cultural* level, society exists as consensus. That is, it consists of a common set of beliefs, values, habits, and attitudes which forms the basis of that collective action which is the mark of the social. This consensus, or "social heritage," emerges only through communication and social interaction. Park believed that the operation of three fundamental forms of social contact—conflict, accommodation, and assimilation—constructs the cultural order.

The counterpart to the cultural for Park is the *biotic*. This represents the sub-social aspect of the human society, technically termed "community." It refers simply to that ecological organization, or system of functional interdependence between units of a locality, which develops as a consequence of the sub-social process of competition. Whereas sociology studies the cultural order of society, human ecology has as its focus the investigation of this biotic sub-structure.

Park observed, as had Haeckel and Darwin, the presence of a balance between different species in the plant and animal worlds. That is, within a particular locale there frequently occurs a process of competitive co-operation among the different types of units, such that all can survive. A primitive division of labour evolves, representing a compromise between the conflicting demands of the various species. Such a precarious balance regulates population growth. A sudden invasion of a new type of species upsets this equilibrium. Competition for scarce resources resumes and ultimately a new division of labour and a balance emerges.

Supporting Durkheim's insight, Park suggested that this process of competitive co-operation occurs not only in the plant and animal worlds, but also on the human level as well, and, in view of its significance, should be the focus of systematic study. He saw competition as determining the territorial and occupational distribution of population. The spatial organization and underlying division of labour found in any community represent a mode of mutual adjustment that mirrors the kinds of accommodations discovered in the plant and animal worlds. In spite of this parallel, Park did see important differences between the human and non-human ecological complexes. Man is not so dependent on his immediate locale. Involvement in an extensive division of labour frees him from the limitations of the surrounding physical environment. More important, the cultural order controls the human biotic level of society. The beliefs, values, and attitudes which represent the consensus governing society limit competition. The spatial patterns and symbiotic relations constituting the structure of "community" reflect this influence. Therefore, although human ecology can employ many of the concepts and general relationships found in plant and animal ecology, it is still necessary to recognize this interaction between the biotic and cultural orders. In Park's view, four factors compose the human community and shape its system of interdependence—population, technology, customs and beliefs, and the natural resources of the locale. A change in any one of these can upset the biotic equilibrium and necessitate transition to a new ecological order.

Park employed this conception of the nature of human ecology in his attempts to analyze the consequences of urbanization. On one level, he argued, the city exists as a natural entity independent of its boundaries as an administrative and legal entity. It is a product of natural forces, particularly competition, that lead to occupational specialization, as well as to territorial distribution. This is essentially an unplanned consequence, just as it is in the plant and animal worlds.

Competition and Natural Areas

Park believed that one of the dominant ecological characteristics of a rapidly growing city is its division into a number of *natural areas*. It represents a "mosaic of minor communities." A "sifting and sorting" of the population into various parts of the city occurs according to class, race, and language:

> Every city has its central business district; the focal point of the whole urban complex. Every city, every great city, has its more or less exclusive residential areas or suburbs; its areas of blight and of heavy industry, satellite cities, and casual labor mart . . . Every American city has its slums; its ghettos; its immigrant colonies . . . These are the so-called natural areas of the city (Park 1952: 196).

This pattern is the result of competition for strategic space. The ability of a particular institution or population to absorb the cost of location in an area determines the distribution of types of land use. Service and retail institutions are better able than the residential sector to locate at the centre of the city where land values are highest. Similarly, the poor concentrate in sections of the city where rents are lowest and costs of transportation minimal. When combined with discrimination and the desire to live among others of the same ethnic group, these sections become ghettos (see Thomas and Znaniecki, 1958 ed.). Like a plant community of a particular locale, the city demonstrates an ordered spatial distribution.

Park believed that each natural area possesses a particular racial or ethnic character. Each is a moral or cultural area with its own peculiar customs and traditions. As such, each develops a normative order which exercises some control over the inhabitants. It is in this way that the "society," as a common set of beliefs and values, emerges within the ecological structure of "community." Park, however, as we noted in the previous chapter, was not fully convinced of the adequacy of this mode of integration, particularly in the immigrant colonies where he believed social control deteriorates in the second generation (Park, 1967 ed.: 27).

Park's theory of natural areas formed the ecological framework within which much of the research of the Chicago School was conducted, such as Thrasher's (1963 ed.) study of the gang and Zorbaugh's (1929) comparison of various inner-city neighbourhoods.

McKenzie and the Ecological Perspective

Within the Chicago School one of the most important attempts to build on Park's delineation of the ecological perspective was that of his student and colleague, Roderick McKenzie. Moving beyond the simple distinction between the cultural and biotic orders, McKenzie sought to define more fully the particular concerns of ecology and clarify the central concepts which it must employ.

McKenzie (1968a: 4) saw the defining character of ecology in its study of the "spatial and temporal relations of human beings as affected by the selective, distributive and accommodative forces of the environment." It attempts to explain the structure of "nexus of sustenance and place relations" which shape the community. Like Park, McKenzie recognized that while the perspective and concepts of plant and animal ecology can be valuable in advancing this study, it is at the same time necessary to recall the distinction between the human and non-human ecological orders:

> The basic difference between human ecology and the ecologies of the lower organisms lies in the fact that man is capable of a higher level of behavior in his adaptation process. As a cultural animal man creates, within limitations, his own

habitat. Symbiotic relations in human society represent adjustments to a cultural as well as to a biogeographic setting (McKenzie, 1968c: 41).

McKenzie identified a series of conceptual tools for examining ecological organization systematically. Contemporary urban researchers frequently employ at least some of these.

McKenzie's central concept was that of "ecological distribution," which refers to the overall spatial distribution of residents, their activities, and institutions in a community or region. Such a grouping forms an "ecological constellation" when it manifests a readily identifiable pattern. McKenzie did not view this distribution from a static viewpoint, but rather emphasized that it is in a continual state of change—a function, in part, of the rate of technological advances. He distinguished between two dynamic dimensions of the community—"mobility" and "fluidity." The former refers to those patterns involving "change of residence, change of employment or change of location of any utility or service" (McKenzie, 1968b: 21). Fluidity, in contrast, designates movement within the community or region, but without alteration in ecological position—illustrated in the daily patterns of commutation between work and home. Degree of fluidity is measured in terms of "ecological distance," or the time and cost of travel, rather than physical distance. Fluidity thus is a function of the state of existing transportation and communication facilities. The overall structure of the community, in turn, is a function of the patterns of ecological distance. Improvements in those facilities strongly influence the growth of the city and its extension outward.

In general, McKenzie (1968b: 23) classified four sets of ecological factors which in their interrelationships determine the underlying spatial organization:

(1) geographical, which includes climatic, topographic and resource conditions; (2) economic, which comprises a wide range and variety of phenomena such as the nature and organization of local industries, occupational distribution, and standard of living of the population; (3) cultural and technical, which include, in addition to the prevailing condition of the arts, the moral attitudes and taboos that are effective in the distribution of population and services; (4) political and administrative measures, such as tariff, taxation, immigration laws, and rules governing public utilities.

These factors are ultimately responsible for the type of ecological distribution which emerges. In its development and change over time, that constellation is characterized by the occurrence of five types of ecological processes:

1. *Concentration.* This process refers simply to "the tendency of an increasing number of persons to settle in a given area or region" (McKenzie, 1968b: 24). The level of concentration reflects the advantages offered by the particular locality and is attained in competition with other regions. Concentration is one prerequisite for large-scale urbanization. McKenzie argued, in addition, that an important concomitant of such a process is the development

of territorial specialization through the existing transportation and communication facilities.

2. *Centralization*. Whereas concentration occurs more at the regional level, centralization actually represents " . . . the process of community formation. The fact that people come together at specified locations for the satisfaction of common interests affords a territorial basis for group consciousness and social control. Every communal unit, the village, town, city, and metropolis, is a function of the process of centralization" (McKenzie, 1968b: 26).

Again, the levels of transportation and communication facilities determine their location and the distance from focal points of centralization to the periphery. As at the regional level, centres compete with one another. Any accommodation between them is only a temporary condition of equilibrium which can be significantly changed with the emergence, for example, of new transportation patterns. That accommodation is also achieved through the evolution of greater specialization, with centres fulfilling different functions and meeting complementary needs.

3. *Segregation*. McKenzie was deeply concerned throughout his work with patterns of ecological change (Hawley, 1968a). He interpreted community growth as a process of increasing differentiation and segregation. The latter term, as both Booth and Park had shown, refers to the tendency of various types of population and land use to concentrate in particular sections of the community. An underlying selection process sifts and sorts the residents and their institutions according to economic and cultural criteria. Their spatial distribution thus reveals an orderly and predictable pattern.

4. *Invasion*. The variety of "natural areas" in a community produced through segregation is not necessarily fixed. It is not uncommon for one type of population or land use to replace another over time. Such a process of invasion reveals the dynamic features of ecological structure. Community growth occurs in "successional sequence," stimulated by a series of invasions and responding to alterations in the existing equilibrium. McKenzie believed the process of invasion evolves through a series of stages, the initial phase of which is marked frequently by a change in land value.

5. *Succession*. The culmination of invasion is the replacement of one population type or land use by another. In its completed form this is a "succession" or emergence of a new natural area with a position in the community's ecological order.

Most significantly, because of extensive improvements in contemporary transportation and communication facilities, these five ecological processes operate, McKenzie argued, within an increasingly less rigid structure, presenting fewer hindrances to their elaboration. The increase in scale of the ecological distribution is thereby insured, and the complexity of the metropolitan community enhanced.

The various concepts and relationships which McKenzie delineated presented human ecology in the form of a "theory of limits." The community attains a "condition of balance between population and resources until a new element enters to disturb the 'status quo,' such as the introduction of a new system of communication, a new type of industry, or a different form of utilization of the existing economic base" (McKenzie, 1968a: 8). The various ecological processes thereby intensify, and a new equilibrium is subsequently sought. Such a framework McKenzie (1933; 1968d) found useful for understanding the emergence and structure of that more recent and complex ecological distribution—the metropolitan community or "super-city"—which he correctly predicted would become the dominant shape of future urban aggregations.

Burgess and the Application of the Ecological Perspective to Urban Growth

Consistent with McKenzie's focus, Burgess (1967 ed.) too identified the growth of large cities as a dominant feature of contemporary industrialized society. This growth is manifested not only in increasing concentration of population, but also through expansion of the urban community. Burgess proposed that this extension occurs outward from the central business district. The underlying processes of invasion and succession enhance the internal differentiation of the city. A series of areas evolve, which can be depicted as a set of concentric zones (see Figure 3).

Zone 1 represents the central business district or downtown core of Chicago. The remaining areas are ordered around the inner district:

> Encircling the downtown area there is normally an area in transition, which is being invaded by business and light manufacture (2). A third area (3) is inhabited by the workers in industries who have escaped from the area of deterioration (2) but who desire to live within easy access of their work. Beyond this zone is the "residential area" (4) of high-class apartment buildings or of exclusive "restricted" districts of single family dwellings. Still farther, out beyond the city limits, is the commuters' zone—suburban areas, or satellite cities—within a thirty-to-sixty minute ride of the central business district (Burgess, 1967 ed.: 50).

This scheme, Burgess proposed, is an ideal pattern which the spatial structures of actual cities approximate in varying degrees. Specific historical, cultural, geographical, and technical factors are responsible for any significant departures from the concentric pattern.

In the process of expansion outward each zone tends to invade the next outer area. Changes in land use and population type occur in similar fashion to ripples in a pond after a stone has been dropped. Immigration is an important stimulus to such expansion, and the distribution of the population among the different natural areas reflects this. Zone 2, as an area in transition responding to the central business district's trend toward expansion, contains many of the

Figure 3: Burgess' Concentric Zone Model

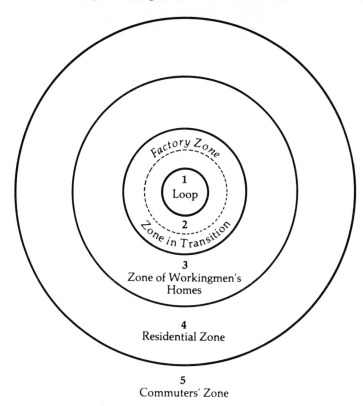

city's slums. Not only is crime disproportionately concentrated there, but also first-generation immigrant colonies. The zone of workingmen's homes, on the other hand, contains second-generation settlements. Movement to this zone frequently represents an attempt to escape from immigrant colonies, as families achieve greater economic security and a higher level of assimilation. Further out are the homes of the more affluent who can afford to live at such a distance from the core. Burgess' scheme, therefore, captures the close relationship between urban spatial and class structures.

Burgess presented his concentric zone scheme linked to Park's theory of natural areas as a general framework within which a series of research projects at the University of Chicago at that time were being conducted. The question of its applicability to other large cities provoked considerable discussion and study in subsequent years.

INITIAL CRITICISMS OF THE CLASSICAL ECOLOGICAL PERSPECTIVE

As it was developed and applied, the classical ecological perspective was subjected to severe criticism because of dissatisfaction with its conceptual framework and empirical relevance. Alihan, for example, in 1938 presented a strident attack on the ecology of the Chicago School. She objected to the theoretical distinction between "community" and "society." Symbiotic relationships are so intertwined with cultural patterns that any analytical separation of the biotic and social orders is a serious error. Indeed, she pointed out that in their actual empirical investigations ecologists themselves failed to sustain this distinction. She attacked the implicit assumptions of ecology—for example, that the division of labour manifests a more strongly organic basis than do human customs and mores, that competition is the most fundamental process, and that the human order represents a mere difference in degree from the non-human—as well as the conceptual ambiguities inherent in its framework.

Alihan's criticisms gained empirical support from Davie's (1961 ed.) study of the applicability of Burgess' concentric zone hypothesis to communities other than Chicago. Delineating twenty-two natural areas in New Haven, he examined the distribution of a series of characteristics among these, and found little evidence of a concentric circle pattern. Substantial diversity in land use and population type existed within each zone. Similarly, Davie's examination of the distribution of land use types on zoning maps of twenty cities in the United States and Canada revealed little support for that spatial model.

A more fundamental criticism focused on the basic premises of the classical ecological perspective:

> Despite its biological terminology, it was actually an application of the paradigm of capitalism to communities in which individual initiative was given a free reign with a minimum of outside intervention to operate competitively in a marked situation. It did very well explaining anything that could be related to market values. . . . It could not in and of itself, tell us why certain things had value. To do this it had to be modified (Bernard, 1973: 40).

Such a modification was suggested in an early study of land-use patterns in Boston. Firey (1945) argued that classical ecology had adopted too narrow a perspective; it posed the relationship between space and "locational activities" solely in economic terms. It assumed that in the free competition for scarce desirable locations considerations of relative cost are the most important factors accounting for ecological distribution. As Alihan had suggested, such a focus ignored the role of cultural values in shaping spatial structure.

Countering the premises of classical ecology, Firey (1945: 140) proposed:

> 1. . . . ascribing to space not only an impeditive quality [that is, a cost-imposing one] but also an additional property, viz., that of being at times a symbol for certain cultural values that have become associated with a certain spatial area;

2. a recognition that locational activities are not only economizing agents but may also bear sentiments which can significantly influence the locational process.

The validity of these modifications is apparent when examining Boston's ecological structure. Beacon Hill continued for many years to function as an upper-class residential area, despite significant alterations in the population composition of other downtown districts. Its "retentive" power derived from strong sentiments the area evoked among upper-class Bostonians. Beacon Hill symbolized historical and traditional values for the city's older and more aristocratic families, who cherished their residence in the district. Similarly, the Boston Common in the centre of the downtown resisted encroachments of the central business district despite a serious land shortage, because it had assumed a sacred and historical status.

These patterns clearly suggest the important influence which sentiments and symbolism can exercise on urban spatial structure. It is evident that "a different order of concepts, corresponding to the valuative, meaningful aspect of spatial adaptation, must supplement the prevailing economic concepts of ecology" (Firey, 1945). Attention must be given to the conditions under which free competition for desirable location does *not* occur—as with governmental intervention through formal planning of ecological patterns (Bernard, 1973: 42).

In conclusion, Gettys (1961 ed.) observed that classical ecological theory represented actually a form of "biological and/or geographic determinism." As with Alihan, he found the fundamental dichotomy between community and society unsatisfactory and the reliance on analogies with plant and animal ecology disturbing. Gettys argued that the Chicago School had failed to present an integrated theoretical system. Their framework required a "thoroughgoing revision and restatement" with more precise delimitation of the exact scope of ecology and with a clearer determination of whether it was to be in truth a *social* science. With such a theoretical revision its value would be certainly enhanced:

> If human ecology will center its attention upon the description, measurement, analysis, and explanation of the spatial and temporal distribution of social and cultural data it may become in truth a significant social science discipline (Gettys, 1961 ed.: 102).

We shall examine how contemporary urban research has extended and modified the classical perspective.

Part Two

Growth of the Urban System

The purpose of this part is to provide a general picture or profile of the Canadian urban system as a whole. This involves a dynamic focus on Canadian urban ecological organization, as well as a partial examination of its structure. We will review briefly the historical development of Canadian urban growth, understood primarily as an ecological process, and consider the major structural features of the contemporary Canadian urban system. This will provide us with a useful background against which we can later explore more specific processes within that system, such as urban immigration and current issues in urban planning.

Chapter 3

Explorations in Canadian Urban Growth

We have seen that by the early 1850s little more than one-tenth of Canada's population could be classified as urban. By the end of the first decade of the present century this proportion had more than tripled. Regardless of the periods of time we compare, however, it is essential that we comprehend the meaning of urbanization as an ecological process. Before we describe several historical dimensions of Canadian urbanization, let us briefly explore that meaning.

THE MEANING OF URBAN GROWTH AS AN ECOLOGICAL PROCESS

A contemporary ecological interpretation of urbanization demands some refinement of the initial insights of Park, McKenzie, and Burgess. In contrast, for example, to McKenzie's rather restricted conception of the field as the study of spatial distributions and correlations, it is more appropriate to see human ecology as concerned primarily with the *organization* of functional relations through which a local population maintains itself in a particular habitat (Hawley, 1950; 1968b; 1971).

We must not define *urban* in primarily spatial terms. The term refers to that organization or set of functional relationships through which a specific population is able to satisfy its daily needs (Gibbs and Martin, 1959). *Urbanization* represents an expansion or elaboration of that organization. It consists, in short, of a process of growth "from the simple, highly localized unit to the complex and territorially extended system"—a process which may assume a similar shape in different societies and cultures (Hawley, 1971). We can measure the degree of "urbanness" according to both the level of integration within a territorial system and the types of linkages that system maintains with the outside world. The historical development of urbanization clearly reveals this.

The earliest towns revealed an extremely primitive organization. The limited capacity of ancient societies for the development of urban centres on a wide scale was a consequence of their inadequate food production and of the

43

lack of advanced transportation and communication facilities. Revival of town life in Europe during the tenth century occurred as these disadvantages lessened. Several significant technological innovations, including the introduction of the moldboard plow which permitted cultivation of the lands in northern Europe, accompanied population growth. The adoption of a more sophisticated rotational system increased agricultural productivity. In addition,

> The development of a supply of grain coincided closely with three almost simultaneous inventions that greatly improved the load capacity of the horse: the horsecollar, the tandem harness, and the horseshoe . . . [As a result] the cost of overland transportation in dry seasons declined to a third of what it had been. Thus towns could obtain their food supplies and maintain relations of other kinds over much larger territories than had formerly been possible (Hawley, 1971: 44-45).

The revival of trade and the emergence of towns as commercial centres strengthened this process of urban development. Yet many of the constraints that had inhibited urbanization in ancient societies were still operative in the Middle Ages. Facilities for short-distance transportation between towns and their surrounding hinterlands, for example, were not yet highly advanced.

Beginning in the latter part of the fifteenth century, urban growth became accentuated, particularly with the rise of modern nation-states. During the eighteenth century, urban development was most pronounced in England. Improvements in transportation—construction of better roads and a variety of canals—partly accounted for this. Agricultural innovations were important: new methods of land drainage and cultivation of pasturage spread widely from the Continent. The increasing commercialization of agriculture encouraged migration to the cities. The emergence of the factory system in England, with industrial production derived from steam power, stimulated concentration of the growing population. The introduction of the railway system in the nineteenth century permitted greater contacts between urban centres and their hinterlands. A broader territorial organization could thereby evolve. Markets expanded, specialization of activities strengthened, and urbanization both in England and elsewhere rapidly became the dominant feature of the modern age.

The urban community that emerged during the early 1800s in Europe and North America formed a dense and constricted settlement—a "pedestrian city." The development of the railway system provided an efficient means of long-distance transportation which, in turn, widened the scope of the city's market and source of raw materials. Methods of short-distance transportation remained relatively primitive, inhibiting the city's expansion outward. Its internal structure reflected a cellular pattern as it contained a number of distinct districts or quarters, ". . . each with its own industries and shops and other institutions. Within each district there was no clear separation of rich and poor.

Employer and employees, if they did not share a place of residence, lived side by side" (Hawley, 1971: 90).

Improvements in local transportation subsequently modified this pattern. The horse-drawn and electric street railways encouraged a wider dispersion of the city's population. As the focus of the urban community's internal lines of transportation and communication, the central business district assumed a dominant position in the local ecological organization.

The fundamental principle of urban development was the process of specialization, operating at all levels. Improved transportation permitted a more extensive territorial division of labour to emerge, frequently covering an area of up to twenty miles within which various communities assumed specific functions. Accompanying that specialization was a wide array of rules and regulations which promoted the overall co-ordination of this system. Increasing functional integration also placed a strong premium on standardization.

The urban system that emerged in the nineteenth century comprised a network of functional relationships among a set of specialized institutions, groups, and local communities. It was a system, however, that reflected primarily a process of "regional and interregional expansion." In contrast, urban growth in the twentieth century represented more fully a process of "local expansion," made possible by the development of even more efficient mechanisms of short-distance transportation and communication. The development of motor vehicles and trucks permitted the local "friction of space" (i.e., the time and cost of local travel) to be more easily overcome than was possible with the railway system. This encouraged deconcentration both of population and industry. As McKenzie had so clearly predicted, this process of diffusion has led to the emergence of the metropolitan community—a dominant trend in twentieth-century urban ecological patterns. Such a territorial enlargement of the urban system represents the culmination of earlier tendencies toward specialization, mobility, integration, and spatial reorganization. It constitutes a vast communication system that integrates wide-ranging groups and institutions. The metropolitan community dominates the surrounding hinterland. Indeed, as the process of metropolitanization advances, the distinction between rural and urban becomes less significant. As urbanization proceeds, the entire society experiences dramatic reorganization. Intricate hierarchies of urban places, based on levels of functional importance, emerge; dominating these hierarchies are the metropolitan centres (Hawley, 1956).

As we observed in the Introduction, urbanization from a demographic perspective means the increase both in the number and size of centres of population concentration in a society. This must be distinguished from the ecological meaning of urbanization as the spread of a more comprehensive and intricate territorial division of labour. As the preceding historical portrait suggests, ecology emphasizes especially how the three variables of population, environment, and technology interact to influence the organization of functional relations at the local, regional, and national levels of a society. These four elements are closely interrelated, and their total pattern constitutes an "eco-system" (Duncan and Schnore, 1959). Spatial distributions of population and land use are important in a derivative sense. That is, they provide "a convenient and invariant set of reference points for observation . . . convenient indicators of structural relationships" (Duncan and Schnore, 1959: 136). For example, the outward spatial relocation of population and industry reflects the evolution of more complex functional relationships between central city and surrounding hinterland characteristic of the rise of metropolitan communities. Examining the interrelations among the four components of the "ecological complex"—population, environment, technology, and organization—provides a useful framework for understanding urbanization. Failure to consider the impact of social values, the significance of how power is distributed, and the influence of such subjective factors as choice and motivation would render this perspective deterministic, positivistic, and unacceptably narrow (Willhelm, 1969 ed.). In reviewing the following historical overview of Canadian urban growth we should keep in mind both the ecological conception of urbanization as well as the need to recognize the importance of the above factors.

HISTORICAL TYPES OF CANADIAN URBAN COMMUNITIES

From the beginnings of permanent European settlement in Canada to the present day urban communities have exercised a central influence on the nation's social, political, and economic landscape. Within the broad range of such communities we can identify at least four central types: (1) the colonial entrepot; (2) the commercial centre; (3) the commercial-industrial city; and (4) the metropolitan community (Stelter and Artibise, 1977). Each of these represented a distinct form of ecological organization and stage of economic development, each a more complex territorial system of functional relationships than its predecessor. Not all Canadian communities experienced each form; nor can we delimit the exact point at which an individual community assumed the character of a new type. This is simply a crude framework through which we might isolate certain patterns that emerge when examining the history of Canadian urban development.

The Early Colonial Town

The distinctive character of the early colonial town was its status as a dependent community (Stelter, 1975; Stelter and Artibise, 1977). It functioned simply as the agent of European metropolitan centres, as a garrison or administrative hub, or as an entrepot. Aside from general military and administrative functions, it collected such staples as fur, lumber, and fish from the surrounding region and transmitted them back to Britain, France, and ultimately to other parts of western Europe (Gertler, 1976). It also was the distribution point for economic and cultural imports from the mother country. Insofar as they preceded settlement of a region, colonial towns formed an urban frontier, a set of "nodes" connecting a relatively unsettled hinterland with an external metropolis. They possessed an undeveloped local economy and their future depended on the potential growth of their own region at least partially.

In their initial state, the colonial towns were relatively isolated from one another. Indeed, one might argue that the emergence of such ties marked the end of the colonial phase of development of a particular community (Stelter and Artibise, 1977). The early colonial town in Canada also typically included a high proportion of the region's population, reflecting its frontier status. In time this proportion declined as the population dispersed and smaller secondary centres emerged (Stelter, 1975). Certain regional variations also occurred. In contrast to the pattern manifested in Lower Canada and in the Maritimes, no single town or group of towns in Upper Canada possessed a commanding proportion of the total provincial population. Because of greater European controls, the movement from colonial status to an indigenous urban economy proceeded more slowly in British North America than in the United States. The foundation of such colonial towns as Kingston, York, Quebec, Montreal, and St. John's established an important basis for the subsequent evolution of Eastern Canada's network of urban communities.

The Commercial Centre

A second major type of community formation, the commercial centre, emerged in Eastern Canada after 1815 (Careless, 1978). The arrival of numerous British immigrants stimulated the expansion of settlements. Internal local markets emerged as places such as York assumed a more vibrant commercial function. Montreal experienced the greatest expansion during this stage of urban commercial development, gaining control over inland trade and commerce along the St. Lawrence River. By the 1830s Montreal had eclipsed Quebec's formerly dominant position (Stelter and Artibise, 1977). Communities such as Saint John and Halifax also combined the functions of a staple entrepot (particularly with respect to lumber) and those of a commercial town.

Like the early colonial town, the commercial centre represented in part a node for the gathering and exporting of such staples as timber, lumber, potash, and wheat to Britain (Bowles and Craib, 1979; Creighton, 1956; Mackintosh, 1967; Marr and Paterson, 1980; Nader, 1975; Watkins, 1963; Wynn, 1979). Its growth was directly linked to the ability of its merchants to exchange primary resources for British manufactured goods. Protected by a mercantilist system, the vitality of such commercial communities as Montreal, Hamilton, and Toronto reflected fluctuations in both the demand for these staples in the mother country and the capacity of the surrounding rural hinterland to meet this demand. An intricate credit system evolved, sustaining the commercial community's exchange relationships (McCalla, 1979). By the middle 1800s the protected market in Britain had eroded (Creighton, 1956). This commercial system underwent radical change as the importance of the market for Canadian lumber and wheat in the United States grew. It is critical to emphasize here, however, the importance of this exporting role for the growth of the nineteenth-century commercial centre.

Later we shall explore the ecological shape of the commercial centre at different points. Here we might note several of its major characteristics. In contrast to the industrial city its economic base derived primarily from its status as a service centre for an expanding hinterland. In addition, it was smaller and more compact than the modern city (Davey and Doucet, 1975). If we take Hamilton, Ontario, in 1851 as illustrative of this type, the following features are also evident (Katz, 1975):

A high degree of population transiency. In Hamilton, for example, less than 10 percent of the work force were born in Canada West; the remainder were migrants from other parts of British North America and immigrants, particularly from the British Isles. The commercial centre was a temporary way-station for a large segment of the population; less than half of Hamilton's residents remained in the city between 1850 and 1860. Such migration was especially pronounced among those who owned little or no property in the community. The more affluent population tended not to move as readily as the less successful.

A high degree of self-employment. This reflects the non-industrial character of the commercial city. Approximately one-third of Hamilton's men worked for themselves in 1851. Many worked at their place of residence. The fairly strict separation of place of work and place of residence that characterizes contemporary urban ecological structure was absent in this type of community.

The small scale of economic enterprises. Most of the labour force worked in small establishments, in small groups. Large-scale economic organizations emerged only with industrialization. The experience and conditions of work were therefore different from those in the industrial city.

Overlapping of social, political, and economic power. A small elite—an entrepreneurial class composed of the most prominent men in business and trade—exercised dominant control of the community. In mid-nineteenth-century Hamilton the most affluent 10 percent of the population controlled almost 90 percent of the property. The entrepreneurs formed the apex of a three-class society; their common interests, mutual ties, and commitment to economic growth, as well as wealth, distinguished them from the artisans and labourers. The latter group especially were politically and economically dispossessed. Such inequality appeared typical of nineteenth-century commercial cities. The rigid stratification system countered the high rates of transiency found among most of the less affluent. Despite a high rate of population turnover, Hamilton, like other nineteenth-century cities, contained a group of prosperous long-term residents who controlled the development of the city.

Residential stability was a reward unequally distributed: "the privilege of class" and "the privilege of stability" were profoundly interwoven (Katz, Doucet, and Stearn, 1978).

The entrepreneurial class sought the economic expansion of their city. They speculated in real estate and exploited whatever opportunities arose to gain access for their community to the emerging railroad network. As we shall see when we briefly review the history of several individual communities, the entrepreneurs not uncommonly experienced economic setbacks and business failures. Downward social mobility was a reality in the commercial city, one the entrepreneurs clearly recognized as evidenced in their continued fear of failure and general sense of anxiety and insecurity (Katz, 1975).

The emergence of the commercial-industrial city and the metropolitan community can perhaps best be analyzed in the context of specific cases. Let us examine in particular the urbanization of Ontario and that of the West, identifying at least some of the factors promoting more complex forms of urban ecological organization.

THE URBANIZATION OF ONTARIO

Earlier we observed that one important component of the complex ecological framework of urbanization is the obvious factor of *environment*. In nineteenth-century Ontario the central lakelands shaped the initial location of urban centres (Careless, 1974a). Towns developed along the rivers and lakes because of the dominance of water transportation. No major community arose inland until the railway system emerged in mid-century; even with the coming of the railways, however, the major Ontario centres remained on the lakefronts. A second environmental factor of some importance was Ontario's physical proximity to the United States. Through the Erie Canal and ties to the railroad system of the United States, Ontario's urban communities were able to benefit from commerce southward.

By 1851 Canada West was 14 percent urban. Such technological innovations as the railroad and the large-scale factory system strengthened Ontario's urban network in subsequent decades. Not all communities benefited equally; some remained small commercial centres servicing a sharply restricted hinterland and others experienced actual economic and population decline. The increasing concentration of industry and tertiary services in Ontario's larger towns and cities destroyed the economy of many local towns, especially after 1871 (Johnson, 1973). These dynamic changes can be seen if we concentrate on specific parts of Ontario's emerging urban network.

South Central Ontario

South Central Ontario represents one of the most highly industrialized and urbanized sections of the country (Spelt, 1972). During the early 1800s, transportation and communication facilities were relatively primitive here, as they were elsewhere in the country (Glazebrook, 1964). Isolation was thereby heightened, and the region consisted primarily of self-sufficient farms with little dependence on urban services. By 1820 urban development was still limited. Only Kingston and York existed as centres of any importance, and even these lacked extensive hinterlands.

This situation began to change significantly after 1820 as transportation facilities improved and a more extensive market system evolved. The development of better roads and a more efficient canal system promoted accessibility and permitted farmers to obtain cash for their produce. Self-sufficiency was no longer as necessary as it had been in previous years. The accumulation of capital in the hinterland provided an economic basis for the expansion of urban service functions. Towns with locations along Lake Ontario or wherever waterpower facilities and good road communications were integrated grew rapidly. This was particularly the case for Toronto, which obtained a major share of the trade with the United States, and which escaped Montreal's dominance by establishing a connection with New York through Oswego and the Erie Canal. In 1851, the urban shape of the region consisted of a series of service centres or central places with differing levels of complexity, measured as follows:

1. *Fully-fledged town or commercial centre*. Contained one member each of the legal and medical profession, a bank, and a newspaper;

2. *Sub-town*. Contained three of the above indicators;

3. *Urban village*. Contained only two of these indicators;

4. *Rural village*. Contained only one of the indicators (Spelt, 1972: 96-97).

Reflecting the important role transportation plays in facilitating urban growth, the "fully-fledged towns" were found along the edge of Lake Ontario.

The trends that had begun prior to 1851 intensified in later decades, especially as a result of the replacement of water transportation by the railway system as the basic mode of communication. Functioning at the centre of this new system assured Toronto's dominance. Towns and villages without immediate access to a railway connection experienced significant declines. The railways encouraged the spread of the money economy, with farmers participating even more deeply in the market system: "Soon the population of the back townships could pay cash for manufactured goods and all kinds of services, which in turn stimulated the urban centres in those townships (Spelt, 1972: 138).

Manufacturing establishments grew in size and were concentrated in larger cities, particularly in Toronto. This city assumed control over the import and export trade, again reflecting its central position in the railway network.

Overall, the years 1851-1881 were characterized by rapid urban growth in South Central Ontario. Urban settlements were distributed more widely through the interior, as access to railways was more critical than access to waterways. Reflecting this, "in 1851, only two inland centers had more than 1,000 inhabitants, but by 1881, there were 26" (Spelt, 1972: 144-45). Smaller centers in close proximity to large urban communities tended to decline as they were unable to compete successfully. Towns that grew had advantageous positions in relation to the railway network and a suitable hinterland.

In the decades following 1881 manufacturing emerged as a primary factor influencing urban development. The concentration of large industrial establishments in Toronto contributed to its increasing dominance in the field. Many smaller centres declined as their industries migrated to this metropolis and other larger cities. Indeed, the service function which had provided such an important basis for urban growth throughout much of the nineteenth century assumed less significance as full-scale industrialization advanced: the commercial centre yielded to the industrial-commercial city. The twentieth century saw the growth of Toronto especially at the expense of other communities in the region. Much of the area's wholesale and retail trade concentrated in that city; smaller centres competed among themselves for control over a more restricted niche in the ecological system.

The Emergence of Toronto as a Metropolitan Community

A central feature of the pattern of urban growth in South Central Ontario was the emergence of Toronto as a metropolitan community. Let us look more closely at its development.

Economic historians such as Gras have proposed that a community evolves into a metropolitan centre through a series of distinct stages. This framework emphasizes the changes in economic functions which occur; it parallels our earlier discussion of metropolitan expansion as an extension of the network of functional relations:

> During the first [stage] the city performs the essential of creating a well-organized marketing system for the whole metropolitan area. . . . The general organization of the market is followed by a second stage—the increased development of manufactures either in the metropolis itself or in the hinterland. The third stage is marked by an active programme of transportation development. The final stage of metropolitan development is the construction of a mature financial system. . . . In this stage by the control of banks, investment houses, and insurance companies the metropolis performs the function of mobilizing capital within itself, radiating capital when required to various points of the hinterland, and facilitating the movement of capital between itself and other metropolitan areas (Masters, 1947: viii).

A strict interpretation of these four stages as occurring is inappropriate when examining the evolution of North American communities (Armstrong, 1977). Instead, the second, third, and fourth "stages" overlapped closely with the first. A city achieves metropolitan status by strengthening its position with respect to all four of the above dimensions concurrently. This is evident in Toronto's case.

The city had not originated as a market and service centre, but rather, as a colonial town, had been established as the capital of Upper Canada. Its initial administrative function exercised a strong influence on the community, and, indeed,

> . . . laid the foundation for its future metropolitan dominance. The inaccessibility of York forced the building of roads, which increasingly converged on the capital and gave historical basis to the convergence of rail routes in the nineteenth century and highways in the twentieth. The function of government brought to York public officials who, with their greater purchasing power, supported more specialized retailing than was found in Hamilton or London (Kerr and Spelt, 1965: 38).

This elite also stimulated the expansion of wholesale trade and financial activities.

In 1825 Toronto was still only a village. During the 1830s it experienced the initial stages of growth that would ultimately culminate in metropolitan status (Armstrong, 1977). Its commercial development strengthened; local manufacturing establishments appeared. By 1833 Toronto was linked to nearby centres and to its agricultural hinterland by a system of stagecoaches. Its growth of population and commerce stimulated the financial sector of its economy. Local insurance companies and banking both prospered. By 1840, six years after its incorporation as a city, Toronto was the largest town in the western part of the province and the dominant marketing centre in the area. In terms of the latter function, it was an important entrepot for the "new staples" of timber, lumber, and wheat (Creighton, 1956; McCalla, 1979). As noted earlier, the economic prosperity of such a community was linked closely to the fluctuations in the market elsewhere for these primary resources. The ability to meet the increased demand for these export staples created "spread effects" throughout the local economy in the form of greater availability of income for investment in other sectors, such as manufacturing (Watkins, 1963).

At mid-century, the city's hinterland was still restricted, extending no further than southern Ontario because of limited transportation facilities. Manufacturing had grown, but not such that the city ceased to be primarily a commercial centre. Nor had it yet gained financial freedom from Montreal: "Five banks operated in the city and of these, three—the Bank of Montreal, much the strongest Canadian bank, the Bank of British North America, and the City Bank of Montreal (an agency) were Montreal concerns (Masters, 1947: 18). Trade relationships with New York provided one potential means by which this domination could be secured.

Toronto in 1850 was a predominantly Anglo-Saxon and Loyalist community, with strong anti-American and anti-French feelings. The city's social structure consisted of several distinct strata, the highest level of which included the "older aristocracy"—that is, the families of those who had come with Simcoe to establish Toronto as the administrative centre of Upper Canada (Cooper, 1956). These relationships were commonly referred to as the "Family Compact" (Saunders, 1957). Although they were politically and socially still dominant, "their position was coming to be challenged by another group [the entrepreneurial class], many of them more recent arrivals in Toronto, the rising commercial and industrial group" (Masters, 1947: 25). Although Toronto contained a number of churches and organizations, it did not evidence any claim to metropolitan status with respect to cultural activities. The community in 1850 functioned as simply an "outpost" or distribution centre for the plays and art that originated in New York and London. The only indigenous literary activities of any consequence were the city's five newspapers.

In the years after 1850 and before Confederation, Toronto moved closer to metropolitan status. Increased prosperity was reflected in a building boom within the city. The Northern Railway was built in 1855 and connections to other routes were also gained (Kerr and Spelt, 1965: 45f.). As a result, the city obtained greater access to the interior, which gave strength to its markets and made its economic position more secure. Manufacturing continued to grow, stimulated by these trends; Toronto was no longer solely a commercial centre, and its industrial base expanded. Attempts to achieve financial autonomy from Montreal intensified. A stock exchange was established in 1855; building and loan and insurance companies proliferated. The failure of the Bank of Upper Canada in 1866, however, indicated that much effort was still needed to achieve economic independence.

In 1867 Toronto became the capital of Ontario, and during the next eight years its economic expansion continued. Throughout this period its increasing prosperity was reflected in the pattern of physical growth and in the development of appropriate municipal services, the basis of which had actually been formed several decades earlier (Armstrong, 1977). The city's retail trade became more extensive, symbolized by the establishment of Eaton's and Simpson's. Toronto's link to its hinterland grew stronger as involvement in additional railway building continued. Although Montreal gained control of the CPR, Toronto's overall financial position was strengthened by the creation of the Bank of Commerce in 1867 and through the Canadian Bank Act of 1871.

During the 1880s Toronto achieved full metropolitanization. The city's population grew by more than four-fifths, matched by a striking expansion in the industrial sector: between 1881 and 1891 the number of industries located in the city increased by well over a thousand. Its marketing, wholesale, and retail functions became firmly established with a secure financial basis, reflected in the growth of the central business district and other changes in the spatial structure of the community. Overall, therefore, Toronto emerged

. . . as the capital of a great metropolitan economic empire. Marketing, manufacturing, and banking facilities were largely centered under its control. It was the focal point for a network of railways and its harbour was the busiest on the Canadian side of Lake Ontario. It had become the great mobilizer of capital within its area and largely controlled capital movement between its own and other areas (Masters, 1947: 165-66).

Emergence as a metropolitan centre was thus facilitated by its geographical advantages, its selection as an administrative centre of Upper Canada, and vigorous leadership in the city, particularly from the dominant entrepreneurial class (Masters, 1947: 208). Its position as the focus of an efficient transportation network permitted the city to achieve a higher level of integration with its hinterland, and also to achieve greater freedom from Montreal's economic influence. It was able to function as an important trans-shipment centre for the export of lumber, potash, and wheat to Britain and the United States. These specific conditions helped to foster the evolution of a territorially extended system of functional relations within this particular region. They were also responsible for the emergence of other metropolitan communities elsewhere in Canada.

The Development of London, Oshawa, and Whitby

Toronto emerged in the nineteenth century as the dominant centre not only of South Central Ontario but of the entire province. Other communities, such as London in Southwestern Ontario and Oshawa and Whitby in Ontario County, sought to expand their economic base from commerce to industry. They were not, however, able to achieve Toronto's preeminence.

London did gain primacy in its region by the late 1880s but not metropolitan status (Armstrong and Brock, 1974). It was sufficiently distant from Toronto to strengthen its local economy. In 1826 London was selected as the administrative centre for the surrounding district. Several other communities had competed for this function, but the apparent radical orientation of their residents was a serious handicap. As with Toronto, London's selection aided its subsequent growth, which a rising entrepreneurial class exploited and guided. Nine years later London obtained the right to establish a public market; this enabled it to become the commercial centre for the agricultural region, especially to its north. In 1838 in response to the threat of a potential American invasion, London became a British garrison town, which strengthened its economy. Improvements in its roads to outside communities such as Hamilton enabled it to expand its market activities. Like Toronto it benefited from the production and exportation of Upper Canadian wheat and sawn lumber which permitted, in turn, the importation of dry goods, for example, from Britain (McCalla, 1979). During the 1850s London gained access to railroad lines, which stimulated growth of its local industries; in addition, its telegraph and newspaper links to the outside allowed it to elaborate a communication system vital to further economic development. Its incorporation as a city in 1855 was an appropriate symbol of its growth. During the following decades London's financial institutions strengthened in response to increasing intensity of market transactions, and enabled it to persist as "the economic hub of southwestern Ontario" (Armstrong and Brock, 1974).

Communities closer to Toronto, such as Oshawa and Whitby, were less able to sustain a pattern of economic dominance over an expanding hinterland (Johnson, 1973). The period 1820-1840 was one of substantial growth in Ontario County, which at that time was part of York County. The total population, containing many immigrants from the British Isles, expanded by 1000 percent. The older townships such as Pickering and Whitby experienced the greatest economic development; the northern areas of the county remained in a pioneer state. By 1840, because of their harbours and the construction of adequate roads, Whitby and Oshawa emerged as the dominant trading centres for the region. At this stage their economies were relatively free of Toronto's dominance. Their merchants increasingly exploited the commercial, grain, and timber trade in the region. The appearance of cabinetmaking and foundry work in Oshawa by 1840 also reflected that community's central economic position.

The continued expansion of population and agriculture during the 1840s, coupled with continued improvement of the system of roads, brought added prosperity to Whitby and Oshawa. Each competed for dominance over the northern areas of Ontario—not only with each other, but also with such northern centres as Prince Albert. Such towns vigorously vied for the allocation of public funds to improve transportation routes that would provide them with a trading advantage.

Whitby merchants sought to have the ten eastern townships in Home District established as a separate district with that community as its administrative centre. They were strongly opposed by their counterparts in Oshawa and Toronto who believed this would strengthen Whitby's control over inland trade. In 1854 Ontario County was separated from York; Whitby successfully competed with Oshawa for county-seat status. Both communities, however, gained from the region's economic growth during the 1850s. Large-scale industries emerged in both Oshawa and Whitby, yet the latter's economy was more fully devoted to trade and administration. After 1857 Whitby stagnated, as it failed to expand its administrative function; its efforts to enlarge Ontario County were unsuccessful. In addition, the County Council balked at granting a loan for the construction of a rail route from Whitby to Lake Huron, which prohibited it from strengthening its market. In contrast, Oshawa's entrepreneurs gave greater attention to industrial growth; during the 1860s many of its factories expanded. This, however, brought only short-term prosperity to the community. By 1880 many of its industries had disappeared—unsuccessful rivals of those in Toronto and Hamilton.

In 1868, Toronto's merchants were able to charter two railways to the northwest and northeast. The latter permitted that city to extend its sphere of dominance over the hinterland previously tied to Whitby. Construction of the

Port Whitby-Port Perry railroad line did not prove to be a significant challenge to this takeover. By 1875 Ontario County existed as part of Toronto's economic orbit. Whitby and Oshawa functioned as subsidiary satellites within the ecological system dominated by that metropolis. The spread of Toronto's "tentacles" spelled doom for the hopes of Whitby's and Oshawa's entrepreneurs to achieve for their communities economic pre-eminence (Johnson, 1973).

THE URBANIZATION OF THE WEST

Between 1870 and 1914 Western Canada experienced rapid urban growth. By the end of the first decade of this century half (50.9 percent) of British Columbia's population was urban. During the thirty-year period from 1881 to 1911 Manitoba's urban population more than doubled. Alberta too reflected this pattern (see Table 3). A variety of factors influenced Western urbanization. Perhaps the most important was the completion of the transcontinental railroad in 1886 (McCann, 1968-69). In contrast to Eastern Canada's major urban centres, which had developed in the age of water transport, such dominant Western communities as Winnipeg, Edmonton, Calgary, and Vancouver were all "creations of the railway." As one historian has observed, the technology of railway transport functioned as the prime mediating factor between environment and population in the ecology of the urban West; railway technology integrated the new Western cities into a continent-wide metropolitan system (Careless, 1977). The influx of immigrants also encouraged urban growth. This process of expansion was, as in the East, directed by an entrepreneurial elite who dominated each community, and sought to insure—at times not always harmoniously (Foran, 1975)—its economic prosperity. As in the East, the latter was a function as well of the extent to which each community was able to function as a trans-shipment centre for the primary resources of the Western hinterland. We shall briefly explore the development of three of these cities—Winnipeg, Victoria, and Vancouver—as illustrative of Western urbanization during this period.

Winnipeg: "Gem of the Prairies"

Winnipeg's growth was as dramatic and significant as that which Toronto experienced. Between 1881 and 1921 its decennial population growth rate averaged more than 135 percent, compared to only 20 percent for the country as a whole (Artibise, 1975). Reflecting this increase, Winnipeg was the sixty-second largest urban centre in the country in 1871; twenty years later it was ranked eighth. By 1911 the city had become the third largest in the country. During the decade 1901-1911 Winnipeg's total population rose by almost 100,000. Such spectacular increase was the result not of annexations of surrounding communities, but rather of a massive influx of native-born migrants—particularly from Ontario—and of immigrants from Britain, Northern Europe, and the Ukraine. This influx paralleled the expansion of the Prairie wheat economy from which the city benefited both directly and indirectly. The arrival of immigrants was of such a scale that by 1916 more than half the city's population was foreign-born.

Since the early nineteenth century a settlement had existed at Winnipeg. But it was only after the monopoly which the Hudson's Bay Company had exercised over trade in the Red River Colony declined that the conditions for growth became more firmly established. Winnipeg's expansion was assured with Manitoba's entrance into the Dominion in 1870 and with the concomitant opening of the entire region to settlement. The city, incorporated in 1874, emerged as a commercial centre, much as Toronto had by 1850, servicing the economic needs of other communities in the provincial hinterland. Paralleling the process of urban growth in Eastern Canada, Winnipeg's prosperity depended closely on the production and export of staples (initially fur and later wheat) in the surrounding hinterland (Morton, 1957). The late 1870s were the years of the "Manitoba land fever"; numerous settlers had arrived seeking to exploit the wheat-growing opportunities in the Red River Valley. Winnipeg emerged as the centre for the western grain trade. That city's leading residents expressed profound optimism for the future of their community, with a strong sense of commitment to achieving full metropolitan status.

In examining the details of how this ambition was fulfilled, particular attention must be given to that small group of residents who directed the city's growth from the time of incorporation through the period prior to World War I. This group comprised an entrepreneurial elite, united through adherence to a common set of values and ideals:

> Accepting the challenge of a vast, underdeveloped domain they saw themselves as agents of improvement. They were practical men, businessmen who were convinced of the desirability of material progress. Setting their sights from persuasive American examples—such as the rise of Chicago—they were optimistic, expansionist, and aggressive (Artibise, 1975: 23).

They believed in the primacy of economic growth, even over social concerns, and sought to achieve this through Winnipeg's struggle for metropolitan status. Their commitment to such a "growth ethic" represented an important force furthering the expansion of this urban ecological organization.

The elite were convinced that the primary function of Winnipeg's municipal government was to support this struggle. Hence, they assumed an active interest in civic politics, and dominated most local elective offices, including City Council. As in Toronto, this group consisted of successful businessmen who were primarily Anglo-Saxon and Protestant. They represented, in addition, a social and cultural elite in the city, participating in common organizations and activities on both the local and regional levels. Between 1874 and 1914 they exercised tremendous influence over Winnipeg's development. The existence of property qualifications for voting and holding elective office strengthened that control, as the majority of poorer residents and members of the various ethnic groups were disenfranchised. The "growth ethic" thus stood unchallenged, despite the continuing presence of serious social problems.

In its quest for economic expansion a major goal for Winnipeg during the 1870s and 1880s was securing adequate rail connections through the region and with the rest of the country: "Railroads were the key to growth, the one essential without which all the commercial elite's plans for Winnipeg would fall" (Artibise, 1975: 63). Railway communications represented an essential channel through which the city might export wheat to world markets (Morton, 1957). Such access would permit it to establish itself as the predominant distribution centre and wheat market for the entire Northwest. The CPR syndicate originally planned to build the transcontinental through Selkirk to the north to avoid the problem of the Red River flooding. This scheme was subsequently changed, and the railway was run through Winnipeg instead, providing the city with that central transportation linkage which it had so desperately sought and which guaranteed it regional preeminence. A building boom ensued for a short time in anticipation of the benefits which this linkage would bring. With construction of this line the city began more fully to assume the functions of a metropolitan centre. As an additional consequence,

> The upsurge in Winnipeg's fortunes that followed the coming of the C.P.R. reaffirmed in the minds of the commercial elite the conviction that railways were the key to rapid and sustained growth. Thereafter City Council did everything to encourage railway development and nothing at all to control it. This attitude had serious long-range consequences for the city's physical appearance and social fabric (Artibise, 1975: 74).

No attempt was made to construct a general community plan within which the location and number of railway lines would be carefully determined.

Efforts to improve the city's connections to an inland navigation system also reflected this concern for attaining adequate transportation and communication linkages. Access to Lake Winnipeg was gained by constructing a series of locks at St. Andrew's Falls. More efficient use of the Red River was also envisioned. As the rail system expanded, interest in these waterways lessened.

Aside from transportation, an additional prerequisite for Winnipeg's rise to metropolitan status was an adequate supply of power at a reasonable cost for the development of manufacturing. This was a serious problem in the city for a time because of the monopoly which the Winnipeg Electric Railway Company held over the community's power supply. Lacking any significant competition, that company maintained its rates at a very high level, which inhibited industrial growth. The prospect of this situation continuing forced the elite to support the move to municipal ownership of a power project. This support did not derive from concern for the public welfare. Rather, the existing monopoly represented a substantial hindrance to the city's economic expansion from which they hoped to benefit.

The elite's "growth ethic" could be fulfilled only through expansion in population and industry. Vigorous efforts were made to attract both. The city supported an extensive publicity program to encourage settlement in Winnipeg itself and in the surrounding communities, from whose trade economic growth could be gained. Immigration agents were appointed to help promote the area. In 1904 the Western Canadian Immigration Association was established to encourage American immigration to the region. Many of the leaders of this association were members of Winnipeg's entrepreneurial elite. Efforts were made to attract industry to the city—for example, through the Winnipeg Development and Industrial Bureau—which proved relatively successful. In all of these schemes, it was evident that economic growth took priority over use of public funds to remedy inadequate housing, educational, and recreational facilities. The pursuit of additional population and industry only served to heighten these problems, which crystallized most dramatically in the strike of 1919 (Masters, 1950).

In sum, the case of Winnipeg's rise to metropolitan status demonstrated the influence a "growth ethic" espoused by a small but powerful elite exercised on a process of ecological expansion. It also suggested the need to take account of cultural factors—in this case an ideology—in attempting to explain that process.

Decline in Victoria, Expansion in Vancouver

As we have seen, one common pattern in nineteenth-century urban growth was the competition between two or more centres for regional dominance. Each sought to capture a wider market than its rival—Toronto versus Montreal, Oshawa versus Whitby, both towns versus Toronto. Economic prosperity for one community frequently meant decline for another. As more complex territorial systems of functional relationships emerged, not all could achieve an equally central position. We can illustrate this competition in the West by examining the fates of Victoria and Vancouver.

Victoria was established as a trading post for the Hudson's Bay Company in 1843 (Ruzicka, 1973; Lines, 1972). It serviced the entire Northwest Coast during the next fifteen years. Its growth was aided by the discovery of gold on the Fraser River in 1858; miners used it as their main supply centre. Reflecting its economic dominance, Victoria was named the capital of British Columbia in 1868. By 1885 its influence extended throughout the province. The main offices of British Columbia's financial institutions were located in Victoria (Ruzicka, 1973). It functioned as the centre of the expanding fishing industry, lumber exporting, and food importing businesses, thus ensuring its economic growth. In addition, it held a key location in the existing transportation system, with local links to the Fraser River and more extensive water routes to San Francisco and Britain. By 1885 the community contained almost 100 businesses involved in secondary industries. Its future seemed secure as a vibrant metropolitan centre, a fact which residents on the Mainland resented.

Their anxieties were premature. In 1887 the CPR's first train arrived in Vancouver, the site chosen as the terminus of the transcontinental railroad. This significantly clouded Victoria's future. Vancouver was now able to mount a serious challenge for regional preeminence and control over the staples trade. By 1891 Vancouver's population had grown to 13,685, only about 3,000 less than Victoria's. Of greater importance, Victoria's financial domination had eroded as Vancouver's branch of the Bank of British Columbia showed greater profits than its counterpart in Victoria. This reflected Vancouver's growing share of total provincial trade; in addition, the CPR established a steamship service linking that city with the Orient. Victoria's businessmen were unable to exploit that market easily.

The Depression of the 1890s reduced demand for lumber, salmon, and fur seal. This affected Victoria in particular. Vancouver's superior transportation facilities and connections allowed it to benefit from the expansion of the Kootenay mining industry and from greater trade with British Columbia's interior; its failure to capture a larger share of the Klondike trade in 1897-1898, when gold was discovered in the Yukon, was not a serious impediment (MacDonald, 1968). Although the Depression ended by 1897, Victoria continued to decline as a major economic centre. Its persistent efforts to gain direct rail connections to the Fraser Valley proved fruitless. By the turn of the century Vancouver, with superior communication facilities, was processing almost double the amount of freight that Victoria did. Vancouver assumed the role of banking, commercial-industrial, and shipping centre of the entire province. Most important, as in the case of the development of other cities we have examined earlier, Vancouver emerged as the dominant trans-shipment point for the export of the region's staples to world markets.

Victoria's decline paralleled Vancouver's expansion. British Columbia's capital failed to obtain adequate transportation facilities that would have permitted that city to maintain control over the staple industries, financial system, and commercial trade of the province. In 1885 Victoria existed as the region's metropolitan centre; by 1901 the city had assumed a subordinate role within Vancouver's sphere of influence (Ruzicka, 1973).

Perhaps as compensation, having lost the battle for provincial dominance, at least some of Victoria's businessmen wished to strengthen her tourist trade (Lines, 1972). As a result of the suggestion of Herbert Cuthbert, a British immigrant to Victoria, the city established a Tourist Development Association in 1901. They sought to exploit the image of Victoria as a "Bit of Old England" and promote an influx of tourists, particularly from the rapidly growing cities of Seattle and Tacoma. Unable to become the terminus of the transcontinental, ironically Victoria did prevail upon the CPR to construct a new tourist hotel, the Empress, in 1908. This interest in tourism reflected the desire to find an alternate channel for promoting at least modest economic growth in the new century.

Vancouver, in contrast, continued to expand its metropolitan position in the early 1900s (MacDonald, 1968, 1970, 1973). From 1900 to 1914 it experienced considerable growth. Many migrants and immigrants, particularly from Britain, arrived, attracted to the diverse economic opportunities in the city. Paralleling Winnipeg's rise, Vancouver's population increased to 115,000, approximately one-third of whom were British immigrants (MacDonald, 1973). Expansion of both local and interurban transportation lines encouraged outward expansion of the population and the construction of numerous single-family homes in many different sections of the metropolitan region. Physically, Vancouver grew to three times the size of Victoria. Its economic activities extended beyond servicing the immediate hinterland. Along with Edmonton and Calgary it began to challenge and erode Winnipeg's position as the leading distribution centre of Western Canada (McCann, 1968-69). As with Winnipeg, however, during this entire process of economic transformation, Vancouver's business elite guided and controlled its rise to metropolitan status. The evolution of more complex territorial systems of functional relationships—i.e., urbanization understood ecologically—throughout the West, as in the East, was correlated with the concentration of economic and political power. Urban political institutions were conservative, with little scope for widespread participatory democracy (Careless, 1977).

THE INSTITUTIONAL CORRELATES OF URBANIZATION: TWO EXAMPLES

Urbanization, as we have stressed, entails the spread of a more comprehensive and intricate territorial system of functional relationships. Accompanying this ecological process are profound changes in the structure of social institutions. The basic principle of urban development is increasing specialization, which influences all aspects of social life—the economy, the political sector, the educational system, even leisure. Bureaucratization, the evolution of more formalized organizations, is a product of enhanced specialization. We may illustrate this by examining the following concrete examples of the "institutional correlates" of Canadian urbanization.

The Taverns of Toronto

Toronto experienced a dramatic transformation in the nineteenth century, from a small commercial centre to a diversified metropolis. Its own labour force grew more specialized as its economy expanded. Yet other parts of Toronto's social environment also reflected specialization.

In the city's early years Toronto's taverns played a central role in its social structure (Christie, 1973). They functioned as more than simply drinking establishments. The tavern was the site for a multiplicity of activities which did not occur elsewhere because Toronto had not yet a variety of buildings devoted to specialized purposes.

The general functions of the tavern included:

1. Meetings. Various groups, organizations and clubs used the tavern as their meeting place. This became less common as halls were constructed.

2. Municipal affairs. Not infrequently court proceedings were held in the tavern. Likewise, candidates for electoral office campaigned in taverns; there too the actual ballots were cast, at least until the temperance supporters put an end to it!

3. Entertainment. Before specialized theatres were built, various types of artistic activities such as plays were presented in taverns.

4. Sport. The tavern also played an important part in Toronto's sporting activities. Particularly in the earlier period of the nineteenth century it was the site for such events as bowling and other non-club activities. Tavern proprietors frequently sponsored matches or competitions off their premises. Participants gathered afterward at the tavern to plan further events.

Paralleling Toronto's population and economic growth, between 1834 and 1874 the total number of taverns in Toronto more than tripled. Nevertheless, the most important change was the loss of many of its functions. By the end of the 1870s the tavern no longer existed as a multipurpose institution; it "specialized" now more rigidly as a drinking and lodging establishment. Many activities now occurred in buildings and sites specifically created for those purposes (Christie, 1973). The tavern's loss of the sporting function occurred some years later, as mass participation in sport intensified (Purcell, 1974).

The Schools of Calgary

The appearance of a greater number of bureaucratic organizations accompanied the expansion of Canadian cities in the late nineteenth and early twentieth centuries. This was evident in most sectors of the urban community—its economy, political system, and welfare arrangements. It was particularly striking in the educational system.

In the mid-1880s Calgary was still a small centre with a population of about 500 (Stamp, 1977). It possessed only a private school which the more affluent residents controlled. No compulsory education yet existed. The city's population increased eleven times between 1884 and 1890, and a public school system was established, reflecting the greater demand for formal education within the city. Stimulating this demand was a sense of civic pride in the community and a desire to expand its indigenous institutions. One central school was built with a formal school board to oversee the institution. During the 1890s, although the population did not expand as rapidly, two additional schools were created, with the entire educational system more thoroughly standardized. New regulations dealing with such matters as student attendance and teacher responsibilities emerged. The gap between school trustees and the citizenry widened.

By 1914 Calgary had become a dominant economic centre in Western Canada. The bureaucratization of its educational system paralleled that status. Its pupil population increased from 12 in 1884 to more than 7000 in 1914, its teaching staff from 1 to 198, and the number of schools from 1 to 34. Any remnants of the earlier non-compulsory approach to education had disappeared. Elementary and high school instruction were separated. A formal administrative system was elaborated, and a full-time superintendent of schools appointed. Significantly, in 1911 the new office of Calgary's school board was moved to City Hall, intensifying the "bureaucratic remoteness" of the educational system (Stamp, 1977). The activities of that system were also extended, reflecting its bureaucratization: the schools sought to deal with broader concerns than merely academic instruction. Business and technical courses occupied a larger share of the curriculum.

Just as the urban network that emerged during these years formed the basis of the contemporary Canadian urban system, so too did the increasing specialization and bureaucratization of urban institutions influence the nature of that urban social structure which we encounter today.

SUMMARY

1. Urbanization, understood ecologically, represents an expansion of the organization or set of functional relationships through which a specific population is able to satisfy its daily needs. It consists of the process of growth from a highly localized unit to a complex, more comprehensive territorial system.
2. Canadian urban history reveals four forms of ecological organization, each more complex than its predecessor. These are: the colonial entrepot, the commercial centre, the commercial-industrial city, and the metropolitan community.
3. The emergence of each form was precipitated by changes within the ecosystem. Increasing population and technological advancements fostered

more complex forms of territorial organization. A variety of factors promoted urbanization in both Eastern and Western Canada. Among these are (a) *Transportation improvements*. In particular, the railroad allowed a more extensive territorial system of functional relationships to emerge; (b) *Expansion of the local urban economy*. Urban centres grew partly as places for the gathering and exporting of such staples as timber, lumber, and wheat from their surrounding hinterlands. The income derived from this permitted cities such as Toronto and Winnipeg to diversify their economies, strengthen their industrial bases, and generate growth in the services they performed for their regions (Jacobs, 1970; Nader, 1975); (c) *Vigorous leadership by a civic elite* (Noble, 1980); (d) *Commitment of that elite to a "growth ethic."* This suggests the need to recognize how the elaboration of a more extensive territorial system of functional relations can be profoundly influenced by cultural variables.

4. A common pattern in nineteenth-century urban growth was the competition between two or more centres for regional dominance. As more complex territorial systems of functional relationships emerged, not all communities could achieve an equally central position. Prosperity for one frequently meant decline for another. Direct access to the railway system was an important factor influencing ultimate success.

5. Urbanization as an ecological process entailed increasing specialization and bureaucratization. As the Canadian urban system emerged in the nineteenth century, a variety of social institutions in the city reflected these features.

Chapter 4

The Contemporary Canadian Urban and Metropolitan System

The contemporary Canadian urban system owes much of its structure to the patterns of growth that emerged during the nineteenth century. The previous chapter sought to identify at least some of those patterns which urban historians have begun to document. The current urban and metropolitan system is far more complex, of course, than that which existed in the late 1800s. In this chapter we shall examine some of its central demographic and ecological characteristics.

A DEMOGRAPHIC PROFILE OF CANADA'S URBAN AREAS

In the Introduction we briefly outlined the overall trends in Canadian urban growth. A more comprehensive demographic profile of Canada's urban areas, however, must include more detailed data on population growth patterns, sex and age composition, and socioeconomic characteristics. In subsequent chapters we shall also look at the ethnic and migration status of Canada's urban population. Such data provide an important base for understanding the variations in Canada's urban social structure, as well as the parameters for future urban planning.

Urban Population Growth

Throughout Canada's history the growth of its population was not evenly distributed across all urban areas. This is apparent when we compare variations in population growth indices for 1961-1971 by region, province, and size of community. Table 4 summarizes the relevant data for all urban areas over 10,000 population in 1971; 70 percent of Canada's total population lived in these communities. We should take note of the following trends:

1. Looking at urban Canada as a whole, during the 1961-1971 period the highest population growth index occurs in the 1,000,000 + size class of urban areas; the lowest relative growth is recorded not in the smallest size class, but rather in communities within the 50,000-99,999 range. Hence, during this period, population growth is not necessarily directly correlated with population size (Ray, 1976: 7).

65

Table 4: Population Growth Index, Urban Canada, 1961-71

Region and province	Size class							All urban areas over 10,000
	1,000,000+	250,000-1,000,000	100,000-250,000	50,000-100,000	30,000-50,000	20,000-30,000	10,000-20,000	
Atlantic			14.69	3.84	14.08	8.96	17.96	12.44
Newfoundland			21.09			4.37	66.79	23.76
Prince Edward Island						13.96	10.42	12.68
Nova Scotia			14.08	-3.32	1.19	8.97	11.97	8.19
New Brunswick			8.46	13.78	27.23		7.11	11.70
Québec	21.28	23.60	4.66	7.31	13.52	18.67	8.42	18.92
Ontario	31.17	22.19	26.58	17.64	13.16	12.27	7.74	24.75
Prairies		25.35	24.29		5.64	18.56	30.03	24.02
Manitoba		12.53			9.62		40.43	14.12
Saskatchewan			24.29		-7.98	16.30	17.45	19.68
Alberta		33.83			14.30	19.72	42.62	32.24
British Columbia	26.77		22.78		53.26	24.33	29.33	29.40
Urban Canada	26.14	23.53	20.52	11.95	20.21	15.48	16.33	22.69

Population Growth Index For 1961-71 is computed as follows:

$$\frac{\text{Population in 1971 - Population in 1961}}{(\text{Population in 1971} + \text{Population in 1961})/2} - 100$$

Thus, the higher the index, the greater the relative population growth.

From D. Michael Ray, ed., *Canadian Urban Trends* Vol. I © Ministry of Supply and Services Canada, 1976. Reprinted by permission of Copp Clark Pitman, Publishers.

2. There are substantial regional variations in relative population growth by size class. Both the Atlantic region and the Prairies show the largest population growth indices in the smallest areas (10,000–19,999); exactly the opposite pattern appears in Ontario. British Columbia experienced growth in all size categories, but especially among communities in the 30,000–49,999 range. Note also the existence of provincial variations within a region; for example, whereas Newfoundland's largest population growth index occurs among the smallest centres, New Brunswick's exists in the 30,000–49,999 category. Similarly, Saskatchewan, unlike the rest of its region, does not show the greatest relative growth among the smallest urban communities. Such variations reflect differences in migration flows, rates of natural increase, and points of destination for immigrants.

3. The total population growth index for all urban areas over 10,000 also manifests significant regional variations. The highest relative growth is found in British Columbia, the lowest in Atlantic Canada. Comparing individual provinces, however, reveals that Alberta attained the highest index, Nova Scotia the lowest. The latter province, indeed, was one of only two throughout the country to show absolute decline in population in one of the size categories.

Metropolitan Growth

As noted earlier, the dominance of the metropolitan community in Canada during the present time is quite evident. The twenty-two metropolitan areas delineated in the 1971 census contain more than half of the nation's total population.

Although the proportion of the population classified as urban has been slightly higher in the United States, Canada has pursued a similar pattern of metropolitan growth to its neighbour since the latter part of the nineteenth century. As Table 5 indicates, over the eighty-year period between 1870 and 1950 in both countries the number of metropolitan areas increased, as did the proportion of the total population concentrated within these urban complexes. As in the United States the rings (or surburban areas) of Canadian metropolitan communities showed higher growth rates beginning in the 1920s in comparison to the central cities. As transportation facilities became more advanced, the outward movement of population occurred on a larger scale (see Langlois, 1961). Since World War I, in North America central cities have held an increasingly smaller share of the total metropolitan population. This represents a later stage in the emergence of more complex ecological units and in the overall urbanization of these two highly industrialized societies. Canada's metropolitan development lagged only slightly behind that of the United States due to "the simple fact that the underlying process of urban concentration got under way earlier in the United States" (Schnore and Petersen, 1958: 68).

Table 5: Growth Data for Metropolitan Areas (MAs), Central Cities, and Rings, Canada and the United States (1870-71 Through 1950-51)

Countries	Number of MAs	Population of MAs (millions)	Percent of natural population		Rate of growth during preceding decade					Percent of total growth claimed by MAs during preceding decade	
			Central cities	Rings	National Total	Area Outside MAs	MAs	Central Cities	Rings	Central Cities	Rings
Canada[1]											
1871	3	0.5	5.9	6.8	—	—	—	—	—	—	—
1881	2	0.5	5.3	5.2	17.2	16.4	24.5	39.1	12.7	10.0	4.0
1891	2	0.6	8.2	4.7	11.8	8.7	37.9	75.1	0.5	33.6	0.2
1901	5	1.0	11.3	7.1	11.1	10.1	16.2	24.6	5.0	22.2	3.4
1911	6	1.9	18.4	8.4	34.2	27.2	57.8	82.8	21.5	32.8	5.8
1921	10	2.8	21.9	10.1	21.9	17.3	33.3	35.7	28.3	32.0	12.3
1931	13	4.2	26.4	13.8	18.1	10.9	30.7	29.5	33.0	39.2	22.4
1941	14	4.8	26.8	14.6	10.9	10.3	11.7	11.0	12.9	27.1	16.9
1951	15	6.2	26.5	19.0	18.6	12.7	26.5	15.6	45.7	22.8	38.1
United States											
1870[2]	21	8.3	12.9	10.6	—	—	—	—	—	—	—
1880	30	11.9	13.5	10.2	41.1	45.7	28.0	36.3	18.4	12.4	5.4
1890	44	17.8	16.9	11.4	25.5	21.8	36.1	45.6	24.0	26.1	10.3
1900[3]	52	24.1	21.2	10.7	20.7	17.2	29.0	45.7	5.2	38.5	3.1
1910	71	34.5	25.0	12.7	21.0	15.0	32.6	35.3	27.6	37.4	15.7
1920	94	46.1	28.9	14.8	14.9	8.1	25.2	26.7	22.4	46.8	20.8
1930	115	61.0	31.8	18.0	16.1	7.1	27.0	23.3	34.2	43.3	32.9
1940	125	67.1	31.6	19.5	7.2	6.2	8.3	5.1	13.8	22.8	34.9
1950	147	84.3	32.3	23.8	14.5	6.3	21.8	13.7	34.8	30.7	48.6

1. Data for Canada from Dominion Bureau of Statistics, *Ninth Census of Canada, 1951.*
2. Data for the United States (1870-90) from Department of Interior, Census Office, *Compendium of the Eleventh Census: 1890,* and Department of Interior, Census Office, *Ninth Census: 1870.*
3. Data for the United States (1900-50) from Donald J. Bogue, "Urbanism in the United States, 1950," *American Journal of Sociology 9,* March 1955. Reproduced by permission of the publisher, copyright 1955 by the University of Chicago; and Donald J. Bogue, *Population Growth in Standard Metropolitan Areas 1900-1950,* Housing and Home Finance Agency, 1953. We have followed Bogue's practice of using "county-equivalent" metropolitan areas in New England. Retrojection of 1950 areas to earlier dates does not imply that these areas were metropolitan in character; our sole intention is to hold total area constant.

Since 1950 this pattern of metropolitan concentration has continued, as Table 6 reveals.

Table 6: Population Growth of Metropolitan and Non-metropolitan Canada, 1951-71

Population	Metropolitan	Non-metropolitan
1951	6,397,680	7,611,749
1961	9,291,305	8,946,942
1971	11,874,748	9,693,563
Percent of Canada's population		
1951	45.7	54.3
1961	50.9	49.1
1971	55.1	44.9
Population growth rate (%)		
1951-1961	45.2	17.5
1961-1971	27.8	8.3
Percent of Canada's population growth		
1951-1961	68.4	31.6
1961-1971	77.6	22.4

From Frederick I. Hill, ed., *Canadian Urban Trends* Vol. II © Ministry of Supply and Services Canada, 1976. Reprinted by permission of Copp Clark Pitman, Publishers.

The total metropolitan population almost doubled between 1951 and 1971. Its share both of Canada's total population and total growth also increased. Nevertheless, it should be noted that the rate of metropolitan growth has declined when examining the total post-World War II trend: "As Canada entered the seventies, her metropolitan areas were growing at only half the rate at which they had grown in the early fifties" (Hill, 1976: 3). This paralleled the slowdown in the rate of population growth for Canada as a whole. Also of interest here is the contrasting increase in the rural population (primarily rural non-farm on the outskirts of urban areas) between 1971 and 1976. During those five years the rural areas gained 8.8 percent, in comparison to the 5.9 percent increase of the urban population: "more urban workers may be prepared to commute to work while opting to live in a rural area" (Statistics Canada, 1980).

Just as we find regional, provincial, and community size variations in the rate of population growth, so too are there significant differences in growth trends when comparing the twenty-two metropolitan areas. Table 7 indicates that during the 1950s the most rapidly growing areas were in the Prairies—Calgary, Edmonton, and Saskatoon. Such communities as Saint John, Quebec, Winnipeg, and St. John's show a far smaller rate of growth. In the more recent 1961-71 period all but two metropolitan areas (Kitchener and Windsor) experienced a substantial decline in that rate; Calgary in particular, however, continued to evidence marked expansion. Chicoutimi-Jonquière, Saint John, and Thunder Bay hardly grew at all. Distinct regional variations in metropolitan concentration have thus emerged, and, as Table 8 suggests, will persist in the future. Atlantic Canada's population will continue to manifest the weakest metropolitanization.

A variety of factors have accounted for metropolitan growth. The rate of natural increase is responsible for at least half of this growth during the 1966-1971 period, with immigration accounting for much of the remainder (Hill, 1976: 5). This too shows substantial variation when comparing individual metropolitan communities. For example, as we shall see later, Toronto's expansion was particularly dependent on the influx of immigrants (Kumove, 1975): in contrast, Calgary experienced a larger net migration with respect to the rest of Canada between 1966 and 1971 than any other metropolitan community (Hill, 1976: 6).

The dramatic growth of Calgary and Edmonton since World War II also reveals the importance of economic factors in accounting for metropolitan

Table 7: Population Growth, Census Metropolitan Areas, 1951-1971 Census Metropolitan Area*

	Growth rate	
	1951-1961	1961-1971
Calgary	96.1	44.5
Chicoutimi-Jonquière	40.0	4.8
Edmonton	85.8	37.8
Halifax	39.7	15.1
Hamilton	42.3	24.3
Kitchener	44.1	46.5
London	35.1	26.2
Montreal	43.9	23.8
Ottawa-Hull	46.7	31.8
Quebec	31.0	26.8
Regina	56.4	23.7
St. Catharines-Niagara	36.4	17.7
St. John's	33.7	23.6
Saint John	21.6	8.8
Saskatoon	71.6	32.3
Sudbury	58.2	22.0
Thunder Bay	38.5	9.8
Toronto	52.1	36.9
Vancouver	41.1	30.9
Victoria	35.6	25.7
Windsor	18.9	19.1
Winnipeg	33.4	13.4

*Oshawa in 1976 became Canada's 23rd CMA.
From Frederick I. Hill, ed., *Canadian Urban Trends* Vol. II © Ministry of Supply and Services Canada, 1976. Reprinted by permission of Copp Clark Pitman, Publishers.

growth. Both of these are regional centres serving a wide hinterland. Parallel-ing the connection between staple exports and urban growth in the nineteenth century, their post-war rate of growth was partly a product of the oil boom that began with the Leduc discovery in 1947 (Baine, 1973; Seifried, 1978). Calgary today is Canada's major oil administrative centre (Zieber, 1975). By the middle of the 1970s the city harboured more than 2,000 companies directly involved with the petroleum industry. Oil producers, explorers, and developers were increasingly attracted to the city because of the existing ser-vices it offered (for example, in terms of financing) and its accessibility to Alberta oil fields and important American centres. The need to co-ordinate joint ventures and common management of oil fields (called "unitization") also heightened the benefits such clustering created, and thereby further encourag-ed it. As Calgary strengthened its position as the head-office city for the oil industry, Edmonton assumed a complementary role (Zieber, 1973); it concen-trated more on the oil operations function, paralleling the shift in oil explora-tion to the north. Whereas service-sales activities within the oil industry clustered in Calgary to meet the needs of oil producers, companies concerned wth oil field construction located more commonly in Edmonton. Such specialization was possible because of the communication-transport links that developed between the two cities.

Rapid economic growth in each, because of the oil boom, led to increased investment in other sectors, such as housing construction. As a result of multiplier effects, new jobs were generated (for example, in the service in-dustries). In 1971 one export worker (e.g., in the petroleum industry) sup-ported two internal workers (i.e., in the service sphere of the local economy) (Seifried, 1978). The establishment of each as a metropolitan wholesale-retail centre has meant that growth is no longer as closely tied to the petroleum in-dustry. Each is at a size now where growth tends to be more self-sustaining (Baine, 1973).

Table 8:   Metropolitan Concentration in Canada and Major Regions, 1961-2001

	Canada	British Columbia	Prairies	Ontario	Quebec	Atlantic provinces
1961[2]	44[1]	53	37	48	50	15
1966[2]	48	53	43	55	52	14
1971	55	58	48	66	56	22
2001[3]	57	58	64	59	61	22

1. Proportion of population in metropolitan centres.
2. The 1961 and 1966 figures are for centres over 100,000.
3. This projection is based on 1971 CMA boundaries, and represents one of several different estimates.

From D. Michael Ray, ed., *Canadian Urban Trends* Vol. I © Ministry of Supply and Services Canada, 1976. Reprinted by permission of Copp Clark Pitman, Publishers.

Age and Sex Composition of Canada's Urban Population

The age and sex composition of any population is a key to understanding rates of natural increase and mortality, labour force entrance, household formation, intraurban migration, and the like. The mounting of effective urban social and economic policies depends on familiarity with these two aspects of the demographic profile of the urban population.

Examining the composition of Canada's urban population for both 1961 and 1971, we should take note of several patterns in Table 9.

1. In each of those years urban Canada contains slightly lower proportions of persons under 14 and 65 and over in comparison to the non-urban population. This partly reflects the age-selectivity of migration and immigration; higher proportions of those in the 25-34 and 35-44 age categories are found in urban areas.

2. Larger cities tend to have slightly larger proportions over 45 than do smaller communities; in contrast, the latter have relatively younger (under 24) residents. Comparing 1961 with 1971 we see that these differences have lessened. We should also note that age composition does not vary greatly among communities across the 30,000 to 1,000,000 size range.

3. Vancouver differs from Montreal and Toronto in that it is the residence of greater proportions of senior citizens. This parallels provincial variations: the urban population of British Columbia as a whole contains relatively more people over 65 than do other provinces. At the other extreme, Newfoundland's urban population is the youngest. Although the data are not presented in Table 9, individual cities and metropolitan communities also show significant differences in their age structure: "The youthful, new resource towns (Labrador City, Thompson, Terrace, Kitimat, Prince George, Williams Lake, Baie-Comeau and Sept-Isles) and the older ones past their prime (Trail, Kirkland and New Glasgow), the towns with military bases (Oromocto, Petawawa and Trenton), the retirement meccas (Victoria, Vancouver, the Okanagan towns and Leamington in Ontario's banana belt) and the smaller towns of the Prairies and Ontario all stand out because of their extremely young or aged populations" (Ray, 1976: 209).

Those cities which experience substantial in-migration frequently contain a relatively higher ratio of young adults than do those centres with limited economic opportunities. The age structure of a community thus often mirrors its economic vitality.

For sex composition, Table 10 indicates one central pattern that has existed at least since 1921 (Stone, 1967: 49). Urban Canada contains proportionately more females than males in comparison to non-urban areas of the country. The latter show a clear pattern of "male dominance" in sex composition. The largest cities (1,000,000+) are as a whole "more female" than the smallest urban communities examined here; yet, even with this variation the non-urban sex ratio remains distinct. As with age composition this too reflects the impact of selective migration streams:

Table 9:   Age of Urban Population by Size Class, 1961 and 1971

Age group	1,000,000+	Montreal CMA	Toronto CMA	Vancouver CMA	250,000-999,999	100,000-249,999	50,000-99,999	30,000-49,999	20,000-29,999	10,000-19,999	Urban Canada	Non-Urban Canada	Canada
0-4													
1961%	11.4	11.8	11.3	10.5	12.2	12.7	12.3	12.5	13.2	13.1	12.0	13.0	12.4
1971%	7.0	7.7	8.1	7.3	8.4	8.7	7.9	8.1	8.2	8.9	8.1	9.1	8.4
5-14													
1961%	18.7	19.4	18.0	18.4	20.3	21.0	22.1	22.1	22.5	22.6	20.2	24.3	21.6
1971%	19.0	19.7	18.8	18.1	20.4	20.9	20.8	21.2	21.9	22.0	20.1	23.7	21.2
15-24													
1961%	13.3	14.5	12.4	12.2	14.0	15.1	15.1	15.0	15.7	15.3	14.1	14.8	14.3
1971%	17.9	18.2	17.6	17.6	19.0	19.7	19.7	19.5	20.0	19.5	18.7	18.2	18.6
25-34													
1961%	15.6	15.8	16.3	13.4	14.6	14.0	13.5	13.4	13.8	13.6	14.7	11.4	13.6
1971%	15.0	15.2	15.3	14.0	14.1	13.5	13.1	13.2	13.3	13.4	14.3	11.4	13.4
35-44													
1961%	14.6	14.2	15.2	14.5	14.0	13.2	13.2	12.9	12.4	12.5	13.9	11.5	13.1
1971%	13.1	13.0	13.5	12.1	12.1	11.3	11.7	11.4	11.4	11.2	12.3	10.4	11.7
45-64													
1961%	18.8	18.1	19.1	19.9	17.4	16.4	16.8	16.8	15.6	16.0	17.6	16.8	17.4
1971%	19.4	19.1	19.1	20.9	18.5	18.1	19.0	18.5	17.6	17.2	18.8	18.4	18.7
65+													
1961%	7.6	6.1	7.8	11.1	7.4	7.5	6.9	7.3	6.8	6.8	7.4	8.1	7.6
1971%	7.7	7.0	7.5	10.0	7.6	7.9	7.8	8.2	7.6	7.8	7.7	8.9	8.1

From D. Michael Ray, ed., *Canadian Urban Trends* Vol. I © Ministry of Supply and Services Canada, 1976. Reprinted by permission of Copp Clark Pitman, Publishers.

. . . a surplus of rural population in Canada has been particularly evident among females, for whom there are relatively few, as compared with males, opportunities in primary economic activities such as agriculture. With the advancing industrialization of Canada since Confederation more and more job openings have been available to females in service activities and, to a lesser extent, in light manufacturing. This long-standing rural-urban differential in the share of economic opportunities for females has probably been a major factor behind the sustained female-selectivity of the net migration gains to urban areas (Stone, 1967: 64).

Again, we must recognize that these general patterns conceal variations among individual cities. Frontier resource and military communities are more likely to be "male-dominant" than are cities with substantial employment opportunities in the service sector.

Table 10:   Sex Ratios and Birth Rates of Canada's Urban Population by Size Class, 1971

Size class	Males per 100 females	Birth rate
1,000,000+	97	15.3
Montreal CMA	96	14.1
Toronto CMA	98	17.2
Vancouver	98	13.8
250,000-999,999	97	17.1
100,000-249,999	98	18.4
50,000-99,999	98	16.2
30,000-49,999	99	16.4
20,000-29,999	98	17.3
10,000-19,999	101	19.0
Urban Canada	98	16.5
Non-urban Canada	106	17.5

From D. Michael Ray, ed., *Canadian Urban Trends* Vol. I © Ministry of Supply and Services Canada, 1976. Reprinted by permission of Copp Clark Pitman, Publishers.

Table 10 also reveals that the crude birth rate is higher in non-urban areas—a characteristic feature of rural society. It is interesting to note that within urban Canada the birth rate does not vary consistently with size of community; nevertheless, the smallest-size class parallels the non-urban more closely than any other urban category. There are significant provincial variations here within Canada's urban population. The highest birth rate is found in Newfoundland, with Quebec (contrary to past trends) second; British Columbia has the lowest crude birth rate—partly reflecting the high proportion of those over 65 in its urban population. A city's birth rate is a product of the age-sex composition of both its "native" and immigrant population. Vancouver's relatively low birth rate, for example, is consistent with its larger proportions of residents over 45 in comparison to Toronto and Montreal.

Socioeconomic Composition of Canada's Urban Population

One central characteristic of Canada's economic system is the continuing existence of provincial and regional disparities in levels of income. Newfoundland's and Prince Edward Island's average family incomes in 1971, for example, were substantially lower than those in Ontario and British Columbia. Table 11 documents additional disparities. The average family income in urban Canada was more than $3,000 higher than that found in rural areas. This is a pattern typical of industrialized societies. Note also that average incomes generally increase with size of community. Cities of 1,000,000+ register a higher income level than do the smallest centres (10,000-19,999). This reflects "the tendency for specialized, high-education, high-income occupations to cluster in settlements at the upper, particularly the metropolitan, levels of the urban hierarchy" (Ray, 1976: 160). The largest communities as a group contain the highest proportion of families with an income of $15,000 or more among all size categories. Note, however, that this is partly accounted for by the relatively larger concentration of such families in Toronto; Montreal's income level is actually only slightly above that found in the 100,000-249,999 size class.

Table 11: Income Distribution Among Families in Canada's Urban Population by Size Class, 1971

Size class	Average family income $	Percent families in income groups			
		Below $5000	$5000-9999	$10,000-14,999	$15,000+
1,000,000+	11,001	16.3	36.0	28.8	18.9
Montreal CMA	10,292	18.4	39.7	25.7	16.2
Toronto CMA	11,841	13.4	32.6	31.9	22.1
Vancouver CMA	10,664	18.4	35.2	29.1	17.4
250,000-999,999	10,750	15.4	37.5	29.5	17.5
100,000-249,999	9,996	17.3	40.9	27.9	13.9
50,000-99,999	9,732	19.0	41.1	26.7	13.1
30,000-49,999	9,282	21.0	42.8	24.6	11.6
20,000-29,999	9,323	20.2	43.9	24.5	11.4
10,000-19,999	9,209	20.8	42.6	25.6	11.1
Urban Canada	10,502	17.0	38.2	28.2	16.6
Non-urban Canada	7,342	38.0	38.6	16.3	7.1

From D. Michael Ray, ed., *Canadian Urban Trends* Vol. I © Ministy of Supply and Services Canada, 1976. Reprinted by permission of Copp Clark Pitman, Publishers.

These data must be read properly: they present proportions only. Thus, although urban Canada's population shows a higher average income with a larger proportion more affluent, it nevertheless contains a large number, in absolute terms, of low-income families than does rural Canada. The problem of poverty is not confined predominantly to the latter.

As we have discovered in other sections of this general demographic profile of urban Canada, within the urban system exist profound differences. Table 12 illustrates this with respect to the country's twenty-two metropolitan areas. Ottawa-Hull has the highest average family income in the country, followed by Toronto. St. John's and Saint John show the lowest levels—more than $3,000 below Ottawa-Hull. Between 1961 and 1971 these disparities sharpened slightly. Such differences among metropolitan areas reflect variations in "industrial structure, the age of the population, labour force participation rate, unemployment rates, and regional location" (Hill, 1976: 41). All of these factors must be carefully examined to explain the income level of a particular metropolitan community.

Table 12: Average Family Income and Education of Nonschool Adult Population, Census Metropolitan Areas, 1971

| Census Metro-politan Area | Average family income | Rank in average family income | Highest Level of Schooling (%) | | | |
			Elemen-tary	Secon-dary	Some uni-versity	Uni-versity
Calgary	$10,943	5	24.2	61.7	6.9	7.3
Chicoutimi-Jonquière	9,162	20	45.1	46.9	4.1	3.9
Edmonton	10,660	10	27.8	60.1	5.7	6.4
Halifax	10,176	12	27.3	59.4	6.5	6.8
Hamilton	10,757	7	34.3	56.8	4.5	4.3
Kitchener	10,661	9	35.7	55.1	4.5	4.6
London	10,763	6	28.4	61.1	4.9	5.6
Montreal	10,292	11	44.0	44.5	5.9	5.5
Ottawa-Hull	12,010	1	28.9	54.7	6.9	9.5
Quebec	10,159	14	42.5	47.4	4.5	5.7
Regina	9,637	18	30.6	56.8	7.0	5.7
St. Catharines-Niagara	9,997	15	37.2	55.5	4.0	3.4
St. John's	8,488	22	37.0	53.4	6.0	3.6
Saint John	8,821	21	38.6	53.2	4.7	3.5
Saskatoon	9,479	19	32.0	53.6	7.4	7.0
Sudbury	11,739	3	40.3	51.9	4.2	3.6
Thunder Bay	10,165	13	40.8	51.4	4.4	3.4
Toronto	11,841	2	31.5	56.2	6.0	6.3
Vancouver	10,664	8	26.3	60.5	7.4	5.7
Victoria	9,921	17	23.2	64.2	7.3	5.4
Windsor	11,281	4	36.4	54.5	5.2	3.9
Winnipeg	9,989	16	31.2	57.2	5.9	5.7
Metropolitan Canada	10,788		34.5	53.8	5.9	5.8

From Frederick I. Hill, ed., *Canadian Urban Trends* Vol. II © Ministry of Supply and Services Canada, 1976. Reprinted by permission of Copp Clark Pitman, Publishers.

It is important to emphasize that income level cannot be understood by reference to one variable alone, such as education. Throughout Canada there is a marked tendency for family income to increase the longer the head of the family remains in the educational system (Ray, 1976: 160). Nevertheless, as the data in Table 12 suggest, the educational level of a metropolitan community is not consistently related to average family income. For example, Sudbury ranks third in family income among all metropolitan areas in 1971; yet, we must go to that centre ranked eleventh (Montreal) before we find one with a larger proportion of the population having completed only elementary schooling. Similarly, Saskatoon ranks nineteenth in average family income, but third in the proportion having completed university. The lowest proportion of this highly educated group are found in Thunder Bay and St. Catharines-Niagara, which rank thirteenth and fifteenth respectively in average family income. Correlations which exist on the individual family level between education and income, thus, cannot be transposed to the community level. To do so is to greatly oversimplify metropolitan income differences.

A FUNCTIONAL CLASSIFICATION OF CANADIAN CITIES

The demographic variations among Canada's urban areas are matched by differences in economic structure, specialization, and function. These can be measured by comparing urban employment patterns. As cities grow, their labour force expands and, most important, diversifies—that is, becomes less concentrated in a small number of industry groupings (Crowley, 1973). Such divergencies can be better understood by classifying cities according to their economic functions (Duncan and Reiss, 1956; Moser and Scott, 1961).

Maxwell (1965) examined the functional structure of all incorporated Canadian cities with 1951 populations of at least 10,000. This was measured in terms of the basic employment structure, which refers to those activities providing goods and services for markets outside the city (Alexander, 1959; Jacobs, 1970). Maxwell determined the minimum labour force required in specific functions to allow the city to survive—these are non-basic functions. That employment in excess of this minimum thus approximates the city's basic employment.

Through this means several important features of urban functional structures can be measured (Maxwell, 1965: 85-87):

1. The *dominant function* of the city, the sector having the greatest share of the city's total excess employment;

2. The *distinctive function* of the city, "an activity whose share of total excess employment in a city greatly exceeds the share it usually has in most cities"; and

3. *Degree of functional specialization*, which increases as the city's excess employment distribution deviates "from the distribution of the city's minimum requirement employment among functions."

Figure 4: City-Types in Canada

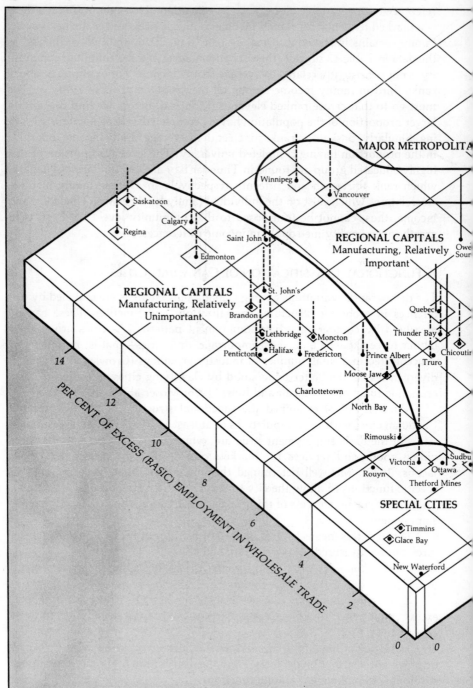

From Maxwell, 1965. Reprinted by permission of the author.

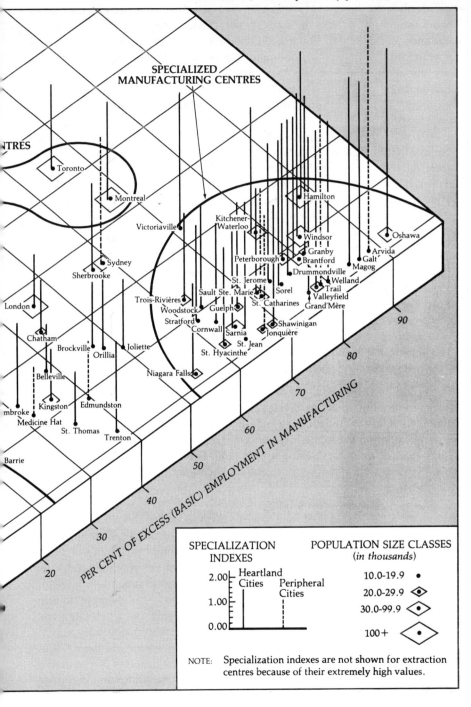

Maxwell's data document how important manufacturing is in urban Canada. It is the dominant function in most cities. This is especially the case in "heartland cities"—those located in the densely populated St. Lawrence Lowlands and Southern Ontario. Forty-three out of the forty-five such cities show manufacturing as their dominant function. In contrast, this is the case in only about one-third of the "peripheral cities"—those located outside the heartland region. Wholesale trade tends to be the distinctive function in the periphery, with extraction centres having the highest degree of functional specialization.

Overall, therefore, an important division exists within the Canadian system of cities (Ray and Murdie, 1972). The periphery cities display significantly different "functional profiles" from the heartland cities. The former are less specialized and less deeply involved in the industrial sector; the latter constitute the nation's "manufacturing belt." These differences reflect the spatial interrelations between cultural and economic characteristics in Canada (Ray, 1971) as well as variations in settlement patterns:

> Whereas great concentration of economic activity, financial power, and population exist in the heartland, the periphery is characterized by huge sparsely settled areas, giving it almost vassal status in its relationship with the heartland. The periphery, because of its involvement with the friction of distance, must devote much more of its "economic energy" to overcoming this friction. In the heartland the friction of distance is comparatively of little consequence. These fundamental differences in situational characteristics are reflected by the functional profiles of the cities in the two regions (Maxwell, 1965: 96).

In addition, we should note that this pattern also reflects the impact of foreign ownership on urban development in Canada (Ray and Roberge, 1981). Many secondary manufacturing industries are subsidiaries of U.S. corporations, and are thus subject to locational decisions made by the latter. American multinationals have established branches in Toronto and Southwestern Ontario because of their market potential and accessibility to American head offices. Such concentration heightens heartland/periphery disparities.

Figure 4 summarizes the types of cities in Canada Maxwell found when examining variations in the importance of manufacturing and wholesale trade, and differences in the level of specialization. Several groups can be identified:

1. Thirty-one cities with high functional importance of manufacturing; wholesale trade occupies a subsidiary position. These are concentrated in the "heartland."

2. Extraction centres which are highly specialized—for example, in mining—but show little importance given to manufacturing and wholesale trade.

3. Cities in the periphery committed largely to wholesale trade.

4. The four major metropolitan centres—Toronto, Montreal, Vancouver, and Winnipeg—which form a distinct group in terms of population size and relatively high values for both wholesale trade and manufacturing.

The remaining cities are fairly heterogeneous with no apparent distinctiveness in terms of the underlying criteria measured. They include a variety of regional capital and smaller cities with insignificant wholesale trade functions.

Considering only the metropolitan areas, we find evidence again of a discernible hierarchy. Stone (1967: 187), for example, ranked metropolitan areas in terms of two " 'partial' indices of specialization in performance of metropolitan functions"—namely, business service receipts per person aged 15+ and the wholesale sales per capita. On both measures four metropolitan communities received the highest score: Toronto, Montreal, Vancouver, and Calgary. Employing these indices he identified four levels in the hierarchy of metropolitan areas regarding specialization in the performance of metropolitan functions in 1961. At the bottom were Kitchener, Victoria, and Sudbury. Stone also explored variations in the distribution of the labour force by industry group, including wholesale trade, finance, business services, and fabricating industries, and found evidence again of a series of levels. Toronto and Montreal occupy the highest level; Vancouver, Calgary, Winnipeg, and London the second level; Edmonton, Saint John, and Windsor the third level; the others are ranked below this. Canada's largest urban complexes vary in the extent to which they specialize in metropolitan economic functions.

Kerr (1968: 532) has argued that actually only two cities—Toronto and Montreal—can claim full metropolitan status, from an economic perspective, with Vancouver on "the threshold." As Table 13 indicates, a relatively large proportion of the nation's financial and industrial sectors are concentrated in both Toronto and Montreal. Each represents a central node in the country's transportation system: for example, much of Canada's domestic air passenger travel is focused on them. The financial interdependence between these centres is also a prominent feature of their positions: "Interaction of these two financial communities is such that they tend to participate, at least in some activities, as one large financial center and are not necessarily the custodians to two separate financial markets" (Kerr, 1968). From this perspective they form "a single dispersed city." Evidence suggests that such economic centralization will not diminish in the future, although the emergence of Quebec political sovereignty may affect this process. The rise of Vancouver to the status of a national economic metropolis also is a not uncertain possibility.

THE CANADIAN SYSTEM OF CITIES

Increasing attention has been given to the need to examine Canada's entire complex of cities as a system (Simmons, 1974a; Bourne and MacKinnon, 1972). Reflecting its highly urbanized character, the necessity of conceptualizing this society as an integrated network of urban nodes has become more clearly evident (Berry, 1964). This notion of a national urban system, however, raises a number of questions which have not been adequately answered. Simmons (1974a: 5-6) lists several of these issues:

Table 13: Value Added in Total Manufacturing Activity (1961), Cheques Cashed at Clearing Houses (1961), Total Income Tax Paid (1963), Assets of Leading Corporations (1965), and Service Receipts and Retail Sales (1961), For Selected Metropolitan Centres as Proportion of Canadian Total (in percent)

Metropolitan centres	Value added in total manufacturing activity	Cheques cashed at clearing houses	Total income tax paid	Assets of leading corporations	Service receipts and retail sales
Calgary	1.0	3.5	2.3	5.0	2.1
Edmonton	1.5	2.3	2.5	— *	2.4
Halifax	0.6	0.9	0.7	0.8	1.2
Hamilton	5.3	2.0	3.2	3.9	2.4
Kitchener	2.0	0.5	0.9	— *	0.9
London	1.6	1.3	1.4	0.5	1.5
Montreal	17.9	26.8	12.7	38.1	13.4
Ottawa	1.3	2.0	3.0	— *	2.7
Quebec City	1.4	2.7	1.5	1.2	2.2
Regina	0.4	1.7	1.0	— *	0.8
Saint John	0.6	0.4	0.4	— *	0.6
St. John's	0.1	0.4	0.5	— *	0.6
Saskatoon	0.3	0.4	0.6	— *	0.7
Sudbury	0.7	0.2	0.6	— *	0.7
Toronto	19.8	37.3	19.0	36.7	13.8
Vancouver	4.0	6.0	6.1	6.3	5.4
Victoria	0.4	0.9	1.0	— *	1.0
Windsor	2.0	0.8	1.3	— *	1.1
Winnipeg	2.2	7.1	3.6	2.0	3.1

*These *together* total 5.5%.
Adapted from Kerr, 1968. Reproduced by permission of Methuen Publications, Toronto, Ontario.

1. How are the characteristics of a particular city and its pattern of growth and change affected by its position in the urban system structured?

2. How fully integrated is the urban system? What proportion of all contacts take place within cities or among them? What is the pattern of intercity linkages?

3. How predictable is growth and change within the system? What can reasonably be modelled?

4. Are the urban system linkages consistent for economic, social, and political activities, or should each be modelled individually?

5. To what degree and in what pattern is the urban system linked to the international system?

6. What is the source and pattern of movement of signals of growth and change? Are they internal? External? Do they flow from large places to small or the reverse?

The urban system represents a more complex and extensive form of ecological organization. A number of levels can be discerned within it—the individual city and its hinterland, a group of cities in a region, and the entire national system itself. As noted above, it is critical that the linkages among these levels be fully explored. The notion of "metropolitan dominance"—giving recognition to the economic preeminence of Toronto and Montreal —represents one attempt to conceptualize these connections with respect to the focus of power in the national system. What Simmons and other geographers recommend, however, is that this be broadened to include the entire range of relationships among cities of differing size and function. The urban system is viewed as an extremely complex unit in which each city is deeply influenced by its economic and ecological position. Moreover, the system itself is characterized by "openness" since it is profoundly affected by the environment.

The Windsor-Quebec Urban Axis: A Sub-System Within the National System of Cities

As we have seen above with respect to "heartland cities," the central core of the Canadian national system of cities is the Windsor-to-Quebec City urban region (Yeates, 1975). An area of almost 70,000 square miles, it contains more than 1,800 municipalities, (in 1971, 55 percent of Canada's total population) and almost three-fourths of its manufacturing employment. Although predominantly urban, the region does include a rich agricultural sector, registering over a third of the value of farm receipts in Canada.

Although the rate of annual increase has declined, during 1961-71 the total population of the axis expanded by more than 20 percent. This growth is concentrated in the Ontario side of the axis in areas around the largest cities. If these trends continue, by the end of this century the region will contain three out of every five Canadians; its population at that point will equal the total for Canada as a whole in 1971. By the year 2001, one out of every three people living in the region will reside within forty miles of Toronto, which will become the dominant node in the axis (Yeates, 1975).

Since 1911 Canada's manufacturing has continued to concentrate here. Between 1961 and 1971 three-fifths of all new manufacturing plants located within the axis, particularly around Toronto and Montreal. In general, the region's cities have been able to claim a disproportionate share of Canada's total economic growth over the last several decades; it is there that much of the nation's economic wealth has been concentrated.

Although the region encompasses numerous municipalities and is under the jurisdiction of two provinces, it functions as an identifiable unit with strong internal linkages. The highest-order centres of Toronto and Montreal economically dominate regional centres, which in turn influence more restricted hinterlands. These ties can be charted using data on telephone calls, rail freights, truck flows, and airline flows (Yeates, 1975: 209). The interaction among communities within the axis is intense. It has emerged as an ecological unit with a complex set of functional relationships. In addition, as a sub-system it exercises profound economic influence over the entire Canadian national system of cities. This pattern will continue in the decades ahead, with implications for urban planning which we shall explore briefly later.

Western Urban Axes: The Edmonton-Calgary Corridor and the Georgia Strait Urban Region

Paralleling the heartland-periphery distinction within the national system of cities are additional urban sub-systems or axes on a lower scale, but nonetheless important, in Western Canada. Earlier we noted the complementary roles which Calgary and Edmonton perform in the petroleum industry. More generally, they function as the two major metropolitan nodes in Alberta's settlement system (Smith and Johnson, 1978; Davies and Gyuse, 1975). Together they dominate a corridor of interconnected communities, in which since 1911 most of Alberta's urban population has been concentrated (Smith and Johnson, 1978). Although containing the majority of Albertans, this corridor occupies only 5 percent of the province's total land area. As with the Windsor-Quebec urban axis, transportation links have helped to shape and integrate the Edmonton-Calgary sub-system. Growth was concentrated in earlier years in these two cities. However, more recently a process of corridor "infilling" is discernible. That is, whereas the growth rates of Calgary and Edmonton between 1971 and 1976 declined, those of Red Deer and adjoining communities elsewhere along the axis increased. An economic revival is evident in many of the lower-order centres within the corridor, as their service functions strengthen and as they become more attractive to the region's workers as places of residence. In short, because of population and economic overspill from Calgary and Edmonton the corridor may increasingly assume the shape of a "lineal megalopolis" (Smith and Johnson, 1978: 30).

Similarly, the Georgia Strait urban region represents an emerging megalopolis of the far West (Hardwick, 1972). This consists of a mosaic of communities, with Vancouver's inner city as the focus, and Victoria, Nanaimo, and New Westminster as additional important nuclei. By the end of this century the region will contain a population of approximately 4 million (Gibson, 1976). This increase is occurring especially in outlying areas. Here too, improvements in transportation systems (road-building, bridges, marine transport) have helped to integrate the region (Robinson and Hardwick, 1973). Each area increasingly assumes a more specialized role. Whereas Vancouver's inner core shows expansion in rented office space and high-rise apartments, industrial and wholesaling plants are rapidly suburbanizing (Gibson, 1976).

Both the Edmonton-Calgary corridor and the Georgia Strait urban region must be viewed as relatively integrated sub-systems rather than as a set of discrete communities. Their formation symbolizes a more complex stage of urbanization understood ecologically.

"QUALITY OF LIFE" VARIATIONS WITHIN THE CANADIAN URBAN SYSTEM

Aside from demographic and socioeconomic differences within any society's urban system, one intriguing question is whether the "quality of life"—however that is defined—varies among types of cities. Is the quality of life significantly "better" in one urban community than in another? This is an extremely difficult question to answer; we cannot devise one single overall measure of quality of life, nor even a set of unambiguous measures. Nevertheless, it is still useful to examine aspects of the condition of life in our cities, and compare their variations.

Table 14 presents data on selected quality of life indicators among Canada's twenty-two metropolitan areas from a recent study by the Ministry of State for Urban Affairs. That research explored variations in a total of thirty-two indicators. Of these we have chosen nine to simply illustrate the differences which exist among Canada's largest urban communities (Stewart et al., 1976).

The first two indicators measure the level of unlawful activity in a city. Given the imprecise nature of criminal statistics generally, these data must be interpreted cautiously. Winnipeg shows the highest rate of juveniles charged, Windsor the lowest. Yet, when comparing rates of Criminal Code offences generally, these cities rank ninth and fifth respectively—Regina has the highest and Chicoutimi-Jonquière the lowest proportion of Criminal Code offences per 10,000 population in 1971. The disparity between these two cities on this measure is quite large. Canada's two largest metropolises, Toronto and Montreal, do not rank high on either crime indicator. Nor is there necessarily a close correlation with growth rate. For example, earlier we discovered that during the 1961-1971 period Thunder Bay and Chicoutimi-Jonquière each showed among the lowest population growth rates of all metropolitan areas (see Table 7). Yet, while Thunder Bay ranks third in rate of Criminal Code offences, Chicoutimi-Jonquière ranks twenty-second or last.

With respect to the education indicator, emphasis is given here to the 20-34 age group: ". . . it is these people who tend not to have the years of experience that might offset their lack of education. With no more than a grade 10 education, it is likely that this group will have difficulty finding satisfactory employment in urban areas. More generally, it is likely that lack of education will inhibit people from participating fully in activities within their communities" (Stewart et al., 1976: 20). Vancouver registers the highest proportion of young adults with low education levels, Montreal the lowest—almost half that of the former.

Table 14: Selected "Quality Of Life" Indicators Among Canada's Metropolitan Areas, 1971

Census Metropolitan Area	Quality-of-life indicators		
	No. of juveniles charged with crimes per 10,000 population	% Criminal Code offences per 10,000 population	% of young adults (20-34) with low education levels (grade 10 or less)
St. John's	40 (3)[1]	828 (6)	29.3 (18)
Halifax	28 (8)	515 (18)	38.7 (12)
Saint John	24 (9)	522 (17)	34.1 (15)
Chicoutimi- Jonquière	24 (9)	286 (22)	28.2 (20)
Quebec	15 (17)	456 (20)	28.7 (19)
Montreal	20 (14)	456 (20)	26.0 (22)
Ottawa-Hull	23 (12)	654	43.0 (7)
Toronto	21 (13)	590 (15)	41.2 (11)
Hamilton	19 (15)	734 (8)	38.0 (13)
St. Catharines- Niagara	12 (20)	678 (11)	35.0 (14)
Kitchener	11 (21)	489 (19)	29.6 (17)
London	14 (18)	658 (12)	43.0 (7)
Windsor	8 (22)[2]	865 (5)	41.4 (10)
Sudbury	19 (15)	547 (16)	26.7 (21)
Thunder Bay	31 (7)	900 (3)	33.5 (16)
Winnipeg	112 (1)[3]	708 (9)	43.0 (7)
Regina	14 (18)	1243 (1)	44.1 (6)
Saskatoon	38 (4)	632 (14)	44.8 (5)
Edmonton	24 (9)	1002 (2)	47.8 (3)
Calgary	34 (6)	765 (7)	48.2 (2)
Vancouver	37 (5)	877 (4)	48.4 (1)
Victoria	50 (2)	682 (10)	45.5 (4)

[*Continued*]

Canada's cities differ greatly in the cultural and artistic opportunities they offer, and in their overall level of cultural vitality. For some this could be a particularly important indicator of the "quality" of urban life. Table 14 presents the data on one measure of the cultural facilities available in the metropolitan communities. Toronto and Ottawa-Hull rank the highest, Sudbury and Hamilton the lowest.

Voter turnout is a partial measure of civic participation in the political process, of interest in and knowledge of governmental structure. St. John's electorate appear more active than that of other cities in terms of voting; Kitchener shows greater apathy. Other data on citizen involvement in public affairs, however, must be examined before this difference can be fully understood.

Table 14 — *Continued*

Census Metropolitan Area	Quality-of-life indicators		
	Square feet of exhibition halls, museums, art galleries per 100 population[4]	Percent of eligible voters voting in elections since 1969	Average income adjusted for taxes and housing costs[5]
St. John's	30.6 (6)	58.6 (1)	$5293 (21)
Halifax	43.0 (5)	45.0 (11)	5699 (14)
Saint John	28.5 (8)	47.1 (6)	5158 (22)
Chicoutimi-Jonquière	2.5 (17)	52.8 (2)	6533 (1)
Quebec	49.3 (3)	51.7 (3)	6031 (6)
Montreal	14.9 (13)	46.9 (7)	6379 (2)
Ottawa-Hull	66.4 (2)	35.7 (18)	6327 (3)
Toronto	70.4 (1)	37.4 (16)	6023 (8)
Hamilton	0.8 (21)	37.6 (15)	5827 (11)
St. Catharines-Niagara	23.1 (9)	32.7 (21)	5541 (18)
Kitchener	1.8 (19)	32.2 (22)	5546 (17)
London	11.4 (14)	38.2 (14)	5762 (12)
Windsor	1.7 (20)	41.1 (13)	6085 (5)
Sudbury	0.0 (22)	45.5 (10)	6026 (7)
Thunder Bay	7.1 (16)	49.0 (4)	5479 (19)
Winnipeg	29.4 (7)	47.3 (5)	5331 (20)
Regina	22.7 (10)	35.2 (19)	5721 (13)
Saskatoon	7.8 (15)	34.5 (20)	5595 (16)
Edmonton	2.4 (18)	42.7 (12)	5940 (10)
Calgary	46.9 (4)	46.4 (8)	6189 (4)
Vancouver	19.9 (11)	36.4 (17)	5978 (9)
Victoria	17.3 (12)	46.4 (8)	5674 (15)

[*Continued*]

Earlier we examined levels of average family income by urban size class and among the metropolitan areas. A more precise measure of "real discretionary income," however, must take account of variations in taxes and housing costs. Table 14 lists the average adjusted incomes based on 1972-1973 data. Chicoutimi-Jonquière ranks first, followed by Montreal and Ottawa-Hull; the lowest levels of real discretionary income are found in two of the three Atlantic metropolitan communities, Saint John and St. John's.

Two other measures of the economic state of cities are the unemployment rate and the cost of new housing. Although Chicoutimi-Jonquière shows the highest average adjusted income, it also has the highest unemployment rate—at least at the time when these data were

Table 14 — *Continued*

Census Metropolitan Area	Quality-of-life indicators		
	Unemployment rate	Average cost of new single-detached dwelling[4] $	Air pollution index (concentration index of suspended particulate matter)
St. John's	5.7 (11)	33,180 (16)	0.78 (18)
Halifax	5.2 (18)	28,073 (18)	0.60 (20)
Saint John	5.8 (9)	35,307 (15)	0.79 (16)
Chicoutimi-Jonquière	8.0 (1)	25,810 (21)	0.84 (14)
Quebec	5.1 (19)	27,382 (19)	1.38 (4)
Montreal	6.5 (4)	28,536 (17)	1.44 (3)
Ottawa-Hull	4.4 (21)	40,969 (10)	1.14 (9)
Toronto	5.3 (17)	62,254 (1)	1.27 (6)
Hamilton	5.6 (15)	47,350 (4)	1.96 (1)
St. Catharines-Niagara	5.9 (8)	40,177 (12)	0.0 (21)
Kitchener	4.7 (20)	46,830 (6)	0.0 (21)
London	5.8 (9)	36,346 (14)	1.23 (7)
Windsor	6.9 (3)	42,086 (9)	1.38 (4)
Sudbury	4.2 (22)	40,367 (11)	0.83 (15)
Thunder Bay	6.4 (6)	57,498 (2)	1.15 (8)
Winnipeg	5.7 (11)	39,177 (13)	1.03 (10)
Regina	5.4 (16)	27,044 (20)	0.79 (16)
Saskatoon	6.5 (4)	25,645 (22)	0.90 (12)
Edmonton	5.7 (11)	42,776 (8)	0.90 (12)
Calgary	5.7 (11)	47,116 (5)	1.47 (2)
Vancouver	7.1 (2)	43,464 (7)	0.94 (11)
Victoria	6.2 (7)	52,985 (3)	0.68 (19)

[1] Presents the rank of each metropolitan area on the particular indicator being measured.
[2] Metropolitan areas receiving the lowest rank are double-underlined.
[3] Metropolitan areas receiving the highest rank are single-underlined.
[4] Based on 1974 data.
[5] Based on 1972-1973 data.

Adapted from *Urban Indicators: Quality of Life Comparisons for Canadian Cities* by John N. Stewart et al. (1976). Reproduced by permission of the Minister of Supply and Services Canada.

collected. *Earlier we saw that Sudbury had a relatively high average family income, as did Ottawa-Hull; consistent with this the unemployment rate in each is lower than in other metropolitan areas.*

The average cost of a new single-detached dwelling varies enormously from a high in 1974 of $62,254 in Toronto to a low of $25,645 in Saskatoon. Housing costs contribute to the overall standard of living *possible in a particular city. They reflect, as we shall explore later, land assembly and construction costs as well as the activities of land development corporations.*

A final indicator of quality of life is the condition of the environment—in this case, an index of air pollution. If these data can be taken as valid, it would appear that Hamilton has a much greater concern here than do Kitchener or St. Catharines-Niagara. There are, of course, many other aspects of pollution which must be compared.

The data presented in Table 14 are interesting but highly tentative bases for making any judgments about the relative conditions of life in different cities. We should emphasize two points:

1. Note the great variation in rank which each metropolitan area achieves across indicators. Hence, depending on the measure(s) used the same city may be judged as "better" or "worse" than other communities.

2. The relationship between rank on these indicators and population size or growth rate is not strong. Even among the larger group of thirty-two indicators only five "have a statistically significant association with the measure of city size and only two with growth rates. This evidence might lead us to conclude that social, economic and environmental issues are peculiar to individual cities and are not associated with population size or rates of growth, as has been advanced by some observers of the urban scene" (Stewart et al., 1976: 85). More precise indicators are needed, and these should be examined across a wider range of communities of all sizes and comparisons made over time if we are to come any closer to a grasp of the variations in the conditions of urban life. The interpretation of such data, regardless of their validity, must still derive from a set of values defining what "quality of life" should include.

SUMMARY

1. During 1961-71 the greatest population growth occurred in the largest urban areas. Yet overall population growth rate is not necessarily directly correlated with size, as the lowest level of expansion is found not in the smallest communities.

2. There are substantial regional variations in relative population growth by size class. For example, whereas both the Atlantic region and the Prairies show the largest population growth indices in their smallest communities, Ontario shows the opposite pattern. Provincial variations within a region must also be recognized, as Saskatchewan's failure to mirror the above trend in the Prairies indicates.

3. The total population growth (1961-71) for all urban areas over 10,000 was highest in British Columbia, lowest in Atlantic Canada; comparison of indivi-

dual provinces reveals that Alberta shows the highest growth, Nova Scotia the lowest.

4. Through the last 100 years the number of metropolitan areas and the proportion of Canada's total population concentrated within them have increased. The total metropolitan population almost doubled between 1951 and 1971; yet that rate of growth has significantly declined during the most recent decade. Individual metropolitan communities differ greatly in their rates of expansion. During 1961-71 Kitchener (followed by Calgary) and Chicoutimi-Jonquière achieved the highest and lowest rates of growth, respectively. Atlantic Canada's level of metropolitanization has continued to remain the lowest of any region.

5. At least half of Canada's total metropolitan growth can be accounted for by natural increase. Immigration is also an important factor.

6. Urban Canada contains higher proportions of those in the 25-34 and 35-44 age categories and lower proportions under 14 and 65+ in comparison to non-urban areas, reflecting partly the age-selectivity of migration and immigration. In terms of sex composition urban Canada contains proportionately more females than males than do non-urban areas.

7. Larger cities have slightly greater proportions of residents over 45 than do smaller communities. The latter have relatively younger residents. These differences declined between 1961 and 1971. The largest cities also are as a whole "more female" than the smallest urban communities. There are provincial variations in age-sex composition of urban communities, such as the contrast between British Columbia and Newfoundland.

8. The crude birth rate is higher in non-urban areas. Within urban Canada the birth rate does not vary with size of community as much as by province.

9. Urban Canada's average family income is higher than that found in rural areas. Average incomes generally increase with size of community, and vary significantly among the country's twenty-two metropolitan areas.

10. The educational level of a metropolitan community is not consistently related to its average family income.

11. Canada's urban areas differ in terms of employment structure, economic function, and levels of specialization. A fundamental division exists between "heartland cities" in which manufacturing is the dominant function and "peripheral cities" which are less specialized generally and in which wholesale trade tends to be the distinctive function. This division partly reflects the impact of foreign ownership on Canadian urban development.

12. A discernible hierarchy exists among Canada's metropolitan areas, with Toronto and Montreal economically most dominant.

13. Canada's entire set of urban areas should be conceptualized as a national system of cities. This represents a more complex form of ecological organization with extensive economic linkages among the different levels ranging from the individual city to the urban region to the national system itself.

14. The Windsor-Quebec City urban axis is the central sub-system within

Canada's national system of cities. It exercises profound economic influence over the country. If current trends continue it will command an increasing proportion of the nation's population and industrial wealth. Toronto will continue to emerge as the dominant node in this axis. Two additional urban axes in Western Canada are the Edmonton-Calgary corridor and the Georgia Strait urban region. Each consists of an interconnected set of communities, forming important sub-systems within their respective provinces.

15. Efforts to delineate "quality of life" variations within the Canadian urban system are still inconclusive. Assessment of relative conditions of life depends greatly on the particular set of measures used. Social, economic, and environmental concerns are not easily correlated with city size or rate of growth.

Part Three

Part Three

Entrance to the Urban System

Two important demographic processes which have contributed to Canada's current position as one of the most highly urbanized nations in the world have been *internal migration* and *immigration*. They promoted that population redistribution which has constituted such a significant part of the country's history in this century.

As we saw in the Introduction, a fundamental aspect of urban sociology is the study of the process of entrance to the urban system. In this part we shall examine urbanization as an assimilation process—a dynamic focus on Canadian urban social organization. With respect to internal migration and immigration to urban communities, it will be useful first to construct a demographic profile of each before analyzing entrance as a social and cultural process.

Chapter 5

Entrance to the Urban System: Canadian Internal Migration

INTERNAL MIGRATION: A DEMOGRAPHIC PROFILE

As we suggested earlier, mass transiency characterized nineteenth-century cities in Canada and the United States. "In almost every place where historians have looked at least half, often two-thirds, of the adults present at one end of a decade had left ten years later . . ." (Katz, Doucet, and Stearn, 1978: 669). The evolution of the new urban-industrial system required such a flow. Similar to what has been found in a number of other highly urbanized countries, transiency has continued. Canada's current population is fairly mobile, with approximately half having lived at their present residence for less than five years (Pineo, 1968: 12; Kalbach and McVey, 1971: 83). Although most of this movement is local—that is, intramunicipal mobility—migration over longer distances is of such a magnitude as to merit careful analysis.

Regional Shifts in Migration

One of the most fascinating features of Canadian migration has been the manner in which it has shifted from one region of the country to another, from one province to another, during this century. These variations in points of destination reflected comcomitant shifts in areas possessing the greatest economic opportunities. Migration patterns, as modes of population redistribution, partly responded to these varying conditions. Such fluidity and changes in direction of population movement are concretely illustrated in Table 15.

The first two decades of this century were characterized by a pronounced in-migration to the western provinces (McInnis, 1969). The opportunities for land settlement and the possible economic advantages that could be derived from wheat production encouraged movement to the Prairies and British Columbia not only of the native-born, principally from Ontario (Keyfitz, 1965: 25), but in even greater numbers the foreign-born as well. In contrast, the Maritimes showed a process of out-migration—as they did through most of the subsequent period—with many residents moving to either the West or to New England. As the development of the Prairies led to an increased demand for consumer goods manufactured in Central Canada, the resultant rise in

Table 15:   Intercensal Net Migration Ratios, by Province, 1901-1911 to 1951-1961

Province	1901-11	1911-21	1921-31	1931-41	1941-51	1951-61
Prince Edward Island	−13.6	−16.4	−11.1	−2.6	−12.4	−11.3
Nova Scotia	−0.6	−7.6	−14.5	0.8	−6.1	−4.4
New Brunswick	−3.8	−7.3	−11.5	−2.9	−8.7	−6.7
Quebec	4.3	−4.0	0.9	0.1	−0.4	5.1
Ontario	9.3	2.3	5.1	2.6	7.2	14.0
Manitoba	41.2	5.1	−1.7	−6.8	−8.4	0.3
Saskatchewan	125.6	15.1	−0.7	−17.3	−23.3	−7.7
Alberta	123.8	20.9	3.8	−5.6	−1.0	12.9
British Columbia	69.4	14.8	18.7	10.7	23.9	18.7

The net migration ratio is 100 times the estimated net migration (in-migration minus out-migration) divided by the average of the beginning-of-decade and end-of-decade population.

Source: Stone, 1969.

employment opportunities, particularly in Ontario, encouraged in-migration there.

As the settlement of the West ended, and with the shift in the economy to new staple products such as pulp and paper and base metals, the economic opportunities in the Prairie region declined during the 1920s. The net inflows which had earlier been so striking were no longer manifested. British Columbia and Ontario, where the new staple products could best be developed, became the primary points of destination.

The Great Depression of the 1930s effected generally a lowered level of movement and a reversal of the earlier pattern. The Prairies now became the leading area of out-migration, as drought conditions seriously restricted the profitability of farming. In contrast, the level of out-migration fell in the Maritimes as subsistence farming became a more viable response to economic conditions—a response less feasible in the West.

This movement out of the Prairies continued through the 1940s. Especially in Saskatchewan, where reliance on wheat had been strongest, out-migration was pronounced. Once again Ontario and British Columbia were the major recipients of this population redistribution, reflecting the range of economic opportunities available in these provinces.

While their dominance was sustained in more recent times, a reversal in the previous pattern occurred again as Alberta once more emerged as an important point of destination for interprovincial migrants. Expansion in non-agricultural employment opportunities, especially in service industries, was an important factor responsible for this gain. Many of these migrants came from Saskatchewan, where rural life was still suffering the effects of the Depression. As Table 16 indicates, during 1966-1971 out-migration from the Maritimes continued at a relatively high level. This movement was directed more toward Central Canada than to New England, which had earlier been an important area of attraction. More recent trends since 1971, however, suggest that the Maritimes have begun to experience net inflows of migrants (Information Canada, 1975: 29). Ontario attained a higher level of in-migration than in previous decades, as its industrial centres rapidly expanded.

As the above trends clearly demonstrate, patterns of internal regional migration evolved in response to the shifting locations of areas offering greater economic opportunities. The current concentration of Canada's population in urban centres underscores this basic relationship.

Table 16:   Rates of Interprovincial Net Migration, 1966-1971

Province	Rate per 1000 population
Newfoundland	− 26
Prince Edward Island	− 19
Nova Scotia	− 29
New Brunswick	− 20
Quebec	− 18
Ontario	16
Manitoba	− 50
Saskatchewan	− 88
Alberta	− 13
British Columbia	65

Adapted from Stone and Signner, 1974. Reproduced by permission of the Minister of Supply and Services Canada.

Migration and Urban Centres

Aside from these variations in interregional mobility, there was an additional significant development in Canadian internal migration during the present century. In more recent times, rural-urban migration has no longer represented the dominant mode of such population redistribution. Rather, interurban flows have become "the most striking feature of the geographic mobility scene in Canada" (Stone, 1974: 272). Whereas in the late 1800s and earlier decades of this century movement from the farm to the city constituted the largest stream of internal migrations, at present mobility between urban centres is the most pronounced pattern (Stone, 1969: 33), as Table 17 documents. Almost two-thirds of all migration in the period from 1966-1971 is of this type. The urban-to-rural stream is actually almost as strong as the rural to urban; the former partly reflects that outward expansion of population characteristic of metropolitan growth. These patterns are characteristic of all highly urbanized and industrialized societies. As the total proportion of rural population declines, the previous dominance of rural-urban movement also necessarily declines.

Table 17:   Internal Migration by Type and Period

Migration Stream*	1956-1961 %	1966-1971 %
Rural to Urban	20.8	16.3
Non-farm to urban	5.5	11.1
Farm to urban	9.4	4.3
Farm to non-farm	5.9	1.0
Urban to Rural	19.1	15.7
Urban to non-farm	14.4	11.1
Urban to farm	2.9	3.5
Non-farm to farm	1.9	1.1
Circular Movement	60.0	68.0
Urban to urban	56.8	63.7
Non-farm to non-farm	2.5	3.5
Farm to farm	0.8	0.8

*Migration stream: "that body of migrants which departs from any area of origin for any area of destination" (Amyot and George, 1973).

From *Perspective Canada II: A Compendium of Social Statistics 1977*. Reproduced by permission of the Minister of Supply and Services Canada.

Aside from this reversal, it should also be noted that the larger Canadian urban centres have obtained the highest net migration ratios. Table 18 illustrates this pattern with respect to the 1951-1961 net migration ratio. In every region of the country the two smaller size groups show much lower levels of in-migration. During this period there was a high volume of out-migration from rural farm areas (Amyot and George, 1973). In Quebec one-third of these moved to a large city such as Montreal. The total in-migration stream was more fully directed toward cities in the 30,000 to 99,999 size group in Ontario, reflecting the fact that "the cities of this group in Ontario are more industrialized than their counterparts in Quebec" (Amyot and George, 1973: 32).

The predominant urban destination of the internal migration flow has responded to the concentration of economic opportunities in these centres. The economic opportunity structure of a community consists of the different ways income can be obtained—the businesses which might be operated and the types of employment present (Bowles and Craib, 1979: 59-60). Migration flows, as we saw earlier with respect to regional shifts, at least partly reflect the location of expansions and contractions in this opportunity structure. Stone (1969: 247-69) verified this relationship by examining how the 1956-1961 in-migration ratio (based on the 1961 population who had lived at a different residence in 1951) varied among the 102 urban complexes with populations of at least 100,000 in 1961. He argued that a migrant evaluated different areas of possible destination according to whether they "could provide him with (a) work opportunities in his occupation at advantageous income levels and (b) an

Table 18: Estimated Net Migration Ratio by Size Group, Canada, and Major
Regions, 1951-1961

Size group (as of 1951)	Estimated net migration ratio					
	Canada	Maritimes	Quebec	Ontario	Prairies	British Columbia
100,000 and over	22.5	8.7	28.2	19.9	34.2	18.0
30,000-99,999	16.6	−3.3	20.7	19.1	38.4	23.3
10,000-29,999	3.2	−5.2	0.8	4.6	19.6	−1.9
5,000-9,999	3.7	−10.4	1.9	8.5	15.0	6.4

Adapted from *Urban Development in Canada* by Leroy O. Stone (1967). Reproduced by permission of the Minister of Supply and Services Canada.

array of services and goods that seems commensurate with his style of life" (1969: 251). He selected six groups of indices of these criteria—including, for example, emphasis in the city's economic structure on the more advanced professional and technical occupations and specialization in manufacturing occupations.

The data show that the in-migration ratio does vary positively when these measures of an urban area's economic structure are considered simultaneously. However, since the variables selected do not directly measure the life-cycle changes that influence mobility, they are not completely predictive of migration patterns. Two factors which emerged by themselves as relatively significant in attracting migrants to a city are tertiary industry specialization and intensity of trading activity—sectors of the economy in which there were important advances in labour demand during the period studied. In contrast, in-migration tends to be negatively associated with degree of specialization in manufacturing when considered separately, reflecting the lack of comparable growth in this sphere of the economy. Aside from regional variations in these correlations, Stone's data also suggest that those factors most strongly associated with in-migration to the largest urban centres—such as income level—are not necessarily the same with respect to the smaller complexes. There thus appears to be complex interaction between in-migration and the regional and size-of-place variables.

Migration and Metropolitan Centres

In the preceding chapter we saw that during 1961-1971 the greatest population growth occurred generally in the largest urban areas, but that growth rates varied substantially among metropolitan communities. Consistent with this pattern, the rate of internal migration, one component of population growth, showed significant differences among these largest cities, as Table 19 reveals.

Table 19:   Internal Migration Ratios, Census Metropolitan Areas, 1966-1971

Census Metropolitan Area	In-migration ratio[1]	Out-migration ratio[2]	Net migration ratio[3]
Calgary	21.4	15.9	7.8
Chicoutimi-Jonquière	8.5	11.8	−3.9
Edmonton	17.9	15.5	3.4
Halifax	16.1	17.3	−1.8
Hamilton	10.0	8.6	1.4
Kitchener	15.9	13.1	4.0
London	16.2	13.8	3.0
Montreal	6.3	6.5	−0.3
Ottawa-Hull	15.5	10.9	5.3
Quebec	11.8	7.7	4.2
Regina	19.0	20.8	−1.6
St. Catharines-Niagara	8.3	8.7	−0.6
St. John's	12.1	11.0	1.2
Saint John	10.1	10.0	−0.6
Saskatoon	23.6	24.2	−0.7
Sudbury	16.2	14.0	2.7
Thunder Bay	10.3	9.7	0.1
Toronto	8.5	9.0	−0.9
Vancouver	13.1	9.1	5.0
Victoria	19.5	13.1	7.2
Windsor	7.9	8.2	−0.4
Winnipeg	11.8	13.3	−1.7

1. In-migrants from the rest of Canada/Population aged 5 and over in 1971 × 100.
2. Out-migrants to the rest of Canada/Population in 1966 according to 1971 boundaries × 100.
3. Net migration (In-migrants from the rest of Canada minus out-migrants to the rest of Canada)/Population in 1966 according to 1971 boundaries × 100.

From Frederick I. Hill, ed., *Canadian Urban Trends* Vol. II © Ministry of Supply and Services Canada, 1976. Reprinted by permission of Copp Clark Pitman, Publishers.

Mirroring its rapid growth, the highest net migration occurred in Calgary, followed by Victoria, Ottawa-Hull, and Vancouver. Conversely, places such as Chicoutimi-Jonquière and Saint John, whose total populations grew more slowly, actually experienced net losses. Despite these correlations, it is important to emphasize again that net migration is actually a less important factor prompting metropolitan population growth than natural increase or immigration. This is documented in Table 20, and illustrated quite vividly in the case of Toronto, which, like Montreal, experienced a net loss of migrants to the rest of Canada. Nevertheless, Toronto had one of the highest growth rates of any metropolitan community. As we shall see in the next chapter, this was due particularly to the large influx of immigrants to that urban area during these years.

There is another intriguing pattern in Table 19 we should note: a high in-

Table 20: Components of Population, Metropolitan and Non-metropolitan Canada, 1966-71

	Metropolitan (,000)	Non-metro-politan (,000)	Canada (,000)
Population, 1966 (1971 boundaries)	10,684	9,330	20,015
Net internal migration, 1966-71	121	− 121	—
Natural increase, 1966-71	588	499	1,087
Immigration, 1966-71	666	158	824
Residual*	− 184	− 172	− 358
Population, 1971	11,875	9,694	21,568

*Includes emigration of those living in Canada in 1966; net internal migration of those born after June 1, 1966; immigrants born after June 1, 1966 residing in Canada in 1971; net migration of those whose municipality of residence in 1966 was not stated; and residual error.

From Frederick I. Hill, ed., *Canadian Urban Trends* Vol. II © Ministry of Supply and Services, 1976. Reprinted by permission of Copp Clark Pitman, Publishers.

migration ratio to a metropolitan community is not necessarily correlated with a low out-migration ratio, as we might perhaps expect. Places such as Saskatoon, Sudbury, and Regina may attract a considerable influx of migrants, yet also experience a significant outflow as well.

Metropolitan areas are also differentiated by their migrant origins and destinations: Figure 5 presents the relative importance of each source of in-migrants for each metropolitan community. This tends to vary during 1966-1971 by population size. That is, the smaller areas of 100,000 to 150,000 residents tend to attract their in-migrants from other non-urban counties in the same province. Those centres that have reached 300,000 receive migrants more commonly from other urban areas. Beyond that size metropolitan areas draw a large number of foreign immigrants along with substantial proportions of migrants from other urban areas. Note also that, comparing the three largest areas, Toronto's in-migration flow is dominated by foreign immigrants, Montreal's by migrants from other non-urban counties in Quebec, and Vancouver's by migrants from other urban areas (Information Canada, 1975: 57-59).

Out-migrants from Montreal are more likely to leave the province, while those leaving Toronto more commonly go to other parts of Ontario:

> The hypothesis that a metropolitan area tends to shoot off satellite communities may have validity for Toronto. If so, one would expect the out-migrants from the city to move to areas immediately adjacent to the metropolitan areas . . . this is precisely what has happened in Toronto. The contiguous counties of Ontario, Simcoe, Dufferin and Wellington absorbed the majority of net migrants from Toronto to other non-metropolitan counties in Ontario . . . (Information Canada, 1975: 65).

Figure 5: Origin of the In-Migrants, 1966-71

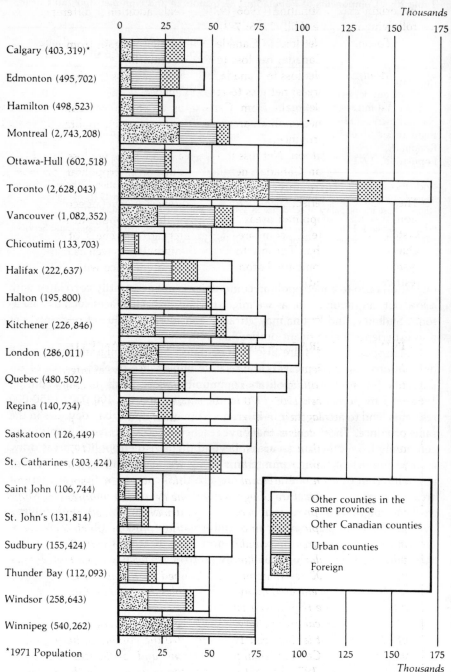

From *Internal Migration and Immigrant Settlement* (Information Canada, 1975). Reproduced by permission of the Minister of Supply and Services Canada.

Comparing the relative proportions of both in-migrants and out-migrants by origin and destination (1966-1971) reveals additional differences, as the following illustrate (Hill, 1976: 7-9).

Toronto. Net loss to Canada as a whole; net gain from metropolitan Canada; net loss to rest of Ontario.

Montreal. Net loss to Canada as a whole; net loss to other metropolitan areas; net loss to rest of Quebec.

Vancouver. Net gain from Canada as a whole; net gain from other metropolitan areas; net loss to non-metropolitan parts of the province.

Regina, Saskatoon. Net loss to Canada as a whole; net loss to metropolitan Canada; net gains from non-metropolitan parts of the province.

These variations reflect such factors as differences in level of economic expansion among metropolitan areas, the role of the metropolis in the provincial system of cities (e.g., compare the greater attractiveness of Montreal to Quebec migrants than Toronto to Ontario migrants), as well as in the national system of cities (compare Toronto's national dominance with Regina's more restricted hinterland).

INTERNAL MIGRATION AND SETTLEMENT SIZE: AN ILLUSTRATION

In Canada as elsewhere it is clear that patterns of internal migration vary to communities of different sizes. We can illustrate this by comparing in-migration between 1965-1970 to three types of centres in the counties of Camrose and Flagstaff, Alberta: incorporated villages with populations of less than 500, towns of between 500 and 1,000 residents, and the city of Camrose with a population of 8,673 in 1971 (Ellis, 1972). This is primarily a farming region which since 1956 has experienced a net loss of rural population. "The rural depopulation has been associated with changes in the structure of agriculture, the decreased importance of this industry in the provincial economy, and with improved opportunities for lucrative employment in other industries, most of which are located in the large centres of population" (Ellis, 1972: xiv-xvi). The smaller villages, particularly, have languished; by 1971 almost one-third of the more than 27,000 residents in the area lived in the city of Camrose, in which were concentrated many of the wholesale, retail and social service functions for the region as a whole.

A hierarchical order characterized the flow of migration in this part of Alberta. That is, between 1965 and 1970 the volume of in-migration was greater for Camrose than for the towns, and for the towns than for the villages. By 1971 one out of every two households in the city contained recent in-migrants—a much higher proportion than in smaller communities—reflecting the economic dominance of Camrose in the region.

This hierarchical pattern was also revealed by differences in the origins of in-migrants. There was a greater proportion of long-distance moves to Camrose than to the towns, and more to the towns than to the villages. Most moves to the latter were short-distance ones, whereas many local migrants to the city had moved up the settlement hierarchy from communities smaller than Camrose—in short, a "step-wise migration pattern."

Table 21:   All Centres; Age of Migrants at Move

Age at Move	Villages %	Towns %	Camrose %
15-39	54.5	49.0	50.0
40-64	34.9	23.5	40.7
65+	10.7	25.5	8.5
Not specified	—	2.0	0.8
	100.0	100.0	100.0

Adapted from Ellis, 1972.

As Table 21 indicates, all categories of centres showed high proportions of migrants in their twenties, who were also female. Yet, whereas Camrose received migrants of all ages, the towns attracted fewer people in middle age and more of those over 65 who had retired from farming. Most of those leaving the farm for Camrose, in contrast, had no intention of retiring but were simply seeking more remunerative jobs; many had not yet assumed the responsibilities of marriage.

Migration streams such as these in a region reveal the varying functions which different-sized communities perform in a hierarchical system. The economic centrality of the city attracts a larger and more extensive flow of migrants than does the village whose position has eroded.

Profile of Internal Migrants

One of the most important areas in migration research is the determination of the individual characteristics of internal migrants. These provide some insight into the motivations for mobility, as well as its possible social consequences. Although greater consideration of this is still needed in the Canadian context, several examples may be cited of the more important relationships which have emerged (Whyte, 1967; Stone, 1969, 1974; Amyot and George, 1973; Information Canada, 1975; Statistics Canada, 1977).

1. *Age*. As Table 22 indicates, Canadian internal migration tends to manifest a pattern of age selectivity. For example, among males the highest rate of movement both within and between provinces is found in the 25-29 age group. For females the greatest proportions of intraprovincial and interprovincial migrants occur, respectively, in the 20-24 and 25-29 age categories. This reflects the influence of stage in the life cycle on mobility. During these periods, "migrants are concentrated in the peak ages for labour force entry, for family formation and childbearing, and in the early years of working life" (Stone, 1969: 78). Their ability and need to migrate in search of adequate housing and employment is greater at this point than in subsequent years when the rate of mobility declines.

Table 22: Percentage Distribution of Internal Migrants by Age and Sex, 1971

	Migrants	
Males	Intraprovincial	Interprovincial
5-14	14.4	4.6
15-19	10.9	3.6
20-24	20.3	7.3
25-29	26.8	8.8
30-34	22.2	7.3
35-44	14.4	4.9
45-64	8.9	2.6
65 and over	8.4	1.7
All males	14.4	4.6
Females		
5-14	14.4	4.6
15-19	13.5	3.7
20-24	28.5	7.8
25-29	26.9	8.3
30-34	19.4	6.3
35-44	12.7	4.2
45-64	9.0	2.4
65 and over	8.5	1.7
All females	14.9	4.4
Total	14.6	4.5

From *Perspective Canada II: A Compendium of Social Statistics 1977*. Reproduced by permission of the Minister of Supply and Services Canada.

2. *Sex*. As Table 22 shows, females migrate at higher levels intraprovincially than males do overall, but particularly in the 15-29 age range. Whereas rural males are more likely, if they move at all, to migrate to other rural areas, their female counterparts tend more frequently to choose urban areas as their point of destination. This pattern has contributed to that "female dominance"

in the sex composition of the Canadian urban population which we documented in the previous chapter. The limited employment opportunities for females in rural areas have encouraged a higher out-migration among males. Note, however, in Table 22 that males migrate greater distances than females. Although relatively more females migrate within the province, males are slightly more likely to move between provinces. This may reflect the higher educational levels of men.

3. *Marital Status.* It appears that the married migrate more frequently than the single. Table 23 illustrates this pattern among migrants from communities of one size to another within Quebec and Ontario. Single persons are underrepresented, while the married are overrepresented within the migrant population for both provinces. This again may be a consequence of exposure "to movement-precipitating life-cycle changes" (Stone, 1969: 79), such as the birth of children, which perhaps stimulate a search for a better job or more appropriate housing.

Table 23:   Percentage Distribution of the Total Population and the Intraprovincial Migrant Population (From One Urban Size Group to Another) by Marital Status for Quebec and Ontario, 1961

Marital status	Quebec		Ontario	
	Total population	Migrant population	Total population	Migrant population
Single	32.0	24.3	22.0	18.0
Married	62.2	70.8	71.2	76.0
Widowed and divorced	5.8	4.9	6.8	6.0
Total	100.0	100.0	100.0	100.0

From *Intraprovincial Migration Streams in Quebec and Ontario 1956-1961* by Michael Amyot and M. V. George (Statistics Canada, 1973). Reproduced by permission of the Minister of Supply and Services Canada.

4. *Education.* Mobility rates vary positively with level of completed education. Table 24 indicates that those who changed residences between 1966 and 1971 have higher educational levels than non-movers. This pattern is particularly pronounced with respect to in-migration to urban areas where those moving into these complexes are more highly educated than the "natives." Several factors appear to contribute to this differential, including the fact that "those with higher education could better afford [than those with low education] the cost of effecting a residence change" (Stone, 1969: 84). In addition, those moving longer distances—between provinces—have a higher level of schooling than do shorter distance migrants, as Table 24 documents. The more educated also move more commonly between metropolitan areas. The loca-

Table 24:   Relationship Between Level of Schooling and Mobility Behaviour, 1966-1971*

		Movers		
Level of schooling achieved	Non-movers %	Same municipality %	Different municipality— same province %	Different province %
Elementary	41.2	35.6	27.0	18.0
Secondary	51.0	55.4	59.5	63.0
University	7.8	9.1	13.6	19.0
Total	100.0	100.0	100.0	100.0

*Change of residence between 1966 and 1971 for population 15 years and over not attending school full-time.

From *Internal Migration and Immigrant Settlement* (Information Canada, 1975). Reproduced by permission of the Minister of Supply and Services Canada.

tion in these areas of employment opportunities which presume advanced training is an important factor contributing to this type of stream.

5. *Ethnicity and Religion.* Socioeconomic status is thus positively related to mobility. Consistent with the observed correlation between ethnicity and socioeconomic status (Porter, 1965), those of British Isles origin have the highest rates of migration. Table 25 shows the French tend to have a lower level of mobility than even those reporting a mother tongue other than British or French. Similarly, given the interrelation between ethnicity and religion, Catholics are less mobile than Protestants and those of other affiliations. The Jewish group is the least migratory of all. While socioeconomic factors may explain much of the variation in mobility among the different ethnic and religious groups, we must not ignore the manner in which specific cultural factors may influence these patterns.

Table 25:   Migrant Population by Mother Tongue, Canada, 1971-1976

	English	French	Other
Total number of migrants*	3,442,545	1,173,010	601,110
Proportion migrants of total population 5 years and over in mother tongue group	26.6%	21.5%	24.9%

*Those who were residing in a different census subdivision in 1976 than five years earlier.

From 1976 Census of Canada. Reproduced by permission of the Minister of Supply and Services Canada.

MIGRATION TO LONDON, ONTARIO: AN ILLUSTRATION OF INTERNAL MIGRATION

The vast majority of the population in Southwestern Ontario live in large urban complexes; less than one-tenth can be classified as rural-farm. Its most urbanized and industrialized counties have had the highest rates of population increase. One significant source of such growth has been the pronounced influx of migrants, particularly young adults (aged 20-24). In Southwestern Ontario the greatest net outflows of members of this group have occurred in its more rural areas. As a result, they tend to be strongly concentrated in its more urbanized counties and largest cities. In addition, these migrants tend to be female, thus helping to lower the sex ratio in their communities of destination.

We can examine these patterns in greater detail by focusing on a small number of such migrants to London, an important regional centre providing employment opportunities in the manufacturing, commercial, and financial sectors (Rego, 1969). Most of these migrants are aged 21 and under, are working at their first job in the city, and have moved there within the previous five years. Most also are female, reflecting the general trend, who tend to be slightly younger than the male migrants. The majority had recently graduated from high school and are now employed in clerical work.

This group had left home not to increase their education but simply in search of work to improve "their occupational and financial situation." Most feel they have advanced their economic position. In addition, some indicate that they had moved to the city to obtain greater independence than had been possible in their home towns. The economic motive was dominant for most, although other factors entered into the decision to come specifically to London, such as the city's cleanliness and accessibility.

These migrants came from small communities within a seventy-mile range of London. Particularly striking is the fact that few migrated from the eastern areas north and south of Lake Ontario. In short, a "migration-field" exists, shaped not only by geographical factors but by the competing influences of other urban centres as well. The greatest inflows to London come from its immediate hinterland to the west and south. In the east potential migrants are more strongly drawn to Hamilton and Toronto.

It is interesting to observe, again reflecting London's relative position vis-à-vis these other dominant urban complexes, that relatively few of these migrants intend to stay permanently in the city. Most view this as one step in a longer process of migration to such places as Toronto. This is especially true for the women. Their eventual move would then

| become part of that interurban migration stream which has become the dominant pattern of Canadian internal mobility. |

ENTRANCE AND THE UPROOTING THESIS

Reflecting a desire to obtain closer collaboration between sociology and anthropology, almost thirty years ago Ralph Beals (1951a: 5) pointed out the need to examine more fully not merely the structure of urban society but the process of urbanization as well—that is, "adaptation of men to urban life." He suggested we view this process as one of acculturation. Contemporary research has sought to follow this lead, and to specify more clearly the dynamic implications of urbanization. In so doing, it has also been following the lines of study suggested by the classical literature on the city. Thomas and Znaniecki (1958 ed.), for example, in their careful exploration of the effects of the process of modernization on the Polish peasant, raised the significant issue of whether entrance to the urban system necessarily involves anomy and disorganization. On the basis of their work it appeared that to some extent it does.

Similarly, Park (1928: 54) proposed that such movement involves not only a change of residence, but also independence from traditional cultural restraints: "Disorganization as preliminary to reorganization of attitudes and conduct is almost invariably the lot of the newcomer to the city, and the discarding of the habitual, and often what has been to him the moral, is not infrequently accompanied by sharp mental conflict and sense of personal loss." The newcomer is a "marginal man," in a period of transition from involvement in a traditional sacred system to absorption into a more individualistic and secular urban order (Park, 1928: 893). The sharp contrasts between rural and urban social systems drawn in the classical typological perspective heightened the expected degree of disorganization accompanying migration.

Criticisms of the Uprooting Thesis

Sufficient contemporary evidence (e.g., Blumberg and Bell, 1959; Tilly and Brown, 1967; Simic, 1973; Safa, 1971; Howton, 1976) from varying contexts, however, suggests that patterns of social support not uncommonly accompany the process of entrance and facilitate adjustment to the urban system. The classical view that rural-urban migration necessarily entails a dramatic uprooting particularly of primary ties appears invalid.

To illustrate, Oscar Lewis (1952) examined the fate of those families who migrated from Tepoztlan to Mexico City. Consistent with his general perspective, a major goal was to demonstrate the inadequacies of the classical interpretation of urbanization and the extent to which its generalizations are culture-bound.

Lewis found little among these Mexican peasants to suggest family disorganization as a consequence of movement to the city. The extended family residential unit became more pronounced in response to the economic constraints of the city. Divorce was uncommon and parental authority remained strong. Ties to kin in the rural village did not weaken, contrary to the classical assumption. Lack of disorganization was also evident with regard to religious participation; in response to pressures within the urban environment, involvement in Roman Catholicism actually deepened.

Hence, Lewis (1952: 39-41; see also Lewis, 1969) concluded that "urbanization is not a simple, unitary, universally similar process, but that it assumes different forms and meanings, depending upon the prevailing historic, economic, social, and cultural conditions. Generalizations concerning urbanization must take these conditions into consideration." Entrance to the urban system need not involve disorganization, culture shock, and anomy. Lewis proposed several explanations for why at least in this case migration cannot be conceptualized as a disorganizing transplantation process. These included the cultural homogeneity of Mexico City, its relatively low level of industrialization, and the fact that Tepoztlan was both culturally and geographically close to this urban centre.

Not infrequently we find that rural migrants may have relatives and friends already established in the city and to whom they turn for help during the initial stages of residence (Browning and Freindt, 1971). Such social support indeed may decrease reliance on the formal institutions of assistance in the urban community (Matthiasson, 1974: 268). Primary relationships also provide rural migrants with avenues for at least partial absorption into the urban occupational structure; specific information about possible jobs as well as appropriate attitudes and values are communicated to migrants through such networks (Young and Young, 1966).

Bruner's study of Toba Batak migrants illustrates the importance of these bonds. They develop new types of clan associations in Medan, the second largest city in Indonesia, which are not found in their rural homeland of North Sumatra. Creative use of the traditional principle of common descent constructs a form of organized aid which facilitates the process of adjustment: "Members assist one another in time of misfortune, but their primary function is to take responsibility for the organization of life-crisis rites that are performed on such occasions as a birth, wedding, a house construction, or funeral" (Bruner, 1970: 130). Membership is restricted to those who can claim a common clan ancestor. This represents an attempt to establish a social group, more extensive than the immediate set of closest relatives, but with many of the same functions. Entrance in this case not only does not destroy extended kin relations, but stimulates their recombination.

Perhaps the greatest challenge to the classical typological interpretation of the consequences of urbanization has come from research by social anthropologists concerned with the fate of tribalism among migrants to the rapidly expanding centres of Africa since World War II (e.g., Mitchell, 1956; Epstein, 1958; Banton, 1957, 1965; Southall, 1961; Gluckman, 1961; Kuper, 1965; Little, 1965; Epstein, 1967). While the typological paradigm would have predicted the decline of tribal allegiances with entrance to the urban system, the actual situation appears to be far more complex.

For example, Mitchell (1956) discovered among the migrants to Northern Rhodesia's mining towns that although tribalism had ceased to represent a corporate social system, as it had in the hinterland, it was still an important basis for establishing social relations. Similarly, Epstein (1958) showed how in Luanshya, a mining town in the copper belt, tribalism as a principle of interaction and control could be operative in one sphere, such as in the native courts, but absent in another—for example, in the political realm. A process of "situational selection" resulted, in which tribal patterns of association were more dominant in some areas of urban social life than in others, where class was perhaps of greater reliance. Both Mitchell and Epstein suggested on a more general level how "folk" patterns persist within the urban system.

Mayer (1961) distinguishes between two levels of urbanization: the "structural," or the development of urban-rooted social networks, and the "cultural," or modification in underlying beliefs and values. These changes are not necessarily correlated with "stabilization" or a prolonged period of residence in an urban community (see also Mitchell, 1969b). Migrants can socially and culturally "encapsulate" themselves, minimizing the need for change in their ways of life. This is precisely what occurred among the Red Xhosa migrants in East London, South Africa. As a result of the conservatism of their culture and the belief in the superiority of their tribal institutions, they extended their home community as much as possible into the urban context. In the areas outside work where choice was greatest, they constructed all-Red social networks which then served to maintain their commitment to the traditional way of life.

Not only is "detribalization" (i.e. loss of tribal allegiance) not a necessary correlate of entrance to the urban system, but the opposite process of "retribalization" (i.e., the strengthening of ethnic tribal ties) may indeed occur, as Cohen (1969) found among the Hausa in Ibadan, Nigeria. Customs and ethnic identities may be exploited by migrants as bases for interest group formations in struggles for power and economic gain within the wider community. In such situations ". . . men emphasize their ethnic identity and separateness and adjust within the contemporary setting, in terms of their enculture" (Cohen, 1969: 194). This occurs not only in many African urban centres, but in other parts of the world as well (Hannerz, 1974).

In short, the uprooting thesis—derived from classical urban theory—may apply to specific groups with respect to how they experience urbanization. Nevertheless, contemporary research suggests that it may be an overgeneralized interpretation of the consequences of the entrance process. To understand fully the complexity of this process, it is necessary to investigate an extensive set of variables (Germani, 1965; Shannon and Shannon, 1968; Lee, 1969; Pahl, 1970).

PREREQUISITE FOCI FOR THE STUDY OF ENTRANCE

Let us briefly review these variables, or what we may term, in rather cumbersome fashion, "prerequisite foci for the study of entrance."

Community of Origin

The social structure and cultural order of the community from which the migrants originate must be examined (Thomas and Znaniecki, 1948 ed.; Kiser, 1967 ed.). These determine, to some extent, the initial impetus of migration and the degree to which entrants are prepared for the specific demands encountered. Earlier in this chapter we noted the relatively high rates of out-migration in the Atlantic provinces during 1966-1971. This has particularly characterized communities having dwindling resource economies (Abramson, 1968a). The slow rate of expansion of employment opportunities coupled with the low average earnings possible in these areas stimulated high rates of rural-urban migration as well as movement to other parts of Canada. The inability of many of these migrants to obtain higher levels of education and skill within their community of origin, however, was a disadvantage in achieving any significant economic improvement after the move. In addition, the rural work environment offered psychic satisfactions which were difficult to replace in the urban context (Abramson, 1968a; Matthews, 1976; Clark, 1978).

Community of Destination

It is likewise necessary to consider the social and cultural systems of the urban centre to which entrance is effected. The assimilation process will be greatly influenced by how different these are from those in the community of origin. Too often attention has been given simply to individual characteristics of the migrants—their educational and occupational levels, for example—without adequate focus on the organization of the community of destination (Shannon and Shannon, 1968: 68). Its stratification system, economic structure, and patterns of ethnic segregation may have a profound effect on the extent to which contact is possible with native residents, and the degree to which participation in its institutions can occur. For example, migrants in Northeastern New Brunswick move to urban centres physically and culturally not very distant from their rural communities of origin (Clark, 1978). At these points of destination they experience little improvement in their housing or in employment opportunities, reflecting the low level of economic growth generally in the region's urban areas. The structure of opportunities in such communities, in short, is restricted regardless of migrants' skills, ambitions, or experience.

Characteristics of Migrants

If the structure of the community of destination establishes whatever opportunities for assimilation are available, the extent to which they can actually be used depends in part on the individual characteristics of the migrants. Age, sex, language, occupation, education, and group membership are all important.

We can illustrate this in the case of the Mennonites (Schellenberg, 1968). When they first arrived in Southern Manitoba during the late 1800s, they sought tracts of land where they could continue their agrarian way of life, sustaining their cultural distinctiveness. Increasingly in more recent decades there has been a significant out-migration of Mennonites from the rural areas to the province's urban centres. In 1951 about one-fifth of Manitoba's total Mennonite population was urban; ten years later this had increased to more than one-third. As the largest city in the province, Winnipeg has been an important centre of destination for this migration stream. The interesting question here is the extent to which the Mennonites have been able to preserve their heritage within their new urban context. One research study (Schellenberg, 1968) has shown that "proneness to acculturation" is greater among younger Mennonites and among those who have lived in Winnipeg for a long time. In addition, with respect to this specific group, receptivity to change appears greater among those who belong to the General Conference Mennonites than among those who are members of the Mennonite Brethren. The former group was founded in the United States and persons of different national origins are affiliated with it. In contrast, the Mennonite Brethren are predominantly of Russian descent. Such homogeneity may have produced stronger group sanctions against modification of traditional norms. Group membership, in this case, can be seen as an individual characteristic that influences the migrant's relationship to the culture of the wider community.

Motivations to Migration

Frequently in the past, the process of migration has been interpreted as a function "of the interplay and balance of expulsive forces existing in the countryside and of attractive forces operating in the city" (Germani, 1965: 159)—in short, the "push-pull" phenomenon. This has increasingly been seen as an oversimplification (Petersen, 1958). It presents too rationalistic a picture of the migration decision, and ignores the social and normative context. Clark's (1978) study of Northeastern New Brunswick showed that the poorer a community, the *less* likely are its residents to leave: ". . . welfare and other mechanisms had served to reduce the forces compelling out-migration to the point where the ties of community could act as an almost decisive counter-force in discouraging such an out-migration" (Clark, 1978: 53-54). Despite economic deprivation, residents live in a rent-free community, receive at least some unemployment insurance and welfare payments, and feel some attachment to their daily routines; this inhibits rates of departure.

We must analyze the process of migration at three distinct levels:

1. *Objective level.* Consideration should certainly be given to push-pull factors—for example, economic decline in the community of origin and the presence of employment opportunities in the centre of destination. Attention should focus on the level of contact between these communities as this will influence the likelihood of migration as well as its direction. McCormack (1968: 4) found among a small sample of migrants from Nova Scotia and New-foundland a readiness to move to Toronto partly because "their destination was not totally unfamiliar to them. At least one member of the family and often both husband and wife had been to Toronto in the past."

2. *Normative level.* Nevertheless, the effects of these "objective" factors are not automatic, as we have seen above. An important intervening variable is the normative system. It is this which determines how situations of economic disparities in communities will be perceived, whether migration is seen as permissible to enhance life chances, and which categories of people are prohibited from moving. Those who leave the rural communities of North-eastern New Brunswick are economically not very successful. Migration is perceived thus by remaining groups of residents as not necessarily offering a viable alternative to conditions at home. For some at least it is defined as a less legitimate channel for advancement, hence discouraging movement out of the community. In other cases readiness to migrate may be strongest among young adults who are expected by the community to explore job opportunities; migration here is almost a "rite of passage" to full adulthood (Abramson, 1968a; Matthews, 1976).

3. *Psycho-social level.* Finally, it is necessary to consider the actual "attitudes and expectations of concrete individuals" (Germani, 1965: 162). These may not coincide exactly with the ideal pattern represented in the normative system. Migration may be strongly influenced by how individuals redefine this ideal pattern. Contrary to the typical characteristic of out-migrants, for example, McCormack (1968: 3) found among her sample of Maritimers living in Toronto a widow who, despite attachments to home, moved there to live with her son after his wife deserted him.

One result of the operation of factors at these three levels is the decision to migrate. There are several aspects of this decision which may have significance for the consequences of the entrance process (Germani, 1965: 172-73):

(a) *Manifest motives*—that is, the overt reasons given for migration (for example, unemployment or desire to be near kin).

(b) *Intentions regarding length of residence in the community of destina-*

tion—whether the move is seen only as a temporary departure to obtain sufficient economic resources to return home permanently, or as one stage in the
process of migration to a more distant city. To illustrate, with the assistance of
Canada Manpower and other agencies a number of young rural migrants are
brought to Winnipeg and Brandon for educational training programs (Monu,
1969). Although they move to these centres for economic reasons, they do not
regard themselves as "real" migrants. Reinforcing this perceived temporary
character of their move is the strong attachment they still feel to their rural
communities. Few stay in the city for the entire week, returning home on
weekends. Their continued commitment to rural living is shown in their lack
of interest in urban affairs and organizations. Their conception of themselves
as only temporary residents of the city thus inhibits full integration into the urban social system. Similarly, among rural migrants to Halifax those of lower
status define their move as a short-term and temporary economic necessity
(Storrie, 1968). Their commitment to the rural social system is strengthened by
frequent visits home and through restricting their contacts in the city to others
with a similar orientation. White-collar, higher-status migrants, in contrast,
define mobility as a means for status enhancement, and interpret their entrance to the urban system as a long-term commitment in which full involvement in city-based organizations is to be pursued. The central point of these
two examples is obvious, but nonetheless fundamental: we must explore the
meaning and definition of migration held by those who move to the city if we
are to understand their subsequent behaviour (Simic, 1973).

(c) *The kind of decision made*—that is, the extent to which it is the result
of careful and deliberate planning or of emotional reactions to particular
events. This may influence length of tenure in the city and strategies of adjustment.

Pattern of Migration

An additional area of research, which Thomas and Znaniecki's study showed
to be important, is the manner in which entrance is effected. We must examine
the channels or "auspices" of migration, defined as

> . . . the social structures which establish relationships between the migrant and
> the receiving community before he moves. We may say that an individual
> migrates under the auspices of kinship when his principal connections with the
> city of destination are through kinsmen, even if he comes desperately seeking a
> job. Likewise, we may say that he migrates under the auspices of work when the
> labor market of a particular firm provides the main organized relationship to the
> new community, even if he also has kinfolk there. Of course, he may migrate
> under several auspices at once, or under none at all (Tilly and Brown, 1967: 142).

"Chain-migration" is an illustration of this. Those migrating to a particular
city in turn encourage and arrange for relocation of kin and friends (Mac-

Donald and MacDonald, 1964). Maritimers moving to Toronto are attracted there because relatives can provide shelter, information about the city, and social support (McCormack, 1968; Abramson, 1968).

Process of Entrance

Finally, consideration must be given to what precisely is involved in the process of entrance itself (Germani, 1965; Eisenstadt, 1952):

1. *Personal adjustment*—the individual's adjustment to the role he performs in the community, the amount of internal stress he feels, and the extent of positive identification with the new social order. For example, among rural migrants to Winnipeg and Brandon, contrary to what might be predicted, those with higher levels of schooling tend to be less well adapted (Monu, 1969). The better educated are less satisfied with urban life. This might reflect a process of "status dislocation": "It could be that the better educated have higher expectations of city life than the less educated and the unfulfillment of these high expectations has resulted in low adjustment" (Monu, 1969: 62).

2. *Institutional integration or social participation*—the extent of involvement in different institutions and social networks in the urban system. Among the rural migrants to Halifax, discussed briefly above, those of higher status showed stronger integration into the rural social system by their severance of rural-based friendships and the cultivation of new relationships in the city (Storrie, 1968). Also important here, of course, is the level of acceptance by resident groups, and the degree of contact maintained with the community of origin. We saw that the low-status migrants to Halifax continued to maintain strong social bonds to rural intimates.

Not infrequently migrants develop allegiances to organizations and groups that readily respond to their particular needs. For example, during the early decades of this century Alberta experienced a marked expansion in membership of a variety of fundamentalist sects and cults (Mann, 1955). These found a ready appeal among those flocking to Alberta's largest cities:

> In the cities, the sects assisted in the adjustment of people of rural background to an urban environment. Their unsophisticated outlook, puritan mores, simple teachings, and friendly informal services made them readily acceptable to persons who had lived a good part of their lives on farms and then moved to the City. In particular, groups like the Pentecostal Assemblies of Canada, the Apostolic Church of Pentecost, and the Church of God assisted in the urban assimilation of the many migrants who poured into Calgary and Edmonton during the twenties and forties (Mann, 1965: 363).

The sects, unlike the established churches, supported traditional rural values and offered the migrants an opportunity to participate in relatively close-knit communities within the cities. The potential strains which accompanied that migration were thereby reduced.

3. *Acculturation*—this is "the process (and the degree) of acquisition and learning by the migrant of urban ways of behaviour (including roles, habits, attitudes, values, knowledge)" (Germani, 1965: 165). Not all cultural patterns are acquired at the same time. Technical skills may be more easily grasped than new patterns of political organization.

There may not be complete correspondence between these levels at any one time. Absorption in the economic sphere may occur, but resocialization in terms of dominant values may be strongly retarded, as we shall later see, through residential segregation of the migrant group.

Measurement of the precise level of assimilation among any group of migrants not uncommonly presents problems: "Sociologists usually develop an instrument based on items selected from the larger culture, with the goal of discerning behavioral or attitudinal modification in the migrant as a consequence of contact with the larger culture" (Shannon and Shannon, 1968: 55). These items—such as higher levels of education, occupation, and various other cultural patterns—tend at times to be far removed from the migrants' previous way of life. As a result, any assimilation which does occur tends to be ignored because it does not dramatically conform with the values of the dominant society.

There are two additional points regarding the study of entrance to the urban system which should be noted. First, it is critical that a dynamic perspective be adopted. For a full understanding of the assimilation process, we need to focus on more than the characteristics of migrants, observed sequentially, at different stages in this process (Shannon and Shannon, 1968: 55). Attention must be given both to the precise means through which adjustment, participation, and acculturation occur, and to the nature of those conditions which discourage integration.

Second, when we examine rural-urban migration, we frequently think in terms of a one-directional adjustment process: the migrant "enters" *the* pre-existing system. We allow the perspective we are assuming—the migrant's—to become confused with the nature of the whole social reality. As a result, we oversimplify this entire process. The urban system itself is frequently profoundly influenced by migration. Abu-Lughod (1961: 23) observed this in Cairo, a city in which more than one-third of the residents are migrants:

> To speak about one-way assimilation to a stable urban culture when so large a minority comes equipped with needs and customs of rural origin is folly. Numbers alone should alert us to the probability that migrants are shaping the culture of the city as much as they are adjusting to it.

As we saw earlier with respect to migration patterns, a parallel situation has existed in Canada's larger cities. Toronto, as we shall see in the next chapter, has in recent decades attracted numerous immigrants. As has occurred in Cairo, they have left a profound mark on the community. In summary, urban social organization must be conceived of as dynamic. Migration, whether of the internal or international variety, is frequently one important factor in determining the shape and direction of its evolution.

THE ADJUSTMENT OF FARM OPERATORS IN SASKATOON: A CASE STUDY

We documented earlier in the demographic analysis the extent of out-migration in Saskatchewan, where farming offered increasingly less economic security. The destinations of those departing were urban centres in the province and in other parts of Canada. Certainly one of the most detailed studies of the consequences of this mobility is Abramson's (1968b) examination of the adjustment problems experienced by former farm operators now living in Saskatoon. Interviewing one hundred of these migrants who had previously owned farms for at least three years and who had not yet retired, she considered the situation they had faced before their removal, the nature of their migration decision, and the specific problems they encountered in the process of entrance to the urban system. She attempted to incorporate as many as possible of those foci presented above as prerequisites for a complete analysis of this phenomenon. It is useful for this reason to review her case study in some detail.

The majority of these migrants had owned farms within a hundred miles of Saskatoon. A number had some familiarity with it, having traded and visited acquaintances there. It was on this basis that they eventually chose the city as the most suitable destination. Most had owned farms that were too small to provide an adequate profit, and most were too poor to purchase additional arable land. They could not afford to purchase the necessary farm machinery. As a result of economic insecurity many were forced to work at other jobs while at the same time trying to maintain their farms. These efforts were not successful. Compounding their difficulties was the distance from such critical services as schools, hospitals, and churches.

Despite these problems, most valued highly many aspects of farm life—its independence and relative freedom, the self-expression which it permitted. Their self-conception was closely tied to the farmer role, which they saw as having an important function in society. In addition, they had derived great satisfaction from the social life of their communities, the frequent exchange of visits and mutual aid between neighbours and relatives. The intensity of this rural integration, however, had begun to diminish before they migrated and this contributed to their eventual decision to move.

These migrants had "*a real commitment to farming as a vocation and a way of life*" (Abramson, 1968b: 32). The vast majority had operated their farms for more than ten years. One-third had never been away for more than a day at any one time. The actual decision to move was a difficult one to make and frequently took some time, often a period of years.

They were realistic about the consequences of their departure. They recognized that they could not hope for any significant upward mobility. Most had relatively low levels of education and did not possess skills highly valued in an urban context. In addition, they were older than Saskatoon's male labour force, but because of their larger families could not contemplate retirement in the immediate future. Most came directly to Saskatoon when they left, hoping to benefit from its employment opportunities and the better educational facilities available for their children. Residence there also permitted maintenance of some ties to their community of origin and to other kin located in the city.

Abramson found that the transition for these farmers to urban residence was not an easy one. The greatest difficulty was obtaining employment. Most had come to the city without offers of definite jobs, and were unemployed for at least some period following their arrival. At the time of the interview (for a large number more than two years after migration) few were unemployed. Yet this still represented a much higher rate than was found for the city's labour force as a whole. Consistent with their lack of training, more than half were in unskilled labour. To compensate for their low level of earnings, their wives commonly also were in the labour force.

Another significant problem which they encountered was in securing adequate housing. Many were forced to locate in undesirable neighbourhoods. Although the vast majority had been able to purchase their own homes—investing all the money they had received from the sale of their farms—they still missed the greater privacy, freedom, and outdoor space of their farms. The material amenities they now possessed in their urban homes did not minimize the loss of these valued features of rural life.

Seeking to ease the transition to the city, many attempted to preserve their social ties to home by visiting friends and kin and returning home for special occasions. These efforts lessened among those who became more assimilated. Supporting to some extent the uprooting thesis, a good number experienced greater social isolation in the city than on the farm. They found Saskatoon impersonal, where status was too often based on external criteria. Contacts with kin living in the city were less frequent than in the rural communities. Their rates of organizational participation tended to be much lower than prior to migration. Disrup-

tion also occurred to some extent within the family as parental authority was weakened through the dominance of competing institutions and groups, such as the school.

The difficulties of this transition were especially pronounced among those migrants who had previously operated relatively successful farms. These had attained higher status positions in their communities of origin. Movement to the city was accompanied by entrance into low-status occupations, which tended to intensify feelings of disorientation.

Length of residence did not appear to exercise any important influence on attitude toward city living. Those migrants who had resided in Saskatoon for a longer period of time were not necessarily more positive. In an attempt to delineate the kinds of attitude change which did occur over time, Abramson (1968b: 90-91) suggested the following phases of adjustment:

"(a) a short period of "euphoria" and "confidence" following the move to the city, related to relief from indecision and the confidence developed from making a move to control their own fate. . . . [under six months in the city];

(b) a longer period of strain associated with their social milieus and physical setting, and with changes in their self image [under two years];

(c) a period of "accommodation" in which they more or less stabilized their position and achieved some security and ways of adapting to the new environment [two to five years];

(d) a period of "adjustment to reality" which may be either favourable or unfavourable, depending on how well their own criteria fit the lines of action available to them in the city [over five years]."

Not all migrants necessarily went through these phases. The time periods represented only approximations. But this scheme does illustrate how positive adjustment or integration need not be effected with a relatively lengthy urban residence, as Mayor also suggested in his distinction between "urbanization" and "stabilization."

Significantly, Abramson's (1968b: 104) study demonstrates quite clearly that:

". . . urban adjustment does not depend in any simple way upon relatively better economic opportunities and living conditions offered by urban occupations and the urban setting. Some of the families who are living at a considerably higher level of consumption in the city, and who eked out a submarginal existence on the farm, yearn to return to an environment where they were more generally satisfied with their lives and had been happier."

Attainment of a more secure economic position need not involve social and cultural absorption in the urban system. As noted earlier, the assimilation of migrants is contingent not only on the structural oppor-

tunities of the community of destination but also on the previous experiences, attitudes, processes of decision making, and individual characteristics of those participating in this demographic movement.

NATIVE INDIAN URBANIZATION

One significant pattern of mobility within Canada has been the increasing
migration of native Indians from the reserves and rural communities to a
variety of urban centres. By 1972 more than one out of every three Indians
(36.3 percent) in Canada was living off the reserve (Stanbury, 1975: 300). The
number of native Indians and Eskimos in urban communities more than tripled
between 1961 (28,382) and 1971 (90,705) (Statistics Canada, 1961: Cat.
92-545, 36-2, 1971: Cat. 92-723, 3-2).

Table 26: Distribution of Native Indian Population by Urban Size Group, 1971

	Number	%
Canada	295,215	
Urban	90,705	30.7
500,000 and over	28,545	31.5
100,000-499,999	18,415	20.3
30,000-99,999	8,585	9.5
10,000-29,999	13,180	14.5
5,000-9,999	5,895	6.5
2,500-4,999	4,800	5.3
1,000-2,499	11,280	12.4
Rural	205,510	69.3
Non-farm	193,005	94.3
Farm	11,500	5.6

Adapted from Census of Canada, 1971. Reproduced by permission of the Minister of Supply and
Services Canada.

Paralleling a trend in the wider society, in 1971, as Table 26 reveals, more
than half of Canada's urban Indians lived in cities of at least 100,000; almost a
third were residents of the largest urban areas. Proportionately fewer lived in
smaller communities. Indians, of course, are still predominantly a rural group;
yet the trend toward increasing concentration in cities is unmistakable. This is
particularly evident, if, as in Table 27, we examine the growth in absolute
numbers of the Indian population in selected cities between 1951 and 1970. In
each of the urban areas listed the increase is quite substantial. Over these
twenty years, for example, Montreal's Indian population expanded tenfold.
Much of this reflects a high rate of rural-urban migration, as well as natural in-

crease. Not all sections of the country have experienced Indian urbanization to the same extent. As Table 28 indicates, in 1971 only a very small proportion of Canada's total Indian population lived in the Atlantic provinces. In contrast more than 40 percent were in the three Prairie provinces.

Table 27:   Indian Population by Selected Cities, 1951-1970

City	1951	1961	1970
Calgary	62	335	5,000
Edmonton	116	995	10,000
Montreal	296	507	3,000
Ottawa	—	180	930
Quebec City	29	58	—
Regina	116	539	1,640
Toronto	—	1,196	24,000
Vancouver	239	530	3,820
Winnipeg	210	1,082	20,000

From Statistics Canada, 1961 Census.

Table 28:   Distribution of Native Indian Population in Canada by Province, 1971

	Number	% of total Indian population
Canada	295,215	100.0
Newfoundland	1,225	0.4
Prince Edward Island	315	0.1
Nova Scotia	4,475	1.5
New Brunswick	3,915	1.3
Quebec	32,840	11.1
Ontario	62,420	21.1
Manitoba	43,035	14.6
Saskatchewan	40,470	13.7
Alberta	44,540	15.1
British Columbia	52,215	17.7
Yukon	2,580	0.8
Northwest Territories	7,180	2.4

From 1971 Census of Canada. Reproduced by permission of the Minister of Supply and Services Canada.

Indian urbanization has been the object of much recent attention not only here in Canada but in the United States as well, where a similar pattern has been occurring (see Graves, 1966; Ablon, 1964; Graves and Van Arsdale, 1966; Snyder, 1971; Garbarino, 1971; Hodge, 1971). On a more general level, it has become clearly recognized that there are important theoretical benefits to be gained from the study of the entrance process among this group of migrants: "The reactions of Indians to urbanization in Canada could indicate the real dimensions of the problems of adaptation by traditional people in complex city environment" (Nagler, 1970: 93).

Urban Entrance

Many Indians may first live off the reserve at a young age in order to attend school. Indian students come specifically to Winnipeg, for example, to take advantage of the variety of courses offered there (Schwartz, 1973). They may be housed in private homes for a time before returning to the reserve. However, it is when they reach at least the age of 16 that Indians are likely to migrate to urban centres on a more sustained basis. Economic necessity is the major reason for movement off the reserve. As Table 29 shows, the search for employment is particularly critical: more than one-fourth of a sample of British Columbia's off-reserve Indians left because there were no jobs for them on the reserve or because the openings they were able to find were at such a distance as to prohibit commuting. This is especially true for young men (Stanbury, 1975: 27). We must recognize Indian urban migration also as something of a life-cycle process (Denton, 1972). Young adults are expected and encouraged to leave home for a time in order to find work and manifest their independence. Many do not intend to remain permanently in the urban centre (Maunula, 1973); they foresee their eventual return to the reserve as a normal and desirable process. Indeed, data on B.C.'s Indians suggest that economic success off the reserve does not necessarily lessen the probability of this return migration (Stanbury, 1975: 43). The reserve is particularly attractive as a place in which to retire, provided of course adequate housing is available.

Conditions of Life in Urban Areas

Surveys of their conditions of life in both large (Boek and Boek, 1959; Stanbury, 1975) and small (Davis, 1965; Stymeist, 1975) urban centres have repeatedly documented the marginal position of many Indians.

Reviewing the situation of Winnipeg's Indian and Metis population in 1959, for example, we find that it was the availability of jobs that made living in the city attractive, although many complained of the noise, overcrowding, poor housing, and cost of living. Commonly, the newcomers first took up residence in a rooming house. They moved often, searching for more adequate living quarters. Some were successful; the housing of most was still inadequate by middle-class standards.

Their occupational and income levels underscored the degree of marginality. Most of those who had come to the city in search of jobs were employed. Yet, most typically, they were engaged in labouring or semi-skilled occupations. Turnover was not infrequent, particularly among the Indians, about half of whom had held their current jobs for under six months (see Mc-

Caskill, 1970). Among the unemployed, sickness was an especially frequent reason for loss of jobs, as were general layoffs and a desire to return to their families. In many households, more than one family member was currently employed. On the other hand, it was not uncommon in an Indian household to have no one working at all.

As an added difficulty many, even though they had generally low status occupations, were responsible for the support of five people, including themselves. As a result, what savings occurred were generally short-term: "Some income would be put aside but soon used for emergencies and other purposes" (Boek and Boek, 1959: 80). Because of the financial burdens they had borne, about one-third had received some type of social assistance during

Table 29: Reasons Given for Living Off the Reserve Among British Columbia Indians, 1971

Reason	Total (%)
No job/distance to job	28.0
Generally prefer life off reserve	23.0
No house on reserve	11.6
With parents, spouse	9.6
At school/children's schooling	8.8
Bad conditions on reserve	4.3
No friends on reserve	5.0
Personal/medical care reasons	6.0
Other	3.8
Total	100.0

Reproduced from W. T. Stanbury, *Success and Failure: Indians in Urban Society*. Vancouver: University of British Columbia Press, 1975.

Table 30: Level of Education: B.C. Indians Off Reserves (1971), Canada (1967)

Level of education	B.C. Indians off reserve age 16 and over %	Canada, age 14 and over %
Some elementary or less	37.5	18.6
Completed elementary	14.5	18.3
Some secondary education	31.0	35.8
Completed secondary	14.7	17.9
Some university education	1.9	5.4
Completed university	0.4	4.0
Total	100.0	100.0

Reproduced from W. T. Stanbury, *Success and Failure: Indians in Urban Society*. Vancouver: University of British Columbia Press, 1975.

Table 31: Median Number of Grades Completed by Age and Sex: B.C. Indians Living Off Reserve (1971) and Canada, Native-Born Population (1965)

| | B.C. Indians living off reserve | | Canada, native-born population | |
Age	Men	Women	Men	Women
55-64	4.63	3.25	8.0	8.0
45-54	7.14	6.33	8.4	8.2
35-44	6.67	6.06	9.2	9.1
25-34	9.16	8.77	9.6	9.5
20-24	10.06	9.71	10.5	10.8

Reproduced from W. T. Stanbury, *Success and Failure: Indians in Urban Society.* Vancouver: University of British Columbia Press, 1975.

the previous two years. Supplementing this were varying patterns of mutual aid through which money was exchanged in times of need. While this helped some to survive in the face of severe deprivation, it was also dysfunctional since it created a drain on the economic resources of the more secure, and thus hindered their advancement.

Many of these patterns of inequality have persisted in more recent years. Table 30 presents data on educational levels among those Indians living off reserves in British Columbia's urban communities. A much higher proportion have minimal schooling than is true for Canada as a whole. Relatively few urban Indians have advanced education. This gap is much greater, however, among older age groups. Table 31 compares the median number of grades completed by age and sex. With declining age group, especially among the men, the difference in education between the Indians and Canada's native-born population narrows significantly. This reflects the rapid rate of increase in level of education among young Indians off the reserve. If this trend continues, the chances for economic success among urban Indians will strengthen.

Nevertheless, other indices also suggest their continued economic difficulties. Table 32 contains data on the income and unemployment levels of urban Indians, again using British Columbia for illustrative purposes. We see that Indians living off the reserve, regardless of age group, have far higher rates of unemployment than are found in the total provincial population. Similarly, more than twice as large a proportion of Indians are in the lower family income categories in comparison to British Columbia's total. Urban Indians are far less likely to be represented at the highest income level. Many are below the poverty line and depend on welfare payments, although over the past decade a larger number of younger and better-educated Indians have been able to enter white-collar occupations. These, however, represent only a minority of the total urban Indian population.

Table 32:   Unemployment (by Age) and Family Income Levels: B.C. Indians Living Off Reserve and B.C.

	Unemployment rate	
Age	B.C. Indians living off reserve (summer 1971) %	Total B.C. non-institutional population (July 1971) %
14-19	59.4	17.6
20-24	50.0	8.0
25-44	39.4	3.7
45-64	55.3	4.2
65 and over	46.5	6.2
	Distribution of income of families of two or more	
Income level $	B.C. Indians living off reserve (1970) %	B.C. total (1969) %
≤ 1,999	9.5	3.5
2,000-3,999	29.3	12.7
4,000-5,999	24.7	11.0
6,000-7,999	16.3	17.0
8,000-9,999	10.7	19.8
10,000-11,999	4.6	13.3
12,000 and over	3.9	22.7

Reproduced from W. T. Stanbury, Success and Failure: Indians in Urban Society. Vancouver: University of British Columbia Press, 1975.

Patterns of Urban Adjustment

There are several aspects of Indian urbanization which we should emphasize if we wish to fully understand the process of entrance among this group of internal migrants:

1. As suggested earlier, Indians frequently move between city and reserve. This influences the extent to which they adapt permanently to city life. Atwell (1969) found, for example, that Indians came to Calgary in search of employment and education. While kinship ties did not exercise a predominant influence on migration to the city, they were significant in the movement back to the reserve. These migrants maintained close contact with relatives who were still residing in the community of origin. Their return migration was a response not only to dissatisfaction with aspects of urban life, such as its perceived impersonality, but reflected continued involvement in the rural social system. In addition, many of these Indians wished to preserve their position on the reserve and sustain the rights and privileges associated with their legal status as settlers there, in anticipation of possible future gains: "One of these days something big is going to happen on or to the reserves and everyone

wants to share in it" (Atwell, 1969: 34). Permanent separation from this refuge was too great a risk. Most significantly, this "pull" affected even those who had attained what appeared objectively to be a secure economic position. As we saw earlier among the Saskatoon farmers, urban adjustment is not a simple function of better employment opportunities. Indian return migration cannot be interpreted simply as a reflection of their "failure" in white society. Rather, it is a manifestation of their continued cultural and social attachments to the reserve. Those who lack these bonds (perhaps because of removal from the reserve permanently at a very young age) or who sever them through inter-marriage, for example, with non-Indians, are less likely to return (Denton, 1972).

2. The level of economic success in urban society does not in itself influence the extent to which Indian culture identity is eroded. There is little evidence, for example, in the British Columbia survey "that Indians living in urban centres must 'go white' in order to be economically and socially successful. Certain non-traditional patterns of behaviour must be adopted, but these need not result in the loss of cultural identity" (Stanbury, 1975: 255). Indeed, readership of Indian newspapers and membership in Indian organizations tend to be more pronounced among the better-educated.

3. The difficulties Indians face in adjusting to the urban system may partly be due to the divergence between their value system and that found in the city (Nagler, 1970). High emphasis on the accumulation of wealth and savings, subordination to a more regimented routine, and separation of work from other spheres of life may be alien to the traditions of the reserve community. This may engender a sense of estrangement among newly-arrived Indian migrants, reinforced by the apparent inappropriateness in the urban setting of customary patterns of mutual aid, creating a cultural gap that is not easy to bridge. Proximity of the community of origin to urban areas partly defines this gap. Those Indians who migrate from reserves near urban centres may be more likely to value and attain higher levels of education, and thus enter skilled or white-collar occupations, than those coming from more remote communities. Proximity results in exposure to urban influences, which allows for greater familiarity with non-traditional cultural patterns.

4. Despite these general patterns it is critical that we recognize the existence of different types of urban Indians, whose relations to the city may diverge sharply:

> The early reports on Indians in the cities seemed to find a single urban way of life for Indians. Today, it is not only useless but absurd to talk about "the urban Indian" in the singular. The adjustment patterns, recreation behavior, employment, and education expectations vary as much for people classified as Indians as similar expectations vary for the general population moving from nonurban to urban life (Garbarino, 1971: 171-72).

In Saskatoon, for example, we can distinguish three classes of Indians: the "affluent" (a small group who hold influential positions in the welfare bureaucracy), the "welfare" (the rapidly growing indigent sector who concentrate on skid row and are significantly estranged from the "urban value system as a whole"), and the "anomic" (marginal men integrated into neither the white social structure nor the native Indian culture) (Dosman, 1972). Similarly, in Toronto, as Table 33 summarizes, there are several types of Indians, distinguished according to class, commitment socially and culturally to urban residence, and strength of ties to the reserve. The exact proportions of urban Indians falling into each of these categories fluctuate over time. Such typologies, however, do serve to remind us of the need to specify carefully the particular groups to which any generalizations about Indian urbanization are applicable. Our earlier discussion, for example, of return migration may be less relevant to the "affluent" or "white-collar" groups than to other categories, although even here, as we noted above, we must avoid stereotypical assumptions.

Table 33:   Types of Indian Residents in Toronto

---

(1) White-collar group;

(2) Blue-collar group—subdivided according to whether they viewed their employment as permanent (the "committed") or not (the "uncommitted");

(3) Transitionals—who had not yet attained permanent urban residence (at least two years), including students, the unskilled, and those who return to the reserve because of cultural estrangement;

(4) Urban users—who only temporarily enter the urban community to make use of its facilities (those coming for supplies, health, recreation, seasonal work to support their families, and the short-term inhabitants of skid row);

(5) Vagabonds—who attempt to find work during the winter in the city, but have no permanent connections with the reserve and do not support families located there.

Adapted from Nagler, 1970.

Indian-White Relationships

One important element in Indian urban adjustment is their relationship with the larger white community. Discrimination against Indians tends to be greater in towns and small cities where they may be more visible (Price, 1975: 44). For example, in Northwestern Ontario the residents of Crow Lake, regardless of their own ethnic affiliations, are all united in their opposition to the Indians (Stymeist, 1975). The natives are discouraged from living and working in the community; many must remain on the nearby reserve as a result. They come to town to shop (but only in certain stores designated specifically for them) and to obtain necessary services from the Indian Affairs Department and the Zone Hospital (which together employ many of the townspeople). The town's economy depends on the continued need of the local Indian population for these welfare services. In general, open discrimination is less pronounced than informal patterns of social distance; social bonds rarely traverse the cleavage between natives and whites.

Regardless of type of community, urban Indians frequently perceive their ethnicity as a stigma in the white world, and feel that "the social category of 'Indian' is a discrediting one among whites" (Denton, 1975: 65). To offset this stigma a variety of "impression management strategies" are adopted by the native migrants. For example, they may encapsulate themselves in all-Indian social networks, avoiding all unnecessary contact with whites and presenting favourable Indian stereotypes in situations where such encounters do occur. This is especially the case among younger migrants. Others may seek to suppress their Indian identity or deny directly the validity of unfavourable stereotypes (Denton, 1975). Whatever strategy is adopted, the extent to which urban Indians can succeed in this process of "deviance disavowal" may influence how well they adjust psychologically and socially to residence in the city.

Formation of Indian Ethnic Institutions

With the rapid growth of the native Indian population in Canada's urban areas has come the gradual development of Indian ethnic institutions. By 1973, for example, there were more than thirty urban Indian centres in Canada, such as those in Toronto and Winnipeg (Price, 1975).

The first institutions that cater specifically to the needs of Indian migrants in the city are the bars. These are frequently tied closely to the skid row sub-community which offers the Indian an urban milieu without middle-class restrictions—a shelter from the discrimination of the wider society (Brody, 1971). During the next stage of Indian ethnic institutionalization, the importance of these bars declines because "(1) other institutions take over the social and educational functions for most new migrants, (2) centres and networks take on the function of receiving new-comers, (3) people move away from the transient skid row area to more stable homes, and (4) people more often drink in their homes and at private parties" (Price, 1975). As the Indian population of a city increases, they evolve more comprehensive kinship and friendship networks and establish their own centres. With the help and direction of more acculturated natives, a greater array of ethnic institutions, including clubs, churches, and political groups, subsequently emerges. This is especially true in cities such as Toronto which have a relatively larger Indian population than places such as Edmonton, where the process of Indian institutionalization is at an earlier stage (Price, 1975). The creation of this urban-based ethnic culture may help counter unfavourable stigma, strengthen Indian identity, and ease the process of entrance for further groups of migrants.

SUMMARY

1. During the present century Canadian internal migration has shown important shifts across regions and provinces, partly in response to the shifting locations of areas offering greater economic opportunities. In more recent years, British Columbia, Ontario, and Alberta have experienced net inflows of migrants.

2. Mobility between urban centres has replaced rural-urban migration as the dominant internal migration stream.

3. The larger urban centres have obtained the highest net migration ratios, partly reflecting the concentration of economic opportunities there. Despite this general trend, Canada's metropolitan areas show significant variations in net migration as well as in migrant origins and destinations. Patterns of internal migration vary to communities of different size; migration streams reveal the varying functions different-sized communities perform in a hierarchical system. Overall, net migration is a less important factor promoting metropolitan population growth than natural increase or immigration.

4. The profile of internal migrants reveals substantial variations by individual characteristics. Among males the highest rate of movement is found in the 25-29 age group, for females the 20-24 and 25-29 groups. Life-cycle stage influences mobility. Female migrants are more likely to choose urban areas as their point of destination than males, although the latter tend to move greater distances. The married migrate more frequently than the single, as do the better-educated than those with less schooling, those of British Isles origin more than the French, and Protestants more than Catholics. Much of this variation may be due to differences in socioeconomic status, although unique cultural factors may also be influential.

5. In interpreting the dynamic implications of urban entrance, the classical typological perspective proposed the uprooting thesis—that urban migration is accompanied by anomy and disorganization. Although this may apply to specific groups with respect to how they experience urbanization, contemporary research suggests that this may be an overgeneralized interpretation of the consequences of the entrance process. Patterns of social support assist migrants in adjusting; traditional ethnic allegiances are not necessarily eroded.

6. To understand fully the social and cultural aspects of the process of entrance to the urban system it is necessary to investigate an extensive set of variables or foci. These include the social structure and cultural order of the communities of origin and destination, the individual characteristics of migrants, motivations to migration analyzed on the objective, normative, and psycho-social levels, the actual decision to migrate, and the manner or pattern in which migration occurs. Finally, with respect to the process of entrance itself, we must explore the migrants' level of personal adjustment, institutional integration, and acculturation, recognizing that there may not be complete correspondence between these at any one time. In examining rural-urban migration we must avoid thinking in terms of a one-directional adjustment process; the urban system itself is frequently profoundly influenced by migration.

7. Positive adjustment or integration need not be effected with a relatively lengthy urban residence. Nor is urban adjustment necessarily a function of improved economic opportunities and living conditions within the city. Attainment of a more secure economic position need not involve social and cultural absorption in the urban system.

8. One notable example of urbanization in Canada is the increasing migration of native Indians from the reserves, especially to larger cities.

9. Economic necessity is the major reason for Indian migration, although it also may represent a life-cycle process: young adults are expected to leave in search of work. Many, however, do not intend to remain permanently in the urban centre. Social and cultural ties to the reserve may remain strong.

10. Urban Indians occupy a marginal economic position. In comparison to the wider population they are concentrated in less-skilled occupations, with lower educational and income levels and higher rates of unemployment. This gap is narrowing among younger Indians off the reserve; data in British Columbia, for example, suggest that their level of education is rising rapidly.

11. With respect to their patterns of urban adjustment we should note that Indians frequently move between city and reserve. Return migration reflects continued involvement in the reserve social system, not necessarily lack of economic success in urban society. Nor does such success in itself weaken Indian cultural identity. The difficulties Indians face in urban adjustment may partly be due to the contrast between their cultural systems and that of the city.

12. As with other groups of migrants, we must recognize that there are different categories of urban Indians, whose relations to the city may diverge sharply.

13. Urban Indians frequently perceive their ethnicity as a stigma in the white world. The extent to which they can offset this through a process of deviance disavowal may influence how well they adjust to the city.

14. Indian ethnic institutions in the city develop through a series of stages. Initially, closely tied to skid row are the bars which meet some of the needs of Indian migrants. In time, as the Indian population of the city increases, they create more comprehensive kinship and friendship networks and a greater array of ethnic institutions. Such an urban-based ethnic culture may strengthen Indian identity and assist in the adjustment of new arrivals.

Chapter 6

Entrance to the Urban System: Canadian Immigration

Immigration has represented an important factor in Canada's national development. It has been estimated that immigration during 1967-1972 "accounted for well over 10 percent of Canada's real economic growth, or that as a result of immigration, each working man and woman in Canada was about $50 richer every year" (Jenness, 1974: 21). Immigration has reinforced the society's pattern of cultural pluralism. Most significantly, it has played a central role in Canada's emergence as an urban nation.

Urbanization in the demographic sense represents partly a process of population concentration. Contributing to this process, especially in the past several decades, has been the clustering of immigrants in Canada's major cities. Ethnicity thus emerges as an important dimension creating that heterogeneity found within the urban population:

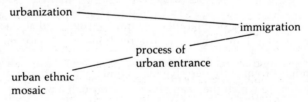

Initially, we must sketch a general demographic profile of who these immigrants are; this will provide us with some sense of the distinctive characteristics of (particularly) more recent foreign-born entrants. We can then proceed to a more detailed analysis of the factors influencing how immigrants adapt to the Canadian urban system. It will be useful here to review several case studies (Toronto's Italians, Vancouver's Greeks, and Calgary's Ugandan Asians) that illustrate in concrete fashion the nature of urban adjustment. The manner in which this process occurs, in turn, affects the structure of Canada's cities. Immigration has produced our rich urban ethnic mosaic. In the final part of this chapter we shall briefly explore the variations in this mosaic across urban Canada, as well as the meaning and fate of ethnicity within the urban system.

132

IMMIGRATION: A DEMOGRAPHIC PROFILE

During much of the previous century, Canada represented a temporary way-station for many immigrants. A number went on to the United States, where economic opportunities were greater (Keyfitz, 1960: 135). Such out-migration declined rapidly as the Canadian Northwest was settled. Figure 6 illustrates the variations in the number of immigrant arrivals since Confederation. Immigration reached its highest peak during the first decade of the present century, a period in which the Prairies exercised their greatest attraction. It was not until after World War II, particularly during the fifties and late sixties, that immigration reached a comparable level.

The overall importance of immigration to Canada's population growth is evident. Those decades in which annual rates of population increase were greatest—for example, 1901-11, 1911-21, and 1951-61—were the same periods, generally, in which immigration achieved higher levels. During the Depression of the 1930s, when immigration was at its lowest point in this century, the rate of population growth also diminished.

During most of these years, "Canada maintained a much more flexible and open immigration policy than the United States" (Jenness, 1974: 7). Since Confederation that policy has shown gradual evolution (Green Paper on Immigration and Population, 1974: Volume 2). Initially immigration was promoted for the purpose of land settlement and agricultural expansion. Those entering under these schemes, however, frequently settled in the urban areas. Subsequent changes in policy were formulated partly in response to pressures from varying sectors of the society, such as French Canada, English Canada, and labour (Petersen, 1965; Hawkins, 1974), and partly in an attempt to fill perceived manpower needs. In the post-World War II period the government sought to foster population growth by encouraging immigration. In addition, a new emphasis was placed on social and humanitarian criteria; "sponsored" immigration emerged as an important trend after 1947. Through the regulations of 1962 and 1967, Canada became "the first of the large federal receiving countries in international migration—the United States, Canada and Australia—to remove racial discrimination from its immigration policy" (Hawkins, 1974: 144). Three categories were distinguished: (1) independent immigrants, or those prospective applicants who expect to become self-supporting after the entry to Canada; they were assessed according to such criteria as education, training, and occupational demand in Canada; (2) sponsored immigrants, or those closely related to persons already in Canada; and (3) nominated immigrants, a "hybrid category" including, for example, grandchildren, uncles, aunts, nephews, and nieces of Canadian citizens or landed immigrants. Both the independent and nominated immigrants, though less so in the case of the latter, are subject to admission through a "points system" in which labour shortages and requisite skills are indentified; an attempt is made to link the country's immigration and labour policies. Spon-

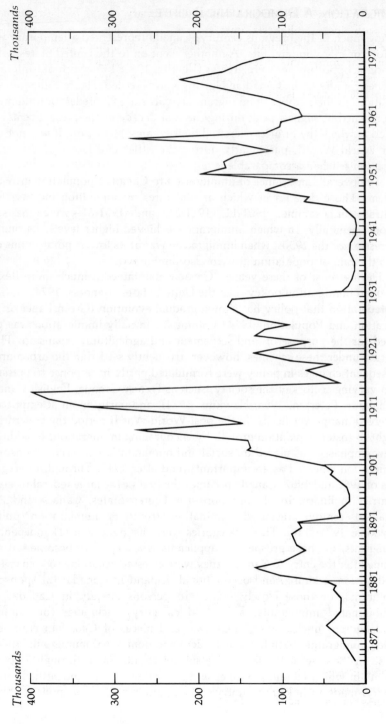

Figure 6: Number of Immigrant Arrivals, Canada, 1867–1971

From *The Effect of Immigration on Population* by Warren Kalbach. Reproduced by permission of the Minister of Supply and Services Canada.

sored immigration, in contrast, has as its primary objective the reunion of those with close familial relationships.

Approximately 3 million immigrants arrived in Canada after World War II. Post-war immigrants differed in many ways from earlier migrants and have had a profound effect upon Canadian cities. In the following section we shall explore the characteristics particularly of the former.

Settlement Patterns

As Table 34 illustrates, the settlement patterns of the foreign-born by region varied during the present century. In the first decade the greatest increases were recorded in the Prairies and British Columbia. In subsequent years the rate of growth declined considerably for the Prairie region in response to greater employment opportunities available in Central Canada. The highest growth rates during 1961-1971 are found in Ontario and Quebec. Among the lowest is that in the Atlantic provinces, which have not constituted a strong locus of settlement for immigrants throughout the century.

What is particularly interesting about the settlement patterns of Canadian immigrants is not merely this regional variation over time. Equally striking is the urban concentration of the foreign-born and the manner in which this has become more pronounced in recent years. In 1971, more than four-fifths of the foreign-born resided in urban areas. This exceeded the rate of urban concentration of the native-born. As Table 35 suggests, the greater urbanization of the foreign-born was evident in 1921. This trend has continued: post-war immigrants are more likely to settle in urban areas than were those arriving in Canada at an earlier time. Such a settlement pattern has contributed to the country's urban transformation.

Table 34: Percentage Increase in Foreign-Born by Decades for Canada and Regions, 1901-71

Region	1901-11	1911-21	1921-31	1931-41	1941-51	1951-61	1961-71
Atlantic Provinces	22.7	17.8	2.5	−7.6	−13.8*	21.4	10.3
Quebec	65.2	28.7	33.5	−11.0	2.2	69.7	20.7
Ontario	56.7	26.4	25.3	−8.8	15.9	59.2	26.2
Prairie Provinces	356.3	23.0	8.2	−19.8	−15.4	4.1	−10.5
British Columbia	182.3	16.8	22.6	−4.6	11.3	24.8	17.4
Territories	−72.0	−67.2	19.7	6.4	19.0	75.0	2.1
Canada	126.9	23.2	18.0	−12.5	2.0*	38.1*	15.9

*Includes Newfoundland.

From *The Effect of Immigration on Population* by Warren Kalbach. Reproduced by permission of the Minister of Supply and Services Canada.

Table 35:   Percent Urban for Foreign- and Native-Born Populations in Canada, 1921-1971

Year	Foreign-born	Native-born
1921	56.4	47.6
1931	59.9	52.0
1941	60.5	53.0
1951	71.0	60.0
1961	81.4	67.5
1971	87.7	74.0

Source: Kalbach and McVey, 1971; 1971 Census of Canada.

Table 36:   Urban Immigrants by Province and Size Class, 1971

Province	Percentage immigrants of total population in urban areas
Newfoundland	3.1
Prince Edward Island	4.3
Nova Scotia	5.6
New Brunswick	4.7
Quebec	10.3
Ontario	24.7
Manitoba	19.0
Saskatchewan	13.4
Alberta	19.2
British Columbia	24.5
Size class (1971)	
1,000,000+	24.6
250,000-999,999	17.6
100,000-249,999	13.6
50,000-99,999	10.4
30,000-49,999	10.3
20,000-29,999	7.7
10,000-19,999	10.1
Urban Canada	18.5
Non-urban Canada	7.7

From D. Michael Ray, ed., *Canadian Urban Trends* Vol. I © Ministry of Supply and Services Canada, 1976. Reprinted by permission of Copp Clark Pitman, Publishers.

Table 36, however, reveals significant variations in this trend. Comparing the different provinces, in 1971 we again find immigrants underrepresented in Atlantic Canada; note, for example, the contrast between urban New-foundland and urban Ontario. In addition, we see that immigrants concentrate not only in urban centres generally and in particular provinces, such as Ontario and British Columbia, but also cluster in the larger urban communities. In 1971 the largest proportion of immigrants is found in the 1,000,000+ category. Between 1961 and 1971 almost 50 percent of Canada's immigrants settled in Toronto, Montreal, and Vancouver. As Table 37 indicates, one out of every five residents of metropolitan areas in 1971 is foreign-born. This varies greatly, however; more than one-third of Toronto's population are immigrants, whereas Chicoutimi-Jonquière contains little more than 1 percent foreign-born. Nor are immigrants of different origin attracted to the same metropolitan areas. Northern Europeans are attracted particularly to Thunder Bay, Sudbury, and Vancouver. Southern Europeans concentrate in Ontario, especially Toronto and Hamilton. Eastern Europeans cluster in the cities of

Table 37: Immigrant Population and Selected Birthplaces, Census Metropolitan Areas, 1971

Census Metropolitan Area	Immigrants as percentage of CMA population				
		Selected birthplaces of immigrants			
	Total	Northern Europe	Southern Europe	Eastern Europe	Asia
Calgary	20.5	0.7	1.9	2.7	1.1
Chicoutimi-Jonquière	1.4	0.0	0.1	0.1	0.1
Edmonton	18.3	0.6	1.7	3.7	1.1
Halifax	7.2	0.2	0.6	0.4	0.7
Hamilton	26.7	0.2	6.5	3.9	0.7
Kitchener	21.8	0.2	4.1	3.9	0.7
London	20.0	0.2	2.9	2.1	0.7
Montreal	14.8	0.1	4.9	2.2	0.8
Ottawa-Hull	12.5	0.2	1.9	1.0	1.0
Quebec	2.2	0.0	0.2	0.1	0.1
Regina	13.1	0.2	0.9	2.8	0.8
St. Catharines-Niagara	22.9	0.3	5.5	4.5	0.4
St. John's	3.0	0.0	0.1	0.1	0.3
Saint John	4.9	0.1	0.2	0.3	0.2
Saskatoon	13.9	0.4	0.7	2.9	0.8
Sudbury	12.4	1.5	3.7	1.9	0.5
Thunder Bay	21.1	3.6	5.0	4.1	0.3
Toronto	34.0	0.5	10.3	4.3	1.8
Vancouver	26.5	1.4	2.4	2.2	2.8
Victoria	24.7	0.8	0.9	1.0	1.6
Windsor	21.5	0.2	7.0	3.5	0.8
Winnipeg	19.9	0.4	2.0	5.7	0.7
Metropolitan Canada	20.8	0.4	4.8	2.8	1.2

From Frederick I. Hill, ed., *Canadian Urban Trends* Vol. II © Ministry of Supply and Services Canada, 1976. Reprinted by permission of Copp Clark Pitman, Publishers.

Ontario and the Prairies. Vancouver, Toronto, and Victoria contain larger proportions of Asian-born immigrants than do other metropolitan areas. Such streams contribute to the distinctive cultural mosaic of these communities.

Immigrants choose to go to particular cities and not to others for a variety of reasons. The greater the average earnings in a city and the lower its unemployment rate, the more likely it is to be attractive to immigrants. Nevertheless, we must recognize the importance of other factors, such as the extent to which the city already contains a large proportion of foreign-born. Reid (1973) compared net new immigrant arrivals to six cities (Halifax, Quebec City, Montreal, Toronto, Edmonton, and Vancouver) over the period 1921-1961. He found that relating immigrant supply variations among cities only to average earning differentials is not adequate. His data reveal that the presence of friends and relatives is actually the most important factor attracting an immigrant to work in a particular city. This reflects that increase in the number of sponsored immigrants which produces a pattern of "chain-migration." In short, "immigrants go not so much where the money is, but also go where other immigrants are" (Reid, 1973: 47). The influence of other factors, such as a province's or city's promotional campaign, on variations in the destination of urban immigrants must also be recognized.

Ethnicity

One of the most significant aspects of Canadian immigration has been its changing ethnic character, comparing pre-World War II and post-World War II entrants. Table 38 clearly demonstrates the lower proportions of post-war immigrants from the British Isles, Central Europe, and Eastern Europe in comparison with the earlier period. Through the years 1926-1945, immigrants from the British Isles represented almost half of all new arrivals; that proportion declined to one-third in the 1956-66 period. Those from Central and Eastern Europe presented a similar pattern. In contrast, Table 38 underlines the increasing proportions immigrating from Southeastern and Southern Europe during the post-war years, as well as from Asia, Africa and the Caribbean. Focusing on absolute numbers rather than proportions, we see that persons of English origin ranked first during the total 1946-1966 post-war period, as they did among the pre-war immigrant ethnic groups (Kalbach, 1970: 157). Italian immigrants ranked second—two-thirds of all those Italians who ever emigrated to Canada came during the decade of 1956-1966 (Kalbach, 1974: 7)—and Germans third, which helped to offset the general decline in those immigrating from Northwestern Europe.

These trends have continued in more recent years, as Table 39 shows. During 1968-1973 the proportion of immigrants from Asia increased significantly, as did those from the Caribbean and South America. Europe, taken as a whole, continued to decline in relative importance as a source of new arrivals to Canada. Paralleling this trend is a rise in the proportion of sponsored and nominated immigrants combined, shown in Table 40.

Table 38: Immigration by Ethnic Origin Groups* for Canada: 1925-45, 1946-55, and 1956-66

Period	Total	British Isles	North-western Europe	Central and Eastern Europe	South-eastern and Southern Europe	Jewish	Asian and others
1926-45	950,944	454,149	232,640	181,193	42,640	32,492	7,826
1946-55	1,222,318	417,164	368,382	184,918	187,437	43,314	21,103
1956-66	1,476,444	486,261	305,953	113,873	441,431	32,490	96,436
Total	3,649,706	1,357,574	906,975	479,984	671,512	108,296	125,365
	%	%	%	%	%	%	%
1926-45	100.0	47.8	24.4	19.1	4.5	3.4	0.8
1946-55	100.0	34.1	30.2	15.1	15.3	3.5	1.7
1956-66	100.0	32.9	20.7	7.7	29.9	2.2	6.5
Total	100.0	37.2	24.8	13.2	18.4	3.0	3.4

From *The Effect of Immigration on Population* by Warren Kalbach. Reproduced by permission of the Minister of Supply and Services Canada.

*This term refers to the group from which an individual is descended. In the past a person's ethnic group was traced through his or her father. This is distinct from country of birth, of citizenship, or of last permanent residence. As a result of changes in immigration regulations in 1967, the latter has become the major basis for estimating ethnic-origin patterns among immigrant arrivals.

Table 39: Percentage Distribution of Immigrants by Source Area,* 1950-1973

Area	1950-1955	1956-1961	1962-1967	1968-1973
Africa	0.4	1.0	2.2	3.3
Asia	2.8	2.7	7.2	16.8
Australasia	0.8	1.4	2.2	2.3
Europe	88.0	84.8	73.5	49.9
North and Central America (except U.S.)	0.7	1.0	2.8	8.4
U.S.	6.3	7.7	10.4	15.2
South America	0.8	1.3	1.6	3.6
Others	0.2	0.1	0.1	0.5
Total	100.0	100.0	100.0	100.0

*Grouped according to countries of last permanent residence.

From Green Paper on Immigration and Population, 1974. Reproduced by permission of the Minister of Supply and Services Canada.

Age, Sex, Marital, and Familial Characteristics

Additional demographic patterns characterized those new entrants to Canada after 1945, in comparison to the current patterns found among the pre-war immigrants and the native-born. Approximately two-thirds of all post-war immigrants are in the younger working age categories (15-44), in comparison to little more than one-tenth of the pre-war immigrants (as expected, perhaps, given the earlier arrival of this group) and less than half of the native-born. As will be seen, such differences have important implications for labour force participation. There are also variations in age distribution among different groups of post-war immigrants (Kalbach, 1970: 179). For example, German immigrants tend to be younger than those from Poland.

Table 40: Immigration to Canada by Category of Admission and Percentage Distribution, 1951-1973

	Total	Sponsored	Nominated*	Independent
1951-61	100.0	36.4	—	63.6
1962-67	100.0	37.6	—	62.4
1968-73	100.0	23.2	23.2	53.6

*The "nominated" category was established in 1967. It does not appear separately in the statistics until 1968.

Adapted from Green Paper on Immigration and Population, 1974. Reproduced by permission of the Minister of Supply and Services Canada.

The foreign-born population of Canada has had a greater number of males than the native-born sector. This was particularly the case during the settlement of the Prairies. However, this difference has been declining rather consistently since 1931, as Figure 7 illustrates. Reflecting this trend, the sex ratio was slightly higher for pre-war immigrants than for post-war entrants. As can be seen, there have been several significant reversals in the sex ratios among immigrant arrivals over the years. During the Depression and World War II, when the overall rates of immigration to Canada were relatively low, there were more females among those entering the country. This pattern was dramatically reversed by 1951 when the sex ratio reached its highest point. This level subsequently declined. In general, such fluctuations occurred in response to modifications in immigration policies and to employment conditions in the country (Kalbach, 1974: 14). Again, we should not lose sight of the variations in sex ratios among origin groups. British post-war immigrants, for example, show an above-average excess of females; the reverse pattern is found among Asiatics under 40 years of age (Kalbach, 1970: 183-85).

Again, comparing their current demographic characteristics, post-war immigrants are slightly more likely to be married than pre-war entrants (as is expected, given partly the greater incidence of widowhood among the latter), and their households and families (with heads under 45 years of age) to be smaller in size in comparison to both pre-war and native-born groups (Kalbach, 1970: 313). Aside from size, an important characteristic to consider is type of family. The census defines "primary" families as those which main-

Figure 7: Sex Ratios for Native and Foreign-Born Populations and Immigrant Arrivals, Canada, 1921-71

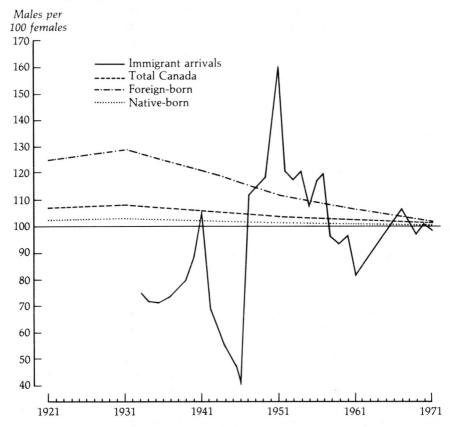

From *The Effect of Immigration on Population* by Warren Kalbach. Reproduced by permission of the Minister of Supply and Services Canada.

tain their own household. "Secondary" families do not. Post-war immigrant families are more commonly of the latter type than are the pre-war immigrants or the native-born. This is particularly the case for those of Asiatic and Italian or other European origins. "Doubling-up" among these ethnic families reflected their limited economic position and reliance on the system of sponsored immigration (Kalbach, 1970: 316). Table 41 presents data relating to more recent changes in family type. As can be seen, the proportion of primary families increased between 1961 and 1971 for both the foreign-born and the native-born. Among the former, the proportion of lodging families declined at a greater rate during this period than did that of the related families. Consistent with the comparison between pre-war and post-war immigrants, Table 41 also reveals that secondary families are more likely to be found among the

Table 41:   Percentage Distribution of Family Types by Nativity of Family Head, 1961 and 1971, and Period of Immigration for Foreign-Born Heads in 1971

Type of family	1961 Foreign-born population	1971 Foreign-born population			Native-born population	
		Arrived prior to 1961	Arrived 1961-71	Total	1961	1971
Primary	93.0	97.4	92.0	96.0	94.7	97.1
Secondary	7.0	2.6	8.0	4.0	5.3	2.9
Related	3.7	2.0	5.4	2.9	3.8	2.2
Lodging	3.1	0.5	2.5	1.0	1.3	0.6
Other	0.2	0.1	0.1	0.1	0.1	0.1
Total	100.0	100.0	100.0	100.0	100.0	100.0

From *The Effect of Immigration Population* by Warren Kalbach. Reproduced by permission of the Minister of Supply and Services Canada.

most recent entrants. This is especially characteristic of those newly arrived families whose heads are at least 55. The apparent lack of time and financial resources discourage the establishment of independent households among this group; many choose to live with close kin (Kalbach, 1974: 69).

Socioeconomic Status

We noted above that immigrants are concentrated in the younger working ages at the time of their arrival to Canada. Consistent with this, post-war immigrants are more likely to be in the labour force than are the pre-war immigrants or native-born. This is also the case among females. "Whether out of choice or necessity, it would appear that a successful economic adjustment on the part of the post-war immigrant family requires the participation of wives to a much greater extent than either the immigrant families with a minimum of 15 years residence in Canada, or the native born" (Kalbach, 1970: 325). This is especially the case among Eastern European and Hungarian immigrants. Even with this contribution, however, total family earnings are lower for the post-war immigrants than for the others. Here too we find important ethnic variations: among all post-war immigrant families, those with British Isles heads have the highest total earnings and the Italians the lowest (Kalbach, 1970: 328).

In terms of educational attainment, the post-war arrivals evidence some superiority as a whole. At every age level beyond 35 they show a higher proportion with at least some university training in comparison to those in the other two categories. Only among the Italians does this pattern fail to appear (Kalbach, 1970: 187-200). Table 42 summarizes changes in the contrasting levels of educational attainment over the 1961-1971 decade. Whereas the proportion of foreign-born with university education almost doubled between 1961 and 1971, the increase among the native-born was only about half as great. This trend was due to the influx of highly educated entrants during that period, and reflected the 1962 and 1967 changes in immigration regulations which "gave greater weight to an applicant's educational attainment and occupational skills in the determination of his suitability" for admission to the country (Kalbach, 1974: 68). Note, however, that Table 42 also reveals that the foreign-born in 1971 have higher proportions of persons with no schooling at all. This may be a product again of an immigration policy which exercises less rigorous controls over the level of training and skill of sponsored entrants seeking to be reunited with their families.

The occupational distribution of post-war immigrants is partly a reflection of the dynamic changes that have occurred in the Canadian economy. Among all ethnic groups they present "larger proportions in manufacturing and construction and smaller proportions in agriculture than observed for the pre-war immigrants" (Kalbach, 1970: 213). In terms of specific occupations, generally, post-war immigrants show greater proportions of craftsmen, professionals, and clerical workers, but fewer numbers of farmers and those employed in transportation and communication. Again, there are ethnic variations in these post-war employment patterns. The British have the greatest pro-

Table 42: Educational Attainment of the Population, 25 Years of Age and Over, by Nativity, 1961 and 1971, and Period of Immigration for the Foreign-Born, 1971 (%)

Level of schooling	1961 Foreign-born population	1971 Foreign-born Population			Native-born Population	
		Arrived prior to 1961	Arrived 1961-71	Total	1961	1971
No schooling	2.8	3.9	3.4	3.8	1.4	1.4
Elementary	50.5	41.7	27.6	38.4	45.9	37.6
Secondary	43.2	50.2	55.2	51.4	49.3	56.0
University	3.4	4.2	13.8	6.4	3.4	5.0
Total	100.0	100.0	100.0	100.0	100.0	100.0

From *The Effect of Immigration on Population* by Warren Kalbach. Reproduced by permission of the Minister of Supply and Services Canada.

Figure 8: Percentage Composition of Immigrant Arrivals by Intended Occupations, Canada, 1955-71

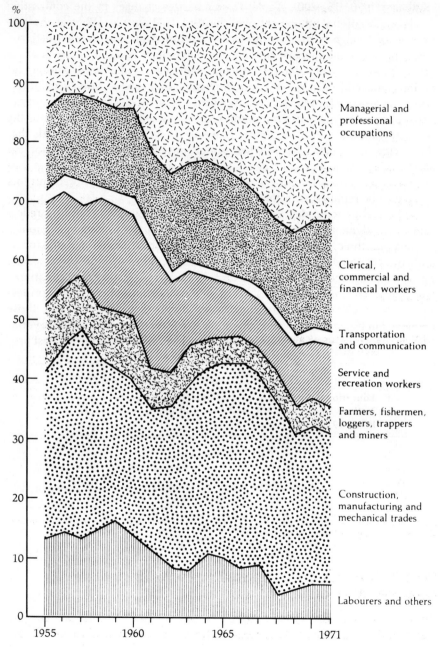

From *The Effect of Immigration on Population* by Warren Kalbach. Reproduced by permission of the Minister of Supply and Services Canada.

portions of any group in clerical and professional occupations, while the Italians are concentrated in the craftsman and labourer categories (Richmond, 1967a: 41). This parallels variations in educational levels.

Figure 8 summarizes trends in intended occupations among post-war arrivals from 1955-1971. Declines in the proportions of transportation and communication, service and recreation workers, farmers, and labourers are apparent. Conversely, the growth of the white-collar groups is rather striking. In all, the white-collar occupations by 1971 "accounted for over half, or 52.5 per cent of all immigrants destined for the labor force" (Kalbach, 1974: 22). This reflected efforts through the "points system" to attract those with higher skills and training.

Despite this general pattern, it is important to note more recent effects of the rise in the proportions of sponsored and nominated immigrants. Insofar as these persons are not screened as rigorously as independent entrants in terms of training and education, the overall skill level shows some decline. Table 43 indicates that in 1966 three-fourths of all immigrant workers were skilled; by 1973 this proportion had dropped to half. Those immigrants classified as semi-skilled show a substantial increase. This perhaps reflects more the influence of nominated than of sponsored immigrants; the latter we find are less likely to intend entering the Canadian labour force (Green Paper on Immigration and Population, 1974: Volume 2).

Table 43: Percentages of Immigrant Workers by Occupational Skill Levels, 1966-1973

	Unskilled	Semi-skilled	Skilled
1966	10.4	15.3	74.3
1967	10.9	19.8	69.3
1968	6.5	28.5	65.0
1969	7.1	27.7	65.2
1970	7.8	30.3	61.9
1971	8.8	33.1	58.2
1972	10.5	32.6	56.9
1973	12.5	36.6	50.9

From Green Paper on Immigration and Population, 1974. Reproduced by permission of the Minister of Supply and Services Canada.

POST-WAR IMMIGRATION: GENERAL PATTERNS OF ECONOMIC AND SOCIAL ADAPTATION

Before exploring more specific aspects of their urban entrance, it might be useful to delineate briefly the general patterns of economic and social adaptation found among post-war immigrants. These generalizations have emerged from careful surveys of their experience and living conditions across Canada, especially in the cities where they have concentrated (Richmond, 1965; 1967a; Green Paper on Immigration and Population, 1974: Volume 4).

Economic Adaptation

The major factor motivating post-war immigrants to come to Canada is the desire to improve their economic position. Although relatives and friends already living in Canada inform them of conditions before, and provide assistance after, their arrival, the desire to be near such intimates is not in itself a dominant motive for emigration.

The process of economic adaptation generally progresses rapidly over the first several years after their arrival. Although most do not have prearranged employment before emigrating, they are able to find a job within the first month. The rate of unemployment is higher among immigrants during their first year in Canada than among the native-born; however, over the next two years the reverse pattern appears, reflecting the concentration, as we observed earlier, of immigrants in the 15-44 age categories. Unemployment tends to be greater among nominated immigrants and among those in occupations for which there is no demand in Canada.

Most post-war immigrants are unable to obtain first jobs on the same level as their former occupations in the country of origin. Many initially cannot use directly those skills which they had brought with them. This is particularly evident for those who held white-collar positions abroad. Such "status dislocation" erodes over time, however; after several years most are in the occupations they had originally intended to enter when they first arrived.

In comparison to other ethnic groups, British immigrants occupy an advantageous position. They are more likely to attain high-status positions during their first year in Canada and to effect subsequent upward mobility, even controlling for level of education.

Immigrants generally do not change jobs frequently. This is particularly the case for those in higher-status management and professional positions. Transience is more commonly found among the less educated and less skilled.

Most immigrants who become self-employed are from Hong Kong and Taiwan. They have a fairly high level of education. After several years their average income is substantially higher than that of other immigrants.

Income levels among post-war immigrants tend to increase rapidly. Indeed, after three years the proportion below the poverty line is lower than for the country as a whole. By this measure many adjust successfully.

In terms of physical mobility, we do find that post-war immigrants change residences more frequently than the national average; their initial housing is typically only temporary shelter. Despite this pattern, immigrants less commonly engage in interprovincial migration. Those who come to Toronto are especially less prone to move elsewhere.

Overall, in terms of the standard of living which they achieved, post-war immigrants are better off here than they had been in their former countries, measured in terms of possession of such minimum material amenities as central heating, running water, and the like. Home ownership appears even among those from poorer countries, who view this partly as a way of achieving security.

Social Adaptation

Although economic adaptation does occur relatively rapidly, post-war immigrants are not necessarily convinced that their social position (measured, for example, in terms of perceived status) has improved in Canada. Those who feel it has actually declined in comparison to their position in the country of origin are most commonly found among the immigrants who have experienced status dislocation and who have not yet entered their intended occupations.

Few post-war immigrants do not feel accepted in their community. This is especially true for those who have achieved economic absorption.

Intermarriage is not a common pattern. Most post-war immigrants select mates from their own ethnic groups; few marry Canadian (i.e., native-born and of a different ethnic origin) spouses, which would have provided a more profound level of assimilation. Those who do tend to be younger immigrants and those from Britain and the U.S.

In terms of informal social relationships, a majority do have at least some close friends who are Canadian-born. The British and Americans are more integrated by this measure; those from the Mediterranean countries, the less well-educated, and newer arrivals less so. Involvement with kin is still rather pronounced for most, particularly among the non-British immigrants, who are more likely to have received assistance for their journey from relatives than are the British.

After several years in Canada, only about one out of every three immigrants participates actively in organizations. The British and those with higher levels of schooling are more likely to become members of Canadian clubs or associations.

Immigrants to English Canada are less likely to become absorbed into the French sector. For example, their knowledge of English is much greater than that of French. Familiarity with the latter is gained more slowly, if at all.

Overall, post-war immigrants are satisfied with the conditions of life they have encountered in Canada, especially the educational and recreational services and the level of earnings. After several years, most do feel at home in Canada and intend to settle permanently here. Naturalization is more likely to occur among groups required to make a relatively severe break with their previous way of life (such as political refugees from Eastern Europe). English-speaking immigrants, especially those from the United Kingdom, are much less likely to become Canadian citizens than are those from other countries. Many of the former are younger people in lower managerial, professional, and technical occupations who had emigrated with the idea of returning to their home countries. They are "part of an internationally mobile labour force, and the return to their former country did not imply any failure on their part to adjust either economically or socially . . . The term 'transilient' may be appropriate to describe such migrants. There is an international market for their occupational skills, . . ." (Richmond, 1967a: 252).

URBAN IMMIGRANT ENTRANCE

In chapter 5 we outlined the array of variables which must be explored to grasp fully the nature of the process of urban entrance. This framework applies to both internal migrants and immigrants to the city. In the case of the latter we must also examine the fate of ethnicity in the urban system. Before dealing briefly with this issue, we shall first explore the nature of urban immigrant assimilation.

The Meaning of Assimilation

Earlier we defined entrance itself as involving personal adjustment, institutional integration, and acculturation. Assimilation thus involves several dimensions or subprocesses. Gordon (1964: 7) identifies seven distinct phases:

1. *Cultural or behavioural assimilation*—acculturation;
2. *Structural assimilation*—absorption into the institutions, primary groups, and social life of the host society;
3. *Marital assimilation*—large-scale intermarriage with other groups and the native-born in the host society;
4. *Identificational assimilation*—evolution of a sense of shared "peoplehood" with the host society;
5. *Attitude receptional assimilation*—diminishment of prejudice by the host society against the immigrant group;
6. *Behaviour receptional assimilation*—absence of discrimination;
7. *Civic assimilation*—erosion of any value or power conflict between the immigrant group and the host society.

Urban immigrant groups experience these different subprocesses in varying degrees. A fair amount of acculturation can occur, for example, without necessarily invoking extensive structural or marital assimilation. Many of these subprocesses do appear strengthened with structural integration, although this generalization needs to be more firmly established. Classical urban theory—in particular, the typological paradigm—tended to assume that assimilation is a unilinear and inevitable consequence of urban entrance. Contemporary research, as we saw earlier with internal migrants, suggests that this is too facile an interpretation: "Different groups at different times may move in either pluralistic or assimilative directions depending upon various factors" (Newman, 1973: 87). Nor do all groups strive for assimilation in the same manner. Any theory of urban immigrant entrance must recognize the possibility of a "multilinear, multidimensional pluralist [i.e., continuation of an ethnically-based social structure and identity] option" (Driedger, 1977: 78). In short, when we speak of "assimilation," we must not only acknowledge the above dimensions, but avoid treating as deviant those phenomena which reflect the opposite process.

The factors influencing immigrant adaptation to the urban system are numerous and interact in complex ways. Indeed, it has been suggested that we should adopt a "multivariate" analysis rather than treating the effects of only one variable at a time. For example, among those immigrants in Toronto with an English mother tongue, acculturation is a function of length of residence; among other immigrant groups, however, level of education is more important (Goldlust and Richmond, 1974: 210). The latter variable, as we saw in our earlier generalizations about post-war immigration, does appear to influence structural integration (Borhek, 1970), as does the similarity of the immigrants' culture to that encountered in the Canadian urban setting (Chimbos, 1972). Nevertheless, these same factors may not encourage an equal degree of identificational assimilation, as the case of the British "transilients" illustrates. To understand this we must take account of additional variables, including the demands of the international labour market as well as these immigrants' own perceptions of the meaning of their mobility.

With these words of caution about both the meaning of assimilation and its study, let us explore several interesting questions about urban immigrant entrance. In particular, we shall examine the importance of social networks and the structure of the ethnic community for immigrant adaptation and whether assimilation does vary among cities. These are specific issues contained within the general set of foci for the study of entrance we outlined in the previous chapter.

Social Networks and Urban Immigrant Entrance

In Table 40 we saw that between 1968 and 1973 sponsored and nominated immigrants together accounted for almost half of all new arrivals in Canada. Many of these originated from the rural areas of Southern Europe. Such extensive chain migration, reuniting relatives and friends, suggests the importance of social networks. This is especially the case for such groups as Jews, Italians, Greeks, and Portuguese who are highly kin-oriented—that is, who place great stress on the maintenance of these bonds (Richmond and Goldlust, 1977).

What is not perhaps fully appreciated is the importance of these networks as channels not only for initial entrance but for subsequent economic improvement as well. For example, Portuguese immigrants in Toronto are able eventually to secure better-paying jobs, even if their educational levels are low, provided relatives or friends are able directly or indirectly to help them find jobs which are "stepping stones" to more highly remunerative positions (Anderson, 1974). The critical factor in attainment of economic success (measured in terms of income) for them is not education nor whether they come to Canada with an urban background. Rather, it is whether their network of contacts directs them to jobs with the potential for further mobility. To illustrate, friends or relatives may refer them to what can be termed "occupational gatekeepers" who may place them in initially low-paying jobs within the construction industry; in time, however, they may be able to move to better-paying jobs in other sectors of that industry. If, in contrast, their networks direct them to jobs that do not offer this possibility, they are far less likely to achieve success. Similarly, among West Indian domestics social networks provide important information about manpower programs and counsellors; this is critical in their quest for educational and occupational improvement: "That many now work in white-collar jobs and have integrated well into the economy is related much more to their ability to make use of the assets of individuals in their social networks than to possession of certain educational and occupational skills at entry" (Turrittin, 1976: 318-19). Neither assimilation theory nor immigration policy has adequately recognized this pattern, which is an essential aspect of the process of urban immigrant entrance in Canada.

The Structure of Ethnic Communities and the Process of Entrance

One significant factor influencing social integration is the character of that ethnic group which the urban immigrant encounters after arrival (Vallee, Schwartz, and Darkness, 1965; Duncan, 1965). Here we are dealing not just with the influence of informal networks, but rather with the broader structure of the ethnic collectivity. Urban ethnic communities vary according to whether they form distinctive cultural, social and institutional systems (Breton, 1961). Social involvement in the networks of the host society frequently will be restricted if the ethnic group attains a high level of cultural distinctiveness.

A second critical factor is the extent to which the existing ethnic community can meet the needs of those arriving—that is, the degree to which it is "institutionally complete":

> Institutional completeness would be at its extreme whenever the ethnic community could perform all the services required by its members. Members would never have to make use of native institutions for the satisfaction of any of their needs, such as education, work, food and clothing, medical care, or social assistance (Breton, 1964: 194).

This extreme condition is rarely met in North America; at least some involvement in native organizations is frequently required. Nevertheless, some urban ethnic groups are able to achieve a higher degree of institutional completeness than are others. For example, in Winnipeg the Poles have fewer ethnic institutions, reflecting their recent arrival, small numbers, and residential diffusion, than do the Ukrainians (Driedger, 1978b). Ethnic groups with a high level of institutional completeness are marked by dissimilarity between ethnic language and that of the dominant society, large proportion ignorant of the native languages, relatively large size, with a high representation of manual workers (Breton, 1961). All of these factors, we should note, contribute to the development of an extensive informal social structure within an ethnic group. This cohesiveness, in turn, encourages the generation of more formal institutions which compete with services offered in the larger community.

The implications of variations in institutional completeness for the process of entrance have been most clearly documented by Breton (1961; 1964; 1965) in a study of male immigrants of different origins living in Montreal. Interviewing most of these at two separate times, Breton focused on the direction of their interpersonal integration—that is, the extent to which their personal relations are confined to other members of the ethnic community or are extended to outside groups.

His data show that the vast majority of those immigrants from highly institutionalized communities (measured in terms of the number of churches, welfare organizations, newspapers, and periodicals in each ethnic community) restrict personal networks to their own ethnic groups. Of the variety of ethnic institutions the most important is the religious "in keeping the immigrants' personal associations within the boundaries of the ethnic community" (Breton, 1961: 135). This indicates that the central role of the churches is sustaining the distinctiveness of, and identification with, the ethnic community. Of least significance are the welfare organizations, which are less relevant to the maintenance of a sense of "peoplehood" among the members of an ethnic group.

It is important to recognize that the degree of institutional completeness has an effect on the personal relations of the immigrants, even if they as individuals do not participate in ethnic associations. Table 44 documents this "structural effect" (Blau, 1960). Those personally involved in ethnic associations, but who come from groups with a low level of institutionalization, are actually less likely to have a majority of their personal relations within their own ethnic group than are those who, although not themselves members of ethnic organizations, are in groups with a high level of institutional completeness.

What accounts for this "structural effect"? Consideration of this question is of extreme importance for grasping the way in which the social organization of the ethnic community can influence the process of entrance. Breton (1961: 190) suggests the following as possible explanations:

1. Extension of their personal networks within the community occurs among the participants in institutions. The immigrants who belong to ethnic organizations value highly their nationality and as we have seen form associations within it. The organizations sustain and perhaps increase this group of "attached" individuals; those in turn nourish the national sentiments of non-participants and include them among their associates.

2. Similarly, ethnic organizations focus on issues of specific concern to the group, emphasizing the need for in-group solidarity, and by strengthening the sense of ethnic identification help to sustain cohesiveness.

3. Frequently, leaders of these associations seek to expand the list of members or support the creation of additional ethnic organizations which revitalize group life.

Institutionalization of an ethnic community is important, then, not so much because it offers substitutes for the organizations in the native community, which would help to channel interpersonal affiliations, but because it stimulates the general social life of the ethnic community. The existence of a formal structure in an ethnic community helps to reinforce the cohesiveness of the group by expanding intra-group relations over time.

There are two additional points with respect to the structure of ethnic communities which we should emphasize here:

First, despite their connection to the overall cohesiveness of an immigrant group, ethnic institutions frequently have different clienteles within the same community. A review of the variety of Russian organizations that functioned in Vancouver over the last several decades provides evidence for this

Table 44:   Institutional Completeness of Community, Individual's Participation in Voluntary Associations and Extent of In-Group Relations Among Montreal Immigrants

Degree of institutional completeness	Individual membership	Proportion of immigrants with a majority of personal relations within own ethnic group
Low	In native associations	.08
	None	.30
	In ethnic associations	.43
High	In native associations	.74
	None	.84
	In ethnic associations	.86

(Tarasoff, 1963). In 1931 the Maxim Gorky Russian Workers' Club was founded to represent the interests of the working class among Russian immigrants and other Slavs. In 1940 it was banned as subversive. During World War II its successor, the Federation of Russian Canadians, was established "to make legitimate and respectable a 'workers' movement' " (Tarasoff, 1963: 43). In 1946 the federation acquired a hall, naming it the Russian People's Home, to serve as a centre in which Russian immigrants and others of Russian origin could become acquainted informally.

Opposed to this organization and serving a more middle-class segment of the community was the Russian Orthodox Society, formed in 1935 initially to help maintain a Russian Orthodox Church in the city as well as to provide a channel through which Russian language and culture could be taught. Members of this society believed the federation to be sympathetic to Communism and sought to discourage others from participating in its activities. Cooperation with what was perceived as a more "leftist" oranization was minimized: "The Society does not notify the FRC of their activities, nor does it make any effort to win their interests. It appears that 'left' wing individuals would be barred from membership in the Society" (Tarasoff, 1963: 99). A relatively sharp opposition between these associations emerged based on differences in attitudes toward Communism and religion. Moreover, they serve members of the ethnic group located at different levels of the class structure. We must not lose sight of the possible internal differentiation of an urban immigrant group when measuring the general level of institutional completeness.

Second, urban immigrant entrance is not only influenced by, but in turn may shape and modify the structure of the ethnic community. For example, Ukrainian immigrants came to Montreal before World War II in two discernible "waves": in 1899-1914 and in 1922-1929 (Kelebay, 1975). These people emigrated primarily for economic reasons. After 1947 a third wave arrived, which included predominantly political refugees. These were strongly committed to preserving a Ukrainian heritage. As a result of their influence the level of institutional completeness in this ethnic community was strengthened during the 1950s and 1960s. Between 1947 and 1967, nine Ukrainian churches were either constructed or renovated, an ethnic credit union movement emerged, Ukrainian language radio broadcasts were established in the city, and Ukrainian schools and organizations proliferated. Post-war refugees thus stimulated "a process of cultural renascence and ethnic re-affirmation" (Kelebay, 1975: 68). Without their influence the structure of the Ukrainian community in Montreal would have languished. Such appears to be the fate among Toronto's Poles (Radecki, 1975). Members of Polish voluntary organizations in that city are drawn from aging immigrants. The organizational structure of this ethnic group does not attract Canadian-born Poles nor is it reinvigorated through the influx of new waves of immigrants. The demise of this structure in a decade or two is a possibility.

The Importance of Ethnic Institutions for Immigrant Entrance: Two Examples

The Institution of Boarding

Historians argue that in studying the evolution of an ethnic community we must distinguish between "sojourning" and more permanent settlement (Harney and Troper, 1975; Harney, 1978; Harney and Troper, 1978; Petroff, 1978). Most of the Italians, Macedonians, and Greeks who arrived in Toronto during the early decades of this century did not intend to stay. Rather, they wished to accumulate sufficient savings that would permit them to return home and raise a family. Such sojourners were frequently unmarried males who clustered together in ethnically-based boarding houses.

To the wider community the institution of boarding was associated with overcrowding, disorganization, and an unacceptable style of life (Harney, 1978). To the immigrant sojourners boarding fulfilled important needs during the process of urban entrance, and indeed helped shape the subsequent structure of their ethnic community. The economic advantages of boarding were evident, both as a mode of entrepreneurship for those who operated the boarding houses and as a means to obtain cheap but adequate shelter and food for the sojourner tenants. The institution of boarding was highly structured with respect to the type of services provided; arrangements for meals and bedding were carefully worked out, as were residents' responsibilities (Petroff, 1978). The immigrants were attracted to boarding houses because here they were able to maintain an ethnic identification while minimizing regional attachments. They prepared the types of meals they preferred, and enjoyed the company of their countrymen. Gradually more formal institutions such as burial societies and mutual aid organizations emerged. The clustering of ethnic boarding houses in a particular neighbourhood attracted additional ethnic businesses and services to the area. During the sojourner phase the roots of a more permanent ethnic settlement were gradually sown (Harney, 1978). The boarding house was less suitable for transplanting immigrants' families; nevertheless, it represented an important institution in easing the initial difficulties of urban entrance.

Ethnic Radio Broadcasts

In the contemporary age of advanced communication technology we must not ignore the influence of media institutions on immigrant urban adjustment. Consider, as an example, the small community of Moslem

Arabs living in a city on the Prairies (Fathi, 1973). Most of these are manual workers with little education. Much of their community life is centred about the mosque. Of particular significance, these Moslem immigrants have little exposure to Canadian mass media. Instead, they rely heavily on Arabic broadcasts from abroad which they are able to receive through shortwave radio. This continued exposure has several important functions (Fathi, 1973):

(a) Listening to these Arab broadcasts to the exclusion of Canadian-based media serves to legitimate their ethnic culture;

(b) This also strengthens their solidarity in the city, as their common cultural and social bonds are continually accentuated through ethnic editorials;

(c) Acculturation is discouraged; failure to rely on Canadian mass media means this group is less likely to learn English quickly or to absorb some of the distinct values of the host society;

(d) Finally, these radio programs help teach the younger members of the community the distinctive aspects of their Moslem Arab culture.

Such ethnic institutions as boarding or mass media do have discernible effects on the process of urban entrance among immigrants. But again we must repeat that their adaptation is multidimensional and is a product of a complex set of factors—including, for example, level of education, length of residence, and degree of difference between immigrant culture and that of the host society.

Variations in Immigration Assimilation Among Cities

We have observed that the structure of the community of destination is a particularly critical factor influencing the nature of the entrance process. For example, a survey in the early 1960s reported that German immigrants achieve greater acculturation and upward occupational mobility in Detroit than in Toronto (Helling, 1962). This reflects variations in the opportunities available for intergration at the time:

> In Detroit where the occupational system is more open and greater substitution opportunities [i.e., transferability of training and skills to new positions] are available, immigrants give evidence of relatively good adjustment. In Toronto, where informal job ceilings are maintained and where the general position of the immigrant is relatively low, a great deal of dissatisfaction and non-integration into the Canadian scene is evident. Unsuccessful immigrants in Toronto are only participating on the fringes of the Toronto community life and are longing for the time when they are back in Germany (Helling, 1962: 219).

Their less successful occupational integration retards the Toronto immigrants' acculturation.

In parallel fashion, insofar as Montreal and Toronto are two dominant areas of settlement for immigrants, we might ask whether these cities have a differential effect on assimilation. Ossenberg (1971) found that in comparison with the immigrants residing in Toronto, those in Montreal show lowered involvement with extended kin. The latter are also more likely to marry Canadian-born spouses and to interact with Canadian-born friends, thus manifesting a higher level of social integration than their Toronto compatriots. The Montrealers' greater assimilation is also revealed by the fact that they are more likely to achieve upward social mobility and thus to be satisfied with their present status.

Such differences may reflect an underlying self-selection process in terms of settlement patterns. That is, the traditional opposition of French Canada to immigration, coupled with the rather extensive out-migration from rural areas to such urban centres as Montreal creating increased competition there for jobs and housing, actually may render that city less conducive to assimilation of post-war immigrants. Nevertheless, despite more extensive economic and cultural conditions in Montreal,

> . . . owing to the freedom of movement of the immigrant, "intact" families may have moved from Quebec to Ontario, where conditions more favourable to permanent settlement may prevail. We may also suggest that the post-war immigrants who, economically, educationally, and psychologically, were less prepared for competition, have also drifted away from Montreal to Toronto, thus partially accounting for the greater upward social mobility of the Montreal sample (Ossenberg, 1971: 57).

There is no direct evidence to substantiate this argument.

Additional structural effects operating in two cities may also produce some of the differences in assimilation. For example, it can be argued that "the more rigid, undifferentiated front of Toronto's Anglo-Saxon population, in conjunction with its 'mosaic' philosophy inspired by Britain, may constitute more of a barrier to assimilation than the vague and often contradictory dualism of Montreal" (Ossenberg, 1971: 53). The historical bias against immigrants in Quebec and Montreal may have concealed a more positive and fundamental acceptance of immigrants by the wider community.

These are simply speculations, however, regarding a fundamental point about urban entrance. The level of immigrant assimilation, even within the same ethnic group, does vary among cities, reflecting such factors as differences in economic opportunities and attitudes toward minority groups.

THREE ILLUSTRATIONS OF URBAN IMMIGRANT ENTRANCE

In the above we have briefly examined urban immigrant entrance analytically—that is, in terms of how such factors as social networks and ethnic community structure influence adaptation. It would be useful now to present holistic profiles of several immigrant groups to illustrate more concretely patterns of adjustment. We shall select for this purpose the Italians of Toronto, the Greeks in Vancouver, and Calgary's small community of Asian refugees from Uganda.

The Italians of Toronto

There have been two major waves of Italian immigration to North America in the twentieth century. Between 1899 and 1910 2.5 million arrived in the United States, settling in the Northeast, especially in New York City (Glaser and Moynihan, 1963: 181-85; Danziger, 1971: 1). The second wave occurred after the Second World War. As noted earlier, of the approximately 3 million postwar immigrants to Canada, Italians represented the second largest group (483,788 between 1946 and 1973) after those of British origin (1,082,971) (Information Canada, 1975: 13). Most significantly, as at the previous stage of arrival, the Italians settled in Canada's urban centres, particularly in Toronto and Montreal. Consideration of their fate as "New Canadians" will help us better understand generally the process of entrance to the urban system within the Canadian context (cf. Helling, 1965; Rees-Powell, 1966; Fenton, 1968; Sidlofsky, 1969; Boissevain, 1970; Ziegler, 1971, 1972; Tomasi, 1977; Sturino, 1978; Jansen, 1978).

Several years ago a journalist (Allen, 1964: 17) poignantly observed: "For a Torontonian of my generation, it's hard to lose the feeling that Toronto is a staid British settlement on the north shore of Lake Ontario, adequately and cautiously run by solidly landed Protestant Scottish-English-Irish aldermen in striped pants and plug hats." This image did not reflect reality even during earlier decades of this century (Harney and Troper, 1975). In terms of population composition, Toronto today represents one of the most cosmopolitan cities in North America. We saw earlier that approximately one-third of the 2.5 million people in the metropolitan area were born outside Canada. Most of these had immigrated after 1945 (Statistics Canada, 1974: 2). Whereas in 1951 more than two-thirds were of British origin, twenty years later this proportion had declined to less than half. While this ethnic group was still the largest in absolute size, the Italians, ranking second, with close to 300,000, contributed greatly to the lessening of the Anglo-Saxon demographic dominance and established Toronto as the largest "Italo-Canadian" city (Johnson, 1971: 18; Richmond, 1967a; Tomasi, 1977).

Italians were present in Toronto during early stages of the city's history (Sidlofsky, 1969: chapter 2). Several years before Confederation five or six Italian families resided there. This number increased steadily in the last fifteen years of the nineteenth century. The first Italian mutual benefit voluntary association, the Primo Umberto Society, was established around 1885, joined shortly by an additional mutual aid society.

In the first two decades of this century the city's Italian population grew eightfold. In contrast to more recent years, few male immigrants came directly from Italy. Instead they spent some time in northeastern sectors of the United States. Toronto, however, proved more attractive for a variety of reasons— access to work, for example, was not controlled by those from any particular region in Italy. (Sidlofsky, 1969: 33). Several ethnic institutions were established—a literary and social club, an Italian newspaper, and additional voluntary associations emerged. The internal diversity of the community was also reflected in the fact that increasingly those from the same regions in Italy tended to move to similar parts of Toronto.

During the 1920s Toronto's Italian population grew by 70 percent. This was due in part to those job opportunities in the city which encouraged inmigration of Italians who had initially settled elsewhere. In the years preceding World War II, this influx lessened. The community became more divided by ideological differences, and conflicting voluntary associations proliferated. The second generation displayed some alienation from their ethnic group. Italy's entry into the war had a profound impact on the Italian community in Toronto. Many lost jobs or contracts for road building. Some were removed to camps. Publication of their newspapers was discontinued, and all the voluntary associations experienced significant loss in membership. Revitalization of the community occurred only with substantial post-war immigration, particularly in the 1950s (Sidlofsky, 1969: 84-85). Experiences during the war heightened the wish to de-emphasize ethnicity, especially among the second and third generations. The Italian presence in Toronto, however, was dramatically renewed, paralleling the Ukrainian experience in Montreal discussed earlier. In 1950 the metropolitan area contained 25,000 residents of Italian origin. During subsequent years this increased more than tenfold.

Several important aspects of the entrance of these more recent immigrants should be emphasized.

1. These immigrants come to Canada for primarily economic reasons. Most originate from the south of Italy and are sponsored by kin. Few ever intend to return home and settle permanently there.

2. We observed earlier that among all groups of post-war immigrants, the Italians as a whole tend to be among the least equipped in terms of educational levels and occupational skills for entrance into higher status positions. A relatively large proportion find initial employment either as labourers or production craftsmen. In time, some degree of occupational mobility occurs, particularly among those at the lowest end of the socioeconomic continuum. However, most do not experience significant improvement in occupational placement during their years in Canada. Despite the fact that incomes are generally low and occupational mobility infrequent, they are economically better off in Canada than in Italy (Ziegler, 1972: 26).

3. Toronto's residential construction has provided a major source of employment for many Italian immigrants having limited skills (Sidlofsky, 1969). Many obtain these jobs while waiting for other kinds of work to open

up. As with the Portuguese and West Indians, social networks perform an important role. Entry into construction work depends on informal help and training from those already in the industry. This constraint restricts their patterns of association. Skills appropriate to that trade in which permanent employment is desired can be obtained only through an informal apprenticeship system that places great importance on intra-ethnic relations. Employment in construction jobs enhances social ties to other Italians in the industry. Leisure activities are shared with workmates and others in similar trades or branches of construction. Through these social contacts future spouses are often met. Insofar as many of their work companions live in the same district of the city, these immigrants become increasingly tied to the immediate area as a source of social activities. In summary, the residential construction industry provides economic adjustment for many Italian immigrants after their arrival in Toronto. It encourages the development of strong intra-ethnic ties. Particularly during early stages of residence this type of employment strengthens ethnic encapsulation, limiting the degree of structural assimilation in the wider society among the first generation.

4. Toronto's Italian community is characterized by relatively high levels of institutional completeness and residential segregation (Ziegler, 1971: 71-75; Richmond, 1967a: 11f; Jansen, 1971; Jansen, 1978). Both are important factors inhibiting absorption into the wider society. Examining a variety of indices we find that overall the level of structural assimilation among Italian immigrants is not high. Most restrict their social contacts chiefly to other Italians, especially kin, even after ten years of residence in the city. Neighbours of the same ethnic background are an important source of friends. Both acculturation and structural assimilation are least likely to occur in any significant degree among those Italians arriving with little prior exposure to urban life and with minimal education or skills. Second-generation Italians in Toronto evidence higher levels of cultural, social, and economic integration (Ziegler, 1972) than the foreign-born; the varied institutions of the community, nevertheless, help sustain general ethnic consciousness and identification (Jansen, 1978).

The Greeks of Vancouver

The Greek community of Vancouver parallels that of the Italians in Toronto in terms of ethnic vitality and level of institutional completeness. In the first years of this century Greeks arrived in British Columbia and Vancouver after attempting to farm unsuccessfully in the Prairies (Lambrou, 1974). These early pioneers frequently opened up small businesses, such as cafes, restaurants, and grocery stores. It was not until 1927, when the St. George Greek Orthodox Hellenic Community was established, that more formal organization of the city's Greeks emerged. Three years later a church was completed. In the years before World War II Greeks increasingly ceased to be sojourners and assumed more permanent commitment to the city. During the 1950s the Vancouver community was strengthened with a relatively large influx of new immigrants. In Canada as a whole the number of Greeks tripled between 1951 and 1961. The core of the city's Greek community was in the Kitsilano area, where ethnic restaurants and businesses provided opportunities for informal social contacts.

Like many urban ethnic communities, Vancouver's Greek community is internally differentiated. We can distinguish the following groups:

1. *The elders.* These are older, pre-1948 immigrants, who came to Vancouver with little education but are now self-employed and fairly successful. This group built the church and supports the traditional belief that religious and secular aspects of Greek life should be closely intertwined.

2. *The entrepreneurs.* This group consists of merchants and more affluent post-1948 immigrants who control the church council (*kinotis*) and other ethnic organizations of the community, but who seek greater separation of the church from secular life. Their influence is greater than that of the elders, who still command some prestige. All fifteen members of the *kinotis* are wealthy businessmen who direct policies for the Greek parish. Something of an elite group, they are distinct from the third and largest segment of the community.

3. *The working class.* These are the mass of newly-arrived immigrants. As in Toronto (Nagata, 1969) their participation in Greek institutional life is limited. Few ever become *kinotis* members; they have little free time or resources to devote to such matters. Nor do they participate extensively in the fifteen Greek voluntary associations in Vancouver. Rather, they restrict their social life to informal networks centred on kin.

We noted earlier that the presence of an array of ethnic institutions strengthens the ability of the community to retain its distinctiveness and influence, especially among the first generation. Such appears to be the case here. Only a small minority of the more than 6,000 Greek residents of Vancouver are active in church affairs. Nevertheless, the *kinotis* supports annual religious events, the celebration of which reinforces ethnic consciousness among a greater number of Greeks than just the dues-paying members of the parish. Similarly, the variety of ethnic organizations and Greek language schools preserves aspects of Greek culture in the urban environment and legitimates ethnic identification even among those who do not directly participate (Lambrou, 1974).

The Ugandan Asians of Calgary

Since World War II one of every ten new immigrants to arrive in Canada has been a refugee (Green Paper on Immigration and Population, 1974: volume 1). Groups such as the Boat People of Vietnam have sought relief from the socially and economically unsettling conditions of their country of origin; others have been forced to leave for political reasons. For humanitarian reasons Canada has permitted entry to these groups. We might usefully review the pattern of adjustment among one such stream for illustrative purposes.

In 1972 Uganda expelled a large number of British citizens of Asian origin. More than 5,000 of these were admitted to Canada. Fewer than 100 came to Calgary on the advice of Manpower and Immigration. Let us briefly examine their patterns of assimilation (cf. Morah, 1974).

Two characteristics of their entrance should be emphasized, since these may influence their subsequent adjustment:

1. In Uganda these Asians were attracted more to European customs and values than to African. They maintained British citizenship and appeared to have acquired at least some cultural patterns found in Canada before arriving.

2. Both official and voluntary agencies took special measures to ease their adjustment. For example, Manpower and Immigration helped them find shelter and employment in Calgary. Similarly, "representatives of the Indian-Canada Association of Calgary were always at the Airport to receive the Asians, talking their ancestral languages to them and making them feel more at ease" (Morah, 1974: 24).

Considering a sample of these Asians living in Canada after a year we find that many had held relatively high status jobs in Uganda but experienced some downward occupational mobility after entry. Nevertheless, they show little desire to leave Canada, although some may not wish to settle permanently in Calgary.

Not surprisingly, in light of the above conditions, these immigrants manifest high levels of acculturation and identificational assimilation. Most speak English, read Canadian newspapers exclusively, and are positively oriented to being "Canadianized." Even after only a year they display strong attachment to this country.

In contrast, structural assimilation is less striking. Only a minority have yet formed close friendships with Canadians. Few participate in the voluntary organizations of the host society. This may reflect the recency of their arrival. Given their small number it is unlikely that they will evolve the type of institutional structure found among the Italians and Greeks. Their potential for further assimilation might be retarded should they be subjected to discrimination and prejudice, as some appear to have been elsewhere in Canada.

Cultural, structural, and identificational assimilation, taken together, are greatest among those Asians with higher educational and occupational status. Their social and cultural absorption have occurred more rapidly; even among the better-educated, however, social networks usually are still restricted to other Asians.

We must be cautious in generalizing these patterns to other refugees or even to other Ugandan Asians (cf. Adams, 1977). Not all enter Canada as culturally "prepared"; not all experience the same degree of initial assistance from the host society.

The three case studies of urban immigrant entrance considered in this section illustrate several basic aspects of the process of entrance. These include: (1) the influence of type of employment, education, and occupation on adapta-

Table 45: Ethnic Origin of Urban Population, by Province and Size Class, 1961 and 1971

Province and size class (1971)	British		French		Italian		Polish		Ukrainian		Asian	
	1971	1961	1971	1961	1971	1961	1971	1961	1971	1961	1971	1961
Province												
Newfoundland	94.5	94.7	2.2	2.1	0.1	0.1	0.1	0.1	0.1	0.0	0.6	0.3
Prince Edward Island	82.5	78.0	13.3	17.6	0.1	0.1	0.1	0.1	0.3	0.1	0.9	0.8
Nova Scotia	80.6	76.3	7.8	9.2	0.8	0.8	0.6	0.7	0.5	0.4	0.9	0.6
New Brunswick	67.3	65.3	26.0	26.9	0.4	0.3	0.2	0.2	0.2	0.1	0.7	0.4
Quebec	12.1	13.0	74.4	75.5	3.9	3.0	0.5	0.8	0.4	0.4	0.9	0.4
Ontario	57.0	57.9	10.6	11.1	7.2	5.4	2.0	2.6	2.3	2.3	1.7	0.8
Manitoba	44.6	46.7	8.4	8.1	1.6	1.1	4.6	5.1	11.6	11.0	1.3	0.6
Saskatchewan	46.8	48.3	5.5	5.4	0.5	0.4	2.8	2.9	9.2	7.6	1.4	0.9
Alberta	49.6	50.4	5.6	5.5	2.0	1.5	2.7	2.9	8.2	6.9	2.0	1.1
British Columbia	59.7	62.4	4.3	4.0	2.7	2.4	1.4	1.5	2.8	2.2	4.3	2.7
Size Class												
1,000,000+	39.8	41.9	29.4	31.0	7.2	5.3	1.3	2.0	1.7	1.6	2.6	1.2
250,000-999,999	45.9	46.0	23.1	23.4	3.7	2.9	2.3	2.7	4.8	4.4	1.3	0.7
100,000-249,999	57.8	55.6	15.5	17.0	2.0	1.7	1.7	1.8	3.1	2.9	1.1	0.7
50,000-99,999	52.1	50.6	33.2	34.7	3.4	2.9	1.2	1.2	1.0	0.8	0.6	0.3
30,000-49,999	42.8	40.6	38.0	40.7	1.6	1.6	1.0	1.2	1.8	1.4	1.1	0.8
20,000-29,999	44.4	44.2	39.7	38.9	0.8	0.7	0.9	0.9	1.2	1.1	0.7	0.5
10,000-19,999	46.6	44.6	32.1	34.1	1.5	1.4	1.2	1.3	2.6	2.1	0.9	0.6
Urban Canada	44.7	45.2	27.5	28.8	4.6	3.5	1.6	2.0	2.6	2.4	1.7	0.9
Non-urban Canada	44.4	41.2	31.3	33.4	0.5	0.5	1.2	1.4	2.8	3.0	0.4	0.3

Percentage ethnic origin (selected groups)

From D. Michael Ray, ed., *Canadian Urban Trends* Vol. I © Ministry of Supply and Services Canada, 1976. Reprinted by permission of Copp Clark Pitman, Publishers.

tion; (2) the key role ethnic institutions play in sustaining in-group allegiances; (3) the manner in which urban immigration promotes the internal differentiation of an ethnic community; and (4) the multidimensional character of assimilation—in the case of the Ugandans, for example, structural assimilation lags behind cultural and identificational assimilation, a pattern which may not necessarily be unique to this group (Gordon, 1964).

THE URBAN ETHNIC MOSAIC

The product of immigration to Canada over time is the creation of an urban ethnic mosaic. The composition of the urban population by ethnic origin varies among provinces, size of city, and across metropolitan areas. Tables 45 and 46 present data illustrating these variations. Only in the Maritime provinces does the urban population show any increase in the proportion of British

Table 46: Average Index of Ethnic Diversity, Census Metropolitan Areas, 1961 and 1971

	1961	1971
Calgary	.642	.657
Chicoutimi-Jonquière	.104	.116
Edmonton	.749	.754
Halifax	.448	.384
Hamilton	.593	.599
Kitchener	.679	.655
London	.446	.461
Montreal	.539	.554
Ottawa-Hull	.633	.638
Quebec	.115	.127
Regina	.719	.719
St. Catharines-Niagara	.696	.676
St. John's	.085	.082
Saint John	.375	.339
Saskatoon	.721	.735
Sudbury	.732	.713
Thunder Bay	.763	.755
Toronto	.600	.646
Vancouver	.598	.635
Victoria	.391	.431
Windsor	.716	.708
Winnipeg	.756	.770

Index of ethnic diversity = $1 - \Sigma p_i^2$, where p_i = the proportion of an urban area's population in the ith ethnic group. Twelve ethnic groups were used: British/French/German/Italian/Netherlands/Polish/Scandinavian/Ukrainian/Asian/Russian/Jewish/Other. The higher the value of this index, the more ethnically diverse the population.

From D. Michael Ray, ed., *Canadian Urban Trends* Vol. I © Ministry of Supply and Service Canada, 1976. Reprinted by permission of Copp Clark Pitman, Publishers.

immigrants between 1961 and 1971. This ethnic group is least prevalent in the Prairie provinces, whose urban areas contain greater representations of Poles and Ukrainians than are found elsewhere. Not surprisingly, in both 1961 and 1971 urbanites of Asian origin are most likely clustered in British Columbia, and Italians in Central Canada. There are urban size differences in ethnic origin, although these are less pronounced. The British are strongly represented in each size category. Note, however, their lowest proportion in 1971 occurs in the very largest class—to which, as we saw earlier, non-British immigrants such as the Italians and, as Table 45 suggests, the Asians, have been particularly attracted.

Taking each ethnic group listed as a whole, regardless of province or size class, we find that those of British, Italian, Polish, and Asian origin are more likely to reside in urban than in non-urban areas in 1961 and 1971. The reverse pattern appears among the French and Ukrainians. In short, each of Canada's ethnic groups are not equally present in its urban centres. In contrast to the Ukrainians, for example, in 1971 almost the entire Jewish population (99.2 percent) in the country were classified as urban (Yam, 1974). Most of these lived in Montreal, Toronto, or Winnipeg.

A useful measure of the urban ethnic mosaic in Canada is the index of ethnic diversity. This summarizes the ethnic composition of a city and "the potential for day-to-day contact of people of different ethnic origins" (Ray, 1976: 258). Metropolitan centres differ in the proportions of their residents who are foreign-born, and we discover in Table 46 significant variations in ethnic diversity. In 1971 Winnipeg showed the greatest diversity, followed by Thunder Bay, Edmonton, and Saskatoon; the lowest levels appeared in St. John's and in two of Quebec's metropolitan communities. Most cities did not experience significant change in ethnic diversity between 1961 and 1971. In both years the range in this index across metropolitan areas is extensive.

The Meaning of Ethnicity

We must grasp not only the demographic dimensions of the urban ethnic mosaic which immigration has produced. Conceptually, what is the meaning of ethnicity? Let us distinguish the following (Stymeist, 1975):

Ethnicity refers to a cultural pattern that distinguishes a collectivity from the wider society. It can include a broad range of cultural traits, extending from dress and food to more comprehensive value systems.

Ethnic affiliation is a social category in which people are placed according to perceived ethnicity and origin. It represents a basis for classifying others and for creating and sustaining social networks.

An *ethnic group* is formed on the basis of a common ethnicity or ethnic affiliation. A relatively clear dichotomy exists between members and non-members; in short, social boundaries emerge that heighten in-group attachments (Barth, 1969).

An *ethnic community* constitutes a more fully developed form of social organization: "within the ethnic group there develops a network of organizations and informal social relationships which permit and encourage the members of the ethnic group to remain within the confines of the group for all of their primary relationships and some of their secondary relationships throughout all the stages of the life-cycle" (Gordon, 1964: 34). These institutions provide channels for fulfilling a variety of needs within the sub-society. They promote a sense of "peoplehood" and shared identification among the members. The ethnic community is an "enclave," a product of four factors— territorial segregation (which we shall examine later), institutional completeness, cultural identity, and social distance (between members and non-members) (Driedger, 1977: 80). Not all ethnic groups achieve this enclavic character. As illustrations of those which do, we might point to the French of St. Boniface, Manitoba, and, as we saw earlier, the Italians in Toronto.

Classical urban theory and the typological paradigm argued, as we observed earlier, that with entrance to the urban system a process of assimilation is set in motion that will inevitably lead to the erosion of ethnicities, ethnic affiliations, ethnic groups, and ethnic communities. This prediction is premature and simplistic. Cultural differences may blur, for example, yet ethnic affiliations may remain vibrant and influence daily social life among urban residents, as Stymeist (1975) discovered in Crow Lake. In situations of ethnic heterogeneity, not uncommonly we find that "it is primarily roles and role relationships rather than entire institutional domains that become ethnically defined. Some segments of the lives and identities of individuals become 'de-ethnicized,' while others remain within the confines of ethnic definitions and expectations" (Breton, 1978: 60). Whereas ethnic affiliations may help shape kinship and friendship networks, they may be less relevant in terms of political or economic ties. Such ethnic fragmentation does not form an adequate basis for the emergence of ethnic enclaves; at the same time it does not render irrelevant the principle of ethnic affiliation in selected sectors of social life. It is in this more "balanced" interpretation that classical urban theory may be lacking. Similarly, it is not inevitable that urban ethnic pluralism will erode, as the continued distinctiveness of the French and Jewish groups in Winnipeg demonstrates. Driedger (1977: 86) argues that initially low-status groups may establish ethnic enclaves in the city. Over several generations, however, they may "shift from an enclavic orientation to a more dynamic regenerational orientation." Such ethnic regeneration is a product of such factors as political or religious ideology and pride in and knowledge of historical traditions. Winnipeg's Jews and Mennonites have preserved their distinctiveness partly through these means. In addition, we might also point to the necessity of improvement in the group's socioeconomic position: "if an ethnic minority can maintain an enclavic foot-hold in the city long enough to groom several generations of urban ethnic identifiers, their socio-economic status can be raised from the low rural status of generations to a status that will enable them to compete on an equal footing with other groups in the city and maintain a pride in their ethnic identity. The Jews and Mennonites in Winnipeg seem to prove this supposition" (Driedger, 1977; 92: 1978).

These speculations point to a general fact about urban ethnicity. We must treat it not as an anachronism, to be inevitably erased, but rather as a variable that can be structurally induced, modified, and even strengthened (Goldenberg, 1977). It is not an ascribed constant; we must conceptualize urban ethnicity as an emergent phenomenon (Yancey, Ericksen, Juiliani, 1976). For example, ethnic identifications and groups are strengthened when they are seen as useful in obtaining scarce resources (Glazer and Moynihan, 1963; Newman, 1973; Goldenberg, 1977). In such a case, "ethnicity is an adaptive and emergent response to disadvantaged location in the existing opportunity structure" (Goldenberg, 1977: 157). Ethnic institutions emerge because access to alternatives is restricted. When greater access is provided, as we observed above, ethnic regeneration rather than ethnic erosion may occur. But again this is a response partly to structural conditions—that is, to Canada's ideology of cultural pluralism and "government support, both fiscal and moral, for the maintenance of ethnic identity in the Canadian mosaic" (Goldenberg, 1977: 157-58). The ultimate fate of ethnicity following entrance to the urban system must be explored in terms of how a group's internal social and cultural structure interacts with external conditions.

FRENCH-ENGLISH RELATIONS: AN ILLUSTRATION OF THE IMPORTANCE OF URBAN ETHNICITY

A fundamental division within the Canadian mosaic is that between the French and the English. This cleavage is strengthened by the differing positions the two groups occupy in the stratification system (Porter, 1965). Class and ethnicity are closely intertwined. We can illustrate the continued importance of ethnicity within Canadian urban social organization by examining French-English relations in one particular community (cf. Hughes, 1963).

Lachute is a small city with a population of approximately 13,000 and is located almost fifty miles from downtown Montreal (Zinman, 1975). The vast majority of the residents are francophone; the English represent only a small minority. The city has attracted few with mother tongues other than French or English.

In contrast to today, in 1900 English was actually the dominant language used by Lachute's residents. English-speaking entrepreneurs shaped the local economy; a paper mill and wool mill were both results of their initiative. Despite their position as a minority the English continue to dominate Lachute's economy. Anglophones control the three largest industries in the community as well as the major managerial positions; lower-status workers are predominantly francophone. Reflecting this economic division, the anglophone average estimated income is higher than that of the francophones.

The two ethnic groups in the community are separated by social not just economic boundaries. Although a numerical minority, one out of every five of the English are able to use only their mother tongue at work, thus insulating themselves further from the majority. Each language group has contrasting religious affiliations; this strengthens the boundaries between them. The community's associations also tend to be exclusively francophone or anglophone, such as the St. Jean-Baptiste Society and the local Orange lodge.

Significantly, sustaining this ethnic division is the separate school system: "French and English relations are described by administrators at the Board level as 'separate but cordial.' French Catholic and English Protestant schools function entirely separately. Any joint venture such as the provision of religious education or the use of any facility is formal and contractual. Teaching staffs are separate; there are virtually no exchange programs. Time schedules, teaching load, unions are different and separate. French students and English students do not mix within this structure" (Zinman, 1975: 153).

Anglophone and francophone teachers evidence the same cleavage socially that exists between their respective students. Across the two school boards there is virtually no intermingling of students, certainly not on a formal basis. With the increase, in more recent years, of the number of francophone students attending the English high school, however, contact between the two groups does occur.

Lachute's social structure, as a whole, reflects a pattern of ethnic "dissociation." All the major institutions of the community are marked by division between anglophones and francophones. This pattern reappears elsewhere, even where the latter are the numerical minority, as in Winnipeg (Driedger, 1977; Cowan, 1971) and Windsor (Mercer, 1974). In the latter city the distinctiveness of French culture is also sustained by continued in-migration from predominantly French-speaking districts in Northern Ontario and Quebec.

SUMMARY

1. Immigration to Canada reached its highest peak during the first decade of the twentieth century. A second large wave occurred in the 1950s and 1960s. Such streams have contributed to Canada's population growth.

2. The settlement patterns of Canadian immigrants reflect a regional variation over time. For example, the largest increases in foreign-born population in 1901-1911 occurred in the Prairies and British Columbia. The highest growth rates during the 1961-1971 period occurred in Ontario and Quebec.

3. Since 1921 the foreign-born have shown consistently a greater tendency to concentrate in urban areas than have the native-born. By 1971 more than four out of every five immigrants resided in urban centres. This varies across provinces; immigrants are underrepresented in Atlantic Canada's urban areas but relatively concentrated in urban Ontario and British Columbia.

4. Immigrants cluster in the larger-sized urban communities. Between 1961 and 1971 almost 60 percent of Canada's immigrants settled in Toronto, Montreal, and Vancouver. The proportion foreign-born varies greatly among metropolitan areas. Nor are immigrants of different origin attracted to the same metropolitan areas. Contrast, for example, the stream of Northern Europeans to Thunder Bay and Sudbury with the relative clustering of Asians in Toronto, Vancouver, and Victoria in 1971.

5. Immigrant supply variations among cities reflect not only differences in average earnings and employment opportunities. The presence of friends and relatives already living in a particular city is an important factor attracting an immigrant to work there.

6. The ethnic composition of Canadian immigrants has shifted over time. The proportions from the British Isles and Central and Eastern Europe have declined among post-war immigrants. During 1968-1973 immigrants from Asia, the Caribbean, and South America increased significantly, as did the proportion of sponsored and nominated immigrants combined.

7. In comparison to pre-war immigrants and the native-born, proportionately more of the post-war immigrants are in the younger working age categories. There have been several significant reversals in the sex ratios among immigrant arrivals over the years. In periods of low overall immigration there tend to be more females among those entering the country.

8.. Post-war immigrants are more likely to be married and to have smaller households and families than are pre-war entrants. The former less commonly maintain their own household; "doubling-up" is especially common for those of Asiatic, Italian, and other European origins, and for newly arrived families with limited financial resources.

9. Reflecting their age composition, post-war immigrants are more likely to be in the labour force than are the pre-war immigrants or native-born. Yet, total family earnings are lower for the post-war immigrants than for the others. Ethnic variations exist here: post-war immigrant families with British Isles heads have the highest total earnings; Italians have the lowest.

10. With the exception of the Italians, at every age level beyond 35 post-war arrivals have a higher proportion with at least some university training than do the pre-war immigrants or native-born. This reflects changes in immigration regulations; "independent" immigrants are now screened partly in terms of educational attainment.

11. In comparison to their pre-war counterparts, post-war immigrants show greater proportions as craftsmen, professionals, and in clerical types of work. Ethnic variations, however, again appear. The British have the largest propor-

tions of any post-war group in clerical and professional occupations, while the Italians are concentrated in the craftsman and labourer categories. The recent rise in the proportions of sponsored and nominated immigrants is reflected in the decline of the overall level of occupational skills among immigrants between 1966 and 1973.

12. The process of economic adaptation generally progresses rapidly for post-war immigrants over the first several years after their arrival. Although many suffer initial status dislocation, they eventually enter occupations more consistent with their skills and aspirations. Economic adaptation is not equally pronounced among all ethnic groups; British immigrants are more likely to experience upward mobility.

13. With respect to patterns of social adaptation, few post-war immigrants marry Canadian spouses. Although some close friendships are formed with the Canadian-born, involvement with kin is still pronounced, especially among the non-British. In contrast to other ethnic groups, the British achieve a higher level of social absorption into the host society. For example, their involvement with Canadian clubs or associations is greater than that found among other groups. Despite this pattern, naturalization is more likely to occur among those required to make a relatively severe break with their previous way of life; English-speaking immigrants, such as those from Britain, are less prone to become Canadian citizens than are other entrants.

14. Urban assimilation of immigrants involves a number of distinct dimensions. These include such subprocesses as acculturation, marital assimilation, and civic assimilation, which need not coincide. Contrary to the assumptions of classical urban theory, we should not see assimilation as a unilinear and inevitable consequence of urban entrance. Nor do all groups strive for assimilation in the same manner. We must recognize the possibility of a multilinear, multidimensional pluralist option. In addition, the factors influencing adaptation to the urban system, such as education, are numerous and interact in complex ways.

15. In examining urban immigrant entrance we should give particular attention to the importance of social networks and the structure of the ethnic community. For immigrants the critical factor in their attainment of economic success is often whether their network of contacts directs them to jobs with the potential for further mobility. This may be even more important than level of education or prior exposure to an urban environment.

Social involvement in the networks of the host society will be limited to the extent the existing ethnic community can meet the needs of those arriving —that is, the degree to which it is institutionally complete. Institutionalization of an ethnic community stimulates its general social life and reinforces cohesiveness by expanding intragroup relations over time, even among those who may not themselves actually participate in ethnic associations.

With respect to the structure of the ethnic community we should also observe that, despite their connection to the overall cohesiveness of an immigrant group, frequently ethnic institutions have different clienteles. In addition, urban immigrant entrance itself may modify or strengthen the structure of the ethnic community.

16. The level of immigrant assimilation, even within the same ethnic group, may vary among cities—reflecting such factors as differences in economic opportunities and attitudes toward minority groups—although more comparative evidence is needed.

17. Holistic profiles of three cases of urban immigrant entrance—Toronto's Italians, Vancouver's Greeks, and Calgary's Ugandan Asians—illustrate the influence of type of employment, education, and occupation on adaptation, the central importance of ethnic institutions in sustaining in-group identification, how urban immigration advances an ethnic community's internal differentiation, and the multidimensional character of assimilation.

18. Urban immigration produces a complex urban ethnic mosaic. The composition of the urban population by ethnic origin, just as with the proportion foreign-born, varies among provinces, size of city, and across metropolitan areas. For example, the Poles are more commonly found in the urban areas of Manitoba, whereas the Asians again cluster in British Columbia. The Asians as well as the Italians are also strongly represented in Canada's largest cities. Regardless of size of centre, some ethnic groups (such as the Jewish) are more likely to live in urban areas than are others (such as the Ukrainians). Employing a summary measure of ethnic diversity we find in 1971 Winnipeg with the highest level and St. John's with the greatest homogeneity.

19. As with assimilation, we must clarify the meaning of ethnicity, distinguishing between ethnicity as a cultural pattern, ethnic affiliation as a social category, ethnic group formed on the basis of a common ethnicity or ethnic affiliation, and ethnic community representing a more fully developed form of social organization. It is incorrect to assume that entrance to the urban system will inevitably lead to the disappearance of each of these. Some sectors of social life may become more fully de-ethnicized than others. In addition, groups may shift over time from an enclavic orientation to an ethnic regenerational orientation.

In general, urban ethnicity should be seen not as an anachronism but as a variable that is influenced by structural conditions. For example, when opportunities for advancement through institutions of the host society are limited, ethnic identification may stimulate the emergence of alternative channels.

20. An illustration of the continued social importance of urban ethnicity is the French-English cleavage that may exist within a given community.

Part Four

Spatial Shape of the Urban System

In Parts Two and Three we examined the creation of the Canadian urban system through a dynamic focus on urban ecological and social organization. We explored the growth and general characteristics of that system, as well as the process of entrance into it. Such growth entails internally a "sifting and sorting," as Park noted, of population in regularized patterns. It is these patterns to which we shall now turn our attention. Specifically, we should consider two questions: (1) How does urban spatial structure evolve over time? (2) What are the resultant characteristics of the spatial structure of contemporary Canadian cities? The city is a socio-spatial system, as we stressed in the Introduction; although we give emphasis here to spatial distribution especially of population characteristics, we must not ignore the connection of that spatial shape to social patterns.

Chapter Four

Evolution and Changing Structure of the Urban System

Chapter 7

Evolution of Urban Structure

In dealing with the evolution of urban structure, we must briefly review the general relation between urbanization and spatial structure. We shall examine the spatial structure of the commercial city and its evolution over time with urban growth. Urban ecology seeks to develop generalizations about this process which might be valid in a variety of contexts. We must move from a descriptive, historical level to a more analytical one. In the second half of this chapter, we shall outline several "urban growth models" which refine the pioneering principles and concepts of the Chicago School. Our emphasis will be on social ecology—that is, the spatial distribution of population characteristics. Urban spatial structure, broadly understood, also encompasses the distribution of a variety of non-residential land uses. Although we shall give some attention to the evolution of these, by focusing on population characteristics we can perhaps more directly illustrate the character of the city as a socio-spatial system.

URBANIZATION AND SPATIAL STRUCTURE

In chapter 3 we defined urbanization from an ecological perspective as the development of a complex territorial system of functional relationships. We saw how such factors as transportation promoted this process, and some of the general patterns that emerged. Here we shall concentrate on the spatial correlates of this process—that is, how the internal spatial structure of the city reflects its growth.

Spatial patterns are indices of underlying functional relationships. The basic principle of urban development is the process of specialization. The emergence of an extensive territorial division of labour is accompanied by important changes in spatial structure. With urban growth, sub-areas become more specialized and differentiated in terms of population and land-use types. Park's theory of natural areas and McKenzie's concept of ecological distribution sought to articulate this process of differentiation; both pointed to the increased sifting and sorting which occurs as urban centres expand. This can be subsumed within a more general theory of increasing scale (Udry, 1964; Clignet and Sween, 1969) which proposes that as a society creates large-scale organizational networks and becomes more thoroughly integrated, internal social and spatial differentiation proceeds.

This process of increased spatial differentiation is revealed when we examine the movement from the commercial centre of the nineteenth century to more complex forms of urban ecological organization.

The Commercial Centre

As we saw in chapter 3, the commercial centre contained a number of distinctive characteristics. Its compactness, small size, and economic base precluded the level of spatial differentiation which the industrial and metropolitan communities were able to achieve subsequently. Nevertheless, the "seeds of specialization" were evident in the spatial form of the commercial centre. Let us take Hamilton again as an example (Davey and Doucet, 1975).

In the early 1850s Hamilton's spatial structure showed some complexity, paralleling its social organization. The community consisted of three sectors: (1) a heavily built-up inner core; (2) a partially developed area around this core; and (3) an undeveloped outer zone. Most of the city's economic activities occurred in the first zone. The core contained both small and large businesses and establishments. What manufacturing there was was located in this inner area also.

Despite this concentration, Hamilton's central core was spatially differentiated along at least the following lines: (1) in an "inner central area," trading, financial, and professional activities congregated; (2) an "outer central area" contained the city's artisans and manufacturers; (3) between these two areas could be found the community's hotels and boarding houses. In short, although numerous types of activities were all concentrated in the core, they were segregated in specific sectors. Such nascent specialization would subsequently strengthen as the city experienced greater industrialization.

A number of constraints influenced residential location. The limited amount of housing available for the growing population, as well as the necessity of living close to place of work or customers meant that there was considerable residential mixing of the classes. Merchants and entrepreneurs were not spatially segregated from the less affluent; both rich and poor lived together as neighbours in the inner core, although as we noted in chapter 3 the poor changed residences far more frequently. Such spatial integration did not correspond to the rigidity of Hamilton's stratification system (Davey and Doucet, 1975). However, as the commercial centre became industrial and metropolitan, this gap between spatial and social structures eroded.

The Evolution of Urban Structure: Toronto and Winnipeg

In chapter 3 we explored the factors enabling Toronto and Winnipeg to emerge as dominant centres in the Canadian system of cities. Let us now see how this growth was reflected in their internal spatial geography, and how their transformation from compact communities brought important spatial changes.

1. *Toronto*. Toronto in 1850 represented a modest commercial centre. Recall that by the end of the century it had emerged as a relatively large metropolitan and manufacturing centre. How did the city's rapid industrial development, changing system of internal transportation, and overall population affect its social geography?

By 1860 Toronto appeared as a city that was "core-oriented" (Goheen, 1970). Land that held the highest commercial and economic value was located in the centre of the community. The city centre constituted an area of high prestige; it was here the higher strata—businessmen and professionals—resided. Unlike the situation in Hamilton, however, Toronto's lowest-status group—the unskilled workers—were not concentrated there. Paralleling this differentiation, the homeowners clustered in the centre. The less affluent were located on the periphery of the city. Thus, residential segregation was most pronounced between the business classes, commercial and professional elite, and the unskilled. Other occupational groups were apparently less segregated, which might have reflected "the relationships which it was necessary to maintain between place of residence in a city having no rapid transit and virtually no public transportation economically available to most of the urban inhabitants. Territorial segregation of the unskilled workers may reflect their inability to compete with any other group for desirable and accessible residential locations" (Goheen, 1970: 128).

In summary, Toronto in 1860—on the threshold of a subsequent rise to metropolitan status—possessed a social geography that manifested a balance "between the tendencies toward segregation by classes and the necessities of proximity imposed by a primitive transportation system which could distribute neither goods nor people efficiently" (Goheen, 1970: 138).

Examining the city's social landscape in 1870 reveals no consistent distribution by family status—measured, for example, by the proportion of large families. In terms of economic status, segregation between the classes did not appear to be especially pronounced. A high-status sector, however, did exist, located outward from the centre to the northern and northwestern section of the city. Religion at this period formed a basis of residential segregation: "to be identified as a Roman Catholic in 1870 was to be segregated from persons of other faiths" (Goheen, 1970: 154).

By 1880, the structure of Toronto had begun to experience fundamental changes as the city advanced economically. With improved local transportation, younger age groups in the population were now locating more commonly than before on the periphery, while the older residents clustered in the centre. Consistent with this trend, family status tended to increase in regular concentric zones with distance from the centre. The core, however, still preserved its high economic value; yet the location of railway facilities rendered the area less attractive for residential purposes. The expansion of the northern part of the city continued, as streetcar lines extended outward from the centre. Overall, the city appeared to be in a "stage of transformation."

These trends continued during the subsequent decade. Toronto in 1890 was characterized by a spatial distribution in which family status was highest on the periphery of that area to which the street railway system had been extended. This was indeed evidence "of a simple relationship between the availability of transportation and the outward movement of large families" (Goheen, 1970: 179). In contrast to earlier years, by this time the downtown waterfront district no longer contained the residences of the higher strata. The area had become completely dominated by commercial and economic forms of land use. Religion had ceased to constitute an independent basis of residential segregation. Economic rank was a more central factor in spatial differentiation: "Unskilled, skilled, clerical and professional persons were segregated from each other" (Goheen, 1970: 194). Yet, as public transportation networks were extended outward, the working class also achieved greater residential decentralization. This trend did not lessen substantially the fundamental pattern of segregation by class.

The 1899 picture of Toronto reveals the final consequences of industrial development, population growth, and transportation improvements. The concentric pattern of increasing values on family status with distance from the centre was firmly established. This did not, however, extend to the actual point reached by the transport lines, suggesting that suburbanization tended to lag behind the development of the local streetcar system.

Similarly, the 1899 map showed a concentric pattern of decreasing property value moving outward, reflecting the influence of accessibility to the city centre. Religion had disappeared entirely as a basis of segregation; differentiation among the classes was clearly manifested in Toronto's social geography by the end of the century. The city assumed at the end of this period of transformation an ecological pattern, as we shall see, typical of the twentieth-century industrial metropolis.

2. *Winnipeg.* Another interesting example of the evolution of urban structure is shown in the changes that occurred in Winnipeg as it achieved metropolitan status (Artibise, 1972a; 1972b; 1975). In 1874, the year of its incorporation, the city consisted of an area a little greater than three square miles, of which only about one-fifth had been built up. By 1914, however, it consisted of more than twenty-three square miles, with a population one hundred times larger. Changes in area and population were not the only indices of transformation. As in Toronto, the internal social landscape was significantly altered.

Winnipeg was a relatively condensed settlement during the 1870s, its expansion restricted by the Red and Assiniboine Rivers and by the inadequate system of local transportation. A majority of the pre-1874 dwellings were concentrated in that section of the city between Main Street and the Red River.

Within this settlement there was little evidence of residential segregation by class or ethnicity. However, with the building boom of the early 1880s, the coming of the CPR, the influx of immigrants, and the general economic expansion of the community, this picture was profoundly revised.

By 1885 the intersection of Portage and Main had emerged as the commercial core of the city. It was here that land values were highest. As Winnipeg's economic functions strengthened, this central district increasingly became the locale in which the city's retail, wholesale, and service establishments concentrated. As Winnipeg assumed dominance over the region's grain trade, institutions connected with it—such as the Grain Exchange Building—located there. Light industry was a not uncommon type of land use. As the central core became increasingly commercial, its traditional status as a residential area declined. By the turn of the century, it contained the lowest proportion of new residential construction in the city. With the expansion of non-residential land uses, the affluent moved outward to more attractive surroundings. Their former dwellings were not reoccupied by working-class people; they settled instead in the North End.

Perhaps the most dramatic revision in Winnipeg's social landscape was the emergence of the North End as the community's working-class and foreign quarter. Before the arrival of the railroad to the city, this area was considered to be a high-status district. Such a reputation was radically changed by the coming of the CPR, which located its yards, shops, and depot there. Workers settled in the surrounding area. A variety of industries located there to be near the railway; this also encouraged concentration of the working class in the North End. The trend was reinforced by the tremendous influx of people after 1896. A large proportion of these were immigrants attracted to the newly constructed and relatively cheap housing of the North End. For example, between 1901 and 1911 Winnipeg's German population increased from 2,283 to 8,912 (Grenke, 1975). A good number were poorer immigrants from Europe without enough money to secure a rural homestead.

The working-class character of the North End was clearly suggested in the many primitive frame dwellings, the excessive congestion, the high rate of infant mortality, and the generally inadequate municipal services. The quarter was relatively isolated from the remainder of the community—a result, in part, of the CPR's main line running through the district, and of the industrial concentration there. The inadequacy of the local transportation network to that area added to this isolation: "By 1914 only two overhead bridges and two subways provided access to the North End. And it was not until after 1908 that the City's street railway had more than one crossing of the CPR yards" (Artibise, 1972b: 121).

Such isolation was not conducive to the assimilation of immigrants concentrated there. As Table 47 demonstrates, by 1916 the North End contained the vast majority of Winnipeg's Slavs, Jews, and Scandinavians. Although the British represented the largest ethnic group, their proportion of the area's

Table 47: Specified Ethnic Groups in Winnipeg's North End, 1886-1916

Ethnic group	1886			1901			1916		
	No.	% of total group pop'n	% of district pop'n	No.	% of total group pop'n	% of district pop'n	No.	% of total group pop'n	% of district pop'n
British	5,965	35.5	80.8	10,174	32.6	64.3	23,624	19.6	38.9
Slavic	240	82.0	3.2	1,422	80.4	9.8	18,280	83.3	30.2
Jewish	3	4.9	—	1,023	88.5	6.5	11,746	86.7	19.4
Scandinavian	579	42.9	7.9	832	25.1	5.3	3,864	66.6	6.4
German	242	44.4	3.2	1,360	59.6	9.3	1,411	22.1	2.3
Others	353	29.5	4.9	771	29.9	4.8	1,691	20.1	2.8

From Artibise, 1972b. Reprinted by permission of the author.

population had declined significantly since 1886. By 1916 less than one-fifth of the total number of British-origin Winnipeggers lived in the North End. These tended to cluster in specific sections of the area. There were, certainly, a large number of non-British groups residing in other parts of the city. These were primarily Germans and Scandinavians, who were not as culturally dissimilar to the British as were the Southern and Eastern Europeans.

Contributing to the increasing class and ethnic residential segregation of Winnipeg was the population movement to other areas of the community. As the street railway system became more extensive after 1900, the upper class concentrated in the South End, while the middle class located in the West End. These districts reported the highest rates of increase of any in the city during 1900-1912. They were primarily residential, with few industrial or commercial establishments locating there; they attracted chiefly persons of British origin and the fairly affluent. In sum, "With the development of South and West Winnipeg as the domain of Winnipeg's largely British upper- and middle-class the City's spatial and social patterns were firmly established. In 1914 there was a distinct north-south dichotomy in Winnipeg which, despite the passage of more than fifty years, has changed but little" (Artibise, 1972b: 128).

An additional consequence of the expansion of the street railway system was the increasing growth of outlying suburban areas. By 1914, however, this trend had not yet become firmly established. It is interesting to note that suburbanization to the north of the city represented the weakest form of diffusion—a product in part of the general desire among many in other areas of the city to avoid the North End and its extensions because of their working-class and "foreign" composition and reputation.

In conclusion, the evidence is clear that as Winnipeg evolved toward the position of an industrial and transportation centre, its internal social geography underwent considerable changes. Segregation of types of land uses intensified. The community became "a City divided": "Beyond the central core three distinct areas of new houses had sprung up. To the south the more affluent and chiefly Anglo-Saxon elements of the population resided; to the west was a large middle-class area of somewhat more mixed ethnic composition; and to the north was the working-class and 'foreign ghetto' " (Artibise, 1972a: 46).

Both Toronto and Winnipeg experienced similar patterns of increasing spatial differentiation. Over time, their central cores assumed more predominantly commercial functions. With the development of improved local transportation systems, their residential populations spread outward. Reflecting patterns of social distance, relative ability to afford housing costs, and level of assimilation, a sifting and sorting of the different classes and ethnic groups occurred to a much greater extent than was possible in the commercial centre. This evolution of spatial differentiation laid the foundations for that ecological structure we encounter in the contemporary Canadian city.

URBAN GROWTH MODELS

It has been a central task of urban ecology to predict the direction in which this evolution occurs. It is not enough to propose that with urban growth, sub-areas become more specialized and differentiated in population and land use types. We must determine whether there are general patterns in this process which outline more fully the precise nature of such spatial differentiation. Let us review the major urban growth models that seek to identify these patterns.

The Burgess Concentric Zone Theory

In chapter 2 we briefly examined Burgess' concentric zone theory, which formed the dominant model of urban growth in classical ecology. Much early ecological research sought to apply this scheme. For example, Dawson (1926) showed its applicability to Montreal. He proposed that this was a useful device for presenting those ecological patterns associated with city growth. With respect to the generality of this scheme, however, he observed the need to take into account those factors effecting deviations from the ideal: "There are, however, factors in every local situation such as rivers, mountains, natural lines of communication and the early position of industrial establishments which tend to press these circles out of their regularity in the growth of any city" (Dawson, 1926: 6). This was clearly illustrated in Montreal. Although the dominant focus of Burgess' hypothesis—radial expansion from the centre—gained support, Dawson found it necessary to represent Montreal's ecological structure, as Figure 9 shows, in terms of a series of concentric "kidneys." Yet each section of the city did constitute a natural area, attracting particular categories of residents and institutions. Dawson proposed, even at this early date, that for the most effective urban planning possible these "natural" lines of growth and differentiation must be given full recognition.

Nevertheless, Burgess' concentric zone theory implicitly assumes several important features that are subject to widespread variations. These assumptions include: (1) a growing city; (2) a city with a fairly heterogeneous population in terms of ethnicity, country of origin, race, and occupational specialization; (3) a particular kind of economic base—that is, a "commercial-industrial" city; (4) the presence of certain economic and cultural factors—for example, private ownership of property and economic competition; (5) a characteristic "geometry of space" wherein, for example, the city contains a single centre; (6) an economic assumption that central areas are more highly valued because of the accessibility which they provide; (7) occupancy patterns distinctive to the varying socioeconomic strata—in particular, the notion that "the more favored classes will ordinarily preempt the newer and more desirable housing areas" (Schnore, 1965b: 353f.; 1972: 7-11). To the extent, therefore, that these assumptions are not applicable to particular urban communities, the concentric zonal scheme will be of limited analytical value.

Figure 9: The Concentric Zone Pattern in Montreal, 1926

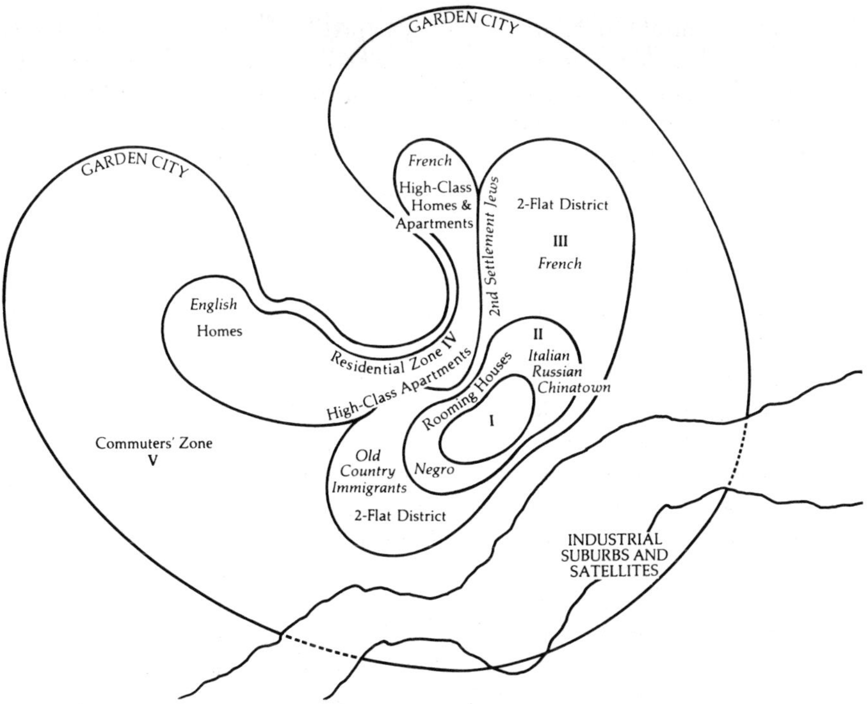

From Dawson, 1926.

The Sector Theory

Burgess' scheme presented the distribution of urban land uses in a relatively rigid geometric pattern. Hoyt (1939) found this an unsatisfactory portrayal of the evolution of urban structure. He noted a number of anomalies this scheme ignored—for example, while a manufacturing zone did perhaps surround the central business district at one point, this is no longer the case. Industries follow railroad lines in elongated bands of growth rather than remaining near the central business district. Similarly, in many cities neither the zone of workingmen's homes nor the high rent area encircles the central core. Rental area maps do not reveal a series of concentric circles with a gradation of rents upward from the centre to the periphery in all sections of the city.

Growth, Hoyt argued, occurs not in uniformly concentric fashion from a central core, but rather along main transportation routes. Similar types of land use and population originate near the centre of the city and migrate outward in discernible sectors toward the periphery. Using rent (house and apartment rents as well as house mortgages or assessments) as an index of the socio-economic composition of the population and of housing conditions, Hoyt

(1939: 112-22) proposed the following principles of urban growth from a comparison of the spatial structure of 142 American cities in 1900, 1915, and 1936.

1. High-rent neighbourhoods do not skip about at random in the process of movement. They follow a definite path in one or more sectors of the city. Movement of the high-rent area is the most important because it pulls the growth of the entire city in the same direction; lower-income groups seek to get as close to the high-rent pole as possible.

2. If one sector of a city first develops as a low-rent residential area, it will tend to retain that character as the sector expands.

3. High-grade residential growth tends to proceed from the given point of origin along established lines of travel or toward another existing nucleus of buildings or trading centres.

4. The zone of high-rent areas tends to progress toward high ground which is free from the risk of floods and to spread along lake, bay, river, and ocean fronts, where such waterfronts are not used for industry.

5. High-rent residential districts tend to grow toward the section of the city which has free, open country beyond the edges, and away from "dead end" sections which are limited by natural or artificial barriers to expansion.

6. The higher-priced residential neighbourhood tends to grow toward the homes of the leaders of the community.

7. Trends of movement of office buildings, banks, and stores may pull the higher-priced residential neighbourhoods in the same general direction.

8. High-grade residential areas tend to develop along the fastest existing transportation lines.

9. The growth of high-rent neighbourhoods continues in the same direction for a long period of time.

10. Deluxe high-rent apartment areas tend to be established near the business centre in old residential areas.

11. Real estate promoters may bend the direction of high-grade residential growth.

12. In the beginning of the growth of a city, high-rent neighbourhoods may have much choice of direction in which to move; this choice narrows as the city grows and low-rent areas expand in particular sectors of the city.

13. Intermediate rental areas tend to surround the highest rental areas or adjoin such areas on one side.

The sector theory of neighbourhood change thus presents a portrait of urban structure as consisting of a set of discernible pie-shaped wedges, not concentric zones. Figure 10 summarizes these differences. Hoyt's alternative model, we should note, is a partial one. That is, it stresses differences in housing and rent, but gives little explicit consideration to the characteristics of those who inhabit the structures in the various sectors of a city (Rees, 1970). Nor does it adequately take into account, as Hoyt (1964) himself recognized, that the automobile and expressway system opened up large regions beyond existing settled areas. As a result, high-grade residential growth need not be confined entirely to rigidly defined sectors.

The Multiple Nuclei Theory

Both the concentric zone and sector theories assume a single centre from which growth of a city extends outward. This assumption is perhaps appropriate for the commercial-industrial city. It is less so for the contemporary metropolitan community. Harris and Ullman (1957 ed.) observed that, contrary to Burgess' and Hoyt's schemes, the land-use pattern of many twentieth-century North American cities is built around several discrete nuclei. The larger the city, the greater are the number and diversity of nuclei.

These nuclei are the basis for differentiated districts (Harris and Ullman, 1957 ed.: 244-45):

Figure 10: Generalizations of the Internal Structure of Cities

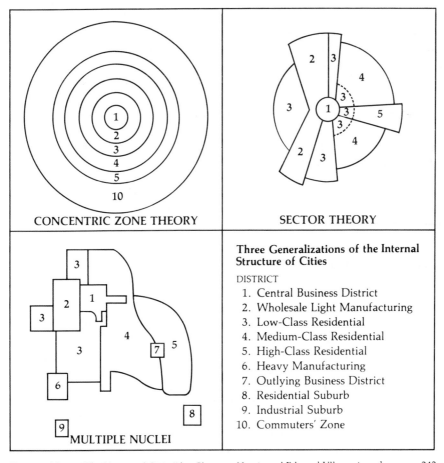

CONCENTRIC ZONE THEORY

SECTOR THEORY

MULTIPLE NUCLEI

Three Generalizations of the Internal Structure of Cities

DISTRICT
1. Central Business District
2. Wholesale Light Manufacturing
3. Low-Class Residential
4. Medium-Class Residential
5. High-Class Residential
6. Heavy Manufacturing
7. Outlying Business District
8. Residential Suburb
9. Industrial Suburb
10. Commuters' Zone

Certain activities require specialized facilities. The retail district, for example, is attached to the point of greatest intracity accessibility, the port district to suitable water front, manufacturing districts to large blocks of land and water or rail connection, and so on.

Certain like activities group together because they profit from cohesion. [For example, retail establishments cluster together for their mutual benefit in terms of attracting greater numbers of customers.]

Certain unlike activities are detrimental to each other. [For example, high-status groups, as Hoyt's theory emphasizes, avoid locating close to industrial land uses.]

Certain activities are unable to afford the high rents of the most desirable sites.

Many large cities, as Figure 10 suggests, contain a number of distinct districts with separate nuclei. These include: (a) the central business district, which is the point of greatest access from all sections of the city and in which many major retail establishments cluster; (b) the wholesale and light manufacturing district, which locates near the focus of extra-city transportation facilities; (c) the heavy industrial district which, because it requires large tracts of land, tends to be near the edge of the city; (d) the residential district, which in different parts of the city assumes a particular class or ethnic character; (e) minor nuclei, such as a cultural centre, park, or university, for example, which may attract a particular type of population to the surrounding area; (f) outlying suburban or satellite communities, which may arise with improvement in local transportation facilities.

The multiple nuclei theory thus seeks to represent the full complexity of spatial patterns characteristic of the expanding metropolis. The sifting and sorting of population and land use occur about an array of nuclei, creating extensive spatial differentiation.

Social Area Analysis

The concentric zone, sector, and multiple nuclei models all tend to treat the city in isolation. They fail to recognize that the city itself is a product of changes in the wider society. Social area analysis acknowledges this link (Shevky and Williams, 1949; Shevky and Bell, 1955). Evolving initially from studies of Los Angeles and San Francisco, this model focuses on the manner in which the level of differentiation within the urban community reflects the extent to which the total society has undergone structural reorganization. Unlike the last urban growth model, this framework (as well as the one following) deals primarily with population characteristics. It approaches urban structure in a more restricted but nonetheless fruitful manner.

As Figure 11 indicates, Shevky and Bell consider the most fundamental change that occurs with the emergence of an urban-industrial society to be a

Figure 11: Steps in Construction and Index Construction: Social Area Analysis and Urban Differentiation

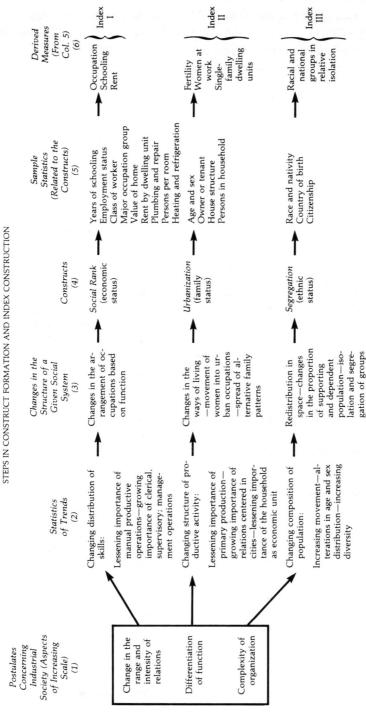

Reprinted from *Social Area Analysis: Theory, Illustrative Application, and Computational Procedures* by Eshref Shevky and Wendell Bell with the permission of the publishers, Stanford University Press. Copyright © 1955 by the Board of Trustees of the Leland Stanford Junior University.

dramatic "increase in scale." Three central processes are involved in this transformation: (a) change in the range and intensity of relations; (b) differentiation of function; and (c) increase in the complexity of organization. Each component of this transformation involves specific trends which provide distinctive forms of social differentiation. Figure 11 summarizes the nature and measurement of these.

The first refers to changing bases of reward and function:

> As societies increase in scale, the nature of income-producing property is altered; land gives way to the enterprise, and ownership of the enterprise becomes less significant than position within a given enterprise. At the same time, the occupations within a society are regrouped: they become hierarchically organized into levels of skill, income, and prestige. Modern society, in contradistinction to traditional societies, is organized on an occupational basis. Only in the modern period has occupation come to have a determining influence upon status and rank; today, no other single characteristic tells us so much about the individual and his position in society (Shevky and Bell, 1955: 9).

Social rank, therefore, forms an identifiable construct, measured by such indices as occupation and education.

The second fundamental aspect of the increase in scale points to certain patterns assumed to be correlated with urbanization. As the "structure of productive activity" becomes modified and made much more efficient, size of population no longer is an immediate function of the supply of food available. Rather, it becomes much more subject to individual decision making and choice in terms of desired family size. The household assumes less importance as a productive unit in the economy. Family structure becomes subject to individual choice of lifestyle, and is not simply a function of socioeconomic status. In short, as the productive capacities of a society broaden, the range of possible ways of life greatly expands. Low family status (or a high position on the urbanization dimension) is associated with lower rates of fertility, greater participation by women in the labour force, smaller household size. A high degree of "familism" is measured by the contrasting characteristics.

Changes in the composition of population constitutes the third component in the overall increase in scale of an industrial society. The widened network of functional interdependence and more efficient means of transportation and communication encourage population redistribution and mobility. Selective migration among age and sex groups occurs, as does increased isolation and segregation of particular ethnic segments of the population. These patterns of redistribution are reflected in the construct of segregation (or ethnic status).

The Shevky-Bell model proposes, therefore, that as the scale of the wider society increases, the urban population becomes differentiated along three separate and independent dimensions—social rank, family status (or urbanization), and segregation (or ethnic status).

Each of these dimensions can be measured, in turn, by available census tract statistics, as suggested in columns 5 and 6 of Figure 11.

THE MEANING OF CENSUS TRACTS

A census tract represents a sub-area in a city, delimited spatially for data-gathering purposes. It ordinarily contains several thousand residents with some degree of social and economic homogeneity. Easily recognized boundaries are used to give the tract a relatively compact shape (Kokich, 1970). A city, with the assistance of a local census tract committee, is divided into a number of such tracts by Statistics Canada. In the 1971 Census, twenty-nine of Canada's urban centres participated in a census tract program. Statistics gathered on each such tract in a city—ranging from housing conditions, to household structure, to level of income —from one census year to the next provide useful measures of internal changes in the urban community which are not revealed in city-wide data. The census tract is a central unit in urban ecological research.

Through these measures census tract populations can be grouped, according to their scores on the various indices of the three factors, into distinct (non-spatial) social areas. Figure 12 depicts the resultant typology. To illustrate, social area 1A contains census tract populations having high family status (or a low position on the urbanization dimension)—that is, fertility ratios are high, there are relatively few women over age 16 in the labour force, and there are relatively many single-family detached dwellings—but low economic status (that is, relatively many persons over age 25 who completed grade school only and who are in relatively unskilled jobs). In contrast social area 4A contains census tracts with correspondingly high family status, but with high economic status as well. Figure 12 suggests sixteen possible types of social areas. Distinctions among tracts having higher and lower ethnic status—the third dimension of differentiation—extends this to thirty-two possibilities.

Each social area thus contains similar types of census tracts, regardless of where these are located physically in the city (Orleans, 1966). The focus of analysis is the underlying social structure of an urban population, not simply its spatial distribution, although it is assumed that residential patterns inevitably reflect the three bases of differentiation.

It is proposed that "persons living in a particular type of social area would systematically differ with respect to characteristic attitudes and behaviours from persons living in another type of social area" (Shevky and Bell, 1955: 20). Social area analysis, therefore, is viewed not only as a useful method for understanding the level of differentiation in an urban population but also an

Figure 12: Social Area Typology

	High	1A	2A	3A	4A
		1B	2B	3B	4B
Family Status		1C	2C	3C	4C
	Low	1D	2D	3D	4D
		Low			High

Economic Status

Reprinted from "The Utility of the Shevky Typology for the Design of Urban Sub-Area Field Studies" by Wendell Bell in *Journal of Social Psychology* 47 (1958) by permission of The Journal Press.

instrument for comparing diverse sub-populations in the city in terms of particular behaviour patterns (Bell, 1961), such as degree of involvement in the neighbourhood. (We shall explore this in a later chapter.)

In summary, the Shevky-Bell model can be used to compare the levels of differentiation among urban populations according to the degree of modernization characterizing the wider society. Its utility extends to comparing subpopulations within the same city. Assuming that urban social and spatial structures are interdependent, social area analysis seeks to delineate the nature of, and changes in, residential patterns among urbanites.

Our earlier review of the evolution of Toronto and Winnipeg lends support to this model's prediction of increasing differentiation along socioeconomic, family status, and ethnic status dimensions. Nevertheless, although an important contribution to ecological research, social area analysis contains several central weaknesses. In particular:

1. It is too closely linked to census tract data gathered with respect to American cities. The model assumes that the three basic dimensions derived from these data are the most important bases of urban differentiation (Hawley and Duncan, 1957).

2. It assumes that census tract populations are relatively homogeneous. This is not necessarily the case; aggregate averages and proportions may conceal significant individual variance within a tract. A social area may therefore be more heterogeneous internally than the scheme suggests (Hawley and Duncan, 1957).

3. The theory of social change which forms the basis of this model needs to be more fully tested itself on a cross-cultural basis (Udry, 1964; Abu-Lughod, 1969). Some have argued that this is an *ex post facto* theory created to justify the three dimensions extracted from census tract data.

4. Most significantly, the model seeks to address the question of how an urban population becomes more socially differentiated over time. It fails, however, to explain fully how this is linked to "the realities of areal residential differentiation within cities" (Johnston, 1971). In short, it does not adequately integrate social differentiation and urban spatial structure (Duncan, 1955; Hawley and Duncan, 1957; Chan, 1970).

Factorial Ecology

In the years following its initial elaboration, social area analysis was subjected to a variety of tests and applications, chiefly in the United States (e.g., Bell, 1955; Van Arsdol, Camilleri and Schmid, 1958; Schmid, MacCannell and Van Arsdol, 1958). This research attempted to clarify some of the assumptions and generalizations derived from that model, but did not necessarily confirm their validity in all cases.

Beginning in the late 1950s, factor analysis was used by urban ecologists to replace the less precise methods of social area analysis (Abu-Lughod, 1969). Factor analysis, as a statistical procedure, is a way of determining the basic dimensions (or factors) which account for most of the variation in a particular data set. Factorial ecology seeks to overcome some of the weaknesses, noted above, of social area analysis. Through the use of factor analysis, it examines the relationships among socioeconomic, demographic, and an array of other characteristics of an urban population. Its goals are twofold: (1) to identify the fundamental dimensions (called "factors") according to which that population is differentiated; and (2) to describe the spatial distribution within the city of those dimensions (Johnston, 1971; Berry, 1971; Rees, 1971; Barrow, 1972; Hunter and Latif, 1973). Factorial ecology has also been used to develop inter-city classificatory schemes (Chan, 1970).

In contrast to social area analysis, factorial ecology is more inductive. That is, it examines a much wider range of variables, and is not directly tied to any previous theoretical assumptions about social change (Schwirian, 1972; Davies and Barrow, 1973). The basic premise in factorial ecology, Berry (1971) observes, is that "meaning in any situation has to be learned rather than posited by aprioristic theory." It can, therefore, "extract" a larger number of factors or dimensions of urban organization than the Shevky-Bell approach.

In recent years factorial ecology research has shown wide variations from study to study in the number of urban characteristics analyzed, the type selected, and the precise factorial methods used (Barrow, 1972). We might classify these studies as follows (Chan, 1970):

1. Those which review generally the underlying dimensions of urban structure and their areal distribution (e.g., Timms, 1971);

2. Those which focus on the changing pattern of the internal structure over a certain period (e.g., Hunter, 1974);

3. Comparative studies of communities within a large metropolitan area (e.g., Rees, 1970);

4. Comparative studies of the internal structure of several cities at the same time (e.g., Clignet and Sween, 1969);

5. Studies of the cross-cultural variation of urban structure (e.g., Abu-Lughod, 1969).

Most of these factor ecology studies have identified more than the three dimensions found by Shevky and Bell (Johnston, 1971). For example, Chicago's community areas are differentiated in terms of a number of factors, including socioeconomic status, stage in the life cycle, race and resources (reflecting the relation between socioeconomic and racial status), immigrant and Catholic status, and Jewish population (Rees, 1970). Cross-cultural comparisons, in addition, suggest that, consistent with what we argued earlier in this chapter, the independence of such dimensions as family status and social rank increases with societal scale (McElrath, 1968). A city such as Calcutta (Berry and Rees, 1969) or Cairo (Abu-Lughod, 1969) fails to show the degree of differentiation among socioeconomic status, family status, and ethnic status that appears to exist in cities of more modernized societies. In Singapore, for example, unlike Western industrial cities where all three of these factors (among others) are important, family status functions as a central basis of differentiation; other characteristics of the population, such as type of housing, are closely correlated with it (Chan, 1970). Similarly, in Cairo we find that such an index of family status as fertility varies directly according to class (Abu-Lughod, 1969). As Timms (1971: 147) has observed: "Only in the modern metropolis, with its emphasis on individualism and its opportunities for expressing individual choice, may it be anticipated that social rank and familism will become fully independent factors. Even here, the degree of their independence is a problem for empirical investigation, rather than theoretical 'fiat'."

With respect to the spatial distribution of the fundamental dimensions of differentiation, factorial ecology has demonstrated that the concentric zone and sector models need not be viewed as mutually exclusive. That is, the two converge insofar as the spatial distribution of factors can be identified in terms of gradients (or zones) and sectors (Schwirian, 1972). In particular, investigations of modern industrial and metropolitan cities indicate that socioeconomic status follows a sectoral pattern, whereas family status varies zonally with distance from the city centre (Berry and Rees, 1969). In addition, ethnic status tends, although not always consistently, to manifest a clustering or multiple nuclei pattern. Recall that Toronto's and Winnipeg's evolution, discussed earlier, reflected such an areal distribution. The sectoral pattern of socioeconomic status partly derives from, for example, the fact that lower-income groups must live close to their work in the core or along rail and water transport lines. More affluent groups have greater freedom and resources to reside in more desirable areas. Similarly, the zonal pattern of familial characteristics partly reflects that single-family homes and greater space for families increase with distance from the central business district (Rees, 1970).

Those groups attracted to a more familistic life style, therefore, are more likely to choose residence in an outlying area. Any clustering pattern that the ethnic status factor reveals, in turn, may be consequences of in-group cohesiveness, levels of social distance among groups, and more explicit efforts to exclude possibly dissimilar residents from the immediate area.

In the following chapter we shall examine and illustrate this "convergence" among such urban growth models within Canadian cities as well as patterns of residential distribution.

SUMMARY

1. Spatial structure is closely linked to the ecological process of urbanization. With urban growth, sub-areas become more specialized and differentiated in terms of population and land-use types.

2. This process of increased spatial differentiation is revealed when we examine the movement from the commercial centre of the nineteenth century to more complex forms of urban ecological organization.

3. The compactness, small size, and economic base of the commercial centre precluded the level of spatial differentiation found in the industrial and metropolitan communities. We must not, however, overlook the "seeds of specialization" within the spatial form of the commercial centre.

4. Examining the evolution of Toronto and Winnipeg, we find similar patterns of increasing spatial differentiation. Their central cores assumed more predominantly commercial functions as these cities expanded economically and in size. With the development of improved local transportation systems, their residential populations diffused outward, but not in random fashion. Segregation among classes and ethnic groups occurred to a much greater extent than was possible in the commercial centre.

5. Urban growth models seek to determine general patterns in this process of increased spatial differentiation.

6. The Burgess concentric zone theory formed the dominant model of urban growth in classical ecology. However, it was based on a number of assumptions—for example, that a city contains a relatively heterogeneous population, or exists within a particular type of economic and cultural system in which private ownership of property and competition for desirable land are legitimized—which may not be appropriate cross-culturally or in varying urban contexts.

7. The sector theory argues, in contrast, that growth occurs not in uniformly concentric fashion from a central core, but rather axially along main transportation routes. Similar types of land use and population originate near the centre of a city and migrate outward in discernible sectors toward the periphery. For example, high-rent neighbourhoods expand in the same wedge for a long period of time; they do not encircle the city core.

8. In contrast to the concentric zone and sector models, the multiple nuclei scheme proposes that the land-use pattern of many contemporary cities is focused on several discrete nuclei. The larger the city, the greater are the number and diversity of these nuclei. We must distinguish, for example, the wholesale and light manufacturing districts, segregated residential areas, and outlying suburban clusters. This scheme seeks to represent the full complexity of spatial patterns found in the expanding metropolis.

9. The concentric zone, sector, and multiple nuclei models fail to emphasize that the level of differentiation within the urban community reflects the extent to which the total society experiences structural reorganization. In recognition of this, social area analysis argues that as the scale of the wider society increases, the urban population becomes differentiated along three separate and independent dimensions—social rank, family status, and ethnic status. This scheme also provides a method for comparing diverse sub-populations (within different social areas) in terms of particular behaviour patterns.

10. Although an important contribution to ecological research, social area analysis suffers from several important shortcomings—including its failure to adequately integrate social differentiation and urban spatial structure.

11. More recently, factorial ecology has emerged as a way of identifying more precisely than social area analysis the fundamental dimensions according to which urban populations are differentiated. Through the use of factor analysis it can explore the relationships among a wide array of population variables and characteristics, without necessarily being restricted to any *a priori* assumptions about the nature of social change. It is a particularly useful tool for comparative and cross-cultural studies of variations in urban structure.

12. Factor ecology studies have identified in many cities more than the three dimensions found by Shevky and Bell. In addition, they support the latter's assertion that the independence of such dimensions as family status and social rank increases with modernization and the intensification of societal scale.

13. Factorial ecology has also suggested, in terms of the spatial distribution of these dimensions of urban differentiation, that there may be a convergence among the previous urban growth models. That is, socioeconomic status frequently follows a sectoral pattern, whereas family status varies zonally with distance from the city centre. Ethnic status represents spatially a clustering or multiple nuclei pattern.

Chapter 8

Contemporary Internal Urban Structure

The internal spatial structure of Canada's cities is a fascinating mosaic. As we observed in chapters 3 and 4, the contemporary urban and metropolitan community consists of a set of sub-areas differentiated in terms of population and land-use types. One major process affecting that distribution, as our earlier portraits of Toronto and Winnipeg reveal, is *decentralization* (Nader, 1975: chapter 3). In the late nineteenth century the extension of streetcar service permitted a greater separation between place of residence and place of work. More important, it encouraged the development of residential suburbs. Such a trend intensified in the twentieth century as the automobile and other forms of local transportation improved accessibility to all parts of the urban region. A variety of urban activities and categories of land use now enjoy a greater freedom than in the past with respect to determining their location (Nader, 1975: 62). Accompanying the outward diffusion of the population has been a redefinition of the functions of the central core. Wholesale and industrial establishments increasingly seek to locate in outlying areas where large tracts of vacant land exist, property taxes are lower, and access to interurban transport lines is available. The creation of numerous shopping centres on the periphery since 1950 has led to an erosion of the CBD's prominence in many categories of retail sales. Compensating for the decline in manufacturing, wholesaling, and to some extent retailing activities in the central city has been an expansion there, especially in more recent decades, in office functions. The cores of most of Canada's metropolitan areas have emerged as the preeminent office districts for their respective regions. Services that require accessibility to the whole metropolitan area find this location attractive, as do those relying on personal contacts with others in allied firms. Downtown Calgary, for example, showed an annual increase between 1960 and 1974 of 600,000-700,000 square feet of new office space (Zieber, 1975: 82-83). Reflecting the city's economic structure, as discussed in chapter 4, oil firms are the primary users of this space. We should note that some categories of office functions have also begun to locate in suburbs as more advanced forms of communication render personal contacts less necessary.

Decentralization is the dominant process. Segregation of land uses is sustained, with the central core compensating for these changes by assuming new functions. Continuing our emphasis on the distribution of population characteristics, we shall sketch selected aspects of their spatial organization, using the urban growth models when applicable to analyze urban form. We shall first examine the general patterns of urban differentiation as revealed through recent factorial ecology studies in Canada. To fully understand the "sifting and sorting" of population which produces the observed spatial structure of a city, however, we must explore in greater detail the process of residential mobility or intraurban movement. Certainly one significant component of the spatial form of the contemporary city, which all urban growth models identify, is the ethnic enclave. We must probe the extent to which residential segregation of different ethnic groups occurs and its social significance. In addition, we must examine the way in which linguistic pluralism, an important part of that ethnic mosaic, is related to ecological structure.

GENERAL PATTERNS OF URBAN DIFFERENTIATION

To identify these patterns let us focus on three questions: (1) What are the fundamental bases of differentiation in Canadian cities? (2) How are these dimensions distributed spatially? (3) Do any changes occur over time either in these dimensions or in their areal distribution?

Paralleling what factor ecologies have discovered in cities of other modernized and industrialized societies, socioeconomic status, family status (or family life cycle), and ethnic status do appear to be important bases of urban differentiation in Canada (e.g., Murdie, 1969; Peucker and Rase, 1971; Haynes, 1971; Bourne and Barber, 1971; Bourne and Murdie, 1972; Schwirian, 1972; Barrow, 1972; Davies, 1975; Davies and Barrow, 1973; Hunter and Latif, 1973; Keith, 1973; Shrimpton, 1975; Hill, 1976; Balakrishnan and Jarvis, 1976, 1979). Despite this general pattern, however, we must recognize that (1) the relative importance of these dimensions varies across urban Canada; (2) additional bases of differentiation emerge frequently; and (3) even the three fundamental dimensions appear to be more complex than initially recognized.

To illustrate, let us compare the bases of differentiation in four cities—St. John's, Montreal, Regina, and Vancouver. Table 48 summarizes the factorial ecologies for each of these communities. In St. John's, family status is associated with stages in the life cycle (pre-family, young family, middle-stage family, and mature family). Contrary, however, to the assumptions of social area analysis, housing type and tenure characteristics do not correlate with this dimension. St. John's, as we have seen, is one of Canada's most homogeneous cities in terms of employment and ethnicity (Shrimpton, 1975: 41). It has not attracted significant streams of immigrants. Hence, ethnic status does not emerge as an important dimension of differentiation in this city, although religious status does. Protestantism appears associated with high family status, Catholicism with low socioeconomic status. In Canada's Prairie cities, the number of women in the labour force is one index of low family status; here, in St. John's, as with housing type, a separate dimension emerges suggesting an increasing proportion of women participating in the labour force between 1961 and 1971.

Table 48: Dimensions of Urban Differentiation in St. John's, Montreal, Regina, and Vancouver.

	St. John's	Montreal	Regina	Vancouver
Basic dimensions of urban differentiation (ranked in importance)	1. Socioeconomic status 2. Family status 3. Religious status 4. Participation in labour force 5. Housing	1. Socioeconomic status 2. Family status 3. Recent growth 4. Ethnic status 5. Household density	1. General family status 2. General socioeconomic status 3. Ethnic socioeconomic status 4. Mobile young adult 5. Established residentialism	1. Socioeconomic status 2. Family status 3. Median income and British background 4. Mobility and population growth
Date to which findings apply	1971	1951-1961	1961	1961

Sources: Shrimpton (1975), Haynes (1971), Barrow (1972), Peucker and Rase (1971).

Additional anomalies appear when we examine social differentiation in the other three cities. Table 7 showed that Montreal's growth rate between 1951 and 1961 was greater than St. John's. Reflecting this, Montreal shows, as does Vancouver, a "growth" dimension. In Vancouver this is associated positively with dwelling occupancy of less than two years, young family heads, and population growth—indices of suburbanization. (In Regina the "established residentialism" dimension is correlated with the stable residential characteristics of older family or post-family groups; the "mobile young adult" dimension is associated with two-family households, lodgers, and young adults—spatially concentrated in the inner core of the city.) We saw in Table 46 that Regina in 1961 manifested a relatively high index of ethnic diversity. Nevertheless, Table 48 shows that a distinct ethnic-socioeconomic status dimension exists—negative scores on which are correlated with male craftsmen/labourers, foreign-born, Lutheran, Roman Catholic, German, and Ukrainian characteristics. Ethnicity and class, in short, are closely intertwined here, as they are in Vancouver. Median income and British background are positively correlated; low income levels are more commonly associated in that city with populations of Asiatic origin. In summary, comparing the structures of these four cities we see broad similarities, especially with the first two dimensions listed for each; yet, reflecting variations in size, immigration experience, and ethnic composition, we must not overlook divergencies. For example, comparative factorial ecology research suggests that the smaller the city, the fewer the dimensions that account for the greatest differentiation in the city's population. This appears to be the case for Regina, in which, in contrast to the much larger city of Edmonton, family status and socioeconomic status together account for much of the variation in its population characteristics (Barrow, 1972).

Apart from these variations, comparative ecological research suggests greater complexity among Canadian cities even within the basic factors of socioeconomic status and family status. For example, examining the three western cities together—Winnipeg, Edmonton, and Regina—we find in 1961 that socioeconomic status is not a single differentiating axis (Davies and Barrow, 1973). That is, a general socioeconomic status dimension appears to be separate from a more specific form of differentiation in the population, distinguishing between those in white-collar occupations and those in poverty. Similarly, a detailed comparison of the 1961 structure of eleven of Canada's largest cities reveals that the familism or family-status variable is actually multidimensional (Schwirian, 1972). Such measures as level of fertility, proportion of women in the labour force, and type of dwelling unit (single versus multiple dwelling) are not necessarily correlated. They appear to represent different aspects of familism. Perhaps this reflects "an even greater variation in life style choice accompanying increase in societal scale than was envisioned by Shevky, Bell, . . ." (Schwirian, 1972: 152). Only in Calgary and Hamilton is there a single familism dimension, incorporating all three of the above measurements. Given the variation in procedures used to identify modes of urban differentiation, such conclusions are only tentative. However, it is clear we cannot necessarily extrapolate from American urban differentiation to the Canadian context.

Spatial Distribution

These dimensions of differentiation are not distributed spatially in a random manner. In most Canadian cities socioeconomic status follows a sectoral pattern, whereas family status, however measured, tends to be distributed zonally in a direct relation to distance from the centre (Balakrishnan and Jarvis, 1976; Robineault, 1970). An analysis of differences among neighbourhoods within each Canadian metropolitan area reveals

a widely known fact that, in most cities, age differences in the population are distributed in a concentric zonal pattern. Peripheral areas tend to be dominated by families in the early stages of child-bearing and child-rearing; inner suburbs tend to have a somewhat older age profile which approximates that of the city as a whole; and inner city areas are less family-oriented and have a disproportionate share of the city's elderly population, young singles who have left their parental home and childless couples (Hill, 1976: 31).

Table 49 illustrates this with respect to Montreal, Toronto, and Vancouver. Family status follows a concentric pattern in urban areas smaller than metropolitan communities (Bourne and Barber, 1971). Nevertheless, these are general spatial trends; cities do vary in the extent to which modifications in such patterns appear. For example, again comparing the eleven largest cities in 1961 if we separate the different familism variables, we find that type of dwelling is distributed in a gradient pattern, with the proportion of multiple-

Table 49: Distribution of Households With and Without Children in Montreal CMA, Toronto CMA, and Vancouver CMA, 1971

	Zone*				
	1 Central business district %	2 Inner city %	3 Mature suburbs %	4 New suburbs %	5 Exurbia %
Montreal CMA					
With children	11.1	26.3	49.3	66.7	71.8
Without children	88.9	73.7	50.7	33.3	28.2
Total	100.0	100.0	100.0	100.0	100.0
Toronto CMA					
With children	9.7	30.9	46.3	67.0	68.9
Without children	90.3	69.1	53.7	33.0	31.1
Total	100.0	100.0	100.0	100.0	100.0
Vancouver CMA					
With children	7.7	17.6	43.0	67.3	55.4
Without children	92.3	82.4	57.0	32.7	44.6
Total	100.0	100.0	100.0	100.0	100.0

*These zones are defined as follows:

Zone 1 *Central business district:* The major focus for much of a city's social and economic interaction.

Zone 2 *The inner city:* The transition zone of mixed and unstable land uses separating the Central Business District from more durable, mature neighbourhoods.

Zone 3 *Mature suburbs:* Encompasses an extensive and varied sector of urban residential land use, developed prior to 1951.

Zone 4 *New suburbs:* Mass-produced suburban developments that emerged in the early 1950's and are oriented to the automobile as the dominant form of transport.

Zone 5 *Exurbia:* The remainder of the Census Metropolitan Area outside the continuously built-up area.

From *Perspective Canada II: A Compendium of Social Statistics 1977.* Reproduced by permission of the Minister of Supply and Services Canada.

dwelling units declining with distance from the city centre. However, in only about half of these cities are the proportion of women in the labour force and the level of fertility likewise distributed zonally (Schwirian, 1972). In addition, we should note that "many cities also have sizable areas in the inner city with a fairly young population. Such areas are often associated with a recently arrived immigrant group, or with public housing projects" (Hill, 1976: 31).

Similarly, variations appear with respect to socioeconomic status. For example, whereas Edmonton shows a relatively clear sectoral pattern, in Winnipeg and Regina we find, in 1961, "a basic city-wide zonation separating the high status west and south areas from the low status areas on the north and east" (Davies and Barrow, 1973: 338).

Finally, ethnic status (the spatial contours of which we shall explore more thoroughly later in this chapter) shows considerable variation in its spatial distribution. Not uncommonly it exhibits a clustered or nucleated pattern, as in Montreal (Haynes, 1971) and Vancouver (Peucker and Rase, 1971). Yet, frequent modifications of this pattern do appear. For example, in Toronto in 1951 a non-British immigrant reception area extended to the northwest of the central business district. During the subsequent decade, several interesting changes occurred (Murdie, 1969). A sector in which Italians were concentrated extended outward toward the northwest, reaching a point of six miles from the centre. An additional sector of Jewish settlement diffused outward, toward the north to Forest Hill Village and North York. The deconcentration of these ethnic groups was increasingly evident; in both cases a sectoral pattern crystallized. Similarly, the St. Boniface area of Winnipeg illustrates the expected ethnic clustering; no such pattern appears in Regina where, as we saw above, a combined ethnic socioeconomic dimension exists that is distributed in a sectoral form.

Patterns of Income Segregation

The urban population in Canada is differentiated partly in terms of education, occupation, and income, as we have seen. In short, it is stratified in terms of a number of economic groupings. The life chances (i.e., opportunities to obtain material goods and other desirable resources) of any individual or family is partly a function of relative position within this stratified order. In examining the spatial distribution of the socioeconomic dimension of differentiation, it might be useful here to review briefly some of the general patterns of residential segregation among income groups within Canada's metropolitan areas. In particular, we should note the following:

1. As Table 50 indicates, in metropolitan Canada middle-income families show the least degree of residential segregation. Families in the $15,000+ category are the most segregated group, followed by those in the low-income (under $4,000) categories. This substantiates the general ecological proposition that residential segregation is greater for those "groups with clearly defined status than for those groups whose status is ambiguous" (Duncan and Duncan,

Table 50: Segregation Indices of Family Income Groups, Census Metropolitan Areas, 1971

Family income group ($)	Average segregation indices*
1- 1,999	.235
2,000- 3,999	.223
4,000- 5,999	.180
6,000- 9,999	.125
10,000-14,999	.135
15,000+	.298
Average	.199

*The segregation index for an income group represents the proportion of the families in that category that would have to move to a different census tract in order for that group's distribution to be the same as the distribution of all other families across the metropolitan area.

From Frederick I. Hill, ed., *Canadian Urban Trends* Vol. II © Ministry of Supply and Services Canada, 1976. Reprinted by permission of Copp Clark Pitman, Publishers.

1970 ed.: 507). Segregation commonly appears among groups at the extremes of the socioeconomic scale.

2. The greater the degree of income disparity among families in a metropolitan community, the greater will be the differences among neighbourhoods in family income (Hill, 1976: 46). In chapter 4 we saw that average incomes increase with size of community. The larger cities also have greater variation in income levels among their populations. Table 51 presents data on the standard deviation of average family income of census tracts, as well as on the mean segregation index of the six family income categories listed in the previous table. With the exception of Windsor, these data document that correlation: cities manifesting higher levels of income differentiation also achieve greater residential segregation among income groups. In such communities the "sifting and sorting" process is more vivid along economic lines; patterns of social distance among income groups are spatially more evident.

3. In most of Canada's metropolitan areas, low income groups tend to be concentrated near the central business district:

> The central business district is almost always poor, and poor areas extend outwards from the core along railway tracks and waterfronts, areas which also include industrial uses which detract from the area as a place of residence. A sectoral pattern is the norm. Often low-income areas also have an ethnic minority . . . . In most cities, areas with a concentration of low-income families are entirely within the older inner city, but pockets of rural poverty are occasionally found on the fringe of the CMA (Hill, 1976: 59).

High-income sectors also extend outward, although they rarely reach the boundary of the metropolitan community. Hoyt's assertion that such sectors are contiguous to intermediate socioeconomic neighbourhoods frequently proves accurate.

Table 51: Intrametropolitan Income Disparity, 1971

CMA	Standard deviation of average family income of census tracts[1] ($)	Mean segregation index of six family income groups[2]
Calgary	2,930	.228
Chicoutimi-Jonquière	—	—
Edmonton	3,156	.208
Halifax	2,936	.201
Hamilton	2,413	.206
Kitchener	2,114	.161
London	3,092	.211
Montreal	4,159	.221
Ottawa-Hull	3,865	.250
Quebec	2,941	.207
Regina	2,237	.222
St. Catharines-Niagara	1,770	.140
St. John's	3,234	.231
Saint John	2,329	.208
Saskatoon	1,889	.175
Sudbury	1,715	.155
Thunder Bay	1,508	.149
Toronto	4,612	.231
Vancouver	3,362	.195
Victoria	2,426	.173
Windsor	2,206	.181
Winnipeg	3,195	.234
Metropolitan Canada	3,732	.199

1. Standard Deviation $= \sqrt{\dfrac{\sum_{i=1}^{n} (X_i - \bar{X})^2}{n - 1}}$

where: n = number of census tracts
X_i = average family income in census tract
$\bar{X}$ = mean of the average family income of census tracts

2. These categories are: $1-1,999, 2,000-3,999, 4,000-5,999, 6,000-9,999, 10,000-14,999, 15,000+

From Frederick I. Hill, ed., *Canadian Urban Trends* Vol. II © Ministry of Supply and Services Canada, 1976. Reprinted by permission of Copp Clark Pitman, Publishers.

Changes in the Dimensions of Differentiation

As we observed in the previous chapter, ecological structure must be viewed as a dynamic phenomenon. Both the bases of differentiation and their spatial distribution can change over time. For example, in analyzing population and housing characteristics of census tracts in Winnipeg we find three fundamental dimensions existing in 1951—social rank, familism (distinguishing between families with children and families without children or single persons), and a single male immigrant factor (Hunter and Latif, 1973). Over the subsequent decade, however, while the importance of the socioeconomic factor in explaining social differentiation remained constant, that of the familism factor increased and that of immigrant status declined. That familism emerged by 1961 as the most significant dimension perhaps reflected Winnipeg's suburbanization. Families with children sought greater space and single-family homes in outer areas; households without children, regardless of class, remained in the highrises and multiple dwellings of the inner core. It has been commonly assumed that increasing modernization of a society creates an urban structure in which social rank is the most dominant dimension. The evolution of Winnipeg between 1951 and 1961 is not consistent with this assumption. Indeed, reflecting the lower socioeconomic level of those immigrants who came to Winnipeg during the 1950s, the social rank and immigrant status dimensions converged. Over the decade, therefore, Winnipeg's overall differentiation actually declined (Hunter and Latif, 1973).

Toronto, too, experienced substantial suburban growth during the 1950s. Population in the outer suburbs expanded by more than 200 percent (Murdie, 1969). In comparison to Winnipeg, Toronto also attracted significantly larger streams of immigrants. By 1961 one-third of Metro Toronto's population was foreign-born; most of these people had arrived after World War II. In contrast to Winnipeg, in 1951, the most important basis of Toronto's differentiation had been family status; by 1961, ethnic status emerged as the most significant dimension (Keith, 1973). As in Winnipeg, educational and income levels became more closely associated with ethnic status. The independence of the social rank factor diminished over the decade. The growing importance of ethnic status in Toronto's structure suggests more generally "that the ecological differentiation of a city is determined by other factors besides the level of scale of the society in which it is located. . . . The volume of migration plays an important role in differentiating sub-areas of the city. The unique elements of the historical background of an urban centre, then, have a very significant effect on its ecological structure" (Keith, 1973: 95).

Changes in Spatial Distribution

It has been commonly observed that the pre-industrial city displays a spatial structure that is the complete opposite of the Burgess model:

> Concentrated in that city "central" area . . . are the most prominent governmental and religious edifices and usually the main market. . . . The pre-industrial city's central area is notable also as the chief residence of the elite. . . . The disadvantaged members of the city fan out toward the periphery, with the poorest and the outcasts living in the suburbs, the farthest removed from the centre. Houses toward the city's fringes are small, flimsily constructed, often one-room hovels into which whole families crowd (Sjoberg, 1960: 96-98; Caplow, 1961).

The commercial centre, as we saw earlier, shows a greater residential mixing of the classes within the inner core. Residential segregation is heightened with the emergence of the industrial and metropolitan community formations. An intriguing research question that emerges is whether urban residential structures can be viewed as evolving in a predictable direction from the pattern of "wealthy at the centre" and "poor at the periphery" to the reverse outlined in Burgess's model (Schnore, 1972: 16). With the growth and expansion of the city accompanying industrialization, and the development of short-distance transportation facilities, a closer approximation to the latter might be predicted. A brief examination of this hypothesized change in spatial distribution over time will enable us to elaborate on the patterns of income segregation discussed earlier.

In a detailed series of research studies beginning in 1955, Schnore (1965, 1972) explored the nature of central city-suburban differences in class composition as an initial step toward establishing the conditions, even in a highly industrialized society, under which Burgess' assertion that the socioeconomic status of residential areas increases with distance from the city centre is applicable. For example, Schnore (1965) examined the structure of 200 urbanized

Table 52:   City-Suburb Differentials in Socioeconomic Status by Size of Urbanized Area and Age of Central City (U.S.) 1960

Size of urbanized area, 1960	Percent of urbanized areas with higher suburban values in:			Number of areas
	(1) Median family income 1959	(2) % completing high school	(3) % in white-collar occupations	
1,000,000 and over	100.0	100.0	87.5	16
500,000-1,000,000	100.0	100.0	86.4	22
250,000-500,000	79.3	75.9	55.2	29
150,000-250,000	72.1	62.8	48.8	43
100,000-150,000	70.3	64.9	40.5	37
50,000-100,000	56.6	49.1	30.2	53
Census year in which central city first reached 50,000				
1800 to 1860	100.0	100.0	100.0	14
1870 or 1880	100.0	100.0	100.0	17
1890 or 1900	86.1	75.0	58.3	36
1910 or 1920	75.0	75.0	54.2	48
1930 or 1940	71.9	56.3	31.3	32
1950 or 1960	50.9	47.2	24.5	53
All areas	74.0	68.5	50.5	200

From Schnore, 1972. Reprinted by permission of the author.

areas (each of which consists of one or more cities of 50,000 population minimum and all the nearby closely settled suburban territory, or urban fringe) in the United States.

As Table 52 reveals, the size and age of the urban area are important factors.

The larger the urban area, the more likely it is that the suburban population will be of higher socioeconomic status in comparison to the central city residents. For example, all of the American urbanized areas in the two largest classes show a higher median family income and a higher proportion completing high school in the suburbs than in the central cities. This becomes much less the case moving down the scale to the very smallest urbanized areas. Among these, a slight majority (50.9%) show the reverse pattern—central cities have a higher educational rank than their suburbs.

The older the urban area, the more likely it is that the suburban population will be of higher socioeconomic status in comparison to the central city residents. Table 52 indicates that suburban fringes manifest higher median family incomes than the central cities of older areas (classified in terms of when the central city first attained a population of 50,000). The newer urbanized areas show larger proportions of central cities with higher incomes. Hence, "the common conception—that higher status people live in the suburbs—tends to be true of the very oldest areas, but it is progressively less true of newer areas" (Schnore, 1965: 209).

Further analysis reveals that age constitutes a better predictor of city-suburban differentials in socioeconomic status than does the size of the urban area. In attempting to explain this, Schnore (1965: 214) observes that the housing stock of older areas is more commonly obsolescent in the central cities. Such housing is unattractive to more affluent and higher-status groups, who seek residence in newer developments on the periphery. In contrast,

> In the newer urbanized areas, the housing stock of the central city itself is neither so old nor so run-down as to be unattractive to potential home-owners of the expanding "middle class" . . . [and] the competition of alternative (nonresidential) land uses on inner zones now appears to be less intense in these newer cities than they were in older cities at comparable stages in the past.

Such differences suggest a possible evolutionary pattern: as urban areas grow and mature, higher-status groups tend in time to shift from central to peripheral residence. Yet, the general applicability of this pattern can be limited because of the continuation of specific high-status neighbourhoods near the centres of the cities—a possibility Firey (1945) emphasized. In addition, renewal of inner-city areas may create stocks of luxury highrise apartments to which particular segments of more affluent groups are attracted. Finally, middle-class residents may themselves seek to renovate housing in formerly working-class neighbourhoods of the inner city.

Beyond these qualifications, however, it is important to determine whether this evolutionary pattern occurs in the Canadian urban context. Here we can cite the results of two recent studies that have tentatively searched for evidence of such a pattern.

Examining 1961 variations in levels of education and income within thirty-seven of Canada's urban communities, Guest (1969) initially found support for that pattern. The higher educational and income groups tended to be overrepresented in the suburbs of older, larger, and extensively suburbanized urban areas. Between 1951 and 1961 this pattern became more pronounced among fifteen of the largest and oldest metropolitan areas in Canada: "higher income and education groups were generally becoming more heavily represented in the suburbs and less represented in the central cities. The opposite process was occurring for lower income and education categories" (Guest, 1969: 275).

Nevertheless, more detailed study of the pattern of these changes reveals inconsistencies. Guest examined differences between 1951 and 1961 in the proportion of university-educated residents within concentric zones around the centres of four cities—Montreal, Toronto, Windsor, and Winnipeg. As Table 53 indicates, no discernible pattern is evident; the changes in proportion university-educated by concentric zone tend to occur randomly. The incomplete congruence between these zonal data and the broad city-suburban comparisons suggests that the latter capture "only very gross changes and that significant variations in change exist within central cities and suburbs" (Guest, 1969: 276). As we noted earlier, changes in socioeconomic composition more commonly follow sectoral paths in Canadian cities, which is consistent with the lack of a discernible pattern in the zonal distributions of Table 53. In any case, Guest's research suggests that Schnore's evolutionary hypothesis is too imprecise a statement of the changes occurring in residential socioeconomic differentiation.

This is confirmed in Balakrishnan and Jarvis's (1979) analysis of changes in spatial differentiation within fourteen of Canada's largest metropolitan areas between 1961 and 1971. Dividing each of these communities into distinct sectors and zones, they found that contrary to the evolutionary hypothesis "the majority of Canadian cities actually increased in the [socioeconomic] status of inner-city census tracts and decreased in the status of outlying, suburban tracts" (Balakrishnan and Jarvis, 1979: 227). Indeed, in ten of these fourteen cities socioeconomic status is distributed more by sector than by distance zones—a pattern ignored in the evolutionary hypothesis.

In contrast, family size (a measure of family status) does increase with distance from the centre of almost all these cities. This spatial pattern became clearer between 1961 and 1971. As cities become older and larger, family status, as we saw with respect to Toronto's growth, assumes more clearly a zonal spatial pattern. Such is not the case, however, for ethnic status. This basis of differentiation does not assume a uniform pattern across all these metropolitan communities in either 1961 or 1971.

Table 53: Percentage of Persons Not in School Who Attended a University, 1961, and Change in Percent, 1951-1961, by Mile Distance Zone from City Centre, for Four Canadian Metropolitan Areas

Miles from centre	Montreal 1961 distri-bution	Change from 1951	Toronto 1961 distri-bution	Change from 1951	Windsor 1961 distri-bution	Change from 1951	Winnipeg 1961 distri-bution	Change from 1951
0 to 1	9.4	0.4	10.9	0.8	4.7	−5.6	6.9	−1.2
1 to 2	6.3	−0.6	7.6	−4.4	5.9	−9.5	6.7	−0.5
2 to 3	11.2	3.3	8.9	−5.7	5.0	−5.1	11.7	1.4
3 to 4	7.1	−2.0	6.5	−7.8	7.2	−5.9	7.8	2.2
4 to 5	7.4	1.2	8.6	−8.2	6.4	−6.7	14.0	0.9
5 to 6	7.7	−0.3	8.0	−9.1	7.0	−2.1	4.7	−4.4
6 to 7	5.0	−1.3	10.4	−10.3	6.8	−2.1	5.7	−3.2
7 to 8	11.3	1.0	7.1	−7.6	—	—	—	—
8 to 9	2.5	−2.8	9.2	−5.1	—	—	—	—
9 or more	17.2	4.2	8.8	−2.7	—	—	—	—

From "The Applicability of the Burgess Zonal Hypothesis to Urban Canada" by Avery Guest in *Demography* 6 (1969). Reprinted by permission of the Population Association of America.

These findings therefore provide little evidence of a tendency toward the Burgess pattern for socioeconomic characteristics as Canadian cities become older and larger; the prevailing sectoral distribution remains pronounced. The evolutionary hypothesis does, however, gain support in terms of family status, which becomes more zonally differentiated over time. Both Guest's and Balakrishnan and Jarvis's research underlines again a point made earlier: Canadian urban ecological structure does not necessarily replicate the patterns found in American cities.

RESIDENTIAL MOBILITY

The spatial distribution of the fundamental bases of urban differentiation is created by regularized patterns of residential mobility. This we might term the "sorting-out" phenomenon: those with similar economic, social, or ethnic characteristics are likely to move to common residential areas in the city (Salins, 1971). That is, "an orderly social geography results as like individuals make like choices, in response to regularities in the operation of the land and housing markets and the collaboration of similar individuals who act to exclude dissimilar people from their neighborhood or to restrict minority groups to particular areas" (Rees, 1970: 313). The decision of where to live is a product of the interaction of such factors as price of the dwelling unit and type and location of residence, as well as such individual attributes as housing needs reflecting stage of the family life cycle, income, and particular lifestyle preferences (Berry and Rees, 1969; Rees, 1970). Certain spatial regularities emerge from that interaction. For example, with respect to the concentric or zonal distribution of family status, as households move through the family cycle (distinguishing such possible stages as single or pre-family, young married couple, young family with children, mature family with older children, mature family without children present, and widowed), their requirements for space change (Salins, 1971). As the number of children in the family increases, the demand for greater space also enlarges. This need can best be met by relocating at greater distances from the city centre. A gradient pattern is thus produced: households in the child-bearing and child-rearing stages more commonly reside on the periphery; pre-child or post-child households are more attracted to core or inner zone areas (Hayter, 1973; Michelson, 1977).

Intraurban migration is also shaped by economic constraints that tend to create that sectoral bias observed earlier:

> The wealthiest class will bid for sites as near the desirable central business district activities (fashionable shops, offices, and so on) as possible; and progressively lower status classes will flank them on progressively less desirable sites near heavy industry, railroad yards, and swamps. This original pattern of settlement sets the precedent for all subsequent locations decisions by class status. As the population of the metropolitan area grows, the increase in the number of families of each class status results in a gradual expansion of each status neighborhood outward, and if the relative proportion of households in each class remains the same, a wedge-shaped or *sectoral* pattern by class will emerge. Each class is kept within the sectoral boundaries because of the preemption of flanking sites by another class (Salins, 1971: 237).

This outward expansion within each class is partly promoted by those seeking greater space to accommodate changes in household composition. Thus, family status is influential here too. Nevertheless, examining economic status and family status as independent dimensions of urban differentiation reveals relatively separate biases toward, respectively, sectoral and concentric spatial distributions. These patterns are, of course, influenced by the spatial location of new housing; any asymmetrical aspects of these distributions are responses to the way in which the housing market may operate in particular cities. Distance from the core in itself, for example, is of less importance than where appropriate dwelling space can be found (Simmons, 1974b).

It might be useful to summarize briefly some of the major generalizations about intraurban residential mobility which illustrate the complexity of this "sorting-out" phenomenon (Simmons, 1968: 1974b; Hayter, 1973; Obright, 1973; Lukomskyj, 1974; McCracken, 1973; Michelson, 1973a, 1973b, 1977):

1. Residential movement is most clearly related to age of household head and household size. Young, growing families are the most likely to change residences within the city, most commonly moving toward the periphery. Economic factors constrain but do not in themselves motivate intraurban migration.

2. Those renting more commonly change residences. Home ownership discourages further mobility.

3. Intraurban migration tends to be greater in larger cities, reflecting the dynamic aspects of the housing market (e.g., the relatively larger number of new housing units constructed, thus encouraging changes of residence among those seeking more appropriate dwelling space). Communities experiencing population growth also provide greater opportunities for housing relocation.

4. Although job considerations may motivate interurban moves, place of employment has far less influence on the choice of destinations in intraurban mobility than does, for example, stage in the family life cycle. This perhaps reflects the expanded system of local transportation in the contemporary metropolis that permits separation of place of work and place of residence without prohibitive "diseconomies." Low-income groups, however, are more constrained than others to seek housing in proximity to their work.

5. Most intraurban moves are of relatively short distance. More affluent residents are able to move longer distances because their economic resources provide them with greater choice and more extensive housing opportunities.

6. Earlier we observed that in metropolitan areas middle-income families show the least degree of residential segregation. This reflects patterns of household movement. Using Toronto as an example, we find that "income groups at both the high and low ends of the scale are segregated and move among a few locations with little net change (high symmetry). Movement of middle income groups are less symmetrical and have a much greater range when plotted. It is the latter who generate observed social change in a neighborhood" (Simmons, 1974b: 71). The lowest-income residents in Toronto relocate within the oldest parts of the inner city; similarly, the most affluent group changes residences, but remains within the North Toronto sector and central Etobicoke.

7. An important factor influencing the search for housing and ultimately the destination of a change in residence is the *mental map* of the city which the intraurban migrant possesses:

> each migrant household begins its search of the housing market with a preconceived image of the city—some areas are deemed desirable, others are avoided, and still others are simply unknown. In short, each migrant household possesses a certain "awareness space", that is, a set of locations within the total urban space about which it has at least some threshold level of knowledge (Obright, 1973: 39).

This mental map or "search space" does not remain fixed; acquisition of new information about the location of housing opportunities, quality of diverse neighbourhoods, etc., will refine that subjective chart (McCracken, 1973). Such a map varies among different classes and among households at different stages of the family life cycle.

8. Reasons for moving within the city vary according to the type of housing and location selected (Michelson, 1977). For example, those moving to

inner-city highrise apartments frequently seek greater access to their work-place, to the downtown area, and to public transportation; they also are at-tracted to recreational benefits within the building and nearby. In contrast, as we have noted, those moving to suburban single-family homes seek extra space within the dwelling and private grounds outside to accommodate their families. Residential mobility commonly reflects a compromise among dif-ferent needs. Suburban dwellers, for example, may have sacrificed accessi-bility to shopping facilities in their quest for more living space.

9. Satisfaction with housing and location after the move does not deter subsequent mobility (Michelson, 1977). This is especially the case among those who choose to live in downtown highrises. Residents in the early stages of the family life cycle see this type of housing as only temporary, and are satisfied with it because they anticipate moving ultimately to the "ideal"—which is widely shared among diverse segments of the urban population—of a single-family, detached house. The analysis below of Edmonton's highrises illustrates this point.

These generalizations emphasize that the "sorting-out" process, which in-fluences the spatial structure of the city, is a product of intricate locational decisions made on the basis of household perception and evaluation of needs and opportunities (Simmons, 1968).

THE HIGHRISES OF EDMONTON

As we noted in chapter 4, Edmonton grew rapidly in the post-World War II period. Internally its population showed marked patterns of suburban-ization and redistribution. The "sorting-out" process occurred in a fashion that was consistent with the generalizations noted above. Moves out to the periphery of the city were more numerous than the reverse (McCracken, 1973). Nevertheless, many did relocate closer to the centre of the city, especially those seeking greater accessibility to their places of work in the core. Despite extensive intraurban movement, Edmonton's high-status residents (at least through the period from 1936 to 1972) re-main clustered in two areas near the central business district and the University of Alberta (Fairbairn, 1978). Executives and professionals find these residential locales attractive because of proximity to their places of work. In addition, housing in these areas has not yet shown that deterioration which would encourage relocation. Consequently, Edmon-ton's high-status residents have not participated in the suburbanization process to the same extent as have other groups (Fairbairn, 1978: 25). (This is consistent with the findings of Balakrishnan and Jarvis's study noted earlier.)

Since the late 1950s Canada's largest cities have experienced a boom in the construction of highrise apartment buildings (Lorimer, 1978). These have clustered partly in the inner areas of metropolitan communities. Edmonton is no exception; the central part of the city contains a number of highrise units. Such dwellings, as the preceding generalizations and discussion suggest, are not equally attractive to all portions of Edmonton's population (Hayter, 1973). Nor can they be; in many cases, for example, management will not rent to households containing children under 12 or 14 years of age. As a result, many highrise households consist of non-related individuals—unattached males between 25 and 34 years old or women over 44 and living alone—or childless married couples. In comparison to the rest of the city, disproportionately few children live here. Reflecting rental levels as well as the desire to live close to work in the downtown area and the university, many of central Edmonton's highrise residents are employed in professional and managerial occupations. Members of older one-person households are no longer in the labour force.

Edmonton's highrises fulfil the residential requirements of those in the early and later stages of the family life cycle (Hayter, 1973). We can distinguish two predominant types of residents:

1. "Hard-core renters": These are older, unattached individuals and married couples over 44 years, who plan to remain here permanently. At this stage of their lives, few would find living in a single-family home desirable. Indeed, with the lessening of their housing requirements—through death of a spouse or departure of children—a number have recently relocated from just such a dwelling (cf. Lukomskyj, 1974). The "hard-core renters" are attracted to the highrise because of the accessibility it affords to the downtown area and facilities, its proximity to friends, and the convenience of amenities within the building. These residents view their present housing as congruent with their housing requirements and few anticipate a further move.

2. "Non-hard-core renters": These are young, mobile persons who aspire to eventual home ownership. Many are single and have moved here from outside Edmonton in search of better employment opportunities or have recently left their parents' homes to establish an independent household. Although they complain about the size, layout, and cost of the apartments they are renting, the location and convenience of the highrise are factors of considerable appeal to them. For this group, unlike households in the later stages of the family life cycle, the highrise is a transitional type of housing, with which they are relatively satisfied for the time being. Most intend moving again within two years, perhaps to rental housing once more, but ultimately, they expect, to a single-family detached home.

> *Because of rental levels, type and layout of units, and their locations, central Edmonton's highrises themselves vary in the extent to which they attract either of the above groups. Some buildings—for example, those on the south side in proximity to the university—draw greater proportions of young, mobile households. Nevertheless, Edmonton's highrises fulfil the needs of those at particular stages in the family life cycle; this illustrates the fundamental point that household structure, residential requirements, and residential mobility are closely interconnected.*

ETHNIC RESIDENTIAL SEGREGATION

One central feature of Canada's urban spatial mosaic is ethnic residential segregation. Ethnic collectivities are not distributed randomly. Since Park attempted to systematize its focus, a fundamental concern of urban ecology has been the patterns of ethnic and racial residential segregation manifested within the city (e.g., Duncan and Duncan, 1957; Lieberson, 1963; Taeuber and Taeuber, 1965). The study of such differentiation contributes to an overall understanding of social geography, and also serves to reveal the level of assimilation among minority groups and to suggest the degree of social distance existing between them and the dominant society (see chapter 8). Frequently, a strong association exists between "institutional completeness and residential segregation—both factors which sustain ethnic solidarity and inhibit assimilation" (Driedger and Church, 1974). In the following we shall briefly explore the formation of an ethnic enclave, using Chinatown as an example. At a more general level we shall document how such residential segregation varies across Canada's largest cities and among ethnic groups. Our understanding of ethnic residential segregation, of the factors affecting it, and of change in its shape will be helped further by a closer look at two specific cities, Toronto and Winnipeg. Our ultimate object here is to identify a series of principles that are applicable to ethnic residential segregation across urban Canada.

In chapter 6 we observed that an ethnic community represents a form of social organization in which informal relationships and institutions develop to fulfil a range of the needs for members. Territorial segregation within the city helps to strengthen such a community, and provides the opportunities for necessary in-group contact. An ethnic spatial enclave is frequently a product of a variety of factors—including, for example, the influence of social networks (friends and kin encourage their intimates to live nearby), the desire to reside with neighbours of similar values and customs, the ability to afford only low-income housing which is frequently concentrated in particular areas of the city, inability to speak the language of the host society, and active discrimination against members of the ethnic group.

CHINATOWN: AN ILLUSTRATION OF AN URBAN ETHNIC ENCLAVE

Perhaps one of the most striking cases of an urban ethnic enclave is the formation of Chinatowns in such cities as Vancouver and Calgary. The gold rush in British Columbia first attracted large numbers of Chinese to the West. They then turned to construction work on the transcontinental CPR. After its completion they sought employment in unskilled jobs, such as domestic labour, selling vegetables, or operating laundries, in both the larger and smaller centres of the West (Voisey, 1970; Baureiss, 1971).

The Chinese frequently encountered hostility and open discrimination from the white society. Labour groups sought to expel them, seeing them as possible threats to their own jobs. Evidence of an anti-oriental prejudice commonly appeared. For example, in Vancouver an Anti-Chinese Pledge Group was established by businessmen agreeing not to serve Chinese customers: "Each of the members placed a card in the window of their establishment which read: 'The undersigned pledges himself not to deal directly or indirectly with Chinese' " (Young, 1975: 60). Mob attacks on the Chinese led to the imposition of martial law on Vancouver for a brief time.

In response to white oppression, and coupled with a desire to construct a familiar social and cultural environment, the Chinese clustered in their own enclaves, separate from the rest of the city's population (Voisey, 1970). In Vancouver, Chinatown was initially located near False Creek; white businessmen sought to restrict its expansion in the early 1900s. From time to time outside groups attacked Chinatown. Issues such as the employment of white girls exposed the enclave to frequent antagonistic action by Vancouver's City Council (Young, 1975).

Because of immigration restrictions most of Chinatown's initial residents were males. The shortage of Chinese women created social disruption (Voisey, 1970). Many of the men saw themselves as sojourners who might eventually return to their homeland. Nevertheless, within their enclave they formed a variety of organizations based on clan, dialect, and locality divisions. The tongs—composed of those with the same last name—emerged as powerful protective and welfare units (Voisey, 1970; see also Light, 1974). Most of the residents' needs could be fulfilled within the enclave.

The Chinatowns of Vancouver and elsewhere have experienced significant change during the later decades of this century. The repeal of the Chinese Exclusion Act in 1947 allowed single Chinese women to enter Canada in greater numbers, providing a more balanced sex ratio and social structure. Greater acceptance of the Chinese on the part of the wider community permitted them to disperse throughout the region (Cho and Leigh, 1972). They are now less segregated than in the past. The Canadian discovery of Chinese food encouraged growth of the Chinese restaurant industry. Post-war immigration brought better-educated Chinese, especially from Hong Kong, who were less willing to accept the traditional social organization of Chinatown based on ascriptive and local ties (Young, 1975). Many of these moved directly into suburban locations (Cho and Leigh, 1972). New types of organizations, concerned with local Vancouver issues, have emerged with young leaders. Tensions between those supporting the Nationalist Party of Taiwan and those more sympathetic to Mainland China have appeared (Glynn and Wang, 1978). Reflecting immigrant youth's lack of identification with China-town's traditional social structure, juvenile delinquency is increasing.

Most significantly, Chinatown has become decreasingly a residential community. Its land-use patterns reflect predominantly commercial functions serving the wider community. In 1971, of the 6,000 Chinese living in Calgary, all but 500 resided outside Chinatown (Baureiss, 1971). The latter are older and less educated than Chinese living elsewhere. Vancouver's Chinatown Chinese are more likely to have been born outside Canada, to have been taught in school in the Chinese language, and to continue to participate actively in Chinese associations and festivals than their ethnic compatriots living elsewhere in the community (Cho and Leigh, 1972). Despite the erosion of its residential function, Chinatown continues to serve the specialized commercial and cultural needs of Chinese throughout the urban community. Even among those who may have lived at one time within the enclave, it remains a centre for shopping and socializing (Nann, 1975). Indeed, vigorous efforts have been made to protect Chinatown from redevelopment and transportation projects that threaten its physical integrity.

Ethnic Residential Segregation in Metropolitan Canada

Not all cities manifest the same level of ethnic residential segregation, nor do all ethnic groups achieve similar degrees of concentration. These variations are illustrated in Tables 54 and 55. Comparing the average segregation (that is, the extent to which ethnic group members would have to move elsewhere in the city to parallel more fully the distribution of the rest of the population) for ten ethnic groups, we find in 1971 substantial differences among metropolitan areas. The greatest segregation exists in Montreal, followed by Ottawa-Hull, Toronto, and Winnipeg. The lowest level is found in Saint John. In addition, we should note the following patterns.

1. In general, the larger the community, the greater its average ethnic segregation. Specialization of land use is more intense in larger cities, and more "sifting and sorting" of ethnic groups occurs here.

2. In chapter 6 we examined the average ethnic diversity in these communities, and found significant variations. Nevertheless, Table 54 suggests that the levels of ethnic diversity and ethnic segregation are not necessarily closely correlated (Balakrishnan, 1975). For example, Thunder Bay in 1971 shows greater ethnic diversity than does Toronto; the level of segregation, in contrast, is much higher in the latter metropolitan area. Diversity in itself, independent of such factors as size of city and ethnic groups and rate of language retention, does not determine level of segregation.

3. Although the data are not explicitly presented in Table 54, it does appear to be the case that cities containing a high proportion of non-British residents also manifest clear patterns of ethnic residential segregation (Balakrishnan, 1975). Toronto, in which many foreign-born persons reside, il-

Table 54: Average Segregation Indices Among Central Metropolitan Areas, 1971

Census metropolitan area	Average segregation index*
Calgary	.213
Edmonton	.258
Halifax	.208
Hamilton	.282
Kitchener	.241
London	.227
Montreal	.520
Ottawa-Hull	.389
Quebec	.292
Regina	.234
St. Catharines-Niagara	.254
St. John's	.266
Saint John	.184
Saskatoon	.208
Sudbury	.261
Thunder Bay	.200
Toronto	.358
Vancouver	.260
Victoria	.206
Windsor	.251
Winnipeg	.332
Average — Metropolitan Canada	.309

*This is the average level of segregation found among 10 ethnic groups—British, French, German, Italian, Jewish, Native Indian, Dutch, Polish, Scandinavian, and Ukrainian. The segregation index "represents the proportion of the ethnic group's population which would have to move to a different census tract in order for that group's distribution to resemble the distribution of the rest of the population in that metropolitan area" (Hill, 1976: 84). Thus, the higher the value of the index, the greater the segregation.

From Federick I. Hill, ed., *Canadian Urban Trends* Vol. II © Ministry of Supply and Services Canada, 1976. Reprinted by permission of Copp Clark Pitman, Publishers.

lustrates this relationship. The pressures to assimilate, we might speculate, are muted somewhat by the presence of residents from other than the British group.

Ethnic groups themselves differ in their levels of residential segregation within Metropolitan Canada. Table 55 reveals that of the ten groups compared, the Jewish population is typically the most segregated, followed by the Native Indians and the Italians. A variety of factors account for these differences. For example:

1. The Jewish pattern is a product partly of their relatively strong cultural identity (Driedger, 1978b).

2. The greater the proportion of a group which (a) retains its own language and (b) is foreign-born, the more likely it is that it will manifest a high level of segregation (as in the case of the Italians).

3. Relative degrees of social distance from the British group are also important here. That is, Eastern and Southern Europeans tend to be more segregated from the British than do Western and Northern Europeans (Balakrishnan, 1975). (The relatively low level of segregation found among the Germans is consistent with this proposition.)

4. Residential segregation, as has been noted earlier, is related to level of institutional completeness. These are mutually reinforcing aspects of an urban ethnic community's existence. (The Jewish and Italian groups illustrate this pattern.)

5. Finally, a group's level of segregation may also be influenced by its socioeconomic status. Urban Native Indians, as we saw in chapter 5, are

---

Table 55:   **Average Segregation Indices of Ten Ethnic Groups in Canada's Census Metropolitan Areas, 1971**

Ethnic Group	Average Segregation Index*
British Isles	.197
French	.224
German	.181
Italian	.378
Jewish	.581
Native Indian	.401
Netherlands	.227
Polish	.239
Scandinavian	.186
Ukrainian	.231
Average	.309

*See Table 54 for definition of the Index.

From Frederick I. Hill, ed., *Canadian Urban Trends* Vol. II © Ministry of Supply and Services, 1976. Reprinted by permission of Copp Clark Pitman, Publishers.

economically marginal. Their segregation partly reflects their lack of resources and freedom to reside elsewhere than in low-income housing. Discrimination against them, of course, may also be influential in restricting this group to concentrated areas.

Ethnic Residential Segregation in Toronto and Winnipeg

The above generalizations are derived from broad comparisons across Metropolitan Canada. It will be useful to focus on two of these communities in greater depth. In the previous chapter we briefly examined the spatial evolution of Toronto and Winnipeg as they were transformed into industrial and metropolitan centres. Let us examine now more clearly the contemporary spatial distribution of ethnic collectivities in each, and what these patterns more generally suggest.

Toronto. We have repeatedly observed in this chapter and in chapter 6 the impact of immigration on Toronto. The multiethnic character Toronto assumed, especially in the post-war period, provides an ideal environment in which to examine patterns of ethnic segregation. In 1970 almost half of the total number of heads of household in the metropolitan area were foreign-born. Less than a third actually were third-generation or more (Richmond, 1972: 15). As we noted earlier, ethnic status emerged as an important and independent dimension of differentiation in the poplation. In 1971 the metropolitan community showed the third highest level of ethnic segregation of all metropolitan areas in Canada.

In considering the residential distribution of Toronto's ethnic groups it should be recalled, as we saw in chapter 4, that the entire metropolitan population grew by more than one-third between 1961 and 1971. As in other cities, this increase was more pronounced in outlying areas. A number of large, inexpensive homes were available in the inner city. These were particularly attractive to the foreign-born. Whereas the British group were far more willing to rent, the Italians and Slavs, even when it was financially feasible, seemed less desirous of residing in the city's highrises. The residential distributions of these ethnic groups reflected such preferences, as well as in-group cohesion, level of assimilation and ethnic identity, intergroup patterns of social distance, and levels of socioeconomic status. Those areas of Toronto in which the Jewish, Slavic, and Italian groups had been concentrated in 1961 maintained their ethnic character in subsequent years. Indeed, it appeared that with the out-migration of those of British origin the city's general level of ethnic segregation had actually become more pronounced during the 1960s (Richmond, 1972). In addition, there was evidence of an expansion outward by ethnic groups to either the northern or western sections of the metropolitan area, as we observed earlier (Murdie, 1969).

To determine ethnic spatial location more precisely, Richmond (1972) divided Metro Toronto into three zones—inner city, inner suburb, and outer suburb—and delineated separate areas within each. Focusing on the Jewish, Slavic, Italian, and British groups, he constructed indices of relative concentrations for each. As we would expect, Table 56 indicates that the various ethnic groups are not concentrated in the same areas of the city. For example, the Jewish group is clustered in two inner and outer suburban areas where non-Jews are strongly underrepresented.

Table 56: Indices of Relative Concentration[1] by Ethnic Group in Metro Toronto, 1970

| Zone | Ethnic Group | | | |
	Jewish	Slavic	Italian	British
Inner city				
1	-83	$+26^2$	-71	-36
2	-85	-31	$+37^2$	-50
3	-26	-32	-36	$+5$
Inner suburb				
4	-87	$+15^2$	-67	-8
5	$+27^2$	-44	-49	-26
6	-53	-22	$+33^2$	-44
7	-91	-58	-65	$+29^2$
Outer suburb				
8	-92	$+4^2$	-45	$+18^2$
9	$+53^2$	-53	$+1$	-42
10	-81	-4	$+21^2$	-21
11	-68	-14	-12	$+17^2$

1. The index of relative concentration measures the degree of representation of a group compared with a hypothetical random distribution in which each group would be found in a given area in proportion to its size and the total population. A positive value, therefore, presents the degree of over-representation; a negative value points to the level of under-representation. This measure controls for the size of the ethnic group in the city's population. It should be noted that in almost all areas the British constitute a majority or plurality, regardless of the level of relative concentration of any minority ethnic group.
2. Areas of concentration by the particular ethnic group.

Adapted from Richmond, 1972.

There are three additional aspects of these spatial patterns which we should emphasize:

1. With respect to their residential distributions, Toronto's ethnic groups tend to be internally differentiated in terms of class, period of immigration, and family status. The pattern of Jewish concentration itself varies by socioeconomic status: "In the inner suburb (roughly corresponding with the Forest Hill area) concentration increases with higher social status, whereas in the outer suburb concentration is greatest among the [Jewish] lower and middle status householders" (Richmond, 1972: 41). Similarly, recently arrived

Italians cluster especially in an inner-city area, whereas Italians of longer tenure in Canada are more commonly found in an inner suburb. Family status is also not without importance. British non-family households, for example, are concentrated in an inner suburb. These variations reflect what we observed generally with respect to intraurban residential mobility. Locational decisions by those even of the same ethnic group will vary according to household requirements and economic and cultural resources.

2. Consistent with the independence of ethnic status as a dimension of social differentiation, variations in ethnic residential segregation cannot be explained by reference solely to differences in socioeconomic status (Darroch and Marston, 1971). To illustrate, those of both the British and Jewish groups are overrepresented at the upper levels of the socioeconomic dimensions; yet, as Table 56 reveals, they are not concentrated in the same areas of Toronto. Likewise, although the Italian and Slavic occupational distributions are not dissimilar, their residential patterns are. Ethnic affiliations and identities thus continue to exercise an important influence not only on urban social organization, as we argued in chapter 6, but also on spatial structure.

3. Expanding on the first point made above, in chapter 5 we distinguished among the concepts of ethnicity, ethnic affiliation, ethnic group, and ethnic community. Typically, as we have seen, ecological research subsumes these within the more general term "ethnic status." This tends, however, to conceal the complexity of this basis of differentiation. That is, contrary to the rather oversimplified approach of social area analysis, ethnic status can be measured in terms of at least six separate indices—national or ethnic origin, race, religion, immigrant status (i.e., period of immigration), birthplace, and language (Darroch and Marston, 1969). Although this is not shown in Table 56, each of these manifests a relatively independent pattern of residential segregation. Residential dissimilarity occurs in significant variations along each dimension, at least in Toronto. For example, with respect to religion, the Jewish group tends to be highly segregated residentially from Catholics and Protestants. A low level of segregation exists between groups from Northern and Western Europe; yet those from Southern and Eastern Europe are not only relatively segregated from both of these, but also from each other.

The various dimensions of ethnic status are independent. One cannot be subsumed within another; each exercises an independent influence on residential segregation. Hence, it can be argued that "a representation of the degree of residential integration and assimilation among ethnic groups may depend to a larger extent on the particular dimension to which reference is made" (Darroch and Marston, 1969: 86). To achieve a comprehensive understanding of the ecological distribution of ethnic collectivities in any city it is necessary to take account of all the components of ethnic status. This has not yet been adequately done in urban ecological research.

Winnipeg. In chapter 7 we saw that, during the growth of Winnipeg in the late nineteenth and early twentieth centuries, the North End emerged as the area in which the foreign-born were concentrated. Such residential segregation profoundly influenced the contemporary spatial structure of this city. In 1941, the French were clustered in St. Boniface, while the Jews, Ukrainians, and Poles were still located primarily in the North End (Driedger, 1978b). It is of interest to examine what modifications in this distribution subsequently occurred.

Fromson (1965) explored the changes between 1951 and 1961 in the city's ethnic distribution. Recall from chapter 4 that this was a period of rapid growth, with the metropolitan area's population increasing by more than a third. Figure 13 presents indices of residential segregation for selected ethnic groups in 1951 and 1961. As can be seen, the level of residential segregation for the British was relatively low; in contrast, the Jewish group—as elsewhere—showed the highest degree of segregation for both years, actually displaying some increase in concentration over the decade. Overall, there were no significant declines in residential segregation of the remaining groups, although most did show some modest decreases. In addition, the overall pattern was maintained during the period: "the relative positions of the ethnic groups to each other with respect to residential segregation were very similar in the period measured" (Fromson, 1965: 42).

Residents of British origin continued to be concentrated in the southern census tracts of the city. What change did occur consisted of greater movement *within* that section—that is, outward migration from the older inner-city areas to new subdivisions on the fringe, but still within the southern sector. It should be noted, however, that all parts of the metropolitan area contained at least a small proportion of residents from this group, thus accounting for the relatively low level of segregation in comparison to other ethnic groups, such as the Jewish and Asiatic.

The North End remained the locale for the city's Poles (Driedger, 1978b). During these years (1951-1961) immigrants from Yugoslavia and Southern Europe, as well as Native Indians, became more evident here also. However, as the Jews achieved higher socioeconomic status they moved out of the North End.

As Table 57 reveals, those of Jewish origin experienced significant change spatially during the decade. They maintained the highest level of residential segregation of any ethnic group in the city; a process of redistribution, however, still occurred. The Jewish proportion in the North End declined substantially. That section of the city adjoining the North End—West Kildonan—showed, on the other hand, a significant increase, as did River Heights in Winnipeg South. In short, "although there has been a change in the areas of high [Jewish] concentration, the degree of concentration has not decreased" (Fromson, 1965: 97).

Winnipeg's French community also sustained a relatively high level of segregation (Driedger, 1978b). Among both the Jewish and French groups residential segregation was correlated with a strong ethnic institutional base.

Figure 13: Index of Residential Segregation* for Selected Ethnic Groups, Metropolitan Winnipeg, 1951 and 1961

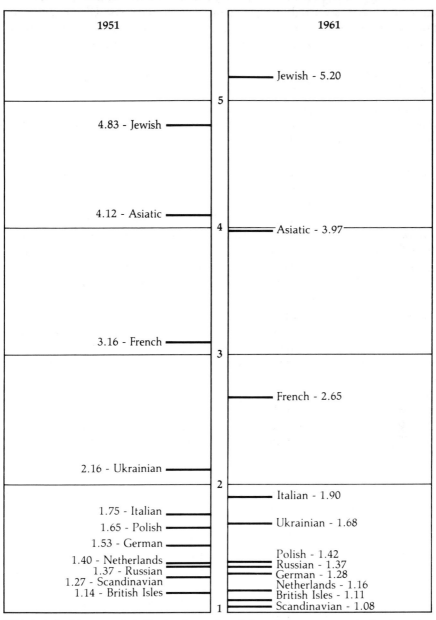

*This is derived from a ratio indicating the number of times the average concentration is greater than the group's percentage in the total population of the area studied: the higher the value of the index, the greater the degree of segregation.

From Fromson, 1965. Reprinted by permission of the author.

Table 57:   Change in the Percentage of the Jewish Group, by Selected Metro Sub-
Areas, 1951 to 1961

Metro sub-areas	Percent of total group		% Change
	1951	1961	
Winnipeg North	66.9	33.7	− 33.2
Winnipeg South	11.9	27.0	15.1
West Kildonan	11.6	31.7	20.1

Adapted from Fromson, 1965.

Each group showed a higher level of institutional completeness than other
ethnic groups in the city (Driedger and Church, 1974). Yet there were important differences between the Jews and the French. Intraurban migration among
the French occurred within the St. Boniface area where they had traditionally
been concentrated, and where many of their ethnic institutions had been
located. In contrast, as we have seen, the Jewish group showed a high rate of
interarea mobility. Despite their mass exodus from the North End, the Jews
maintained their ethnic cohesion by transferring their institutions to the new
areas in the city where they concentrated. Unlike the French, Jewish religious
congregations "are not organized around a spatial parish; also many of their
parochial schools and synagogues are relatively small in size so they can afford
to move them. More important, however, with their emphases on endogamy
and choice of Jewish friends, the Jews tend to seek out neighbourhoods where
their ingroup members may congregate, bringing their institutions with them"
(Driedger and Church, 1974: 49). The Jewish and French groups thus represent
two different "segregation-mobility" patterns. In both cases, however, a
strong association was manifested between institutional completeness and
residential segregation—factors which sustained their ethnic solidarity and inhibited assimilation. With respect to other ethnic groups, these factors were
less pronounced. For example, the weak institutional base of Scandinavians
was reflected in the fact that when they moved from their area of concentration, unlike the Jews, they did not re-establish their pattern of segregation
elsewhere. Similarly, other groups not exhibiting institutional completeness
(such as the Germans) were less likely to be residentially concentrated. Both
the Scandinavians and Germans, over time, culturally and spatially merged
more fully with the wider community. Such contrasts between the French and
Jews on the one hand and the Scandinavians and Germans on the other suggest
the close connection that exists between the institutional viability of an ethnic
social system and its ecological distribution. Both factors are mutually supportive, and together influence the ultimate fate of any urban ethnic group.

The continued residential concentration of the French and Jews from 1941
to 1971 fails to support the contention of population succession theory

—proposed within the classical ecological paradigm—that an ethnic group will over time inevitably disperse throughout the urban area, leaving the locale of first settlement to newer immigrant groups (Matwijiw, 1975: 4). Winnipeg does not show a consistent "pattern of sequential occupance in specific areas by different ethnic groups." The Asians, for example, are increasingly concentrated in the city centre; they are not, however, invading a pre-existing ethnic enclave. Similarly, the French enclave in St. Boniface has been able to retain its boundaries despite the appearance in Winnipeg of newer ethnic groups. We have observed some change in the North End's composition; however, Jewish relocation did not signify residential dispersion. The population succession theory is too facile a model of changes in urban ethnic location.

Summary

We have examined in some detail the patterns of ethnic residential segregation in two of Canada's major metropolitan communities, although we might have selected others (see, for example, Chandler, 1965; Walhouse, 1961; Villeneuve, 1971) for illustrative purposes. Some general themes emerge from the above review:

1. In terms of residential distribution, ethnic groups may be internally differentiated in characteristics such as socioeconomic class, length of residence in Canada, and family status.

2. The overall level of residential segregation of an ethnic group is not simply a function of its socioeconomic composition. Spatial distance or "residential dissimilarity" among urban ethnic collectivities is not necessarily a product of class or status differences.

3. The level of residential integration among ethnic groups ultimately can be understood only by measuring all the components of ethnic status—ethnic origin, race, religion, etc.

4. The exodus of members of an ethnic group from an area of concentration in the city does not necessarily lead to spatial diffusion. Particularly when coupled with a high level of institutional completeness, redistribution may lead to re-creation of a new area of concentration.

5. Sequential occupancy of the same area by different ethnic groups does not perforce occur. Once an ethnic enclave—such as the French community of St. Boniface—is established, it may resist encroachments by other ethnic groups. Again, the presence of a strong institutional base, enhancing a sense of cultural identity, strengthens the enclave's boundaries (Gale, 1972).

LINGUISTIC PLURALISM AND ECOLOGICAL STRUCTURE

To understand fully Canada's urban spatial mosaic we must examine the importance of linguistic pluralism. Linguistic segregation is an increasingly important feature of Canadian social structure. One striking manifestation of this trend is the concentration of Canadians of French mother-tongue within what has been termed the "Soo-Moncton area," an area 1,000 miles long, bounded on the west by a line drawn from Sault Ste. Marie through Ottawa to Cornwall and on the east by a line from Edmundston to Moncton (Joy, 1967: 23). The majority of Canadians who use French in their daily lives reside within this region. Those of French origin living in other parts of the country are increasingly being assimilated, relying solely on the English language. This sharpens language boundaries and promotes the segregated character of Canada's pattern of linguistic pluralism. As Table 58 indicates, the rate of French assimilation appears to be particularly pronounced in the metropolitan areas outside the Soo-Moncton line. Relatively few in numbers and faced with the necessity of adapting to local social and economic conditions, the French become bilingual. Without adequate institutional supports for the preservation of their language, the likelihood of young persons maintaining the native language at all diminishes considerably. Despite this trend, the overall distribution of the population in the two dominant language groups during the present century has not varied significantly: "Among those 5 years of age and older, between 1901 and 1961, the percentage able to speak English either alone or with another tongue increased from 78 to 81, a change of 3 per cent. During this period, the population able to speak French, either monolingually or along with English, remained unchanged at 32 per cent" (Lieberson, 1970: 31). Similarly, the proportion of bilingual persons remained at slightly more than one-tenth of the total population. Such stability has not been upset by the vast influx of post-war immigrants. Indeed, between 1931 and 1961 the proportion whose mother tongue (that is, the language first learned in childhood and still understood) was neither English nor French declined, showing a tendency toward greater homogeneity of the Canadian population in terms of mother tongue (Report of the Royal Commission, 1967: 27). Many of these immigrants, although contributing to the nation's ethnic diversity, adopt English as their second language and transmit this as the mother tongue to their children.

In view of the increasing political and social importance of language differences in Canada, it is essential that we grasp the nature of linguistic maintenance and change. Two basic issues must be distinguished (Lieberson, 1970): (1) What are the factors which lead to bilingualism? (2) What are the conditions under which a second language is transferred to children of bilingual or multilingual parents? The two sets of factors are not necessarily identical: bilingualism and mother-tongue intergenerational shifting cannot be viewed as inevitably correlated in all situations.

Bilingualism is a product of more than a single factor. It is affected by the patterns of segregation at the community and neighbourhood levels; this illustrates the influence ecological structure can have on individual characteristics. One central independent variable appears to be the type of community context or the mother-tongue composition of the local population.

Table 58: Language Retention Rate of French Ethnic Group, Census Metropolitan Areas, 1971

Census Metropolitan Area	Language retention rate*
Calgary	7.8
Chicoutimi-Jonquière	98.8
Edmonton	20.0
Halifax	12.9
Hamilton	17.4
Kitchener	17.0
London	7.4
Montreal	95.8
Ottawa-Hull	80.4
Quebec	98.6
Regina	7.7
St. Catharines-Niagara	38.7
St. John's	7.9
Saint John	24.6
Saskatoon	13.3
Sudbury	67.6
Thunder Bay	10.1
Toronto	17.0
Vancouver	11.2
Victoria	7.2
Windsor	18.3
Winnipeg	35.3

*The language retention rate is the percentage of an ethnic group's population which reported the corresponding language as the language most often spoken at home.

From Frederick I. Hill, ed., *Canadian Urban Trends* Vol. II © Ministry of Supply and Services, 1976. Reprinted by permission of Copp Clark Pitman, Publishers.

This can be readily demonstrated by examining the patterns of bilingualism in a small number of selected cities which vary according to the degree to which the French mother-tongue residents form a minority (Lieberson, 1970).

Edmonton and Toronto. In both of these cities French represents the mother tongue of only a very small minority of the residents. Almost all of these are found to be bilingual, with little difference between the sexes. Significantly, the French learn English at a young age because of the necessity of adapting to the English-dominated local institutions and social life. The acquisition of this second language occurs well before entry into the labour force—indeed, before beginning elementary school. What little bilingualism exists among the English, in contrast, is a result of pressures stemming from particular occupations. Hence, sex differences in bilingualism are more likely for the English.

Quebec City. This community represents the other extreme. French is the mother tongue for the vast majority of residents. Yet, reflecting a national pattern, bilingualism is "far more frequent among the French mother-tongue residents of Quebec than is the acquisition of French among the English residents of Toronto or Edmonton" (Lieberson, 1970: 111). Community pressures to adopt a second language appear less effective among the English in Quebec than among the French in Toronto and Edmonton. As an additional contrast to the situation in the latter, Quebec's French who are bilingual do not become so at an early age. Their bilingualism appears to be a result solely of occupational pressures. White-collar jobs in many cases demand fluency in English as a condition of employment, reflecting the dominance of English in the nation's economic institutions. Since French-speaking men in Quebec are more subject to these pressures, their rate of bilingualism is higher than that for women residents. Such a difference between the sexes does not appear in Toronto or Edmonton because they both are subject to the same neighbourhood and community pressures.

Sudbury and Ottawa-Hull. In both of these cities the French and English mother-tongue groups are approximately equal in number. Yet, there are interesting differences in the pattern of bilingualism between the two communities. French children in Sudbury are more frequently bilingual than their Ottawa-Hull counterparts. On the other hand,

> . . . the job market in Ottawa, which is greatly influenced by the federal government's requirements, provides a strong incentive to acquire English. Consequently, despite higher bilingualism among the early ages in Sudbury, the rates are almost as great in adult working years for men in Ottawa-Hull. . . . Consistent with this interpretation is the fact that there is more of a male-female gap in the French bilingualism rate in Ottawa compared to the very slight gap in Sudbury among adults. This may be interpreted as reflecting the greater importance of occupational pressures in Ottawa as an impetus to the acquisition of English (Lieberson, 1970: 114).

Although the rate of bilingualism appears higher among French mother-tongue children in Edmonton and Toronto because of their minority status, French adult residents of Sudbury and Ottawa are as frequently bilingual as those in the other two centres.

These findings clearly suggest that variations in community composition correlate with the differences in patterns of bilingualism. Additional research is required to explain these correlations more fully.

In order to examine the consequences of population composition at a more immediate level, it is useful to explore the relationship between bilingualism and degree of residential segregation between French and English ethnic groups. It can be hypothesized that a high level of segregation will be correlated with a low bilingualism "because it reduces the need for acquiring another language for residentially based activities such as shopping, neighboring, and the like" (Lieberson, 1970: 129). Data from thirteen cities confirm this. French is less commonly the mother tongue of those residents of French ethnicity in communities where segregation is not pronounced. Relatively high levels of ethnic segregation, conversely, are correlated with low bilingualism. These patterns hold not only for the French, but for residents of non-French ethnic groups as well. Although the importance of this ecological factor is confirmed overall, it does appear that the influence of segregation on bilingualism varies according to the mother-tongue composition of the whole city. For example, "In wards in which 70 to 90 percent of the residents are native speakers of French, the acquisition of French among the remaining residents varies from about a third in Ottawa (where only 30 percent of the total residents had French as their mother tongue) to 47 percent in Montreal (two-thirds had French as a mother tongue) and 67 percent in Quebec (90 percent had French as a mother tongue)" (Lieberson, 1970: 133). The acquisition of English as a second language, in contrast, is more likely in Ottawa than in Quebec. Thus, the influence of residential segregation on bilingualism can be lessened or strengthened by community-wide pressures deriving from the general mother-tongue composition of the city's population. Female bilingualism is more closely a function of the level of residential segregation, perhaps reflecting women's greater integration into the local neighbourhood. Male bilingualism, in contrast, is more closely linked to occupational demands which exist regardless of locale. This difference between the sexes is not equally pronounced among all cities.

Turning next to patterns of intergenerational shifting in mother tongue among children of bilingual parents, community composition and residential segregation again appear important. Intergenerational shifting in mother tongue among French bilinguals is less common when they are more segregated from those who speak English only than from French monolinguals. In general, the level of retention appears to vary inversely with "the probability of bilinguals interacting randomly with English monolinguals in their residential neighborhood" (Lieberson, 1970: 216).

The overall pattern of residential segregation among bilinguals, English monolinguals, and French monolinguals varies significantly from city to city. To illustrate, in Montreal both British and French bilinguals are residentially integrated with monolinguals of their respective ethnic groups (Lieberson, 1965). Each is relatively segregated from the monolinguals and even bilinguals of the opposite ethnic group. This pattern is repeated to a lesser degree in Ottawa. In Edmonton, however, a complete reversal is evidenced among French bilinguals. These are "actually less segregated from those British who speak only English than they are from the small number of ethnic compatriots who speak only French" (Lieberson, 1970: 218). This is a community, it will be recalled, in which the French constitute a very small minority. Such a residential pattern is not particularly functional for the preservation of their language. In contrast, Edmonton's British bilinguals are segregated from French monolinguals. Through all these three cities, therefore, the British residential pattern is such as to encourage intergenerational mother-tongue retention. This is less true for the French.

Reflecting these patterns, British monolinguals and bilinguals do not differ substantially in terms of socioeconomic status in these cities. Such close homogeneity facilitates residential integration, which in turn strengthens the retention of English as mother tongue in the next generation. French bilinguals do manifest higher levels of income and occupational status in comparison with French monolinguals (Report of the Royal Commission, 1969). Differences in class, however, promote "greater [residential] segregation among the French segments in the very same cities in which, demographically speaking, they are most vulnerable to intergenerational language shift, namely where English is the numerically dominant language. Hence the cities where bilingualism among the French is greatest also have considerable segregation between the two linguistic components of the group" (Lieberson, 1970: 220-21). This spatial distribution, as has been seen, discourages retention of French as a mother tongue among children of French bilinguals who are residentially integrated with the English. Class differences weaken the ability of common ethnic membership to serve as a basis of residential location, which, in turn, has important negative consequences for the maintenance of French in the next generation.

SUMMARY

1. Socioeconomic status, family status, and ethnic status are important bases of urban differentiation in Canada.

2. Nevertheless, depending on such factors as size and homogeneity of an urban community, the relative importance of these dimensions varies among cities. Additional bases of differentiation frequently appear.

3. The three fundamental dimensions are also complex. Socioeconomic status is not necessarily a single differentiating axis across urban Canada, nor is family status one-dimensional.

4. With respect to spatial distribution in most Canadian cities socioeconomic status follows a sectoral pattern, and family status is arrayed zonally in direct relation to distance from the centre. Departures from these general patterns, however, do occur. The spatial patterns that ethnic status manifests fluctuate among cities.

5. Residential segregation is greatest among groups occupying extreme positions on the socioeconomic dimension.

6. Cities with a higher degree of family-income disparity will manifest greater residential segregation among income groups.

7. In most metropolitan communities, low-income groups are clustered in proximity to the central business district.

8. The bases of social differentiation may be modified over time in response to such factors as urban expansion and the volume of migration and immigration.

9. The spatial distribution of these dimensions of differentiation also may change over time. One possible model of these changes argues that as cities grow and age their residential structures will evolve in a predictable direction from the pattern of "wealthy at the centre" and "poor at the periphery" to the reverse outlined in Burgess's scheme. Although evidence appears to substantiate this in the American context, such a prediction does not gain clear support in Canadian cities where changes in socioeconomic composition more commonly follow sectoral paths. The evolutionary hypothesis is applicable, however, in terms of family status which over time assumes a clearer zonal distribution.

10. The "sorting-out" of those with similar economic, social, or ethnic characteristics through residential mobility accounts for the spatial distribution of the fundamental bases of urban differentiation.

11. Intraurban mobility is a function especially of changes in household size and composition or stage in the family life cycle. As the number of children in the family increases, the demand for greater space encourages relocation at greater distances from the city centre. The gradient distribution of family status thus emerges.

12. Economic constraints also influence intraurban migration and help shape the sectoral distribution of socioeconomic status. Middle-income families move within a greater range of locations than those at either end of the socioeconomic dimension; this accounts for the lesser degree of residential segregation found among the former.

13. The motivations for intraurban mobility vary according to the type of housing and location selected. Central city highrises, for example, attract those in the early and later stages of the family life cycle because this type of housing best satisfies their need for accessibility to the downtown.

14. The formation of a spatial enclave within the city helps to strengthen the cohesiveness of an ethnic community.

15. Ethnic residential segregation is more intense in Canada's larger cities. It is not, however, necessarily correlated with the level of ethnic diversity in a community, although cities which contain a high proportion of non-British residents do manifest clear patterns of ethnic residential segregation.

16. Ethnic groups themselves differ in their levels of residential segregation. The Jewish population tends to be the most segregated in metropolitan Canada, followed by the Native Indians and the Italians. Such variations reflect an array of factors, including strength of cultural identity, proportion of a group retaining its own language and which is foreign-born, and level of institutional completeness.

17. More precise examination of patterns of ethnic segregation in Toronto and Winnipeg reveals several interesting themes—for example, that the residential distribution of those in the same ethnic group varies by class and family status, that an ethnic group's overall level of residential segregation is not solely a product of its general position on the socioeconomic dimension, and that all the components of ethnic status must be measured to grasp fully the com-

plexity of ethnic segregation. These themes must be explored more widely on a comparative level across urban Canada.

18. The language retention rate of the French ethnic group is significantly less among residents of metropolitan areas outside the Soo-Moncton area. Loss of mother tongue is greatest among those living in cities where the French form a small minority.

19. Type of community context or mother-tongue composition of the local population correlates with degree of bilingualism. For example, the acquisition of English by the French occurs at an early age in cities such as Edmonton and Toronto where French is the mother tongue of only a small minority. However, community pressures to adopt a second language appear less effective among the English in Quebec than among the French in Toronto and Edmonton.

20. The greater the degree of residential segregation, the lower the level of bilingualism.

21. The influence of residential segregation on bilingualism can be strengthened or offset by community-wide pressures from the overall mother-tongue composition of the city's population.

22. Female bilingualism is more closely linked to the level of residential segregation than is male bilingualism.

23. Community mother-tongue composition and residential segregation both influence intergenerational shifting in mother tongue among children of bilingual parents.

24. Residential segregation among bilinguals, English monolinguals, and French monolinguals varies across urban Canada. In a city such as Edmonton, French bilinguals are more segregated from French monolinguals than they are from British who speak only English. Such a pattern discourages French intergenerational mother-tongue retention.

25. French bilinguals tend to be of higher socioeconomic status than French monolinguals. Such differences promote greater residential segregation between them, which in turn discourages retention of French as a mother tongue among children of French bilinguals who live in anglophone neighbourhoods.

Part Five

Urbanism

As we observed in the Introduction, another major area of study in urban sociology is the structure of urban social organization. In this Part we shall survey selected aspects of "urbanism," or the social life found within cities. We shall look first analytically at the fate of kinship and community in the urban system; this will be balanced with a more holistic view of the structures of inner-city and suburban communities.

In chapter 1 we noted how the classical analyses of urban social organization generated a typological perspective elaborated, for example, in the work of Robert Redfield. In contrasting the urban with the non-urban, emphasis is given to the decline in significance of the local community and all primary intermediate groups. Like kinship, the neighbourhood is seen as increasingly of little importance. The assumption is that intimate and familial-like relationships are now no longer pronounced. Urbanites are related functionally rather than by close moral ties. In addition, this paradigm emphasizes the problem of social order in the city. With the demise of the traditional bases of social solidarity, concern is manifested for the apparent disorganization of the city and for the manner in which the individual can now be integrated into the urban system.

It is important to recall that Redfield, in particular, emphasized that his theoretical scheme represents only one step toward a more comprehensive understanding of urban social structure. Subsequent research has indeed demonstrated the inadequacies of that model and the need to take fuller account of the complex ways in which urban residents organize their social lives. Despite the proliferation of secondary relationships in the city, primary group ties continue to be important to urbanites. In the following chapters we shall examine the fruits of this research.

Chapter 9

The Fate of Kinship and Community in the Urban System

A central task of urban sociology is the delineation of those types of relationships and institutions which structure the social life of city residents. An added goal is the explanation of any variations in these social patterns. A significant research interest related to this task has been the fate of kinship and community in the urban system, which we shall explore in this chapter.

URBAN KINSHIP

The fate of urban kinship represented an important topic in the classical literature on the city. Toennies, for example, saw the kinship bond as one of the clearest manifestations of Gemeinschaft. He proposed that with the increasing dominance of the Gesellschaft mode of life, the centrality of the family and its integration into a wider kinship network were becoming less apparent. This theme reappeared in the works of many others considered to be the founders of urban sociology as a discipline. Wirth (1938: 21) summarized this position:

> The transfer of industrial, educational, and recreational activities to specialized institutions outside the home has deprived the family of some of its most characteristic historical functions. In cities mothers are more likely to be employed, lodgers are more frequently part of the household, marriage tends to be postponed, and the proportion of single and unattached people is greater. Families are smaller and more frequently without children than in the country. The family as a unit of social life is emancipated from the larger kinship group characteristic of the country, and the individual members pursue their own diverging interests in their vocational, educational, religious, recreational, and political life.

Redfield found evidence to support this position in his comparison of the Yucatan communities. Tusik, the tribal community, displayed strong familial organization, integrated extended family systems, and the wide applicability of kinship terms. Urban Merida manifested the opposite. From this Redfield delineated an ideal type of folk society in which kinship relations occupy a dominant position; the urban counterpart de-emphasizes such bonds.

This typological perspective crystallized in the formulation of the isolated nuclear family thesis, espoused particularly by Talcott Parsons.

The Isolated Nuclear Family Thesis

Parsons' (1959; 1964a; 1964b) primary interest was in the delineation of the place of kinship in modern industrial-urban society. Through a formal, cultural analysis he proposed that the contemporary kinship system is characterized by a set of interlocking conjugal families. The uniqueness of this arrangement rests especially in "the absence of any important terminologically recognized units which cut across conjugal families, including some members and excluding others" (Parsons, 1959: 242). The nuclear family is, in short, structurally isolated, not being integrated into any wider kinship unit.

As Figure 14 illustrates, Parsons depicted this system as an "onion"-type structure. The inner circle is composed of the two conjugal families within which "ego" (the individual from whose perspective this system is traced) holds membership—the "family of orientation" (which he enters through birth) and the "family of procreation" (which he enters through marriage). Despite this pattern of common membership, the two families are structurally separated. Tracing through the linkages in the outer circle reveals an essential symmetry. The conjugal units are interconnected by a common member. No predominant emphasis is given to either the patrilineal or matrilineal side. Except for the prohibition of marriage between kin, the whole system is characterized by an underlying openness. The formation of a family of procreation establishes new linkages between previously unconnected kinship groups.

The structural isolation of the conjugal family is further revealed in that it constitutes the ordinary unit of residence, geographically and economically independent of other kin. This is most fully realized in the urban middle class. It is among this group, Parsons believed, that the nuclear family isolation thesis has greatest applicability. Particularly within this segment the marriage bond holds prime importance over other possible kinship ties. This demonstrates the close interrelation which exists between the kinship and occupational systems of contemporary society. Parsons argued that as a consequence of the emphasis on functional achievement, the occupational system requires that other sectors containing contrasting orientations be segregated. The kinship structure, especially with its emphasis on ascribed roles (such as that of son, acquired without individual choice) and particularistic relations (involving obligations specific to these roles), needs to be restricted in its sphere of influence. Parsons proposed that isolation of the nuclear family is the most func-

Figure 14: Parsonian Depiction of Contemporary Kinship System

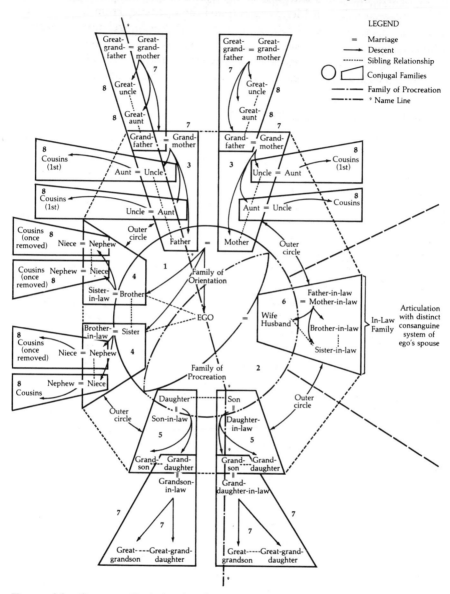

Types of families: 1 = Ego's family of orientation; 2 = Ego's family of procreation; 3 = First-degree ascendant families; 4 = First-degree collateral families; 5 = First-degree descendant families; 6 = In-law family; 7 = Second-degree ascendant and descendant families; 8 = Second-degree collateral families.

tional pattern in a society marked by high levels of urbanization and industrialization. The rapid rates of social and residential mobility in such a context demand the lessening of any inhibiting kinship bonds beyond those found within the immediate family. Detachment from strong allegiances to kin, in short, constitutes an important prerequisite to the most efficient functioning of that occupational structure characteristic of the modern industrial-urban community. Substantially the same conclusion was drawn by several others (Linton, 1959; Schneider and Homans, 1955) who supported the isolation thesis.

The isolated nuclear family thesis represents a continuation of the classical and typological view of the fate of kinship in the urban system. It constitutes a translation of that interpretation into a general position on the role of kinship in the contemporary city, characterized by high levels of role specialization and mobility (cf. Gibson, 1972).

The Rediscovery of Urban Kinship

Just as in time there emerged empirical evidence to challenge other features of the typological perspective of urban social organization, so too was the isolated nuclear family thesis the object of substantial critical review. Urban kinship was "rediscovered" and the complexity of this bond more fully appreciated (e.g., Axelrod, 1956; Sharp and Axelrod, 1956; Greer, 1956; Coult and Habenstein, 1962; Adams, 1968; Aiken and Goldberg, 1969; Firth, Hubert and Forge, 1970; Carns, Goldenberg, and Greer, 1973; Rosenberg and Anspach, 1973; Stack, 1974; Goldenberg, 1977).

To illustrate, in a series of studies conducted in Cleveland and elsewhere, Sussman (1959: 334; 1953) provided evidence suggesting "that many neolocal families are closely related within a matrix of mutual assistance and activity which results in an interdependent kin related family system rather than the currently described model of the isolated nuclear family." Sussman found that almost all middle-class and working-class households interviewed were engaged in patterns of mutual aid with their kin. Parsons had proposed that the isolation of the nuclear family reached its fullest development among the middle class. Yet Sussman (1959: 338) found that it was precisely among this group in which the amount of help exchanged among kin was greatest:

> The middle more than the working class are in a better position to give financial help and expensive gifts; and non-working middle-class grandmothers are more likely to be "free" to take care of grandchildren. The offering of advice, most likely to be given by the parent to the child, reflects middle more than working class occupational status and child rearing patterns.

In short, the isolated nuclear family thesis is "more fiction than fact." Reflecting a traditional bias emphasizing urban social disorganization, it fails to give full recognition to the manner in which urban families are linked with kin in "complicated matrices of aid and service activities" (Sussman and Burchinal,

1969: 362). A more appropriate view is that of an interdependent kin-related family system to replace the stereotype of the atomized family. In such a system, Litwak (1960a, 1960b) has shown, ties with kin are not necessarily disrupted by occupational or geographical mobility. In a wide variety of metropolitan areas, involvement in kinship networks appears to be an extremely important part of many residents' patterns of social participation. Such links provide urbanites with material and psychological support, and are sustained by the sense of obligation to maintain contact and by mutual concern for well-being. Ties with parents remain strong, as do those with siblings. Relations with more distant kin are more selective and respond to differences in personal compatibility (Carns, Goldenberg and Greer, 1973; Adams, 1968; Firth, Hubert, and Forge, 1970).

Historical Analysis of Urban Kinship

Examination of the significance of kinship relations in urban social organization is not restricted merely to the contemporary scene. More recently, attention has been given to this from a historical perspective, filling a critical gap (Hareven, 1977). As Laslett (1972a: 2) observed, there has been generally a lack of interest in the history of the family:

> Sociologists of the family have evidently been satisfied with contemporary materials and have tested their hypotheses about familial attitudes, the institution of marriage, and even the size and structure of the domestic group itself, with no more than occasional reference to the past.

Frequently, there has been the tendency to project from the present to the past by identifying family systems in underdeveloped countries as the predecessors of contemporary forms in more industrialized societies. This, Laslett pointed out, involves inappropriate assumptions.

One important consequence of this lack of historical research on the family is acceptance without question of the notion "that in the past the domestic group was universally and necessarily larger and more complex than it is today in industrial cultures" (Laslett, 1972a: 5). The view of a "classical extended family," existing prior to the emergence of the industrial-urban community—proposed in the isolation thesis—is derived from this assumption.

Laslett (1972b: 130) demonstrated that at least for England this interpretation is unwarranted. Examining the records of a large number of English parishes, he discovered that the mean household size remained at 4.75 persons from the late sixteenth century to the first decade of the twentieth century. This covered a span from the pre-industrial social order to a point well after industrialization and urbanization had become solidly established. Decline in household size, evident especially after 1911, occurred only in the later stages of industrialization.

In addition, traditional English households, prior to the industrial-urban age, did not appear to contain resident kin. Only a small minority of the households had members representing more than two generations. The largest households were found among the upper socioeconomic strata, reflecting the presence of many servants.

Although much more research in this area is needed, the relative constancy of mean household size from the late 1500s to the early 1900s cannot be dismissed, nor the more general implications of this pattern ignored:

> There is no sign of the large extended coresidential family group of the traditional peasant world giving way to the small, nuclear conjugal household of modern industrial society. In England in fact, . . . the large joint or extended family seems never to have existed as a common form of the domestic group at any point in time covered by known numerical records (Laslett, 1972b: 126).

Such a historical clarification suggests, as do the initial empirical challenges discussed above, the need to revise significantly the isolated nuclear family thesis. Indeed, extending this historical analysis, on the basis of his study of kinship in the Union Park community of Chicago during the late 1800s, Sennett (1970) concluded that the nuclear family was *not* more adapted to the constraints of the urban-industrial order. On the contrary, it represented a means of retreat from the perceived disorder and complexity characteristic of the rapidly growing city.

During the latter half of the nineteenth century, Chicago underwent dramatic changes in demographic and economic structures. Its population doubled each decade after the Great Fire of 1871 and, concomitantly, its status as a marketing centre, initially oriented to the immediate area, assumed much broader regional and national concerns. Its economic activities were increasingly conducted in highly bureaucratic organizations. The instability of class position across generations, the emergence of large, bureaucratized structures, and "the shifting character of the division of labor in the work force" all created a sense of fear among many in the middle class. Involvement in the small intense or nuclear family was a means by which some sense of security could be attained. It was not, however, conducive to upward mobility. Those living in nuclear families were unable to respond to opportunities for status advancement and to pass on this capacity to their sons: "in the intensive families the father did not exhibit to the sons a pattern or a model of successful adaptation to work in a way that was present in the other homes" (Sennett, 1970: 178-79). Not only were sons of nuclear families less likely to be upwardly mobile than those in extended families, but they were also much less likely to move out of Union Park. This retreat from participation in the city's rapidly expanding economy was paralleled by their physical attachment to the place in which they had spent their childhood.

Such patterns suggest that the Parsonian assumption as to the greater functionality of the isolated nuclear family in the emerging industrial-urban system is open to question on historical grounds (cf. also Anderson, 1971;

Shorter, 1975; Griffen and Griffen, 1975; Hareven, 1975, 1977; Hareven and Langenbach, 1978).

CANADIAN URBAN KINSHIP PATTERNS

In examining the fate of kinship in Canadian cities it is important that a historical perspective be adopted, as Laslett and Sennett have done. Although a detailed history of the urban family (cf. Young and Willmott, 1973; Shorter, 1975) remains obscure, we must recognize that, with respect to the Parsonian thesis, industrialization initially affected families in the commercial city (Katz, 1975). In a community such as mid-nineteenth-century Hamilton, the vast majority of households were simple in structure. Nevertheless, many expanded for a time to include relatives, boarders, or servants; as these left, the households contracted. Only among the relatively wealthy were households extended on a more stable basis. As Hamilton became industrialized between 1851 and 1871, a larger proportion of young people remained at home with their parents for a longer period of time. Young men went to school longer and entered the labour force later. Their dependency on their immediate kin thus increased during early adulthood. The implications of these patterns in the commercial city of the nineteenth century for understanding the role of kinship in urban social organization are at this point ambiguous.

In contrast, the importance of that role in contemporary Canadian cities is clear. For example, a recent survey of residents in the metropolitan Toronto borough of East York reveals that half of all their intimate ties are with kin (Wellman, 1978, 1979), many of whom are spatially dispersed. Through such links mutual assistance and support are exchanged (Shulman, 1976), particularly between parents and their children. The significance of kinship for urbanites persists, even though it may not function in the form of a large, closely integrated network of extended kin relations (Wellman, 1978, 1979).

PARENTAL TIES OF ADULT URBANITES

Let us illustrate the importance of urban kinship ties by examining the relationships among a small sample of young, native-born, Anglophone, lower-middle-class couples, most of whom have been married less than nine years, and their parents and parents-in-law (Irving, 1972). Little support for the isolation thesis exists when we review residential patterns, frequency of interaction, and the exchange of assistance.

Residential Proximity

Geographical integration between the generations is indeed quite high. Almost three-fourths of the sample have parents residing in the metro-

politan area, many in the same neighbourhood as their children. Such proximity reflects the fact that most of the young adults are native Torontonians. "Bilateral symmetry" is manifested in that no differences exist between husbands and wives in terms of parental proximity. Geographical closeness to the older generation is not something which these young adults evaluate negatively. Most actually prefer that their parents live nearby—that is, within the metropolitan area, but not necessarily in the same neighbourhood. One apparent reason for this is their "desire to control the frequency of interaction with parents. They wanted parents and parents-in-law close enough so that if and when they chose to visit them, they would be readily available" (Irving, 1972: 45-46). This points indirectly to the significance their parents have for them.

Interaction Frequency

These Torontonians are in close contact with their parents. Three-fourths having these kin as co-residents of the city or neighbourhood visit them at least weekly. The minority, whose parents live farther away, see them less often. Reflecting the underlying sense of obligation to keep in contact, the degree of interaction is not a direct function of feelings of closeness toward parents. Yet, those who do rely on their parents for emotional support are in more frequent contact.

Consistent with the importance of this kinship bond and their stage of life cycle, it is the young married couples who initiate contact. Participation in common ritual activities, such as birthdays and anniversaries, are important foci of interaction. The significance of such contacts for these young adults in their daily lives is clearly revealed in that almost one-third see their parents socially more frequently than any other persons. The telephone also serves as a common means of maintaining contact.

Both husbands and wives are in more frequent contact—personally, by telephone, and through letters—with their own parents than with parents-in-law. Parelleling the symmetry with regard to residential proximity, husbands and wives do not differ in terms of frequency of contact with their own parents. In contrast, as Rosenberg and Anspach (1973) found among the working class of Philadelphia, husbands appear to spend more time with their in-laws than wives do with theirs. One reason for this "is that the wives' mothers visited more frequently than the husbands' mothers . . ." (Irving, 1972: 56). Additional differences between the sexes also emerged. Wives telephone their parents more frequently than do husbands. Significantly, mothers and mothers-in-law respond more commonly with the wives. Finally, wives write to their parents-in-law on a more sustained basis than husbands do to theirs. In short, "wives represent the emotional or expressive element of the family and *are therefore expected to be the locus for interaction with parents and parents-in-law" (Irving, 1972: 58).*

Mutual Aid

Considering both instrumental aid and emotional support, the importance of parents to these urbanites is clear. Almost half had lived with their parents or in-laws during the early years of their marriage. Although this had been necessary for economic reasons, it was not viewed as the most satisfactory arrangement. As soon as it had become feasible, they established their own households.

The most common type of aid parents offer their adult children is care during illness—especially at the birth of grandchildren. Sussman (1959) found the same in Cleveland. In addition, parents—chiefly the wives' mothers—frequently function as babysitters. Not unexpectedly, more recently married couples receive greater help from parents than those married for at least five years. However, many prefer not to discuss major decisions with their parents for fear "that there would be bad feelings if they chose not to take their parents' advice" (Irving, 1972: 68). During times of crisis, on the other hand, parents are seen as quite helpful. These young couples reciprocate. While they are less prone to give direct financial aid to their parents, they seek to help them in turn by doing home repairs or caring for them when they are ill.

Overall, these patterns clearly demonstrate what research in other contexts has also shown (e.g., Pineo, 1965): the significance of the parental bond to these urban residents and the inappropriateness of overemphasizing their social and functional isolation.

Geographical Mobility and Urban Kinship Patterns

The isolation thesis assumed that the high level of mobility in an urban society encourages the loosening of kinship bonds. Such an assumption is not supported by research done, for example, in Montreal and Fredericton. Osterreich's (1971) and Butler's (1967) examinations of this hypothesis reveal:

1. Geographical mobility does not necessarily reduce the size of the "kin universe"—that is, all consanguineous relatives still living whom the individual recognizes (cf. Cowley, 1972).

2. The average number of kinsmen with whom some form of contact is at least minimally maintained does not differ significantly between mobile and non-mobile urbanites.

3. Non-mobiles do have greater face-to-face contact with relatives. An-

nual visits and communicating by letter are more important forms of contact with kin for mobiles.

4. Geographical mobility does not weaken the sense of obligation to give assistance to kin, especially parents and siblings, when they are in need. Mobiles and non-mobiles show no differences in "kin-orientation"—that is, in recognition of the special features of the kinship bond. Both gain some psychological support from kin and rely on them for assistance in time of need.

5. In spite of less frequent face-to-face contact, mobiles may retain close ties with extended kin because they provide a sense of emotional security and belongingness which may not be derived from the immediate community.

6. Factors other than geographical mobility—such as the death of central "connecting" relatives (or "kin keepers")—may be much more significant in terminating kinship ties.

French-Canadian Urban Kinship Patterns

In view of the traditionally large size of French-Canadian families (Henripin, 1972: 170f.; Lamontagne and Falardeau, 1947) particular attention has been given to the fate of kinship ties among urban residents from this ethnic group. Garigue's (1956) exploratory research, for example, does not confirm the isolation thesis.

The range of genealogical knowledge in Garigue's sample is much greater than that reported elsewhere. An average of 215 relatives are recognized, with the majority from the individual's own or parental generation. The range of kinship knowledge decreases with age, but varies especially between the sexes. Women know a greater number of kin: "Not only was their knowledge of the total kin group greater, so that in a number of instances wives knew more of their husbands' kin than the husbands themselves did, but they also had a much greater knowledge of the affairs of the kin group" (Garigue, 1956: 1092-93). Reflecting such differences, women also have more frequent interaction with relatives. As a result, they form the major links among these households.

The tie between siblings represents the most important kinship bond for these French Canadians. Contact with both parents and siblings is sustained regardless of their geographical location. Beyond meeting the obligations to preserve their ties to immediate kin, location and personal preference govern the degree of contact with other more genealogically distant relatives. Visiting at Christmas or seeing them perhaps at an annual family reunion is frequently the most that is expected.

The significance of the kinship bond is also demonstrated in that many receive important services from relatives, including in some cases employment. Exchange of services is especially pronounced among consanguine kin of the same sex.

Garigue (1956: 1097-98) found evidence to suggest that while upward social mobility leads to some loss of contact with particular relatives, it does not, on the contrary, effect a total disruption of kinship ties:

> Certain formal ties are still recognized, and informants reported instances of a person helping his entire sibling group to move upward. Furthermore, a new kin group forms rapidly at the higher level. Social mobility does not seem to imply a complete loss of the recognition of kin obligations, but merely the movement from a kin group at one level to another kin group at a different level.

This underlines the "elasticity" that characterizes the French-Canadian urban kinship system. While formal ties are maintained with a core of close kin—that is, those in the individual's own and spouse's families or orientation—personal preference operates on a stronger basis in ties with other relatives. This is also manifested in the case of those who take Anglo-Saxon spouses: patterns of association are disrupted only with more distant kin.

The flexible character of this kinship system, Garigue argued, heightens its adaptability to the urban system. Kinship awareness and participation are not negatively affected by the urbanization process, as the classical view had proposed. The particular cultural values of the French Canadians help maintain these bonds:

> The hypothesis is offered that socialization in a family of many full siblings results in special perception of kinship obligations . . . children raised in large families accepted as normal the fact of having many children and the implications of multiple kinship recognition. French Canadians, one of the most prolific groups in the Western world, have made the tradition of a large sibling group one of the ideals of family life (Garigue, 1956: 1100).

As a result of the force of such values, urbanization in itself does not exercise a major independent influence on the kinship system.

Although Garigue's analysis has not been accepted by all (e.g., Rioux, 1961), more recent evidence has continued to confirm the importance of kin relations among urban French Canadians. For example, consistent with our earlier generalizations, Piddington (1965) found that geographical mobility does not disrupt these bonds among residents of St. Boniface, Manitoba. Several different "agencies of kinship liaison" are instrumental in helping them maintain contacts with kin in distant places. "Kin keepers" (cf. Firth, 1970) represent one such category:

> They are usually elderly women and keep up an extensive correspondence with geographically remote kin to whom they provide information about kin in Manitoba in return for news of the migrant and any kin who may be living in his vicinity (Piddington, 1963: 150).

The clustering of migrant kin in these distant places is a product of chain-migration. In addition to kin keepers, contacts are sustained by visits in the course of work. For example, those employed in train crews or as truck drivers stop off during their trips to visit relatives. As with kin keepers, this represents a means of indirect contact as well. That is, the visitors report news about relatives still residing in St. Boniface, and on their return provide additional information about kin living in other parts of Canada and the U.S. The size and significance of the sibling groups among French Canadians help to ensure the vitality of these bonds: "If a person has a large sibling group and his parents and cousins are members of similar groups, the chances are high that one of the individuals will sooner or later visit more remote parts of Canada and the U.S.A., and so establish the kind of indirect contact mentioned" (Piddington, 1965: 152). Intermarriage among distant kin is not uncommon within this group and also helps to sustain ties. Indeed, it may be the case that geographical distance is even less of a negative factor in kinship involvement among the French Canadians than among those of Anglo-Saxon origin. This remains to be tested.

This brief portrait reveals how the kinship system is adapted to the geographical and social mobility which occurs within the urban system. Social ties with kin are sustained through both direct and indirect means. They thus continue to form important sources of support and involvement.

THE FATE OF COMMUNITY IN THE URBAN SYSTEM

Almost twenty-five years ago Edward Shils (1957: 131) expressed a profound rejection of the classical image of urban society:

> As I see it, modern society is no lonely crowd, no horde of refugees fleeing from freedom. It is no "Gesellschaft", soulless, egotistical, loveless, faithless, utterly impersonal and lacking any integrative forces other than interest or coercion. It is held together by an infinity of personal attachments, moral obligations . . .

Criticizing nineteenth-century sociological thought for having ignored the place of primary groups in complex society, he pointed to the increasing recognition being given at the time to the role of "informal and intimate relations." In such areas as industrial sociology, sociometry, and social psychology, the research of Mayo, Moreno, and Lewin all demonstrated the need to see primary groups as not dated remnants of an earlier age, but integral parts of larger ongoing social structures. In short, there appeared to be a renaissance of the study of primary groups which was "leading to a more realistic awareness of the dynamic components of social life which operate in all spheres, those which are informally organized as well as those which are formally organized" (Shils, 1951: 69). Such a "renaissance" had important implications for the study of urban social life.

The Community of Limited Liability

Illustrating that "renaissance," one of the most significant initial challenges to the typological conception of urban social organization was Morris Janowitz'

The Community Press in an Urban Setting (1952). At the time of this study, the city of Chicago contained eighty-two community newspapers with a total weekly circulation of close to one million readers. This represented a substantial increase since 1910; during those years circulation had grown over 700 percent. These were English-language publications oriented to specific local areas within the metropolis. Adopting the classical typological perspective, this growth would have been puzzling. Such a counter-trend would have been explained away as a mere rural survival "destined to be eliminated in the so-called 'long run' " (Janowitz, 1967 ed.: 2) with the general decline in significance of the local community in the urban system. In contrast, Janowitz argued that the persistence of the local community press was indicative of the central functions it performed. It represented an important means through which the individual was integrated into the urban social structure and consensus on the local level maintained. Readership was concentrated especially among those closely tied to the local area: women, married couples, households containing children, long-time residents, and those whose own socioeconomic status parelleled that of their local community.

The local press, it is important to note, was not a substitute for the city-wide mass media. Insofar as the local press concentrated on events in the immediate area, it represented "an auxiliary not a competing news source with the daily press." Local involvement, in short, did not exclude broader orientations: urban residents effected a balance between involvement in local and non-local institutions. This demanded revision of traditional conceptualizations:

> Social scientific efforts to analyze community involvement have been dominated by a typology involving a sharp distinction between those individuals who display local community orientation and those who are reputed to have a broader or metropolitan outlook. At numerous points, the data at hand question the advisability of considering urban personality in these sharply opposing terms (Janowitz, 1967 ed.: 199)

An either-or framework is less appropriate generally than one which stresses *relative commitments* to both local and non-local social systems.

That the community press was read by most of the urban residents also suggested the need to recognize the importance of intermediate institutions within the local community. These exercised control over many individuals, and integrated them into the larger society. Janowitz found, for example, that those who were highly attached to the local area were also those with the greatest political knowledge and competence. Participation and confidence in the wider political structure were encouraged, not discouraged, by local community identification.

In summary, contrary to the typological scheme which assumed the demise of the local community as a significant social fact, Janowitz' research pointed to its continued role as an agent of integration and control. A more appropriate view is that of a community of limited liability. That is, "in varying degrees, the local community resident has a current psychological and social investment in his local community" (Janowitz, 1967 ed.: 211). Such involvement is particularly pronounced among those households faced with problems of child rearing, yet is limited by their need to take account of non-local institutions. The individual's allegiance to the local area is contingent on the community's ability to serve his needs. Should that not occur, what social and psychological investment has been developed is withdrawn.

Generalizing on the basis of this model, therefore, Janowitz (1967 ed.: 212) proposed:

> The resulting balance of social control at the local community level is one which leaves relatively untouched only a minority of residents, heavily involves another perhaps smaller group in the community, and creates varying degrees of involvement for the bulk of the residents.

As with urban kinship, the local community was "rediscovered," but the need to recognize the complexity of involvement in it among urban residents was also emphasized. Janowitz' research and that of others (e.g., Smith, Form, and Stone, 1954; Stone, 1954) pointed to the need to reconsider the fate of community in the urban system and thereby modify some of the assertions in classical urban theory.

Much the same conclusion was reached by other students of urban social life at the time. For example, Greer (1962: 21) observed that, in part, the crisis of the city is actually an intellectual one. The traditional images of the urban system reflect more nineteenth-century "laissez-faire" liberalism than they do current reality. Similarly, Gans (1962a: 628-29) attacked Wirth's characterization of urban life, noting that it is actually valid only for particular areas in the inner city, and can be challenged on three points:

> (a) the conclusions derived from a study of the inner city cannot be generalized to the entire urban area;
> (b) there is as yet not enough evidence to prove . . . that number, density, and heterogeneity result in the social consequences which Wirth proposed;
> (c) even if the causal relationship could be verified, it can be shown that a significant proportion of the city's inhabitants were, and are, isolated from these consequences by social structures and cultural patterns which they either brought to the city, or developed by living in it.

These criticisms parallel those made of the general folk-urban scheme.

In an attempt to clarify the fate of community in the urban system, an important area of concern has been the social significance of the urban neighbourhood. Attention has focused on the extent to which the neighbourhood is an important source of social participation and integration for city dwellers. As Mumford (1968: 59) has observed, the bond between those living near one another

. . . is perhaps the most primitive of social bonds, and to be within view of one's neighbors is the simplest form of association. Neighborhoods are composed of people who enter by the very fact of birth or chosen residence into a common life. Neighbors are people united primarily not by common origins or common purposes but by the proximity of their dwellings in space. This closeness makes them conscious of each other by sight and known to each other by direct communication, by intermediate links of association, or by rumor.

An important empirical issue, however, is the extent to which such *physical* proximity is translated into *social* propinquity. Janowitz' model of the "community of limited liability" only partially resolves this question.

Variations in the Urban Neighbourhood as a Local Community

Extending that model, we must analyze the urban neighbourhood as a multidimensional phenomenon. The various aspects of locality-based relationships include (Keller, 1968; Hunter, 1974, 1975):

1. *definition of the neighbour role*—that is, the set of norms that reflect and guide the type of contact among co-residents of a specific area in the city (cf. Useem, Useem, and Gibson, 1960);

2. the type of *neighbouring interaction* that actually occurs among co-residents;

3. the *symbolic-cultural* dimension of the neighbourhood, which includes *cognitive* definition of what the neighbourhood is, its *assessment* or evaluation (in terms of meeting particular needs, for example), and the sense of *attachment* it engenders among its residents.

As has been seen, classical urban theory proposed that the neighbourhood's social significance for urbanites has eroded (cf. McKenzie, 1968e; Roper, 1964; McClenahan, 1942). Yet subsequent research clearly demonstrated that any generalizations about the urban neighbourhood as a social fact must be derived not only from investigation of all the above dimensions but also of the various types of local areas within the urban community. With respect to the latter, for example, Bell and Boat (1957) found in San Francisco that informal participation with neighbours is more common among those residents of areas where family life especially is a dominant daily concern. Generalizations about "the" urban way of life, therefore, are imprecise if they fail to recognize that the social significance of the neighbourhood does vary systematically among different parts of the city.

Additional confirmation of this point came from a series of studies done in Los Angeles (Greer, 1972). Greer's analyses suggest

. . . that the disappearance of the "local community" and neighborhood in the city is far from complete. It is most nearly true in the highly urban area [i.e., one containing few children, few single-family detached dwellings, and many women in the labour force], but in those neighborhoods characterized by familism there is considerable vitality in local associations. This is evident in neighboring, local organization and church participation, readership of the local community press, and ability to name local leaders. It is accompanied by an attitude of commitment to the area as "home"—a place from which one does not want or expect to move. In participation and in felt permanence, the highly urban areas had a much weaker hold on their residents (Greer and Kube, 1959: 46-47).

Just as there was concern for identifying variations in the urban neighbourhood as a local community, so too was consideration given to those individual characteristics that appear to be most closely associated with high levels of involvement in the locality as a social system (e.g., Shuval, 1955, 1956; Tomeh, 1967). This research, again, was stimulated by the desire to refine the generalizations of classical urban theory. For example, Caplow (1964) found that neighbouring is most intense among San Juan women living in the best housing, from families with high socioeconomic status. Those most fully involved locally were also long-time residents of the area (cf. Kasarda and Janowitz, 1974).

In exploring generally the fate of the local community in the urban system it is particularly necessary to integrate these strands of neighbourhood research—that is, to articulate the relative influence of social contexts and individual characteristics on degree of involvement with neighbours.

The Theory of Opportunity Structures

One attempt to take both of these factors into account and thus provide a more comprehensive explanation of the apparent variations in neighbouring behaviour is the theory of opportunity structures (McGahan, 1972a; 1972b). In chapter 8 we explored the bases of urban internal differentiation. Contemporary factorial ecology has demonstrated that the city is a mosaic of subareas differentiated along such dimensions as socioeconomic status, family status, and ethnic status. Here we are examining the *social* consequences of this *spatial* structure (cf. Scheu, 1975). The following "model" consists of a series of empirical generalizations which emphasize the importance of family status:

1. *The ecological structure of the urban community in part consists of sub-areas differentiated in terms of familism* (Greer, 1962: 80-97). As we noted in chapter 8, it appears that in many Canadian cities this variable may be multidimensional. It is, in any case, a measure of lifestyle divergences: contrast, for example, the highly familistic way of life—in which orientation to child rearing and family living has predominance—with a type of career orientation in which child rearing is less central. Thus, a highly familistic sub-area in the city might be one in which there is high fertility, relatively few women in the labour force, and many single-family dwelling units. Recall again from

chapter 8, however, that at least in the Canadian urban context these three indices are not necessarily correlated.

In that chapter we also observed that the spatial distribution of the bases of urban differentiation is created through a "sorting-out" of those with similar economic, social, or ethnic characteristics in regularized patterns of intraurban residential mobility. In particular, individuals wishing to pursue a similar lifestyle tend to choose similar places to reside within the urban community, if their social rank and ethnicity permit (Fava, 1956: 37). Those who are committed to a familistic way of life tend to choose peripheral and suburban areas within which to reside. The consequence of similar locational choices is the ecological differentiation of lifestyles; that is, the development of primarily familistic areas as contrasted with other areas that are less so (Schmidt, 1975).

2. *The structure of opportunities for interaction of the neighbouring types varies directly according to the degree of familism of the specific subarea* (Nohara, 1968: 186-87; Greer and Orleans, 1968: 204). Interaction in spatially defined groups is encouraged by the following conditions, which are found most frequently in highly familistic neighbourhoods (Greer, 1962: 111-12): (a) "intersecting trajectories of action"—that is, the use of common or overlapping space for daily household tasks; (b) common routines during the day; (c) common needs (for example, maintenance of safety of children) which stimulate some degree of functional interdependence among households; and (d) the presence of children who, through mutual play, encourage interaction among their parents.

In general, the more familistic the neighbourhood, the more important the dwelling unit as a site for everyday life because of the large number of daily activities that centre on it. Surrounding households assume greater importance for the successful functioning of the resident's own home. This situation and the factors listed above serve as conditions for the occurrence of what Festinger (1950: 34) refers to as "passive contacts" among neighbours—that is, casual or involuntary meetings among the residents of an area.

3. *Since in a highly familistic area the opportunities for neighbouring are greater, the level of social contact will be greater than among those living in a less familistic area.* This assumes, however, a certain degree of homogeneity among neighbours (Gans, 1968: 154). In short, the greater the opportunities for interaction, the greater the actual neighbouring among those individuals so predisposed. In addition, a highly familistic neighbourhood gives rise to a normative and value environment in which even the less predisposed are stimulated to interact.

4. *Whereas the degree of familism determines, to some extent, the structure of opportunities for neighbouring, access to that structure may be determined by such critical individual characteristics as class, length of residence, marital status, age, and personality type.* Many studies (cf. Keller, 1968) have found that these variables do tend to affect the individual's potential for neighbourliness. As a result, within the same type of area there can be wide

variations in the levels of neighbouring among residents because not all are equally predisposed to engage in this form of interaction. However, those with similar social characteristics are more likely to interact in a highly familistic area where the opportunities for this form of contact and its encouragement are greater (Fava, 1958: 125; Nohara, 1968: 187).

5. *Apart from the degree of familism of an area, there are additional aggregate characteristics which may influence the opportunities for and actual level of neighbouring interaction.* Some of the more important of these appear to be:

(a) *Degree of class heterogeneity among the area residents.* Bracey (1964: 86-87), for example, found that neighbouring is less intense in areas containing residents from different social classes. Gans' (1967: 161-62) research also documented this.

(b) *Degree of residential mobility among the area's residents.* Contrary to the assumptions of classical urban theory, Fellin and Litwak (1963) have pointed out that this may not retard local social involvement if neighbourhoods are structured to deal with high residential turnover.

(c) *Ecological location of the area,* that is, whether it is located in a suburb, central city, or on the periphery of the city. Fava (1958: 124-25), for example, found that suburban residents have higher neighbouring scores than inner-city residents—even when controlling for such individual characteristics as sex, age, and marital status (cf. Tomeh, 1964).

(d) *Length of settlement of the area.* With respect to the influence of this variable, Keller (1968: 68) has noted: "Two phases of neighboring and socializing may be identified according to available data on communities in transition and on new communities. The first phase is characterized by eager interaction and mutual helpfulness, whereas the second is characterized by restricted interaction, selectivity, and withdrawal." Gans' (1967: 45f.) study of the evolution of Levittown tended to validate the existence of these phases.

(e) *Population density of the area.* Wirth proposed that high density breeds superficiality and impersonality in social relationships among neighbours. Kasarda and Janowitz' (1974) recent comparative analysis of communities in England fails to support this: length of residence is a far more important factor than community size or density in influencing local social bonds and attachments. Later in this chapter we will examine the role population density does play in urban social organization.

(f) *Physical structure of the area.* Festinger (1950: 37f.) has documented the influence of physical design features on the likelihood of initial "passive" contacts and the formation of friendships among neighbours. The necessity of examining the impact of physical structure—for example, layout and spatial distribution of housing—has been demonstrated in a number of different contexts (Merton, 1948; Kuper, 1953; Whyte, 1957; Stevenson, Martin and O'Neill, 1967).

The preceding generalizations represent one means through which some of the variations in urban neighbouring can be explained and the differences among urbanites with respect to their involvement in the local community better understood. Although certainly limited—for example, this "model" does not fully address the interrelations among the three aspects of locality-based relationships we identified earlier—and in need of much further refinement —particularly if additional ecological research does demonstrate and elaborate the multidimensional nature of family status—this theory of opportunity structures does attempt to go beyond the broad generalities proposed in the typological tradition.

VARIATION IN THE SOCIAL SIGNIFICANCE OF THE NEIGHBOURHOOD: A CANADIAN EXAMPLE

Systematic investigation in the Canadian context of variations in locality-based relationships among urban residents has been rather limited. However, one attempt to test the theory of opportunity structures compared patterns of neighbouring among women living in two different sections of Saint John, New Brunswick (McGahan, 1972b; 1973). Both of these neighbourhoods contain predominantly upper-working-class and lower-middle-class residents. They differ, however, in terms of family status. Located in the centre of the city, the first area is characterized by a greater proportion of multiple dwellings and tenant-occupied households. It also contains many childless families, has one of the lowest rates of children per family of any section in the city, and many of its women residents are in the labour force. The second neighbourhood, located on the edge of the city, is marked by the opposite features, and by less residential turnover. Examination of residents' conception of the neighbour role as well as level of neighbouring reveals several important patterns.

The neighbour role, as we noted earlier, represents a set of norms for behaviour among those living in proximate households. Knowledge of such expectations is useful for understanding the social life of any residential group. Most of these Saint John women can be categorized as "sociables"—consistent, for example, with what Shulman (1967) found among those living in the Lower Town East community of Ottawa-Hull. That is, most in each neighbourhood appear to expect a balance between social distance and friendliness in their relations with neighbours. As Lorimer and Phillips (1971: 45) discovered in the locality relationships of a downtown Toronto working-class neighbourhood, not defining a good neighbour as a close friend is functional in that "once someone is friendly with a neighbour it is far more difficult to withdraw from the friendship than from family or friends who live in different locations." Nevertheless, for a rather large minority within each area of Saint John the neighbour relationship is expected to be far closer. Approximately one-third of the women are "intimates," seeing co-residents as an important source of friendship—demonstrating again, as Janowitz found in Chicago, the continued social significance of the local area for many urbanites. In contrast, very few of the Saint John women are "isolates." In terms of mutual aid expectations, for the majority the neighbour relationship is defined as a source of assistance and routine help. They define a good neighbour as someone with whom frequent borrowing and exchanging can occur when household needs dictate. Although they may not articulate it exactly in these terms, the neighbour relationship is one means through which they expect to adapt better to the urban system. Despite variations in family status, there are no substantial differences between the two areas in conception of the neighbour role. Within each neighbourhood, in addition, greater reliance is placed on kin than on any category of intimate. Almost three-fourths of the women indicate that in general they would rely first on some member of their family and relatives for help. This dominance of the kinship bond is sustained regardless of how the neighbour role is defined. Such a pattern is consistent with what research elsewhere has shown (e.g., Bell and Boat, 1957). Neighbours are generally least likely to be named as a superior source of assistance to other categories of intimates. Irrespective of how the neighbour role is defined, the kinship role has priority in times of critical need. This certainly suggests some degree of structuring in urbanites' relationships to different social networks.

While the neighbour role is that set of expectations or norms that ideally reflects and influences the manner in which residents interact with each other, it is important to test whether this is the case in reality. As Keller (1968: 30) has observed: "Neighboring activities and relationships thus include predictable core elements based on the neighbor role and additional non-predictable elements reflecting the social and personal context in which neighboring typically takes place. The second aspect cannot be deduced from a knowledge of the role but must be observed and assessed from case to case."

In Saint John we find an extremely close correlation between role conception and interaction—especially among women residents of the outer-city familistic neighbourhood. "Intimates," for example, are far more likely to have strong local bonds than are "isolates." Such a correlation, nevertheless, does not appear to be the case for those living in the inner-city area; this suggests the limited opportunities for contact that exist in this type of environment.

A central hypothesis contained in the theory of opportunity structures is that those with similar individual characteristics neighbour more in the "familistic" area than in one having lower family status. If this is the case, it can be taken as partial and indirect evidence for the existence *of greater opportunities for local social involvement in the familistic area, and thus provides some additional support for the theory. The data presented in Table 59 confirm this hypothesis. Controlling for specific individual characteristics, the residents of the outer-city neighbourhood, with few exceptions, are more likely to be highly involved with neighbours than are people living in the city centre.*

It should be recalled that one other factor which might affect the opportunity structure for neighbouring, aside from level of "familism" of a local population, is degree of residential mobility among an area's residents. As Rossi (1955: 31, 39) observed: "A neighborhood whose residents are stable is likely to be characterized by the growth of close interpersonal relations within this area . . . The more mobile the neighborhood, the less likely are its residents to form personal ties with their neighbors." The downtown area is characterized by a greater rate of residential mobility than its outer-city counterpart. This may have influenced the lower levels of involvement in the neighbour network among the inner-city residents. It may be the case that the greater the mobility within an area, the fewer the opportunities for extensive and close contacts with co-residents. The between-area differences in neighbouring, when controlling for individual characteristics, may also partly reflect this.

One final point: recall that conceptions of the neighbour role do not vary between residents of the two areas. This is significant in that it can be argued, contrary to the above, that a specific type of neighbourhood—for example, an inner-city area—attracts residents who are not predisposed to become involved in neighbour relationships. Thus, it might be this self-selection process and not variations in opportunity structures that explains differences in degree of neighbouring from one area to the next. This argument—though it may undoubtedly apply to some residents—is not supported with respect to the two areas as a whole. Approximately equal proportions of residents from each neighbourhood define the neighbour role—a normative reflection of that predisposition—in a similar manner. A self-selection process is in itself, therefore, not an adequate explanation for the patterns revealed in Table 59.

In summary, if these findings are generalizable to other urban contexts (cf. Wayne, 1972; Gates, Stevens, and Wellman, 1973), they suggest:

1. With respect to the neighbour role, most urbanites expect a balance between social distance and friendliness in their relations with neighbours. In addition, the neighbour relationship is seen as a viable source of assistance and more routine help.

2. The urbanite attempts to order the neighbour relationship in view of other forms of social involvement. In particular, reflecting its

Table 59:   Proportions of Saint John Women Who Show High Intensity of Neighbouring[1] by Individual Characteristics and by Neighbourhood

Individual characteristics	Neighbourhood			
	Inner-city (Low family status)		Outer-city (High family status)	
Life-cycle characteristics				
Marital status	%	$(T)^2$	%	$(T)^2$
Married	28.1	(57)	44.8	(96)
Single	19.0	(21)	25.0	(8)
Widowed	20.0	(20)	36.4	(22)
Presence of children				
One or more	32.6	(46)	45.8	(83)
None	16.7	(60)	32.6	(46)
Age				
Under 25	18.2	(22)	0.0	(10)
25-34	38.9	(18)	36.0	(25)
35-50	32.1	(28)	54.2	(48)
Over 50	13.2	(38)	39.1	(46)
Residential and occupancy characteristics				
Length of residence				
Less than 6 mos.	12.5	(16)	0.0	(3)
6 mos.-2 yrs.	16.7	(24)	25.0	(16)
2 yrs.-5 yrs.	33.3	(21)	27.8	(36)
5 yrs. and over	26.7	(45)	53.4	(73)
Ownership status				
Owner	14.3	(14)	42.9	(42)
Renter	24.2	(91)	40.2	(87)
Type of occupied dwelling				
Single attached	16.7	(6)	56.1	(41)
Single detached	0.0	(3)	40.6	(32)
Two-family	42.9	(14)	36.4	(22)
Multiple	21.7	(83)	26.5	(34)
Community of socialization				
All or part of youth spent in Saint John	27.9	(43)	34.6	(81)
All of youth spent outside Saint John	21.3	(61)	52.2	(46)
Socioeconomic status				
Education				
High school+	22.2	(36)	40.9	(44)
Some high school	30.3	(33)	43.3	(53)
8 or fewer years	17.1	(35)	38.7	(31)
Occupation				
White-collar	23.5	(51)	45.8	(59)
Blue-collar	26.1	(46)	38.5	(65)

1. Intensity refers to the degree of intimacy associated with neighbouring interaction; it is measured in terms of such indices as extent of mutual aid and discussion of personal problems with neighbours.
2. This refers to the total number on which the percentage is based; e.g., there are 57 married women interviewed from the inner-city neighbourhood.

Adapted from McGahan, 1972b.

central importance, the kinship bond has priority with respect to the exchange of assistance in times of need.

3. In general, the conception of the neighbour role reflects and
influences the manner in which residents interact with each other. Such
factors as opportunity for contact and mutual compatibility can affect
this level of correspondence.

4. The level of neighbouring varies according to individual characteristics. Reflecting the greater opportunities available, residents of a
familistic neighbourhood are more likely to be highly involved with
neighbours than are those who possess the same characteristics but live
in an area where familism is not predominant.

Conception of the Neighbourhood

As early as 1921 Roderick McKenzie (1968e: 73) observed: "Probably no other
term is used so loosely or with such changing content as the term neighbourhood, and very few concepts are more difficult to define." Viewing the
neighbourhood from an ecological perspective would lead one to define it "as
an area or a place within a larger entity, [which] has boundaries either physical
or symbolic and usually both—where streets, railway lines, or parks separate
off an area and its inhabitants . . ." (Keller, 1968: 88-89). On the other hand,
the neighbourhood can be viewed as a social unit in which there are "shared
activities, experiences, and values, common loyalties and perspectives, and
human networks that give to an area a sense of continuity and persistence over
time" (Keller, 1968: 91). These definitions of neighbourhood as physical and
social units are not necessarily incompatible, but they are distinct.

We have briefly examined the nature of variations in neighbourhoods as
social units. It has, however, been increasingly recognized that attention must
also be given to the local area as a spatial unit within which social networks
are developed. Particular concern has focused on the subjective conception
that urban residents have of their neighbourhood—the symbolic-cultural component of locality relationships. As Strauss (1967: 89) observes, an important
task of contemporary urban theory is "to develop categories and related hypotheses about the differential symbolism of space, and the differential behavior
associated with that symbolism." It is necessary, in short, to consider not only
the individual resident's involvement in the local community, but also his conception of what that area constitutes, as this may reflect or influence that
degree of involvement (Hunter, 1974). In the Fleetwood section of Surrey,
British Columbia, for example, the mental map (or subjective social space) of
the area held by long-term residents is more compact and organized than is
that of those who have only recently moved there (Cromwell, 1972). Similarly, newcomers to Edmonton—perhaps partly reflecting their as yet limited

involvement in the city's institutions—do not have as detailed a mental map of the downtown area as do those who have lived there for a long time (McGillivray, 1974).

A subjective conception is termed by Lee (1968: 248) a "socio-spatial schema":

> . . . space is effected by what fills it, the social relationships are influenced by space, and the physical objects are closely identified with the people who live in them or make use of them. This complex interdependence results in a mental organization that functions as a unit.

This mental schema emerges in an intricate manner:

> Repeated transactions with people and places in the urban environment leads, by a process of differentiation, to the separation of an organized socio-spatial whole . . . People, buildings, and space are articulated into a figure which is well-defined and stands out from the ground, and the space within is continuous; it appears "different" from the remainder; it has familiarity and "meaning."

This neighbourhood schema is also a product of the resident's past experience in the urban environment and in other spatial settings. It constitutes only one part of a comprehensive set of images of the city which most urbanites develop. With respect to this, Lynch's (1960: 85-86; also Lynch and Rivlin, 1970) detailed investigations of patterns of urban imagery showed that

> rather than a single comprehensive image for the entire environment, there seemed to be sets of images, which more or less overlapped and interrelated. They were typically arranged in a series of levels, roughly by the scale of area involved, so that the observer moved as necessary from an image at street level to levels of a neighbourhood, a city, or a metropolitan area.

Conceptions of neighbourhood may be strongly influenced by these other sets of images (cf. Tuan, 1974; Lofland, 1973).

WESTMOUNT: VARIATIONS IN THE PERCEPTION OF THE NEIGHBOURHOOD AS A STATUS SYMBOL

One important source of the subjective conception of neighbourhood is its potential function as a status symbol. The "socio-spatial schema" that is constructed can influence, reflect, and sustain the urbanite's particular status (Hunter, 1974). Although research on this process is not yet extensive in the Canadian urban setting (cf. Baskett, 1970; McGahan, 1972b), one interesting attempt to explore it is Seabrook's (1964) analysis of the perceptions the residents of Westmount had of their neighbourhood in the early 1960s.

Westmount is located in the west-central section of the Island of Montreal. The district achieved the legal status of city in 1908. Over the years, as its population grew, it developed many of its own civic services, which gave the area some measure of independence. What was particularly characteristic of Westmount, however, was its ethnic composition. In contrast to the larger metropolis, its population remained of British origin. The majority of Westmount's residents were also in the middle and upper-middle classes; many were professionals or managers. In short, Westmount was the area "where the more successful of Montreal" resided, and it acquired the image of a high-status residential community.

Seabrook was particularly concerned with the basis on which residents perceived Westmount as a status symbol and the significance of any variations in this. The area contained excellent facilities for its residents and manifested a high level of achievement in its physical planning. In addition, its population included a relatively large proportion of those in high-status positions. Hence, its physical or social attributes, or both, could have formed the basis for the residents' perceived "eliteness" of the community.

In order to examine which of these was dominant, Seabrook interviewed more than one hundred residents located in several different sub-areas of Westmount. The lower section of the district was zoned for shopping and commercial facilities, and for highrise apartment units. It was here that those residents who were lower on the socioeconomic scale concentrated. Farther up the mountain, the homes were more expensive. In the upper section zoning regulations permitted only single-family dwellings, which had better landscaping and larger lot sizes. Only higher-status residents could afford to live there.

Significantly, Seabrook found that all residents did not perceive the neighbourhood as a status symbol in the same manner. Those from the lower classes seemed to emphasize much more the physical eliteness of Westmount, while their upper-class counterparts were concerned more with the social eliteness of the city. This suggested that the status needs of each group were not the same. One possible explanation was that the community's class structure permitted more the imitation of higher-status positions than actual entrance by those lower in rank. Since their social contacts with the upper classes tended to be restricted, those of lower social rank emphasized the overt physical characteristics of Westmount in order to symbolize their own success and to suggest equality with the residents of higher rank. The latter could afford to be less concerned with such tangible symbols of status. Emphasis was placed on social eliteness—"the factors that ensure social acceptance and status equality of one's neighbours" (Seabrook, 1964: 96-97).

Residents of the lower and poorer sub-areas in Westmount were also particularly likely to stress physical eliteness. Area of residence within the city had an independent effect on perceived status. The upper classes were more likely to stress social eliteness if they lived in the better sec-

tions of Westmount. On the contrary, residents of lower social rank living in the same places were less likely to emphasize social eliteness. The difference between the classes in perceived social eliteness, therefore, was greatest in the "better" sections of the city. In short, area of residence appeared here to act "as reinforcer to the original attitude" (Seabrook, 1964: 99-100). This may have partially reflected the fact that in the better sections the upper classes, being more prevalent, had greater opportunities for developing social contacts with co-residents of the same status. The emphasis on social eliteness would have been consistent with this more intense level of involvement with status equals. On the other hand, those residents lower on the socioeconomic scale might have experienced a heightened sense of isolation from their upper-status neighbours. This would have encouraged a lesser emphasis on social eliteness, and reliance instead on more tangible signs of status, such as those derived from the physical aspects of the environment.

There were additional variations among Westmounters in their perceptions of the neighbourhood as a status symbol. For example, the newest residents had not yet developed strong ties within the area. As a result, they were less inclined than the longer-term residents to employ a status conception based on social acceptance. They relied on external symbols of status—"the architectural qualities, the cost, the palatialness of the homes in the neighborhood" (Seabrook, 1964: 121). One interesting pattern was the apparent decline in perception of both physical and social eliteness among those who had resided in Westmount between four and eight years. This could have reflected their increased sense of security in the new surroundings, as well as a more critical eye toward the "values and images of the neighborhood" (Seabrook, 1964: 129-30). As the period of residence increased, the individual became more closely involved socially in the local area. This encouraged greater attachment to the neighbourhood. More pronounced internalization of the area's status values—especially those relating to its social composition—occurred as greater social acceptance was attained.

This research illustrates the variations among residents in their conceptions of the neighbourhood as a status symbol. In particular, it points to the fact that the status needs and interests of different groups are not identical. As a result, their perceptions are dissimilar.

THE STUDY OF URBANISM:
NETWORK ANALYSIS AND SUBCULTURAL THEORY

This chapter has examined the fate of kinship and neighbourhood involvement separately. Yet there is a need to better articulate the nature of urban social organization as a whole, to better grasp the complexity of urban social life without the assumptions and biases of the classical typological perspective. Two recent attempts to do this are social network analysis and subcultural theory. These are not incompatible approaches; they emphasize different components of urbanism.

Social Network Analysis

The classical typological paradigm, it will be recalled, assumed that urbanization, modernization, and the large-scale division of labour in a society erode primary groups (Wellman, 1978, 1979; Fischer, 1977). This chapter has shown that such an assumption is an oversimplification. That assumption also does not give adequate recognition to the restructuring of primary ties which characterizes contemporary urban social life. Social network analysis has emerged as a valuable alternative. The approach developed partly through the efforts of urban anthropologists to understand the nature of social order in African cities despite the fluidity and transience of their populations. Sociologists have increasingly found equal value in this orientation for analyzing North American urbanism.

Any urban community contains three general orders or types of social relationships (Mitchell, 1966: 51-56): (1) *structural relationships*—that is, those within such organized groups as a factory, a mine, or a governmental agency, which are relatively ordered through clearly defined roles and positions; (2) *categorical relationships*—where social contacts are directed more through broad visible criteria or stereotypes, such as ethnicity or race; and (3) *personal networks*—the personal linkages which individuals have established with others. Such networks are frequently composed of members from different spheres of the urban social system, such as the locality and kinship contexts. We must delimit this third order of relationships because of the frequent blurring of group boundaries and the "interpenetration between different systems of groups, classes, and categories" (Srinias and Bereille, 1964: 165) particularly characteristic of rapidly expanding communities.

In concentrating on the nature of these personal links, network analysis is able to "bridge the gap" between the individual and the collective level of social life (Fischer, 1977). Groups consist of networks; connections among them through higher-order networks form institutions. The total social structure, thus, consists of interrelated sets of interpersonal networks. Changes in the networks are influenced by both the choices of the individual actors within them as well as aggregate characteristics (such as network density). In short, "networks influence individuals, individuals influence networks" (Fischer, 1977: 30).

NETWORK ANALYSIS TERMINOLOGY

Insofar as social network analysis does represent a theoretical orientation, it employs an interrelated set of concepts with which we should be familiar. Although there is not complete agreement on these, some of the central aspects of social networks include the following (Mitchell, 1969a; Barnes, 1969, 1972; Mayer, 1966; Fischer, 1977):

Morphological *characteristics refer to the shape and general structure of social networks:*

1. Anchorage—*the individual from whose point of view a network at the immediate level might be examined;*

2. Reachability—*the extent to which an individual can establish indirect contact with other members of a network (hence its relative compactness);*

3. Density—*the number of links actually existing among those in the same network, as a proportion of the maximum possible number of such ties;*

4. Range—*the number of persons in direct contact with the person on whom the network is anchored;*

5. Zone (or partial network)—*any particular section of the network—for example, restricted to the bonds among kin—including a delimited number of members and the relations among them.*

Interactional *characteristics refer to the nature of network bonds:*

1. Content—*the meaning of the linkages to the participants;*

2. Multiplexity—*whether the social bond involves more than one relation (for example, kin who work together); "single-strand" ties do not;*

3. Directedness—*the balance of power and resources, and whether linkages are reciprocal;*

4. Durability—*derived from mutually recognized rights and obligations;*

5. Intensity—*the perceived significance of the linkages;*

6. Frequency—*the number of times interaction occurs among those in the network.*

Apart from these characteristics, there is the problem of determining the boundaries of social networks—that is, "the number of steps in the links radiating out from ego that need to be taken into account" (Mitchell, 1969a: 40). Ordinarily, it is the nature of the particular research question that indicates the extent to which indirect linkages are to be examined. If all possible mediated connections are included, the result would be a study of the "total network" of the community which encompasses its entire social life. It is to avoid such an unmanageable task that ego-centred networks are delineated (Barnes, 1969).

In addition, it is important to distinguish between potential linkages
in personal networks and those that are activated in particular situations
for specific purposes. The latter are termed "action-sets" (Mayer, 1966):
"An action-set may be looked upon as an aspect of a personal network
isolated in terms of a specific short-term instrumentally-defined interactional content: the personal network itself is more extensive and more
durable" (Mitchell, 1969a: 39-40). For example, in times of economic
crisis an individual turns for assistance to only a selected number of kin
and friends, while still maintaining some bonds, direct or indirect, with a
wider aggregate of people (Boswell, 1966). There is an underlying pattern
of choice in the construction of the action-set; the same potential linkages
are not necessarily activated in different circumstances.

Social network analysis is a useful means for determining, for example,
(a) processes of communication and control in the urban community and how
norms are sustained or transformed; (b) patterns of mutual aid and assistance
which facilitate adjustment during entrance to the urban system; and (c) how
ethnic ties can be sustained while at the same time other types of linkages are
created—by virtue of the fact that all participants in ego's network are not
necessarily known to one another, or are not all mobilized for similar purposes.

Most significantly, network analysis does not interpret the nature of urban social organization from the perspective simply of the fate of distinct primary groups (Shulman, 1976), as did the classical typological paradigm. The
latter assumed that with urbanization and the erosion of dense and multiplex
networks, social relationships are less intimate and enduring. Such an assumption is not supported by contemporary research (Fischer, 1977). Wellman's
(1978, 1979) detailed analysis of East Yorkers' social networks shows that their
intimate ties are sparsely knit and spatially dispersed; they are not confined to
a single densely knit, tightly bounded solidarity.

It has been commonly observed that the continued expansion of urbanization has increasingly demanded a rethinking of the notion of community. Improvements in transportation and communication facilities have enabled
widely dispersed groups and institutions to be more fully integrated (Webber,
1968). Constraints imposed by geographical distance are no longer as significant as they once were. In Webber's (1970) terms, "interest communities" now
rival "place communities" in the degree of attachment they elicit from urban
dwellers. Communities marked by despatialization and specialization of interest have become more common. Intimacy is no longer totally dependent on
spatial propinquity (Fischer, 1977).

Network analysis represents, as we have seen, an alternative perspective
in the study of the city's social life. The urban community is seen as a complex
of social networks in which individuals and collectivities are linked (Wellman,

1973). These ties, although generally differentiated, overlap and are not necessarily spatially restricted, nor are they static. Significantly, *indirect* bonds among members of networks provide essential functions in terms of communication, assistance, and control which cannot be ignored (Lee, 1969; Granovetter, 1973).

Urbanites are viewed from this perspective as involved in "personal communities" or segments of networks "characterized by both a high density of ties between network members, and a relative paucity of ties outside these areas" (Craven and Wellman, 1973: 34). Since they are ego-centred, no two personal communities are exactly alike. The city dweller's typical involvement in multiple communities has important implications for the overall integration of the contemporary metropolis. These multiple bonds link diverse sectors of the population. As a result, the city itself can be seen as "a network of networks" (Craven and Wellman, 1973: 50). Through their elaborate linkages social networks provide a basis for the co-ordination of urban activities and the attainment of order despite the city's heterogeneity and diversity. Social network analysis therefore represents a fresh approach to the study of urban social organization distinct from the traditional typological perspective. It holds much promise in furthering our understanding of the process and consequences of urbanization (cf. Wellman et al., 1971; Wayne, 1971; Shulman, 1972, 1975).

Subcultural Theory

A central thesis in classical urban theory was that size and density exercise an independent effect on social life. Wirth argued that alienation, impersonality, and isolation are more likely to be found in the city (Fischer, 1972). Comparative research fails to support this thesis (Fischer, 1973, 1976). For example, Booth (1976) found that neither objective nor subjective (perceived) crowding at both the household and neighbourhood levels affects social integration or participation. Indeed, crowded living conditions in themselves appear to have few consequences in areas such as health, reproduction, family relations, or level of political activity.

THE EFFECTS OF RESIDENTIAL CROWDING

Since the 1920s the manner in which urban density affects behaviour has been of significant interest. The initial wave of research proposed crude correlations between levels of areal density and various forms of pathology. Their conclusions, however, were based on faulty methodologies, and were thus premature. A second wave of more sophisticated research is underway, correcting earlier biases and leading to more precise propositions in this area (Aiello and Bauzn, 1979).

This recent research has established several important themes regarding the effects of residential crowding, among which we might cite the following (McGahan, 1980):

• *We must be careful about what we mean by "density". We should distinguish* spatial density *(the number of square feet of floor space in a particular unit),* social density *(the number of individuals in a housing unit),* perceived social density *(the subjective evaluation of social density), and* crowding *(the condition of social or spatial density experienced as aversive).*

• *Spatial density in itself has few negative behavioural consequences. Only when it is accompanied by the perception of a loss of control over the physical and social environment (that is, the inability to predict and manipulate what occurs in such a setting and to avoid unwanted social contacts) does the negative experience of "crowding" occur.*

• *Prolonged exposure to perceived uncontrollable situations creates profound dissatisfaction with the particular environment, social withdrawal or alienation, and such motivational "deficits" as a sense of helplessness. The latter may, in turn, influence how an individual adjusts to settings other than the one from which that sense originated.*

• *Our understanding of how and why particular categories of individuals may have a greater tolerance of crowding than others is still incomplete. In some settings, for example, women appear to be more sensitive to density and more conscious of crowding than men.*

• *It is incorrect to assume that an individual will adjust to high density conditions over time. Perception of and tolerance for crowding do not necessarily diminish the longer one stays in such a setting; indeed, the reverse may occur.*

• *We must refrain from overgeneralizing from one type of residential setting to another. The nature and consequences of crowding vary according to the characteristics both of individuals and situations.*

These themes are guideposts for further research. Obviously, we are far from a comprehensive theory of residential crowding. The implications of these themes for environmental design are also seminal. If the construction of high-density residential buildings continues, it can be argued that the environment should be designed to minimize the perception of uncontrollability and the sense of crowding. This might suggest such strategies as, for example, incorporating semiprivate buffers architecturally that regulate intrusions into private spaces, creating more cohesive residential units by reducing the number of inhabitants who must share a common facility, and producing a flexibly congruent fit between the environment and the functions to be performed within it (Michelson, 1970).

Population concentration may influence social life by supporting the emergence of distinctive subcultures. This effect is proposed in the subcultural theory of urbanism (Fischer, 1975, 1976). As with the theory of opportunity structures, this model consists of a set of interrelated hypotheses in need of further testing (Fischer, 1975). They include the following:

1. *The more urban a place, the greater its subcultural variety.* "Urban" is defined here in terms of population concentration: the greater the size and density of a community, the more urban the place. This subcultural variety is a product of the structural differentiation which, as we have seen, accompanies urban growth. For example, in chapter 8 we noted that such dimensions as socioeconomic status, family status, and ethnic status emerge as significant bases of social differentiation. These also form the roots for distinctive subcultures. Large cities also attract diverse streams of migrants; this heightens subcultural variety.

2. *The more urban a place, the more intense its subcultures.* Large cities are more likely to achieve that "critical mass" of population necessary if any given subculture is to develop its own institutions. (Chinatowns, for example, are more commonly found in Canada's largest cities.) Such institutional completeness will, in turn, enhance attachment to the subculture's values and beliefs. The clash and contrast among subcultures in large communities also foster in-group cohesion and strengthen the central norms and values of each subculture.

3. *The more urban a place, the more numerous the sources of diffusion and the greater the diffusion into a subculture.* The co-existence of a number of diverse subcultures initially leads to an intensification of each; nevertheless, over time some degree of diffusion of beliefs or behaviours—particularly with respect to less central elements, such as style of dress—will occur from one group to the next. Such intermixing encourages social and cultural innovations (for example, new forms of music).

4. *The more urban a place, the higher the rate of unconventionality (attitudes, values, and behaviour that diverge from the central norms of society).* This follows from the preceding hypotheses: the greater the variety and intensity of subcultures, the greater the likelihood that some will support behaviour that is defined as "deviant" or unconventional. Large cities encourage the congregation of those with similar interests; the emergence of vital subcommunities will sustain activities that depart from mainstream norms. Deviance is thus not a consequence of anomy and alienation, as Wirth argued, but of subcultural strength and of innovations arising from subcultural intermixing: "With size comes 'community'—even if it is a community of thieves, counter-culture experimenters, avant-garde intellectuals, or other unconventional persons" (Fischer, 1975: 1328-29).

This model does not minimize the importance of individual factors such as social class and stage in the family life cycle in accounting for social relationships among urbanites, nor of type of residential area. It simply seeks to present possible consequences of the sheer size and density of urban communities. The verification of this model requires a comparative study along a wide rural-urban gradient (Fischer, 1972).

We should note that social network analysis and subcultural theory are complementary. That is, by reference to the structure of urbanites' social networks we can understand better how particular subcultures in the city are integrated and sustained. The persistence of ethnic communities, which we discussed in chapter 6, is a product of ethnically based social linkages, for example. In addition, the diffusion process which occurs across subcultures in the city is effected through the interlocking of networks. These bonds, directly and indirectly linking diverse segments of the population, serve as channels for the transmission and intermixing of subcultural elements. The mosaic of networks thus forms the social basis for the mosaic of urban subcultures.

SUMMARY

1. A central proposition in the classical typological interpretation of urbanism was the decline in significance of such primary intermediate groups as kinship and the local community.
2. The isolated nuclear family thesis represents a continuation of that paradigm's interpretation of the fate of kinship in the urban system. It argues that detachment from kinship networks is an important prerequisite to the efficient functioning of that system.
3. That thesis is not supported by contemporary analyses of urbanism. In a wide variety of urban communities, involvement in kinship networks appears to be a central part of many residents' patterns of social participation. Kinship ties provide urbanites with various types of assistance and support. Such ties—particularly among parents and their adult children and among siblings—are sustained by both mutual concern and the obligation to maintain contact.
4. The isolation thesis may also be challenged on historical grounds. For example, the assumption that a classical extended family existed prior to the emergence of the industrial-urban community does not appear to be correct. Examining patterns of social mobility during Chicago's industrialization in the nineteenth century also casts doubt on the necessarily greater functionality of the isolated nuclear family.
5. Within the Canadian urban setting little support for the isolation thesis exists when we examine the nature and content of residents' intimate ties.
6. Contrary to the isolation thesis, geographical mobility does not in itself loosen kinship bonds. Although the frequency of face-to-face contact may decline, migrants sustain their involvement with kin through alternate means of communication and their sense of obligation to give assistance in times of need. In analyzing why a particular kinship network may have eroded, other factors, such as the loss of a central connecting relative, are more influential than simple mobility.
7. Among urban French Canadians the tie between siblings is a particularly

central kinship bond, perhaps reflecting the cultural values of this ethnic group. Neither social nor geographical mobility significantly disrupts their kinship ties.

8. As with urban kinship, the typological interpretation of the fate of the local community in the urban system has been challenged. One alternate model initially proposed was that of the "community of limited liability." The urbanite typically shows a limited social investment in the local community insofar as it exercises some control and partially fulfils household needs. Thus, it is more correct to speak of relative commitments to both local and non-local social systems than the complete demise of the former as a significant social fact.

9. The urban neighbourhood is a multidimensional phenomenon, which includes the way in which the neighbour role is defined by local residents, the type of neighbouring interaction that occurs among them, and the subjective conception of the neighbourhood.

10. The theory of opportunity structures argues that social involvement in the neighbourhood varies according to type of area as well as individual characteristics. The degree of familism influences the structure of opportunities for neighbouring. Those with similar social characteristics are more likely to neighbour in a highly familistic area where the opportunities for this form of contact and its encouragement are greater. This is not to deny the importance of other "contextual" characteristics beyond family status, such as extent of residential turnover in the neighbourhood, in affecting the level of local social participation.

11. With respect to the neighbour role, most urbanites appear to expect a balance between social distance and friendliness in their relations with co-residents. Exchange of assistance and routine aid is also expected. However, most commonly the kinship bond has social priority over the neighbour relationship. The extent to which the latter corresponds to conception of the neighbour role is influenced by the opportunities for contact and level of mutual compatibility among co-residents.

12. The symbolic-cultural or subjective dimension of the neighbourhood includes the cognitive, evaluative, and affective responses to it of its residents. The neighbourhood subjective "schema" is a product of the form of local relationships developed, as well as of past experiences in other spatial settings. It is part of a comprehensive set of images of the different levels of the urban system. One central function of the neighbourhood "schema" is that of a status symbol. Perception of the neighbourhood varies according to the status needs and interests of different groups.

13. In an effort to grasp the nature of urban social organization as a whole, social network analysis has emerged in recent years as a useful alternative to the classical typological paradigm. This theoretical approach examines the structure and content of urbanites' personal networks, and provides a better understanding of the processes of communication and control as well as the flow of mutual aid and support within the urban community. Urbanites' in-

timate ties, contrary to the classical assumption, have not eroded, but rather tend to be sparsely knit and spatially dispersed. The overlapping of social networks provides a basis for the co-ordination of urban activities and the attainment of order despite the city's heterogeneity and diversity. Urban social structure is seen as a set of interrelated networks in which intimacy is no longer as dependent on spatial propinquity as in the past.

14. In an attempt to refine the typological paradigm, subcultural theory argues that population concentration in itself may influence social life by supporting the emergence of distinctive subcultures. The larger and denser the community, the greater the structural differentiation which, in turn, encourages subcultural formation. Reinforcing this process is the influx of migrants from a variety of places. Large cities are also more likely to attract sufficient numbers to support the institutions needed for each subculture's vitality. The co-existence of diverse sets of subcultures will strengthen the central basis of each, but at the same time allow for diffusion of peripheral elements from one to the other. Subcultural theory depicts the city as a mosaic of social worlds, some of which may support unconventional or deviant behaviour; the latter, thus, must not be interpreted as a symptom of anomy or disorganization.

15. Subcultural theory and social network analysis can be usefully integrated. Urbanites' social bonds are patterned in such a way as to create and sustain distinctive subcultures, including, for example, viable ethnic communities. The images of the city as a set of interlocking social networks and as a series of differentiated subcultures are complementary rather than contradictory.

Chapter 10

The Fate of Community
in the Inner City
and the Suburbs

Classical urban theory frequently generalized about the nature of urban social organization on the basis of what was observed in the inner city. Park's concern for the disintegrating influences of the urban system, for example, was derived from his analysis of the processes occurring there. Redfield's implicit characterization of the urban type embodied those traits which supposedly marked particularly the inner-city way of life. Indeed, much of the work of the Chicago school (e.g., Zorbaugh, 1929; Thrasher, 1963 ed.) was devoted to exploration of the variety of social patterns found in this setting. The previous chapter, however, has demonstrated the increasing importance that has been given to the fact that there are systematic variations in the social significance of the local community within the urban system. It is thus inappropriate to generalize from what might be found in the inner city to the entire urban area: such global characterizations of urban structure are imprecise and over-simplified.

An additional task of contemporary urban research, it should be noted, is a more rigorous investigation of social patterns within the inner city as well. In an attempt to modify and develop the generalizations of classical urban theory, attention has been given to the structure of social life found in the working-class neighbourhood, the slum, and the highrise apartment building, all three of which form central parts of the inner city's "mosaic of minor communities." In this chapter we shall briefly review a selected sample of the fruits of this research and its significance for our understanding of the nature of urban social organization. To complement this survey, we shall also examine the structure of communities at the other spatial extreme in the metropolitan area—the suburbs. In a sense, we shall explore the "micro-ecology" of each of these types of living areas and the consequences each has for patterns of social life.

THE INNER CITY

In earlier chapters we observed that ecologically the metropolitan area represents an extensive territorial division of labour. Sub-areas within it assume diverse and specialized functions, and attract particular types of residents. The distinctive characteristics of the inner city (as well as the suburbs) can be inferred from our previous analyses of the patterns of urban expansion and residential mobility.

As we observed in chapter 8, the central areas of many of Canada's metropolitan communities are undergoing change in their land-use patterns. As the population expands outward to the periphery in search of available housing, the central core also experiences a decline in its proportionate share of total metropolitan employment (Nader, 1975). Manufacturing and wholesaling are no longer as prominent in the centre as they once were. Those losses are compensated for by gains in office functions. For example, more than 75,000 workers are employed in downtown Vancouver offices (Collier, 1978). Between 1965 and 1975 more than 5 million square feet of office space were added to the core.

In addition to office functions, the downtown area typically contains the highest land values and the most intense land use in the city. Retail activities serving some of the daily needs of those employed in the area locate there, as do highly specialized establishments requiring accessibility to the whole metropolitan population. Some industries also remain here, requiring access to other services and firms, for example, job-printing industries (Nader, 1975).

Linked to the commercial core are the highrise apartment buildings, which house those who are at certain stages in the life cycle. By the middle 1980s Vancouver's downtown (broadly defined) will contain a residential population of approximately 100,000 (Collier, 1978). Many of these will continue to locate in highrises in the west end—the most densely populated square mile in Canada (McAfee, 1972). Such a location is attractive to many because of its accessibility to places of work and nearby entertainment facilities. Highrise apartment construction is also occurring in some suburban areas.

While one might no longer go so far as to call it the "heartbeat" of the metropolitan region, the downtown area remains one of the most vital parts of the urban system. We shall now look more closely at the population characteristics and heterogeneity of the inner city.

Definition of the Inner City

The inner city represents the central core of an urban area (McLemore, Aass, and Keilhofer, 1975). Since it is ordinarily the first part of the community to be settled, it contains the oldest housing stock. It is a dense, congested area, into which the central business district expands, thus corresponding to Burgess' zone in transition. Not infrequently, it functions as the point of initial settlement for new groups of immigrants and migrants.

Table 60 summarizes some of the central demographic characteristics of inner cities in the metropolitan areas of Edmonton, Vancouver, Montreal, and Toronto. Typically, in comparison to the wider metropolitan area the inner city is marked by these characteristics (McLemore, Aass, and Keilhofer, 1975):

1. A smaller proportion of the young, and an overrepresentation of the elderly;

2. Lower average household income (a pattern noted in chapter 8);

3. Smaller average household size (see also Kumove, 1975; Lioy, 1975);

4. A greater proportion of the population with little education;

5. A higher unemployment rate;

6. A larger proportion of the population foreign-born (except for Montreal and cities that are ethnically relatively homogeneous);

7. A lower proportion of single-family homes;

8. Lower average number of rooms per dwelling, as well as lower average gross rent.

These demographic features are consistent with our earlier portrayal of urban spatial structure in Canada. It is important to note that the inner city is not characterized by a pronounced proportion of overcrowded dwelling units. This partly reflects the outflow of population from such areas.

The statement of these general features, however, conceals the heterogeneity which does exist within inner-city areas. The core contains diverse sections, neighbourhoods that have experienced not necessarily similar consequences of urban growth and development (McLemore, Aass, and Keilhofer, 1975):

• *Declining areas.* These might be viewed as "slums," that is, parts of the inner city undergoing physical deterioration. The threat of urban renewal and transition to non-residential land uses discourages maintenance and improvement of the buildings. Those residents who are able to achieve some economic mobility are apt to leave; among the remainder of the population major social problems are especially evident.

• *Stable areas.* The inner city frequently contains socially and physically stable neighbourhoods, such as the working-class community and the ethnic enclave. These are "viable" neighbourhoods, containing housing that is not dilapidated—communities to which the residents are attached.

• *Revitalized areas.* Certain sections of the inner city may experience a return of the more affluent middle class, who perhaps desire to live in proximity to the downtown core. They frequently purchase and rehabilitate older homes there, competing with lower-income groups for available housing. In Toronto this process is called "whitepainting" (McLemore, Aass, and Keilhofer, 1975); other terms are used to describe it elsewhere:

A real-life urban drama with as many turns of plot as a "play within a play" is being acted out in many U.S. cities.

Table 60: Characteristics of Inner City and Census Metropolitan Areas—Edmonton, Vancouver, Montreal, and Toronto, 1971

	Edmonton		Vancouver		Montreal		Toronto	
	Inner city*	CMA	Inner city*	CMA	Inner city*	CMA	Inner city*	CMA
Population	48,775	495,725	236,320	1,082,310	644,400	2,743,185	642,290	2,628,070
(% of CMA)	(10%)		(22%)		(23%)		(24%)	
Age groups:								
under 19	28%	39%	22%	32%	29%	35%	28%	34%
65 and over	12%	6%	15%	10%	11%	7%	10%	8%
Average household size	2.5	3.3	2.4	3.0	2.9	3.3	3.2	3.3
Average household income	$6,718	$10,168	$8,547	$9,932	$8,525	$9,881	$10,104	$11,911
Education:								
less than grade 9	40%	28%	28%	27%	52%	44%	42%	32%
university graduates	3%	6%	8%	6%	6%	6%	6%	6%
Occupational groups:								
blue-collar	27%	25%	20%	26%	24%	25%	26%	25%
white-collar	43%	42%	47%	43%	39%	40%	41%	42%
professional	12%	20%	19%	17%	18%	20%	16%	19%
Unemployment	12%	7%	12%	9%	11%	9%	9%	7%
Born outside Canada	31%	18%	37%	26%	15%	15%	45%	34%
Type of dwelling:								
Single-detached	44%	62%	35%	63%	3%	24%	22%	46%
Apartments	55%	31%	63%	33%	51%	51%	43%	37%
Dwellings owner-occupied	32%	55%	33%	59%	13%	35%	43%	55%
Rooms per dwelling	4.4	5.4	4.4	5.2	4.6	5.0	5.2	5.6
Average annual gross rent	$1,041	$1,310	$1,312	$1,391	$1,082	$1,156	$1,438	$1,559
Overcrowding (over 1 person per room)	6%	6%	5%	5%	9%	9%	9%	6%

*Includes all census tracts in the core where the percentage of housing built before 1946 is more than double that for the metropolitan area as a whole.

From *The Changing Canadian Inner City* by R. McLemore, C. Aass, and P. Keilhofer (Information Canada, 1975). Reproduced by permission of the Minister of Supply and Services Canada.

At stake is who will live in once-genteel, now shabby inner-city areas that are being refurbished. Will it be the present residents, most of modest income and humble backgrounds, or will it be the young-to-middle-aged, affluent whites who now want to live near the shiny office towers in which they work?

Over the past years, this "new gentry" has been squeezing poor whites, blacks, and Hispanics out of choice property in neighborhoods that are bouncing back in New York; Washington; Savannah, Georgia; and many other cities.

This trend is called by those who oppose it "the Georgetownization of America." Washington's Georgetown section was a slum before it was transformed into one of the most expensive, exclusive, and desirable residential areas in the District of Columbia (Morehouse III, 1979: 6).

Such an influx can erode the cohesiveness of inner-city working-class and ethnic communities.

• *Areas subject to massive redevelopment.* Both public and private renewal programs have in the post-World War II period physically transformed many downtown areas. Highrise apartment and office buildings, for example, have replaced older residential communities. This has permitted the expansion both of the managerial-administrative sectors in the downtown and of housing attractive to those employed in such jobs (Hardwick, 1974).

In summary, although we can draw a broad demographic profile of the inner city, we must also recognize its internal richness; it serves the needs of a range of residents (McLemore, Aass, and Keilhofer, 1975). Canadian literature, we should note, captures that richness in the portraits presented by a number of novelists of central city neighbourhoods (e.g. Roy, 1969 ed.; Lemelin, 1965 ed.; Wiseman, 1956; Fennario, 1974; Carrier, 1973; Richler, 1955; Richler, 1969). Gabrielle Roy, for example, in *The Tin Flute*, writes of the Saint-Henri section of Montreal as "an antheap with the soul of a village!"

> During the day it knew a life of relentless toil. In the evening it had its village life, when folks gathered on their doorsteps or brought their chairs out to the sidewalk and exchanged gossip from door to door. (Roy, 1969 ed.: 202).

Roy and other Canadian novelists show us the influence of economic insecurity on family life among disadvantaged inner-city residents, their transience, and the difficulties they encounter in their quest for upward mobility. Similarly, Lemelin (1965 ed.) portrays the localism, provincialism, and relative separation from outside institutions among those in working-class neighbourhoods. We will explore analytically the "content" of these synthetic portraits in the following.

The Working-Class Neighbourhood

In the inner city the working-class neighbourhood functions partly as a transitional community, "helping to absorb low status migrants who are economically necessary but socially neglected participants in urban, industrial life" (Fried, 1973: 44). It provides a context in which new entrants and their children can gradually adapt to the demands of the urban system, and thus become more fully prepared for social mobility within the wider society. It represents, in short, "a vast 'processing mechanism' . . . a port of exit as well as a port of entry" (Fried, 1965: 128). That many of its residents are at least second-generation, however, clearly suggests that such "processing" is not completed within a relatively short period of time.

Although much of the housing in a working-class neighbourhood may be relatively old, it is a source of satisfactory shelter for less privileged groups in the city. Indeed, contrary to the stereotype frequently held of such low-rent areas,

> the image of slum residents as people largely incapable of maintaining decent conditions of housing is manifestly at variance with the great care and attention lavished upon the dwelling units by many working-class tenants (Fried, 1973: 68).

Most significantly, the urban neighbourhood is an extremely meaningful and satisfying community for many of its residents. This is most pronounced among older adults, relatively long-term residents, and members of the community's dominant ethnic group.

Such attachment is revealed also in the locally-based social relationships which develop (Young and Willmott, 1957; Bott, 1957; Gans, 1962b; Fried, 1973). Not uncommonly, residents of the working-class community have kin living nearby, whom they rely on and see very frequently. Bonds between parents and adult children are relatively close; the tie between mother and daughter is particularly strong. In addition, involvement with neighbours appears to be a central source of localism. The vast majority of the residents develop close relationships with others in the area; such contacts encourage frequent exchange of assistance in day-to-day situations.

Locally based patterns of association tend to assume the form of dense or close-knit networks in which social ties directly or indirectly overlap. The centrality of the relationship among neighbours is due to the fact that it provides an avenue for further contacts with other residents to whom each is linked. Thus, "one contact or one relationship or one form of participation readily leads to others. In this sense, the close knit network, locally based within an urban working-class community, provides the framework of social organization and the basis of inter-personal commitment and stability in the working-class world" (Fried, 1973: 114). Kin, friends, and neighbours are, as a result, all joined in the same local relationships. These constitute an important source of gratification for the majority of residents whose options are limited because of their economic position (Fischer, 1977). Non-local social ties are dominant among the small number preparing to move "beyond the urban village."

That intense localism of the working class is also reflected in the "spatial identity" they construct. We noted in chapter 9 the importance of analyzing such a subjective conception for a full understanding of the locality relationships of urban dwellers. Residents of this type of inner-city area feel, in a very real sense, that this area is their "home" and that it belongs to them. Conversely, they feel estranged from places beyond its boundaries. Their conception of local space, therefore, seems somewhat different from that found among the middle class:

> While people in the working class are comfortable primarily in "places," in areas in which they can function, middle-class people quite readily accept the impersonality of many areas of the city as passageways between places they know or want to. It is a fundamental difference in the sense of spatial identity, in the conception of the physical environment as a personal region. The spatial identity that characterizes working-class people is a "territorial one," based on and largely confined to a particular, bounded area. The spatial identity of higher status people is more generally a highly "selective" one, defined on the basis of desire or interest rather than propinquity or contiguity (Fried, 1973: 104; Fried and Gleicher, 1967: 131).

The significance of the local community is also revealed—perhaps most dramatically—in the case of those forced to move from such an area because of urban renewal. For example, interviewing several hundred former residents of Boston's West End after their removal, Fried (1963: 152) found that a large number had experienced a severe sense of loss, approaching real grief. Many were deeply dissatisfied and unhappy with their involuntary departure. This was particularly true for the majority of working-class residents unprepared for such change (Fried, 1965: 159). Relocation disrupted the spatial and social bases of their sense of community. The feelings of grief they so clearly manifested were the psychological fruits of this loss. It was also evident that post-relocation experiences were important. Many were unable to "re-establish all or any significant part of the West Ender close-knit ties with the same individuals" (Fried, 1965: 150). Even if they had, after the move, developed new relationships with kin and neighbours, these were frequently not sufficient to increase satisfaction. Objective improvement in residential status did not really compensate for the loss suffered through social dislocation. The West Enders' sense of grief was socially and spatially rooted. Movement to a "better" neighbourhood in itself did not temper this feeling. Relocation from the West End thus constituted a traumatic experience for a large proportion of the ex-residents. This crisis underlined the deep significance the local community has for the social and spatial identities of the urban working class.

In summary, the working-class neighbourhood represents a locally based social system in which close-knit networks centred within the area elaborate a distinctive subculture. Such localism reflects in part residents' class position, and forms a basis of social support in dealing with the institutions of the wider society.

THE WORKING-CLASS NEIGHBOURHOOD IN TORONTO: AN ILLUSTRATION

More recent attempts have been made to examine the social structure of the urban working-class neighbourhood within the Canadian setting (e.g., Crysdale, 1968; Grayson, 1972). Such analyses, centred chiefly in Toronto, have sought to determine implicitly whether patterns discovered, for example, in the West End of Boston and elsewhere are generalizable to other contexts. This research, although not extensive, has given us a better understanding both of the dynamic processes in the urban stratification system and of the organization and impact of this type of local community. To illustrate, let us briefly consider the "East of Parliament" area in Toronto (Lorimer and Phillips, 1971)—in previous years rather pejoratively known as "Cabbagetown" (Garner, 1968 ed.).

This neighbourhood is located near the centre of the city, and is clearly delimited by natural boundaries. The vast majority of the employed males are in blue-collar occupations, chiefly unskilled and semi-skilled, with below-average incomes. The large proportion of the 7,000 residents are of Anglo-Saxon origin. Although the housing is fairly old, new residents of more middle-class status are moving into the area, renovating some of the buildings, and taking advantage of the neighbourhood's convenient proximity to the downtown core. In short, it is experiencing flux—a formerly "stable area" is now undergoing some "revitalization" through the efforts of new middle-class entrants.

As is true in other working-class communities, such as Boston's West End (Gans, 1962b, Fried, 1973), within these East of Parliament working-class families, roles are clearly and separately defined. Conjugal role segregation seems the dominant pattern. The husband is expected to work and to provide and maintain shelter. In contrast, the wife is charged with the responsibility of carrying out daily household activities as well as caring for the children. Such separation of duties is generally not questioned: "Not only do the families we know adhere to this division of functions and responsibilities but they also accept it as being perfectly legitimate and appropriate, an attitude quite different from that of many middle-class families where, even if both husband and wife adhere in practise to this pattern, there is a good deal of uncertainty and doubt about how appropriate it is" (Lorimer and Phillips, 1971: 36).

Again, reflecting a general working-class pattern, East of Parliament families are primarily adult-centred. Children are not strongly controlled, but are expected to lead independent and separate lives. The extent to which all members of the families engage in common activities is extremely limited. The central role of the peer group is also evident:

"Men have men friends, women have women friends, and there often are an intimacy and frankness between friends of the same sex which rarely exists amongst married couples" (Lorimer and Phillips, 1971: 43). The circle of close friends includes kin, especially parents and adult offspring. Involvement is not necessarily matched by intense positive feelings toward them. A sense of mutual obligation seems sufficient to maintain these ties. An additional category of close friends is that of neighbours. This type of social bond occurs more often when those with close ties eventually move to the same immediate area. It is less common for friendship to emerge merely through physical contiguity. Overall, perhaps reflecting its state of flux, the neighbourhood social life does not appear to be as intense in the East of Parliament district as that characteristic of other working-class communities—such as London's Bethnal Green (Young and Willmott, 1957) or Boston's West End (Fried, 1973). Contacts among neighbours are friendly, but not necessarily close. There are very few voluntary associations located in the area. The residents, having no sense of it as a neighbourhood, do not agree on a name for the area. The small number of middle-class renovators who have recently moved into the neighbourhood tend to be avoided by the older working-class residents:

> *"Relations between long-term residents and townhouse renovators on the street were cautious but edgy. Behind them was an unspoken mutual recognition that the old residents found the townhouse renovators quite different from the rather disreputable tenants who for a long time had lived in many of the houses now being renovated and from the respectable but friendly working-class homeowners like themselves who they might have expected to move onto the street. The renovators were a disruption in normal neighbourhood life, and though in some ways they were a relief to long-time residents because they didn't bring with them the noise and trouble which some of the previous tenants had caused, in other ways they were an annoyance and trouble themselves in the way they fussed about parking on the street, or about John's truck, which he left in front of his house every night" (Lorimer and Phillips, 1971: 27-28).*

Despite this influx, the working-class residents still derived satisfaction from living there, as shown by their organized opposition to the city's renewal plans.

In general, the economic and political conditions of these working-class urbanites' way of life are sharply distinct from what is found among the middle class. The vulnerability of their limited skills, together with their low and unstable wages, heighten the insecurity of their position. Savings are difficult to accumulate, as most of their earned income is ex-

pended on necessary items. They idealize the benefits of self-employment, with little chance of achieving them.

They perceive "themselves and people like them as being a distinct and separate category of people" (Lorimer and Phillips, 1971: 107). They view themselves as "working people." Although they recognize that the larger society defines them as inferior, they have a sense of their own worth. This is manifested in their reluctance to embrace a more middle-class style of life, even if in time it becomes more economically feasible to do so. Indeed, they distinguish between "respectable" working residents and those categorized as "welfare bums." The latter are viewed negatively because of their failure to meet what is considered the most central obligation of the male role—employment. The "respectable" working-class view other low-income groups of a different racial or ethnic origin as inferior. In this way, they maintain some sense of their own value.

As with Boston's West Enders, these Toronto working-class residents take little interest in the political institution. They manifest a similar withdrawal from, and hostility toward, governmental agencies that assume a middle-class "care-taking" orientation. The staffs of those agencies frequently seem to display a lack of respect for those living in the area.

The East of Parliament people perceive politics as based more on special interests than on moral principles. Governmental institutions are seen as instruments serving the rich and powerful, and thus unresponsive to the needs of ordinary citizens. Reflecting this sense of alienation, the residents vote less often than the average for the city as a whole. The churches and labour unions are the only organizations that attract them. They are more positively oriented toward the local school system—an attitude developed during their youth—but lack detailed knowledge of its operation.

Limited involvement in public agencies is correlated with a sense of their own powerlessness. Except for their immediate efforts to thwart a proposed urban renewal scheme for the area, they are very reluctant to engage in organized and collective attempts to communicate their views to the various governmental bodies. Such isolation from political life sustains their economically deprived condition.

Consideration of the East of Parliament area and the Canadian urban working-class community generally suggests that structural impediments, including lack of adequate education, are central factors inhibiting substantial upward mobility. Such neighbourhoods provide important functions for the variety of types of residents (Crysdale, 1968: 211-12). For the native-born, it offers some security in a familiar social and residential context. For immigrants it provides an opportunity to acquire their own homes, and thus security and status in their new homeland. Political isolation, however, renders such an enclave vulnerable to external agencies.

The Urban Slum

Paralleling the study of the social structure of the urban working-class neighbourhood are attempts to understand how those inner-city areas containing high proportions of low-status residents frequently living in dilapidated housing are socially organized. Such areas are often designated as "slums" (Hunter, 1968), and have been the targets of a variety of redevelopment and renewal projects in a number of North American cities.

Increasing recognition has been given to the need to delineate more carefully the existing functions which urban slums provide for their residents. In addition, the necessity of distinguishing among the various categories of slum dwellers according to these functions has become apparent. Seeley (1959), for example, identifies twelve types of residents in slums. The central criterion is whether slum residence occurs because of necessity and lack of alternatives, or instead represents a means for the attainment of some ultimate goal. Slum dwellers vary in the meaning which they attach to their presence in this type of urban area; they do not all derive the same benefits or disadvantages from living within it. Destruction of the slum through urban renewal necessarily has different consequences—not all inevitably favourable—for many of these diverse categories of residents.

Even with such a possible diversity of residents, however, and with evidence of social problems (such as high rates of unemployment), there still appears to be some underlying order in the urban slum which has not, perhaps, been fully recognized in the past (Kerr, 1958; Lees, 1969). A common assumption—particularly in classical urban theory—is that the physical deterioration in such areas is matched by pronounced social disorganization. This assumption has been challenged; it represents more an evaluative impression than a conclusion derived from empirical analysis—which indeed provides contrasting evidence. One form of social organization that can evolve in such areas is that of "ordered segmentation." Slum dwellers are able to achieve some degree of mutual predictability and thus co-ordination by successfully meshing the principles of territoriality and ethnicity as bases of association and differentiation. Although evidence of the bases of social order in Canadian slums (Mann, 1970; Rowley, 1978) is incomplete, we can illustrate this type of social structure by examining the Near West Side community in Chicago (Suttles, 1968; 1972).

"ORDERED SEGMENTATION" IN A CHICAGO SLUM

The "Addams area" is no more than one-half of a square mile in size; it contained in the mid-1960s almost 20,000 residents. It was in this section of the city that Jane Addams had originally established the community settlement house called Hull House. The district represents a typical "zone of transition." As in many other cities, those of low socioeconomic status concentrate there. To the wider community it is seen as a dangerous slum, a place to avoid except when passing through to work. Although the majority of residents are Italian, more recently blacks, Mexicans, and Puerto Ricans have begun to settle there. Despite the increased heterogeneity, and contrary to the wider impression of the area as disorganized, an underlying social order exists that successfully meshes the principles of territoriality and ethnicity as bases of association and integration.

A central problem facing the residents of the Addams area is the determination of their mutual trustworthiness. In the practical search for moral order they develop relationships among themselves, providing greater personal knowledge of one another and, consequently, mutual predictability. The instruments through which this order is elaborated are the various ethnic, territorial, age, and sex units into which the community is divided. This type of slum social structure represents a form of "ordered segmentation," which is supported in the ecological, institutional, and cultural patterns through which groups of residents arrange their daily lives.

The Addams area is divided into four relatively separate ethnic sections—the Italian, Puerto Rican, black, and Mexican. Each of these, in varying degrees, tends to be divided into additional territorial, age, and sex sub-groupings. Significantly, while on one level the different segments are opposed to one another, at times they co-operate in resisting a common adversary. The congestion of the Addams area ensures that co-residents frequently encounter one another on a daily basis. It is expedient for them to render assistance during a dispute and direct their most intense enmities to those outside the neighbourhood.

The central pattern of ordered segmentation that characterizes this slum community's social organization is reflected in the various types of institutional arrangements in the area. Churches, local business enterprises, and recreational sites become the exclusive preserves of particular ethnic groups. These informal claims of "ownership" are respected by the different segments of the population. The ethnic divisions in the Addams area are culturally sustained as well. Differences in language, dialect, non-verbal gestures, clothing, and modes of personal display represent concrete indices of the ethnic cleavages that exist.

Within the various segments of the community, residents gain personal knowledge of each other's characters. Going beyond public definitions of morality, they develop more particularistic mutual expectations. Street life represents a very important context in which these personal acquaintanceships are achieved. It provides an opportunity for this type of knowledge to be extended to other segments. Personal knowledge is also gained through the informal contacts that occur in the various local business establishments frequented by particular age, sex, and ethnic groupings. Sanctions are imposed not when residents deviate from public morality, but when they depart from what their age, sex, ethnic, and territorial associates expect them as individuals to be and to do.

Fundamental components of that "ordered segmentation" which characterizes the Addams area are the adolescent street-corner groups (cf. Dawley, 1973). The members of each are primarily males of relatively the same age. They tend generally to be from the same ethnic and territorial groups, thus reinforcing these cleavages within the community. Within the groups, the boys are able to establish their own personal identities, according to which expectations of their behaviour are developed by other members. Such groups are also effective in reducing anonymity. Personal acquaintances can be extended among the boys only to a certain point, beyond which the names of the various street-corner groups become instruments through which useful categorical knowledge of others can be attained.

In summary, the Addams-area slum manifests an underlying order in which ethnic, age, sex, and territorial groupings are established as bases of association and differentiation. The segmentation of this community is in part a response to the conditions within the inner city. Such a "zone of transition" is subject to rather abrupt changes in residential patterns—due, for example, to urban renewal. One part of the Addams area has recently been demolished. The remaining sections continue to function without significant change. In short, "the Addams area and its adjacent neighbourhoods are like a multicellular animal whose separate members can be severed without major loss to the survivors" (Suttles, 1968: 143). "Ordered segmentation" represents on one level a mode of adjustment to processes affecting the zone of transition, and, in addition, a means of organizing social life within an inner-city slum neighbourhood.

The Urban Highrise

An important change in inner-city housing has been the development of high-rise apartment buildings during the past several decades. Construction of public housing projects and luxury apartments has created a new physical environment for various segments of the inner-city population. Since 1945 at least 450,000 highrise apartment units have been constructed in Canadian cities (Lorimer, 1978: 129). This trend is especially pronounced in the largest metropolitan areas, and has occurred outside their central cores as well. The rapid rate of highrise apartment construction is a function of the increased demand for this type of accommodation among those, for example, with small households (Nader, 1975). Highrises are economically attractive to developers because of the revenue rentals bring, coupled with tax benefits. (McAfee, 1972). An intriguing area of study is the social patterns manifested in these new types of housing.

In an effort to improve the living conditions of slum dwellers, public housing projects have been constructed in which low-income inner-city residents are frequently concentrated. An example of this is Blackmoor, a thirty-building complex located in the centre of an American midwestern city (Moore, 1969). Constructed to replace a slum, this highrise project offers no significantly greater advantages. Although the physical structure of the housing does represent an improvement, many of the same problems remain. Overcrowding is still pronounced within many individual apartments. The noise level is intense, services and facilities are not maintained, and the residents still lack relative control over their total life situations.

More important, the tenants are subject to the general stigma of living in public housing. They are, in a sense, victims of their locale: "It appears that mere residence in Blackmoor makes the tenant suspect. Many people in Midwest City believe that all the tenants in Blackmoor receive welfare, that all the children are illegitimate, that all the homes are broken, and that most of the residents are criminal" (Moore, 1969: 30-31). This negative stereotype tends to be internalized by the residents themselves. A manifestation of this is the shame they feel about where they live.

Almost two-thirds of "project" households are without a male head. Overall, the fathers who are present occupy a marginal role. A large proportion are unemployed. Most are unskilled, and with the declining job market are unable to obtain a secure wage. In view of the generally insecure position of most of the adult males, the daily life of the families in Blackmoor is characteristically unpredictable (cf. Rainwater, 1970). This is intensified by their subordination to the local housing authority whose rules cannot be ignored because of the threat of possible eviction. Despite their common situation, the relationships among these project families do not seem particularly close. This is perhaps partly a consequence of the high rate of turnover among the tenants, and the absence of some focus for local involvement.

Similar difficulties appear in Lawrence Heights, a Toronto public housing project (Delegan, 1970). Tenants improved their physical accommodations when they moved to the project from other neighbourhoods, but they view it unfavourably in terms of social considerations. They see "The Heights" as "a swearing, drinking, fighting, noisy, destructive population with few controls (particularly over children); therefore, control must be imposed from outside by the Housing Authority, police, social agencies, etc." (Delegan, 1970: 81). As a result few consider the project as home, and indeed, the vast majority do not believe that residence there is a good experience for their children, whose chances for upward mobility are viewed as limited. As in Blackmoor and other public housing projects (Rainwater, 1970), there is an underlying anxiety that violations of various housing regulations might be reported by neighbours. This fear heightens a sense of distance toward one another, discouraging community cohesiveness.

In contrast to the public housing projects, an increasingly important type of dwelling in the inner city is the "luxury" highrise in which more advantaged segments of the urban population reside. For example, "Manhattan Towers" represents an extremely large highrise complex in New York City (Zito, 1974). It consists of eight 29-storey buildings in which 12,000 residents live. Most of the tenants are middle-aged and Jewish. Reflecting the levels of rent in the complex, the majority are at least middle-class. A significant proportion are employed in professional occupations, earning substantial incomes. Although most are married, few households contain children, and fewer still contain teenagers. Reflecting the pattern we saw in chapter 8, young newly married couples tend to move away when their children reach school age. Similarly, older couples move in after their children have been reared.

In general, a relatively high degree of anonymity is manifested in Manhattan Towers (cf. also McGahan, 1972a). Most residents have superficial contacts with neighbours, and the complex is not generally seen as a source of friendships. This certainly reflects the lifestyles of the majority of tenants. Few are at home during the day, and therefore they have less opportunity and need to cultivate local contacts. Such anonymity also serves a "latent function" by permitting "privacy among the propinquitous":

> In a chokingly close, urban environment, a high level of pervasive sociability could be psychically suffocating. Anonymity not only provides psychological distance, it also allows more freedom to come and go without interruption, thus permitting time-pressed residents to maintain their life routines and meet their preferred social obligations (Zito, 1974: 262).

That there is some appreciation of the value of this function is revealed by the low incidence of loneliness among these highrise tenants. There is no evidence that they find this anonymity dissatisfying.

In contrast to a neighbourhood of single-family dwellings a highrise apartment complex such as Manhattan Towers manifests particular physical and social characteristics that influence the patterns of interaction and the general degree of normative formation found there. For example, Reed's (1974: 473) comparative analysis of residential environments in Toronto suggests that the highrise possesses much less "symbolic information content" than single-family homes:

> While the exteriors of the single-family homes were quite expressive of their inhabitants' socioeconomic status, tastes, and living patterns, there were, typically, no differentiating characteristics of unit exteriors in the HR [highrise] building. People living in the SF [single-family] neighborhood could easily ascertain who were desirable neighbors or interactants, and which families or individuals did

not fit this category; HR residents could not evaluate their fellows so easily because everyone lived behind an identical door.

The highrise residents, in short, are less able to manifest their particular identities through manipulation of their dwellings. The absence of open areas makes it difficult for the tenants to observe one another's life routines. These conditions mean that co-residents do not obtain extensive information about each other. As a result, there is an underlying uncertainty regarding the benefits to be gained in cultivating relationships with neighbours. The greater heterogeneity of the highrise also fosters this uncertainty. The sharing of walls, floors, and ceilings means that the tenants have less control over noise, cooking odours, and so on. Domestic arguments can at times be overheard, thus providing neighbours with private and perhaps discrediting information. The possibility that neighbours possess this knowledge only serves further to restrict social contact. This pattern reflects "the almost universal inverse relationship between control of physical distance or boundedness and control of social distance: the greater the amount of physical distance (or control over it) between people, the less the need for devices to control or signal social distance" (Reed, 1974: 475). The greater mobility or turnover among the highrise tenants also represents an important factor discouraging social contacts, and creates an undeveloped informal normative structure—an extremely "precarious social order" at the informal level. In contrast, the residents of the single-family neighbourhood are able to develop greater consensus regarding these norms. Highrise tenants are, as a result, more dependent on agents of formal authority to secure order; strong reliance is placed on the superintendent to mediate relationships among them.

To summarize, in contrast to the social order achieved in the working-class neighbourhood and slums such as the Addams area, the public housing project and the luxury highrise both evidence a precarious informal normative structure.

While the public housing project may offer improved physical accommodation for its low-income residents, it does not necessarily eliminate many of the social problems they experienced in their previous locale. They must contend with the stigma attached to living in public housing, which is frequently isolated from the surrounding neighbourhood. More significantly, the residents often appear unable to establish a cohesive social life. Extensive solidarity is inhibited by their mutual distrust, inability to co-operate, and subordination to the external control of a housing authority. A viable practical moral order—such as ordered segmentation—is not fully developed. Territoriality does not emerge, for example, as a feasible basis of association and differentiation because of the physical structure of the public housing project. The residents recognize their economic deprivation and inability to achieve the success goals of the wider society. Confined to what they view as a relatively dangerous and socially unsatisfactory environment, they manifest caution and distance in dealing with one another to protect what limited resources they possess.

The luxury highrise, increasingly evident in many North American cities, offers housing for residents at the opposite end of the socioeconomic continuum. Its tenants are primarily middle-class. Just as in the public housing project, relationships among the residents are not close. This, however, is due less to feelings of deep distrust and fears of potential exploitation than to the limited opportunities in the highrise for mutual contact. It is also a reflection of the lifestyle of most of the residents: propinquity is not viewed as an important factor in the formation of social ties. In both the public housing project and the highrise the lessened control over physical distance fosters social distance. In each the lack of extensive relationships among the residents, coupled with the high rates of transience, discourages the formation of clear sets of informal norms. Greater dependence must therefore be placed on agents of formal authority to secure order.

THE SUBURBS

One central feature of North American urbanization in the twentieth century has been the increasing growth and settlement of suburban areas. The term "suburb" has been most commonly applied to "an urban place (usually an incorporated place) outside the corporate limits of a large city, but either adjacent thereto or near enough to be closely integrated into the economic life of the central city and within commuting distance of it" (Duncan and Reiss, 1958: 45).

Although the settlement of suburbs has been extensive in recent decades, they did exist on a more modest scale in Europe centuries before the emergence of the industrialized city. Indeed, as Mumford (1961: 483) has shown, the suburb became visible "almost as early as the city itself, and perhaps explains the ability of the ancient town to survive the unsanitary conditions that prevailed within its walls." Particularly for the upper classes the suburb presented a means of escape from the physical and social dangers of urban civilization: "From the thirteenth century on, the dread of plague prompted a periodic exodus from the city; and in that sense one may say that the modern suburb began as a sort of rural isolation ward" (Mumford, 1961: 487).

As we saw in Part Two, it was not until transportation and communication facilities had become more fully developed with industrialization that large-scale dispersion of population became feasible (Warner, 1962). The metropolitan community expanded beyond the confines of the earlier, more concentrated "pedestrial city" without lessening the net of functional interdependence. Stimulating that dispersion as well was the expanding demand for housing, fuelled in turn by the growing urban population. The availability of large tracts of vacant land on the periphery permitted construction of numerous single-family dwellings. This is illustrated by the rapid growth of Vancouver's suburban municipalities (Evenden, 1978); with the better placement of bridges and construction of access routes across the Fraser delta, suburban

Table 61: Percentage Change in Population for the Central Cities and Remaining Parts of the 1961 Census Metropolitan Areas, Canada, 1951-61.

Census metropolitan area	Percentage changes in population[1]				Percentages of 1961 MA population			
	MA	Central city[2]	Other centres of 10,000+[3]	Remainder of MA[4]	MA	Central city	Other centres of 10,000+	Remainder of MA
All MAs	44.8	23.8	57.0	110.7	100	61.9	5.8	32.3
Atlantic	31.9	11.7	78.6	70.6	100	57.1	16.4	26.5
St. John's	32.4	20.4	—	72.8	100	70.0	—	30.0
Halifax	37.3	8.1	101.1	78.0	100	50.3	25.5	24.2
Saint John	22.0	8.6	29.5	57.5	100	57.7	14.5	27.8
Quebec	41.1	27.9	53.6	117.7	100	75.0	3.8	21.2
Montreal	43.3	30.9	71.9	141.9	100	79.6	3.1	17.3
Quebec	29.4	4.9	24.1	76.3	100	48.1	8.2	43.7
Ontario	45.8	15.5	54.5	116.3	100	53.4	4.4	42.2
Hamilton	41.0	21.8	148.5	103.7	100	69.3	11.9	18.8
Kitchener	44.1	53.5	31.2	31.0	100	61.9	18.0	20.1
London	40.6	40.9	—	35.9	100	93.5	—	6.5
Ottawa	46.9	34.2	—	150.6	100	81.4	—	18.6
Sudbury	49.9	40.8	—	80.7	100	72.4	—	27.6
Toronto	50.7	-0.5	30.7	125.0	100	36.8	3.9	59.3
Windsor	18.2	-4.7	—	81.3	100	59.2	—	40.8
Prairies	61.6	50.2	70.4	133.0	100	72.9	10.9	16.2
Winnipeg	33.4	12.6	70.4	78.6	100	55.8	25.0	19.2
Calgary	96.1	87.0	—	233.5	100	89.5	—	10.5
Edmonton	91.0	74.9	—	251.4	100	83.2	—	16.8
British Columbia	39.9	10.9	29.3	90.7	100	46.5	6.1	47.4
Vancouver	40.6	11.5	29.3	101.6	100	48.7	7.2	44.1
Victoria	36.2	7.0	—	60.3	100	35.6	—	64.4

1. The 1961 areas of the MAs are held constant.
2. Groups of incorporated centres are used in some cases: Montreal—all cities of 10,000 and over (in 1961) on Montreal Island; Kitchener—Kitchener and Waterloo; Ottawa—Ottawa, Hull and Eastview.
3. As of 1951.
4. Portion of MA outside of cities of 10,000 and over in 1951.

From *Urban Development in Canada* by Leroy O. Stone (1967). Reproduced by permission of the Minister of Supply and Services Canada.

Table 62:   Population Redistribution, 1951-1971 in Montreal CMA, Toronto CMA, and Vancouver CMA

	I (Central business district)	II (Inner city)	III (Mature Suburbs)	IV (New suburbs)	V Exurbia	CMA total
Montreal CMA:						
1951	26,150	190,670	1,052,315	146,370	123,160	1,538,665
1966	9,385	138,890	1,338,820	739,110	344,770	2,570,975
1971	7,535	116,400	1,266,370	937,065	415,735	2,743,105
Percentage change 1951-1971	−71.2	−39.0	+20.3	+540.2	+237.6	+78.3
Toronto CMA:						
1951	21,225	122,285	897,135	114,345	105,870	1,260,860
1966	15,395	107,190	1,060,755	807,110	298,450	2,289,900
1971	15,835	108,965	1,072,405	1,058,210	372,715	2,628,130
Percentage change 1951-1971	−25.4	−10.9	+19.5	+825.4	+252.0	+108.4
Vancouver CMA:						
1951	13,835	60,515	355,065	108,755	48,005	586,175
1966	9,465	67,360	451,770	308,740	95,755	933,090
1971	7,355	76,680	476,520	383,490	138,325	1,082,370
Percentage change 1951-1971	−46.8	+26.7	+34.2	+252.6	+188.1	+84.6

Zone*

*See Table 49 for explanation of these zones.

From *Perspective Canada II: A Compendium of Social Statistics, 1977.* Reproduced by permission of the Minister of Supply and Services Canada.

expansion intensified among those seeking improved housing on the Lower Mainland. In the United States those living in suburban areas constituted little more than 15 per cent of the nation's population in 1900. From 1940 onward, however, this suburban proportion grew rapidly, as mass housing outside central cities became more readily available. The result of this redistribution is striking: "The 1970 census counted more than 75 million Americans as suburbanites, comprising 37.6 per cent of the total American population; only 31.4 per cent of Americans lived in the central cities of metropolitan areas . . ." (Fava, 1975: 11; cf. Hawley, 1956).

In chapter 4 we observed a similar pattern in urban Canada. Table 61 indicates, for example, that between 1951 and 1961 the population residing within Canadian metropolitan areas but outside incorporated centres of 10,000 and over more than doubled. In contrast, the central cities of these areas increased by only one-fourth during the same decade. Such suburban expansion was repeated in each region of the country. The central cities in the Prairie provinces actually were the only ones to grow by more than 30 percent. No region showed a suburban growth rate of less than 70 percent—a level found in the Atlantic provinces, where metropolitan expansion was more limited. Focusing on the three largest census metropolitan areas—Montreal, Toronto, and Vancouver—Table 62 shows the rapid growth that occurred between 1951 and 1971, especially in the "new suburbs"—the mass-produced

Table 63: Proportion of Total Metropolitan Toronto Employment by Area, 1956-74

| Year | Total employ- ment in Metro Toronto | City of Toronto | | | Other munici- palities[3] | Total |
		I	II[1]	III[2]		
1956	630,200	25.5%	18.9%	29.8%	25.8%	100.0%
1960	674,700	24.7	16.0	25.8	33.5	100.0
1964	711,700	23.4	14.0	23.9	38.7	100.0
1970	920,000	21.1	11.4	18.5	49.0	100.0
1974	1,057,600	21.2	10.8	16.6	51.4	100.0
% change in total employment 1956-74[4]	+67.8%	+39.5%	−3.8%	−6.5%	+234.0%	—

1. Does not include tracts 86 and 87 but includes Tracts 1, 2, 8, 9, 10 and 20.
2. Includes tracts 86 and 87 but does not include Tracts 1, 2, 8, 9, 10 and 20.
3. Includes East York, North York, York, Etobicoke, and Scarborough.
4. These figures indicate increases or decreases in the percentage of individuals who have their place of work in these zones.

From *Perspective Canada II: A Compendium of Social Statistics, 1977.* Reproduced by permission of the Minister of Supply and Services Canada.

suburban developments that emerged in the early 1950s, oriented to the automobile as the dominant form of transport.

It is important to recognize that not all suburbs are "dormitory towns"—
that is, not all function simply as residential havens for workers employed
elsewhere (Schnore, 1965a: 154-55). As metropolitan areas expand, many
economic activities disperse as well, paralleling the decentralization of population (Hardwick, 1974). "Suburban cities," for example—such as Toronto's
Erin Mills or Edmonton's Mill Woods—seek to develop their own employment
opportunities (Pressman, 1975). Table 63 illustrates this trend in Metropolitan
Toronto. Between 1956 and 1974 the proportion of total Metro Toronto
employment concentrated in outlying suburban and exurban areas increased
significantly.

Considerable attention has been given to the demographic and planning
implications of this suburbanization process (Whyte, 1958; Carver, 1962;
Lithwick, 1970). Of greater relevance here, increasing consideration has been
given to the social organization of suburban communities in order to determine whether it is significantly different from the social patterns displayed in
cities. This research has particular importance for the elaboration of more
comprehensive and precise theories of urbanization (Popenoe, 1977).

The Myth of Suburbia

The initial understanding of the social structure and social consequences of the
suburban community was strongly influenced by several investigations in the
mid-1950s (Spectorsky, 1955; Seeley, Sim and Loosley, 1956; Whyte, 1957).
These studies so captured the public mind that a "myth of suburbia" was unconsciously constructed, much as the theme of urban disorganization had been
emphasized within the earlier typological tradition. Subsequent research
sought to modify and test more rigorously the contents of this myth.

Certainly one of the most influential portraits of suburban society is
Whyte's (1957) analysis of Park Forest, Illinois. Focusing on this "package"
suburb because it houses many aspiring executives of large companies, or what
he terms "organization men," Whyte examines the sense of community, the
patterns of association and consumption, and the general institutional life
found among the residents. Many of these patterns, he believes, can be generalized to similar types of new suburbs that emerged during the post-war period
and in which the young organization man is dominant.

Significantly, Whyte argues that a suburb such as Park Forest represents
more than newly constructed mass housing. The influx of the mobile middle
class creates a "new social institution," a communal way of life in which adjustment and group involvement are highly valued. The residents of Park
Forest moved there seeking better housing at a reasonable price and adequate
facilities for themselves and their children. After arriving, "they created something over and above the original bargain. Together, they developed a social
atmosphere of striking vigor" (Whyte, 1957: 314).

A central characteristic of the organization men is their transience and mobility. Park Forest represents a temporary way station from which they would move shortly, responding to the demands of their careers and the wishes of their companies. Since they are not deeply integrated on a permanent basis into one local community, they can be viewed as truly "rootless." Yet they adapt somewhat to this condition. In Park Forest they participate in a relatively intense social life which partially compensates for the disruption resulting from their transience. They develop, in short, a sense of home in their temporary locale.

The dominance of locally based social attachments is clearly apparent. An ethic of sociability and conformity to group norms is stressed. Class distinctions based on family background are minimized. New entrants to the suburb who are not yet fully middle-class in their mores are socialized. It appears that such a community actually represents "the second great melting pot" in which the patterns of behaviour displayed by the organization may become the model for others to follow. Changes in political affiliation are not uncommon: "people from big, urban Democratic wards tended to become Republicans and, if anything, more conservative than those whose outlook they are unconsciously adopting" (Whyte, 1957: 332). Changes in religious affiliation also occur as do modifications in standards of personal taste.

The stress on an "outgoing" way of life is manifested in communal coordination of patterns of consumption. It is the locally based group that appears to determine when certain luxuries are redefined as necessities. Displays of conspicuous consumption are not encouraged. Those residents significantly surpassing the income levels of their neighbours are pressured through social isolation to move elsewhere. The emphasis on social involvement is seen in the extent to which the search for greater privacy is discouraged, in the variety of local organizations and civic activities that are developed, and in the stress given in the community schools to adjustment and getting along with others. Even in the religious sector, formal doctrines are less important than opportunities for social activities. The intense social life in the suburb is facilitated also by residents' mutual tolerance and strong desire to seek common values. The result of this social immersion is the group's rather formidable control over the individual. In exchange, the latter gains a "foster family." Common interests and needs heighten mutual attachments, and render the residents' search for community fruitful. Although Park Foresters view neighbourliness and social participation as a "moral imperative," they are also conscious of the conflicts and costs involved in such cohesiveness. On the one hand, they gain social support in their transient state of life. At the same time, pressures toward conformity infringe on their individuality and make unclear whether their social adjustment constitutes "selflessness, or surrender." This dilemma, Whyte argues, is central to the entire existence of the organization man.

Whyte's portrait of Park Forest strongly affected the general image of suburbia that was held for a time. Several additional studies of other suburban communities, such as Toronto's suburb of Crestwood Heights (Don Mills)

(Seeley, Sim, and Loosley, 1956), enriched that image (Stein, 1965: 199f.). Crestwood Heights grew as part of Toronto's outward expansion after World War II: "Less than three miles from downtown, with ready access to urban improvements, and adequate separation from interior housing and from industry, it furnished suitable conditions for an elite dormitory" (1956: 38). The availability of single-family homes with adequate access to downtown Toronto attracted affluent residents. In this upper-middle-class Canadian community, great emphasis is placed on the attainment and maintenance of social status. The residents manifest deep commitment to a fundamental theme in North American cultures—"the great North American dream, a dream of a material heaven in the here and now, to be entered by the successful elect" (1956: 6). Consistent with this ideal is the perceived connection between status and material affluence as a basis for judging others. This orientation permeates the institutions and cultural traits of the community. The type of house owned as well as its specific location in the suburb represent important bases for securing esteem. Memberships in the proper clubs and associations serve as additional instruments for declaration and enhancement of relative status.

Correlated with this pursuit of status is the emphasis placed on the male career as a means of attaining success. The residents' whole conception of time is fundamentally influenced by the dynamics of a career. Tradition is consequently devalued. Family ancestry is not an appropriate basis for status claims. Social ties, particularly those to kin, are viewed as expendable; career demands take precedence. Pursuit of a career is presented to young males as the dominant goal of their lives. Achievement and competition are firmly established as guiding standards of conduct.

Such concerns deeply mold the entire process of child rearing which represents the core focus of Crestwood Heights' institutions. The ideal of a functioning personality, according to which a child is expected to develop, is "that of the individuated person who can and wants to separate himself from his kinship group and establish a new family unit" (Seeley, Sim, and Loosley, 1956: 61-62). Beginning in nursery school and extending through the early years of childhood, the skills and attitudes viewed as necessary for the attainment of success are disseminated both formally and informally. The child is expected to manifest maturity and individual responsibility, as he would be required to do in adulthood. Nevertheless, there does appear to be confusion and ambiguity regarding the most appropriate methods of child rearing among many of the residents.

A critical feature of familial life overall in Crestwood Heights is the extent to which members' bonds to institutions and individuals outside the home come to dominate over those within the family. This is clearly manifested in the increasing control over, and responsibility for, the socialization of the young by the community's secondary institutions. The most influential institution appears to be the school. As in Park Forest, it has become the major agent concerned with the social, ethical, and emotional development of Crestwood

Heights' youth. It represents the community's "major industry," since no other sector is as physically and socially dominant. The school system increasingly contains a variety of experts—such as educational psychologists and counselors—who exercise an important influence on the values disseminated. The product of this socialization system is marked by ambivalence. The child is encouraged both to compete and co-operate, to manifest humanitarianism and maturity while at the same time achieving success and ultimately enhancing his status. The family and school systems do not fully insure that both these sets of values can be easily achieved. This creates an ambiguity that permeates the suburb's entire culture.

The picture which these and other writings present of suburbia, though not necessarily consistent with each other, generated a great deal of criticism. In the years following World War II, as the settlement of mass-produced suburban housing increased rapidly, a number of commentaries appeared condemning and attacking that style of life suburbanites were said to lead. Mumford (1972: 7), for example, views the evolving mass suburb with disdain, accusing it of "snobbery, segregation, status seeking, political irresponsibility." It represents, in his judgment, an unfortunately artificial environment in which homogeneity, uniformity, and standardization are all dominating features. Reisman (1964: 235), in turn, interprets suburbanization as "a tremendous but tacit revolt against industrialism." Although defences of the suburban community are not lacking (e.g., McGinley, 1959), an emphasis on the negative features of suburbia predominates.

Donaldson (1969: viii) offers several possible reasons for this pessimism:

> First of all, the "post hoc" fallacy accounts for much of the attack. Critics in the 1950s watched conformity spreading across the land, for example, and attributed its spread to the concurrent phenomenon of suburbanization. People moved to the suburbs, such arguments ran, and the suburbs made the people conformists . . . Another source for the attack was provided by the many writers who tended to generalize about all suburbs from the sample of a single one. This practice frequently resulted in unjustified conclusions, and explains why some critics found too much neighboring in the suburbs, while others found too much loneliness.

At a more fundamental level, the attack on suburbia derives from a recognition that such an environment does not embody that Jeffersonian ideal— stressing "a return to nature, a return to the small village, a return to self-reliant individualism"—to which many of the critics unconsciously adhere (Donaldson, 1969: 22). Just as the city had earlier been seen as a disorganizing force, now the suburb itself is viewed in a negative light (Bell, 1968: 143).

Implicit in these criticisms is a set of images of suburbia, derived especially from Whyte's analysis, that "coalesced into a full-blown myth, complete with its articles of faith, its sacred symbols, its rituals, its promise for the future, and its resolution of ultimate questions" (Berger, 1960: 3-4). Insofar as it does form a "myth," the degree to which it accurately reflects reality is ignored. The meaning of suburbia becomes standardized and stereotyped in the popular mind. Suburbs are believed to be

1. Warrens of young executives on the way up;
2. Uniformly middle class;
3. "Homogeneous";
4. Hotbeds of participation;
5. Child-centered and female dominated;
6. Transient;
7. Wellsprings of the outgoing life;
8. Arenas of adjustment;
9. Beulah Lands of returns to religion;
10. Political Jordans from which Democrats emerge Republicans (Dobriner, 1963: 6).

These features are viewed as particularly characteristic of the mass-produced tract developments in areas surrounding many North American cities. Implicit in this myth is the belief that there exists a distinctive suburban way of life which contrasts with what is manifested in the city. This interpretation represents a continuation of the typological perspective (Fava, 1975: 15). Just as the city has been viewed as containing unique social patterns that set it apart qualitatively from the non-urban, so too is "suburbanism" identified as unique to these outlying areas. New entrants to these settlements are socially and culturally transformed, paralleling changes urbanites are believed to have undergone (Dobriner, 1963: ix). The suburban and urban products are qualitatively different. Yet in each case the process of transformation is similar: type of settlement, it is implicitly believed, constitutes the dominant force in the emergence of a unique style of life. This popular assumption subsequently became the object of scrutiny in more rigorous investigations of the nature of suburban social life. For example, Berger's (1960) study of working-class suburbanites in San Jose, California, demonstrates that they are not transformed to a middle-class way of life. The supposed attributes of suburbanism are not manifested in a working-class suburban tract. While this suggests the over-generalized nature of the portrait of suburbia that has been drawn, it also points to a need to determine whether and in what manner the suburban type of settlement gives rise to a unique style of life.

The Suburban Lifestyle: From Myth to Attempted Explanation

Three alternative interpretations of the relationship between suburban residence and lifestyle patterns have emerged (Dobriner, 1963: 61f.; Marshall, 1973; Fischer, 1976). Each stresses a separate set of factors to account for whatever differences appear to exist between suburban and urban social life. Each attempts to explain the essential social structure of the suburban community.

The structural interpretation. From this perspective, the specific structural and demographic characteristics of the suburb encourage a distinct style of life. For example, Martin (1956) distinguishes a set of "definitive" characteristics of the suburb which constitute the dominant factors affecting its social life:

1. Ecological position: The suburban community is located outside the central city but within its hinterland. As a result, suburbanites are "less active than urban residents but significantly more active than farm residents in social events located at the city center" (Martin, 1956: 447). Those living in outlying areas are less able to take advantage of the different social opportunities in the central city.

2. Commuting: Because of the ecological position of the suburban community and its residential specialization, commuting to work is a necessity. This structural feature, too, has important social correlates:

> Commuters participate less than non-commuters in voluntary associations and informal groupings in the residence community. Commuters participate more than non-commuters in the affairs of some community other than the residence community. As a result of the daily commuting of males, women play an unusually important role in voluntary association and other interaction situations in the suburbs (Martin, 1956: 449).

As Dobriner (1963: 16) has pointed out, however, the need to commute to work is not restricted to suburbanites. Those residing in central cities also frequently are required to travel daily to their place of employment. Commuting, therefore, more correctly seems "a national, not a suburban, pattern." Nor is there conclusive evidence, as Martin himself admits, that the above correlates are actually a function of commuting, rather than some other factor, such as length of settlement or type of suburb.

3. Size and density: Paralleling Wirth's analysis of the demographic sources of urbanism, Martin argues that the size and density of the suburban community are also important in accounting for specific lifestyle patterns. Although this has not been adequately documented, he proposes "that the relatively small size and low density of most suburban populations would provide a social situation conducive to certain types of relationships (e.g., neighboring, visiting, and primary types of relations in general) and disadvantageous to others (e.g., gatherings of individuals with extremely rare interests ordinarily occur only in urban centers large enough to include several such persons) . . ." (Martin, 1956: 450). To these characteristics of small size and low density, Dobriner (1963: 9) adds the heightened "visibility" which accompanies residence. The openness and spaciousness of suburbs permit residents the opportunity to observe more readily one another's behaviour. This, in turn, allows for clearer recognition of any common interests as bases for further social contact. An important problem overall is to determine whether particular aspects of suburban lifestyles can be explained by reference to such factors as size, density, and visibility, apart from ecological position and commuting.

Although he recognizes the importance of secondary and "derivative" features of the suburb (such as its socioeconomic composition), Martin still proposes that the structural "definitive" features exercise an independent influence on behaviour patterns, and thus account in part for particular components of suburban life styles.

The selective migration interpretation. A second attempt to explain the nature of suburban lifestyles places greater emphasis on the selectivity process than on any structural differences between urban and suburban communities. Particular types of families are attracted to the suburb because of the opportunities it affords for the fulfillment of certain types of needs and values. Their behaviour patterns simply reflect these attitudes.

Bell (1968), for example, distinguishes three dominant types of lifestyles between which an increasing proportion of the population in urban-industrial societies are able to choose:

1. Familism: This lifestyle places "a high valuation on family living, marriage at young ages, a short childless time span after marriage, child-centeredness . . ." (Bell, 1968: 147).

2. Careerism: Here the emphasis is given to the pursuit of a career. Involvement in activities not directly related to the attainment of increased status and wealth is restricted.

3. Consumership: Within this lifestyle individuals focus "their effort, time, and money on 'having a good time,' 'living it up', or enjoying life as much as possible, and they do so in ways that are unconnected with family or career goals" (Bell, 1968: 148). Individuals do not necessarily pursue the same lifestyle throughout their lives. An emphasis on one does, however, tend to preclude simultaneous commitment to the other.

Bell argues that suburban residence does not appeal equally to persons manifesting these different lifestyles. It is most conducive to the pursuit of familism:

> the move to the suburbs expresses an attempt on the part of the movers to find a location in which to conduct family life that is more suitable than that offered by central cities, i.e., that persons moving to the suburbs are principally those who have chosen familism as an important element of their life styles as over against career or consumership (Bell, 1968: 151).

His examination of the motives people have for moving to Chicago's suburbs confirm this.

Nevertheless, Marshall (1973: 141) has argued that this research is actually inconclusive, partly because of the methodological weakness of its approach:

> It is not clear that the reasons given by people for moving to suburbs—at present, the principal technique for evaluating the selective migration hypothesis—correspond to their "real" reasons. While respondents tend to give "familistic" answers such as "better for children," "more space," and so on, they may in fact be pro-

viding *themselves* with an ad hoc interpretation of behavior, the causes of which involve such factors as availability of suitable housing.

In addition, it is not altogether certain that this research adequately controls for all the structural factors which might influence the patterns found.

A slightly different attempt to validate the selective migration thesis is illustrated in Fava's (1956, 1958) investigations of urban-suburban variations in levels of neighbouring. She selected sub-samples of residents from Manhattan, Queens, and suburban Nassau County within the New York metropolitan area. These were matched on a number of different characteristics—including, for example, marital status, education, and length of residence. Despite these controls, those living in suburban Nassau still manifest higher levels of neighbouring than their Manhattan counterparts. One possible explanation for this, she proposes, is that those moving to suburbia possess specific values and attitudes—one of which is a positive orientation to neighbouring—that distinguish them from urbanites. In short, "selectivity on the basis of non-rational elements of habit, feelings, and experience, which may be called social-psychological, should be added to standard ecological factors in explaining suburban social characteristics" (Fava, 1958: 126).

Class and life-cycle stage interpretation. A third perspective proposes that suburban lifestyles are simply the function of class and life-cycle variables and not of suburban residence *per se*. Hence, if these variables are held constant in comparing behaviour patterns of urbanites and suburbanites, no significant differences will emerge. This interpretation minimizes the importance of the structural features of the suburb. It also can be distinguished from the selective migration approach:

> Advocates of the selective migration hypothesis argue that selection is *not* solely on the basis of class and life-cycle stage. Rather, they seem to be contending that "segments" of the middle and working classes in particular age categories value such things as family life and social involvement to a much higher degree than their class and life-cycle counterparts in the city . . . some families may choose to remain in the city, even though they have children and are middle class, in order to maximize access to various activities which can only be found there . . . (Marshall, 1973: 126-27).

Among those emphasizing this third perspective are Gans (1962), Berger (1960), and Dobriner (1963). Dobriner, for example, argues that attention to the class factor will provide "a major key with which to unlock the suburban riddle" (Dobriner, 1963: 38). Like Berger, Dobriner believes that many of the earlier descriptions of the suburban way of life are nothing more than portraits of middle-class behaviour patterns. The fact that families of this still rather heterogeneous stratum concentrate in various outlying areas only serves to heighten awareness of those patterns. Dobriner does admit that particular structural features of the suburb have some influence on residents' social activities. As noted earlier, its greater spaciousness enhances mutual "visibility," which in turn encourages greater interaction among those with similar interests. Similarly, there seem to be greater opportunities for the middle class to pursue their child-rearing ideals in the suburban community. Nevertheless, he emphasizes, these differences must not be exaggerated:

> The urban and suburban upper-middle-class share many more significant characteristics between them than either shares with the working class. The similarities in their views of education, political ideology, family organization, religion, and life style in general are far more numerous than the differences . . . But the massive intrusion of class variables into the entire complex of relationships and values in the suburbs clearly indicates the primacy of class over place variables. In the final analysis, suburbanites and city dwellers are joined together by common class bonds, and relatively few factors separate them. It is unfortunate that the emphasis given to the few uniquely suburban situational features have blinded so many to this basic fact (Dobriner, 1963: 59).

As Berger clearly demonstrated, a similar conclusion can be drawn generally with respect to working-class suburbanites and urbanites.

In evaluating these three perspectives, there are still several fundamental issues to be resolved, such as the underlying typological orientation inherent in the first two approaches:

> Indeed, it may be that we are asking the wrong question—that the question of urban-suburban variations in life styles is irrelevant. Given our interest in determinants of particular life styles, perhaps we ought to be more concerned with specifying and evaluating the types of variables which affect them, rather than with the simple comparison of "suburban" and "urban" behavior—a comparison which inevitably confounds a variety of possible causes (Marshall, 1973: 143).

A similar criticism, as we saw earlier, was directed at the more general typological perspective derived from classical and urban theory. In addition, we should note the frequently arbitrary and ambiguous meaning of a suburb—for example, it is not uncommon to exclude from this category low-density areas *within* a city's boundaries despite the fact that they are quite similar to "suburban" communities in terms of a variety of structural features. Finally, there is a clear need for more rigorous research, employing adequate controls, to distinguish "the independent, joint, and interactive effects of structures, social-psychological selection, class, and family composition" (Marshall, 1973: 143). Insufficient attention has been given to this methodological imperative (Popenoe, 1977).

The Canadian Suburb

During the past two decades, a number of empirical investigations of particular suburban communities have emerged (e.g., Willmott and Young, 1960; Gans, 1969; Zelan, 1968). These studies attempt to move beyond the facile generalizations promulgated in the mass media and in the initial explorations of suburbia discussed earlier. They prove invaluable in demonstrating the complexity of suburban social life and the need to integrate more rigorously the alternative interpretations noted above.

Concern for the social structure of suburban communities in Canada has not been lacking. However, the amount of detailed research comparable to the study of Crestwood Heights has been quite limited. One initial attempt to fill this gap is Clark's (1966) analysis of the suburbanization process in the Toronto area during the 1950s. Paralleling the findings of others, the results of this research are not entirely consistent with the portrait drawn in the suburban myth.

Clark sees the process of suburban development as one in which the country becomes transformed into the city (cf. also Carver, 1962). The suburban community represents a society in transition, hence lacking definable form or structure. It is "an urban society not yet complete." Clark analyzes some of its social features, manifested particularly in the mass-produced suburban areas outside Toronto.

The dominant motivation for the move to such areas is the desire to obtain a house and adequate living space. Change of residence does not appear to represent an attempt to escape from the city. Nor does it manifest for more than a small minority an attempt to relocate in a prestigious setting. There is a certain self-selection, however, involved in the types of population participating in this suburban influx. They are not from the extremes of the economic continuum, but are primarily young middle-class families—native-born, Protestant, and of British origin. Nor are they as deeply attached socially and culturally to the city as those who stay behind: "It was people with no great stake in the urban society, no heavy commitment to urban values, who were prepared to move to the suburbs without regard to what the suburbs were like" (Clark, 1966: 83). Urbanites such as newly arrived immigrants, dependent on the ties of social support they have forged in the city, are less prepared for any such change of residence. Consistent with their less intense attachment to urban social life, those moving to the suburbs are also characterized by the relative absence of any pronounced sense of community or strong involvement in groups beyond the family. Such an orientation influences social patterns evolved after the move, particularly since the residents have much greater interest in establishing a new home than in constructing a new way of life.

In direct contrast to the image of suburbia portrayed by Whyte in his analysis of Park Forest, Clark emphasizes more the Toronto suburbanites' desire to be left alone. The young families concentrate primarily on their new homes and are not interested in assuming constraining obligations at the neighbourhood and community levels. There is little evidence of intense neighbouring or participation in local life. Far from the stereotype of suburban hyperactivity, a general tone of social apathy is present in these communities. Clark argues that the "sameness" of the suburban population contributes to this lack of close relationships: "Everyone is too much like everyone else. Where there were no means of discerning who among the neighbors could be claimed a good friend, neighborhood associations necessarily assumed a character of casualness and ephemerality. There were few with whom secrets could be shared or intimacies exchanged" (Clark, 1966: 143). The absence of a distinctive physical character in the suburban neighbourhood discourages the development of close bonds among those within the same local area. The set of mutual obligations developed among those living on the same street, for example, are extremely limited and have a minimal impact on behaviour. The conception of the "good society," to which the suburbanites appear to be attached, "was the society that made no demands upon them." The new suburban community is characterized by little organized activity outside the home. In its incomplete and transitional state, it is, in a sense, a society of strangers. In time, as it loses this character and a definable structure emerges, it assumes less the status of a "suburban" society, and becomes more fully "urban."

The validity and generalizability of Clark's analysis of suburbia have not been extensively investigated. There have, however, been several additional tentative explorations of particular aspects of the Canadian suburban community (e.g., Rush and Mansfield, 1973). One important example is Michelson's (1973a; 1973b; 1977) long-term study of the social consequences of the suburban residential setting in Toronto. This is part of a more comprehensive comparison of four different residential environments in which a metropolitan area's population is housed—downtown apartments, downtown homes, suburban apartments, and suburban homes. In examining the social correlates of these four types of housing and location combinations, Michelson's research addresses the following questions:

> (1) To what extent does a particular residential environment tend to attract a particular type of resident?
> (2) To what extent does a particular way of life become pronounced in a particular physical setting? Do aspects of the environment influence "what people do, with whom they do it, and where they do it", or all else being equal, do they merely repeat the round of life which they formerly pursued in a physically different environment?
> (3) If a typical way of life emerges in a particular setting, what happens to the new resident who fails to adopt it?
> (4) What effect does the passage of time have on people's adjustment to their environment? (Michelson, 1977: 5).

These research foci parallel closely other earlier attempts, discussed above, to explore systematically the social implications of urban and suburban residence, and to explain more fully any apparent differences.

A large number of families were interviewed several times during an eighteen-month period—Phase I occurred at the point of signing a lease or agreement to purchase, Phase II two months after the move, and Phase III one year later. Michelson (1973a: 7) argues, for a fuller understanding of the social consequences of an affluent family's location in any of the four types of settings, it is necessary to focus on more than the mere move itself. Attention must be given to the stage "where a family falls within its own successive pattern of residential movements." The motivations for different moves as well as the types of satisfactions experienced can thereby be more clearly grasped.

Michelson identifies three fundamental stages in the "family mobility cycle": (1) *the baseline stage*—this constitutes the first stage in establishment of a family or its entrance to a metropolitan community. Residential choice is determined less by previous experience than by consideration of such factors as distance from work; (2) *the stage of incremental change*—during this stage, the family may move several times in response to practical considerations, but without realizing the ideal of a single-family home in a low-density setting; (3) *the approximation of the ideal*—here that ideal is attained with settlement in a suburban single-family home.

Families in Stage 2 living in highrise apartments are found to be satisfied with their housing, even though it does not represent their ultimate aspiration. They view it as a temporary compromise, and believe that in due time they will attain their ideal. Those in Stage 3 are also satisfied—they have achieved some approximation of that ideal. They are unlikely to move again, except as required by job changes. The conception of the family mobility cycle, therefore, reveals "how both groups of movers could be reasonably satisfied while maintaining basically the same housing aspirations, but while living in very different objective situations" (Michelson, 1973a: 15).

Michelson's research also clearly demonstrates some selectivity in the types of population attracted to the four residential settings. Those moving to downtown housing are more likely to be highly educated, with both husband and wife employed as professionals. The proximity of cultural facilities is one important reason for the decision to live there. Downtown highrises attract residents who are in the early stages of their careers. As our discussion in chapter 8 suggested, familism as a lifestyle orientation is not pronounced, a fact reflected in the high proportion of females in the labour force. Ultimately, these women expect to move to their own detached homes in outlying areas.

In contrast, families moving to suburban homes tend to be more highly oriented to neighbours. One central reason for this is that "most of them are moving from situations where they feel socioeconomically superior to their old neighbors and to one where they feel that their neighbors are equal or superior to themselves and are personally compatible" (Michelson, 1973a: 24). This influences the subsequent degree of contact among co-residents. With respect to suburban highrises, Michelson found a greater concentration of families with children among these than is true for their downtown counterparts. These suburban families appear more uncertain as to when they would move, reflecting their lower economic status. These represent the least satisfied, and illustrate a case of "families in Stage II of the family mobility cycle, whose movement into Phase III is potentially blocked" (Michelson, 1973a: 25).

Consistent with this pattern of selectivity, residential satisfaction is a function of the level of "congruence" between types of housing context and in-dividual orientation (Popenoe, 1977). Working wives living in downtown highrises are more fully satisfied after a year than are those not employed. In the case of those living in suburban single family homes, levels of satisfaction are highest among residents who arrived with a greater interest in establishing relationships with their neighbours.

In addition to such patterns of selectivity, there appear to be a variety of post-move differences in social contacts, daily activities, and leisure patterns, among the residents of the four settings. Those living in suburban single family homes are much more likely to develop close relationships with their neigh-bours, including patterns of mutual aid. Michelson interprets this intensive level of contact as a sign of their "vulnerability." These suburban homeowners do not adjust as readily to their new residences as do those in other settings. This, along with their greater spatial isolation—especially among the wives—encourages social ties with neighbours.

One year after arrival, suburban wives appear least satisfied with the way they spend their time. This is partly the result of their not being employed; but another important factor is the distances they are required to travel for various activities. Although they had not foreseen this as a problem prior to the move because of their preoccupation with the greater space and more intense social life afforded by suburban settlement, they are extremely dissatisfied with such inconvenience. Over time the suburbanites feel this even more strongly, although they do become more satisfied with the social aspects of their residen-tial setting. As a consequence of their location, the "paths of travel" followed by these families are quite different from those downtown:

> people living in centre city concentrate their trips . . . to traditional downtown destinations . . . Suburbanites, particularly those living in towns, not only travel further to get anything but once underway are very likely to go all the way downtown. At the least, suburbanites exhibit a far greater diversity in the loca-tions where they choose to shop for clothing or to seek entertainment (Michelson, 1973a: 43).

This diversity is partly a function of their greater reliance on the automobile. Distance is also a factor in discouraging suburban housewives' involvement in organizations located elsewhere. As a result, despite their greater contact with neighbours, they still spend more time alone during the week than those living elsewhere.

The variety of housing types and locations—of which the suburban home is one example—thus offers different opportunities for behaviour patterns (cf. also Popenoe, 1977). The advantages of each benefit selective segments of the population. In particular, Michelson (1973a: 51) argues:

> . . . the primary benefits intended and realized by the respective environmental choices focus on the wife for the downtown apartment (to alleviate her travel time, in the perspective of her career pursuits and the postponement of children),

on the husband in the downtown house (reflecting his emphasis on his job and on cultural pastimes, usually shared by his wife, but not as strongly), and on the husband for the suburban single family home (he is the one believing most strongly in the virtues of the suburban location as desirable for his family, at the same time suffering few obstacles in escaping this location to reach his daily place of employment, leaving his wife to encounter the negative aspects of this setting)
. . .

Satisfaction is less, therefore, among the family members who do *not* benefit the most from the housing choice.

In general, such comparisons of the suburban residential setting with other types of housing environment will enable us to understand better the relative importance of structural and selectivity factors in accounting for suburban lifestyle patterns. This has the potential for significantly advancing our understanding of the social correlates of suburban residence.

SUMMARY

1. In comparison to the wider metropolitan area the inner city typically is marked by such characteristics as lower average household income, a greater proportion of the population with little education, and a higher employment rate. The Canadian inner city, however, does not contain a higher degree of overcrowding.

2. The inner city is internally heterogeneous. It includes such diverse neighbourhoods as declining areas (or slums), stable areas (such as working-class communities), revitalized areas (due to re-entry of middle-class renovators), and areas subject to massive redevelopment (through public and private renewal projects).

3. As part of the inner-city mosaic the working-class neighbourhood provides important functions for its residents—satisfactory shelter, security in a familiar social and residential context to which they are strongly attached. It forms a locally-based social system in which close-knit networks centred in the area channel that attachment. Involuntary relocation from such a neighbourhood disrupts the spatial and social bases of residents' sense of community. That such relocation can easily occur reflects the political vulnerability of working-class residents.

4. Classical urban theory assumed that the physical deterioration in inner-city slums is matched by pronounced social disorganization. Such an assumption, however, overlooks the subtle and diverse ways social order is achieved in declining areas. One way is by ordered segmentation, in which territoriality and ethnicity can be combined to form bases of association and differentiation among slum dwellers.

5. Public housing projects and luxury highrise apartments provide accommodations for residents at opposite ends of the socioeconomic continuum. Neither type of housing is confined to the inner city. In each, lessened control over physical distance fosters social distance among residents. High rates of transience and the lack of extensive relationships among them inhibit the development of clear sets of informal norms. To achieve order they must rely heavily on agents of formal authority, such as the housing authority or the superintendent of the building.

6. As metropolitan areas expand and become more internally differentiated, suburban communities emerge as more visible parts of the territorially extended system. During the last several decades, as in the United States, Canadian suburbs have experienced significant growth in population. We must recognize, however, that not all suburbs are primarily residential communities. Many offer significant employment opportunities.

7. With respect to the social consequences of suburbanization, a "myth of suburbia" was initially developed that proposed, much like the theme of urban disorganization within the classical typological paradigm, that this new type of settlement fostered a distinctive style of life among its residents. This included such traits as child-centredness, almost frenetic involvement in local social life, and conformity to middle-class standards or symbols of status and success. Such a portrait of the suburban way of life has been found to be overgeneralized and stereotypical—just as Wirth's depiction of the urban way of life was.

8. In attempting to understand the nature of suburban social organization three alternative perspectives have emerged, each stressing a different set of factors. The structural interpretation argues that the specific structural and demographic characteristics of the suburb—including its ecological position, size, density and distance from the workplace—exercise an independent and important influence on social life. In contrast, a second perspective emphasizes that any distinctive features of suburban social organization, such as high involvement in local social relationships, are products simply of the fact that the suburb attracts particular types of families and individuals who value such involvement. In short, social patterns found in suburban communities are not structurally induced but rather reflect a process of selective migration. The third interpretation proposes that suburban social structure is shaped predominantly by the class and life-cycle composition of its population. Urban and suburban residents of the same class are far more similar to each other than are suburbanites with different class backgrounds.

9. More recent research—for example, that in Toronto comparing the social consequences of a variety of residential environments—suggests the importance of all three approaches and the need to synthesize them more fully. A residential setting such as a low-density suburban community does attract particular categories of persons because of its congruence with their desired lifestyles. Such a setting also provides both opportunities for particular behaviour patterns after the move—for example, relatively active contact with neighbours is facilitated in the suburban setting—as well as disadvantages, such as the need to travel some distance to various facilities. Not all residents

benefit equally from living in this environment. In summary, suburban social structure is influenced by the class, life-cycle composition and lifestyle orientations of the population it attracts, as well as by the nature of its residential environment. Rather than view these three perspectives as mutually exclusive, we must explore on a comparative level how the factors they emphasize interact in complex ways.

Part Six

Regulating the Urban System

In examining urban social and ecological organization from both a dynamic and a structural perspective, we must recognize that the growth, development, and resultant structure of the urban system are influenced by how power is distributed and exercised. Not all groups are equally effective in shaping the city's spatial and economic patterns for their own benefit. Concern for regulating the urban system, as we observed in the Introduction, is increasingly the focus for formal planning efforts on the part of the three levels of government. A variety of issues—ranging from the shape of urban redevelopment to the role of citizen participation in city government, the value of new community formation, and the possible benefits to be gained from political restructuring of metropolitan communities—have emerged with important social and ecological implications for both understanding and directing urban growth.

Chapter 11

Power and Planning in the Urban System

POWER AND THE URBAN SYSTEM

Classical urban theory, proceeding with a consensus model of the social order, tended to ignore the patterned conflicts of interest that are a vital part of urbanism (Cox, 1978). The city can be seen as "an areally localized resource system" (Harvey, 1973) to which groups vary in their accessibility depending on the amount of power, influence, and wealth they can command. The spatial and social form of the urban system reflects the clash of interests and the quest for dominance by specific groups, classes, and organizations. Let us first define the meaning of power, survey briefly some of the types of participants in this clash, and explore as an example the influence of the "property industry."

The Study of Community Power

In studying the nature of power in any community it is useful to distinguish the following terms (Clark, 1968):

1. *Power* refers to the potential capacity to affect the "life chances" of other groups and to achieve desired change in the existing social and political structure.

2. *Influence* is the actual exercise of that capacity in specific situations.

3. *Power structure* is the overall distribution of power among groups, classes, and individuals in any community social system.

4. *Decision-making structure* consists of the relative distribution of influence in the community.

A major issue in the study of community stratification systems has been the manner in which power and influence can best be measured. There are three general approaches (Clark, 1968; Hawley and Svara, 1972; Bonjean and Grimes, 1974; Domhoff, 1978):

• *The positional or structural approach:* The leaders of a community are designated according to who occupies the key positions or offices in the central community organizations. The assumption here is that an individual's power derives from the formal position he holds. Yet this approach does not measure directly the level of influence, nor does it identify those who may possess power in the community although they do not occupy a formal position.

• *The reputational approach:* Here key informants are simply asked to designate those whom they believe to be powerful in the community, whether they hold formal positions or not. This approach, however, has several critical weaknesses—it may provide information on the reputation of power rather than its actual possession or exercise, and it fails to distinguish levels and relative scope of leadership.

• *The decisional approach:* To overcome the above weaknesses, an alternative strategy is to select important issues in the community's history and examine who is most influential in resolving them. Although this approach may help to identify some of those who actually exercise power in the community, it may overlook the importance of "non-decision" in revealing who are the influentials. In addition, the sample of issues it analyzes may not be representative of the most important decisions made, and may thus create a biased portrait of a community's leaders.

Adoption of one of these methods to the exclusion of the others, it has been discovered, may significantly affect the findings. That is, those employing the positional or decisional approaches are more likely to discover a pluralistic power structure (power and influence distributed relatively equally among a number of competing groups). A monolithic power structure (in which power and influence are concentrated among a few central leaders) is particularly likely to emerge if one adopts the reputational approach, which tends to assume the existence of such a structure. It is generally agreed at present that a comprehensive analysis of the power and decision-making structures of a community requires a combination of these approaches. In addition, it is important to compare how these structures vary among communities distinguished in terms of size, rate of growth, and function. Most important, we must not ignore the consequences of particular leadership formations—for example, with respect to policy "outputs." Hawley (1968c) has shown that the greater the concentration of power in any city, the greater the probability of success in undertaking and completing any collective action such as a program in urban renewal (cf. Lincoln, 1976). Such concentration provides a greater chance of mobilizing the necessary personnel and resources to deal with the specific issue. This, however, is still too imprecise a generalization as it fails to include the relative importance of other factors such as the community's rate of growth in affecting policy outputs. Finally, we might note that a common problem with many community power studies in the past "is their failure to consider local power in relationship to the national ruling class and the needs of the national corporate economy" (Domhoff, 1978: 152). How decision-making structures are linked across communities is a critical empirical issue that has only recently begun to be explored.

INFLUENTIALS IN A SMALL URBAN COMMUNITY: AN ILLUSTRATION

Banff is a small resort community in Alberta with a total year-round population of 3,000 (Koch and Labovitz, 1976). One central issue in this town has been the extent to which it can achieve relative autonomy from the federal government. The latter assumed control in the past over most of the major activities in the community because of the nearby national park. Residents have sought to establish a municipal government that would provide greater local influence over laws and regulations.

Using a combination of the various methods noted above to study patterns of power, we find that this community is dominated by a small group of individuals who hold overlapping executive positions in community organizations. Through these positions these persons are able to tap a variety of resources to influence decision making. They not only exercise power and leadership with respect to such critical issues as greater local control; they also have a corresponding reputation for power in these matters.

Reflecting the economic function of Banff, most of this "ruling elite" are either owners or managers of hotels, motels, and restaurants. They are long-term residents of the community, and tend to have a higher level of education than those with more limited organizational connections. Although they may not have a distinctive set of values, they do appear to have formed a greater number of social ties to each other and to those whom they perceive as powerful than have the other members of the community.

It would be inappropriate to generalize from this community to larger urban areas where a less concentrated or elitist power structure might be found. A similar analysis of the leadership structure in a larger city in the U.S. midwest found that it does appear to be the case that "in a smaller community less interlocking organizational executive positions are required to effect the same degree of power as more do in a larger community" (Koch and Labovitz, 1976: 10).

Political Participants in the Urban System

In Canada, municipal government was first established in Ontario (Higgins, 1977). Municipal institutions have primarily been the responsibility of the provinces. As a result, their development has been erratic. One major theme that characterizes the history of municipal government is the continued erosion of its financial position. With urban growth and expansion the provinces have assumed greater influence in municipal affairs, as has the federal government. By the mid-1970s more than half the revenue of local governments came from these sources (Higgins, 1977). Although they traditionally have dealt with the provision of routine or "housekeeping" services, Canada's cities have at the same time increasingly found themselves faced with more challenging and controversial issues, such as the need to curb undirected physical expansion. Since 1954, one response to this has been efforts to restructure municipal government—especially in the larger cities. We shall examine this response at a later point.

The structure of municipal decision making varies greatly across urban Canada. In smaller cities we find city council linked to standing committees which oversee the activities of municipal departments. This permits council members to concentrate on particular areas. For larger cities, however, this is a less efficient structure. Such committees tend to be inadequately connected to one another. The process of making decisions is retarded by the need to discuss at the council level what each committee has already thoroughly reviewed (Higgins, 1977). Larger communities require a more co-ordinated, less diffuse structure, as we shall see later in this chapter. In the West, boards of commissioners co-ordinate programs and services at the local level. Other communities employ a board of control or city manager system to facilitate co-ordination of the administrative responsibilities of the municipality. The relative power of the mayor varies greatly among these municipal structures. Although our understanding of the relation between them and the manner in which power and influence are distributed in Canada's cities is as yet only at a rudimentary level, it is apparent that not all segments of the population are equally likely to be represented at city council or its equivalent. A survey of council members in Toronto in the early 1960s revealed the following traits of the typical "successful politician": conservative, Protestant, affiliated with a business group, about fifty years old, married with two children, owns his own house, has lived in the community for at least fifteen years, and is employed in a professional or managerial position (Joyce and Hossé, 1970: 16). Women, poor people, and members of minority ethnic groups tend to be underrepresented on city councils (Higgins, 1977; Keiner, 1973). The question of which groups are excluded from the process of political recruitment is an important one for understanding the possession and exercise of power and influence in urban Canada. (Recall our portrait in chapter 10 of the political orientation found in one of Toronto's working-class neighbourhoods.)

POLITICAL RECRUITMENT IN URBAN ALBERTA

Political recruitment on the municipal level refers to the process whereby elected officials are selected from the eligible citizens in the city. The manner in which this process operates is particularly of interest in urban

Canada because of the ideology of non-partisanship that still exists in many cases at the local level. Unlike the United States, Canada's municipal candidates frequently run without explicit and direct endorsement by the national political parties.

Let us examine the characteristics of aldermen and mayors in five Alberta cities—Edmonton, Calgary, Lethbridge, Red Deer, and Medicine Hat (Slemko, 1974). In each case their campaigns and victories were not linked to the efforts of organized political parties. Nor, reflecting their own belief in non-partisanship, did they actively solicit the support of local civic associations. The public, they felt, would not have viewed as appropriate close association with particular interest groups.

Consistent with what has been found elsewhere, these aldermen possess distinctive characteristics not necessarily shared by the wider population. Most are male, over thirty-five, of high socioeconomic status, fairly well educated, and hold white-collar jobs. This group of elected officials, however, forms more of a "class elite" than an "ethnic elite" (Slemko, 1974). That is, they are not predominantly Anglo-Saxon Protestants, although they are of more affluent social standing than the average residents of their community.

Of particular importance, most had prior involvement in community business and service organizations, where they obtained experience and skills that could be transferred to elective office. Such participation indeed provided them with the sense of "personal competency" which enabled them to think seriously of seeking such an office. The social networks they formed through involvement in these associations encouraged them to make that decision, and were an indispensable resource in their success. In short, these community associations performed "diffuse recruitment functions" and served as "entry channels into civic politics" (Slemko, 1974). That the membership of these associations is composed primarily of more affluent members of the community suggests that, unless alternate recruitment channels are established, municipal government in these cities will continue to be dominated by those with characteristics similar to these elected officials. Local community associations link the community's stratification system with the formal political structure.

The urban political system is, of course, influenced by more than the persons formally occupying municipal offices. It includes a broad variety of actors ranging from special purpose boards (such as the board of education) to various corporate and non-corporate special interest groups—for example, the local chamber of commerce, a grass-roots association established to oppose construction of an expressway, and the media (Higgins, 1977). Of particular importance here is the ideology of non-partisanship. Beginning in the early years of this century an anti-party orientation was established at the local level. Reflecting the influence of the American municipal reform movement, it was strongly argued that urban government should be treated as a business, that municipal issues are not inherently political, and local parties would foster patronage and corruption. The non-partisan ideology also reflected the balance of power between provinces and municipalities; the latter's subordination to the former was not conducive to involvement at the local level by political parties (Lightbody, 1971; Anderson, 1972). Exceptions to this did occur. During the 1920s and 1930s in Western Canada socialist and labour groups fielded candidates in municipal elections to counter the rule of the more affluent business elite (see also Taraska, 1975). Non-partisanship in many cities permitted the middle-class business and professional segments of the population to sustain their formal and informal power and influence.

This tradition of non-partisanship has eroded in recent years. The formation of Mayor Drapeau's Civic Party in Montreal in 1960 encouraged the emergence of party politics at the municipal level (either through local parties or through affiliation with provincial parties) elsewhere in urban Canada. Increasing recognition has been given to some of the advantages of civic parties, which include the following:

- Civic parties are better able to achieve a consensus in council on some issues.
- The electorate has an opportunity to vote on a series of proposals and programs—rather than simply voting for individual personalities.
- Party platforms tend to be broader and more comprehensive than the view of one independent candidate.
- Party discipline facilitates implementation of politics. Civic parties improve voter turnout and community involvement in local problems.
- Parties are able to select and screen the best candidates (Joyce and Hossé, 1970: 22f).

If a civic party gains control of the council, however, its policies may not be equally responsive to the needs of all segments of the population. The extent to which municipal parties encourage patronage is uncertain, as is the degree to which the above advantages actually do occur. The number of local civic parties appears to be increasing, frequently emerging around a specific issue. Not all, of course, survive from one election to the next. Those that initially adopt a relatively non-partisan orientation find they become over time increasingly partisan (that is, they develop an articulated policy, and employ caucusing and bloc voting as instruments for defining and implementing that policy).

The continued growth of urban areas, the emergence of more complex metropolitan municipal systems, and the shift in municipal governments from "non-controversial decision making to more politicized policy making" (Higgins, 1977) have encouraged the national parties to become more directly involved in the urban political system (Lightbody, 1971). Their entry may offer several advantages over local civic parties:

- Local civic parties may be less democratic than national political parties operating at the municipal level in that the former are dominated by a small active elite.
- National civic parties want their members to devise party policy whereas local parties, in contrast, leave the creation of platform and policy with the party representatives on council.
- Some local parties do not select candidates democratically; national civic parties choose their candidates at open nomination conventions.
- Knowledge that a candidate is a member of a certain national party gives the voters some indication of the candidate's philosophy.
- National political parties have the resources to carry out their programs at the municipal level. Local parties, in contrast, tend to be more unstable; they frequently dissolve after election defeats (Joyce and Hossé, 1970: 59f).

Again, whether these advantages truly exist is an issue that has not been fully resolved. In any case, the involvement of mainstream parties, particularly the NDP and the Liberals in municipal politics, such as in Toronto, is a relatively new political phenomenon which will become more pronounced in the years ahead—especially in the larger cities where the need for co-ordinated political action is increasingly evident.

The Urban Community as a Political Economy

At various points in preceding chapters we have argued that the city must be analyzed as a socio-spatial system. Social and spatial structures are closely intertwined. In chapter 8, for example, we explored how in urban Canada the fundamental bases of social differentiation are in turn spatially expressed. An additional and equally important illustration of this interrelation is the conception of the urban community as a political economy (Harvey, 1973, 1978; Molotch, 1976; Pickvance, 1976; Castells, 1976, 1977). That is, urban space and land are structured according to the distribution of wealth and power within the city. Any parcel of land represents an interest for a particular segment (Molotch, 1976). The urban locality consists of an aggregate of interest groups competing for the most advantageous land-use patterns. Simply put, politics at the local level has to do with distribution of valuable resources, of which land is the most important. The more powerful groups and individuals in a community frequently are committed to local growth and development, and form a loosely structured coalition to advance their common interests. For them the city is a "growth machine" which must compete with other localities for economic expansion. Municipal government is viewed by local businessmen, property owners, and investors as the political instrument through which growth is to be sustained, the costs for which may have to be borne by the wider public. The costs are justified ideologically by reference to the number of jobs that will be created by growth. In more recent years the extent to which growth may be a liability has emerged as an important issue. Population and economic growth as well as physical expansion of the city may benefit only a small proportion of the residents, and may impose greater financial hardships on many taxpayers (Molotch, 1976).

The portrait of the urban map as "a mosaic of competing land interests capable of strategic coalition and action" (Molotch, 1976) argues that urban structure must be more explicitly linked to capitalistic market processes (Castells, 1977; Harvey, 1973)—a point which classical urban theory did not adequately articulate. That is, urban policies and political structures reflect and sustain the concentration of power and wealth characteristic of advanced capitalism (Harvey, 1973). For example, the city as a "growth machine" does not include within its municipal government, as we saw earlier, representatives of all segments of the population. Businessmen and those oriented to local growth dominate municipal affairs (Molotch, 1976). Such a proposition, consistent with an urban political economy paradigm, is a central tenet within a controversial argument recently advanced about the power and influence of the property industry in urban Canada.

The Property Industry and the Urban System

Since World War II Canadian cities have experienced a dramatic physical change. With metropolitan growth and expansion five major types of development projects have become increasingly visible. These include large-scale suburban developments, highrise apartment buildings, industrial parks in outlying areas, office towers, and shopping centres (Lorimer, 1978). Such a trend reflects the evolution of a complex and financially concentrated urban development industry in this country. Beginning at the level of small entrepreneurs, with the financial and other assistance of the federal government, this industry has expanded to such an extent that it now controls approximately $18 billion in real estate, with annual operating profits of about $1 billion. It is increasingly dominated by investor-owned, professionally managed development corporations such as Trizec, Cadillac-Fairview, and Genstar. Smaller development firms are unable to compete with these corporate enterprises (Barker, Penney, and Seacombe, 1973).

As in the other sectors of the Canadian economy, foreign ownership and foreign capital have played an important role in this industry. British property companies, banks, and insurance interests, for example, have exercised an important influence on Canadian urban development. A major source of real estate capital in past years in Montreal, for example, has been Italy (Aubin, 1977). Foreign property investors own over one-third of downtown Vancouver, and the proportion is increasing (Gutstein, 1975). Foreign developers have helped to intensify the trend toward greater concentration in the industry; their activities have also enhanced the price of urban real estate (Lorimer, 1978).

If we examine the sixty largest land development companies that produce most of the new residential land in metropolitan Canada, we find many operating in various sectors of real estate across the country (Spurr, 1976; Lorimer and Ross, 1976). Their land holdings are quite large. In cities such as Toronto, Thunder Bay, Calgary, and Edmonton they dominate the local new housing market. For example, there are approximately 40,000 acres of land available on Toronto's fringes for residential development; more than four-fifths of this is controlled by only nine firms (Spurr, 1976). These companies are able to bear the costs of site acquisition and preparation, and they have access to large amounts of capital through their ties (and interlocking directorates) with financial institutions. Such resources provide them with a significant advantage over smaller development firms. That competitive advantage is also enhanced by the major types of integration that major developers manifest. These include (1) *vertical* integration, where development firms control a number of subsidiaries that provide the necessary supplies and services to produce new urban accommodation (for example, a cement or construction company); (2) *horizontal integration*, where a corporation's activities and interests are spread across various sectors of the urban real estate market (from highrise office towers to single-family suburban dwellings); and (3) *conglomerate integration*, where joint ventures are undertaken with other large developers such as occurred in the Erin Mills project west of Toronto (Spurr, 1976). Such strategies reduce costs, increase profits, and allow these firms to reduce their risks involved in large-scale development projects. Although the data to support this contention are incomplete, the dominance over real estate market they achieve appears to contribute to the rising cost of residential lots in many cities. Holding a monopoly on the supply of new house lots, it is argued, allows these major developers to continue raising prices to support increased profits (Lorimer, 1978).

It has been contended that such dominance extends to city hall. The economic power of the property industry is matched by its political power and influence—especially at the local level (Lorimer, 1972, 1978; Barker, Penney, and Seccombe, 1973; Caulfield, 1974; Gutstein, 1975; Lorimer and Ross, 1976). Let us examine in greater detail this thesis which involves a combination of the approaches to the study of community power discussed earlier in this chapter.

The property industry, as it operates in Canadian cities, consists of a coalition of all the businesses and professions that own, manage, or service existing urban property, or supply new urban accommodation (Lorimer, 1972). These include, for example, property-owning businesses, lending institutions, insurance companies, construction businesses, lawyers, real estate agents, insurance agents, and civil engineers. The various segments of this industry have a common set of interests which derive from their conception of the city as a "growth machine"—as a source of profit from investments in urban property.

They seek to maintain and develop the value of that property through, for example, controlling the supply of new residential land, and opposing any attempts to tax more heavily their operating profits. Most important, it is argued, the property industry pursues a political program that helps to promote its interests. With respect to the senior levels of government, the industry has sought mortgage-lending and tax policies that would not restrict the flow of capital necessary for its investments. The Central Mortgage and Housing Corporation (CMHC) has functioned as an important ally in the industry's expansion—for example, by not strongly advocating in past years the creation of non-profit companies providing low-cost housing that might affect the general value of urban property, and thus lower the industry's profits.

It is at the municipal level where the power and influence of the property industry are especially visible. City government, it is argued, represents "the political arm of the industry" (Lorimer, 1972). Control is exercised over city council through a variety of measures, including the following:

- Persons oriented to the interests of the property industry frequently are members of city council;
- Contributions are made to political campaigns in the hope that the elected officials will give serious attention to the concerns of the industry;
- Informal social ties are cultivated among city politicians and those in various segments of the industry;
- When leaving city politics, officials may be offered lucrative positions within the industry.

As a result of these ties, city council will be more likely to support policies and programs that will coincide with and advance the interests of the property industry, such as permitting massive construction and development of the downtown core of a metropolitan area without adequate planning controls or concern for the fate of inner-city neighbourhoods (Caulfield, 1974). The influence of the development industry extends to special-purpose agencies and the municipal bureaucracy. City planning boards support policy proposals and modifications in existing plans from which the industry benefits, such as amendments to zoning by-laws that might permit placement of a new shopping mall in a residential area. Even the urban media support the industry's interests. Growth and expansion are portrayed as inherently good for any city. Indeed, the media themselves, through their dependence on advertisement revenues from businesses in the industry and their own real estate holdings, are economically linked to those interests.

The political strength of the property industry has generated citizen opposition in a variety of cities. Citizen groups have sought to challenge that influence by opposing specific projects (such as the Spadina Expressway in Toronto) and seeking to elect to city council those who might be more responsive to the need to balance the economic goals of the development industry with concern for the viability of existing neighbourhoods and for establishing greater controls over land and housing costs. The relative success of these groups in attaining their ends has varied greatly across urban Canada.

The thesis that the property industry dominates municipal decision making is a compelling one. Nevertheless, it is in need of much further verification and elaboration. It assumes a more monolithic power structure at the local level than may be the case—that the various sectors of the property industry act in concert and co-ordinate their efforts to achieve common goals. This may underestimate the clash of interests *within* the industry—for example, between the media's need to respond to citizen groups' demands for critical journalism and developers' desires for "boosterism" reporting. In addition, this thesis does not adequately analyze in a systematic manner how the influence of the property industry over municipal government might vary according to the size and functional structure of a city. There is a need to employ more carefully the positional, reputational, and decisional approaches in a variety of urban settings to determine in greater detail how power is exercised, and whether the variety of measures noted earlier used to influence city council are equally prevalent and successful. The roles local and national civic parties play in supporting or challenging the interest of the property industry must be more thoroughly explored. It has been argued that with the late 1970s many of Canada's cities may have entered a "post-developer era" (Lorimer, 1981). The downturn in post-war economic growth in Canada on the national level has curbed development at the municipal level. Developers may therefore have less control over city councils than in earlier years.

Indeed, one recent test of this thesis, employing a combination of the decisional and positional approaches, fails to document the dominant influence of private land developers in the regional municipality of Ottawa-Carleton (Sesay, 1978). Focusing on several important decisions made by the regional council, including the development of an official plan, no single group or sector of the community gained more advantages than did others. The region's official plan, for example, presented both benefits and disadvantages for private land developers in the area. Examining, in addition, the composition of the 1974-76 regional council reveals that only about one-fourth of the members have property industry occupational affiliations. Nor is there any evidence of a close link between how a councillor voted on issues relating to development and whether he had such an affiliation. In short, at least in this context it is incorrect to attribute significant political influence to the property industry. Rather, there exists a more pluralistic pattern in the distribution of influence. The extent to which this is the case elsewhere has been strongly debated. At times the argument that such influence does exist has been advanced more in terms of illustrations of its existence than by systematic and comparative analyses of how the municipal decision-making structure operates. The need for such analyses in Canadian urban studies is obvious.

PLANNING AND THE URBAN SYSTEM

Urban planning represents the formal, institutional attempt to regulate the physical, ecological, and social dimensions of urban growth and structure according to specific objectives and interests. Stated more simply, it seeks to "harness" systematically urbanization (understood both demographically and ecologically) and urbanism. Urban planning policies and techniques frequently reflect and even sustain the manner in which power and influence are distributed. In many instances planning can be seen as "the intervention of the political in the different instances of a social formation to assure the interests of the dominant social class" (Castells, 1977: 261). North American urban renewal projects, for example, in many cases appear to have benefited more the commercial and corporate interests encouraging these projects than the inner-city residents forced to relocate. Planning policies also reflect how the urban community is conceptualized, according to the social model used to portray its structure. The British garden-city movement that emerged in the early years of this century and sought to achieve a balance between town and country living in rebuilding cities perceived urban structure as based on a fundamental consensus of interests and values, as did classical urban theory:

> In the old city these theorists saw many evils, but they saw victims rather than villains. They tended to blame the evils not on class exploitation but on historical inheritance of poverty and poor buildings, on institutional inadequacies, or at worst on ignorance or apathy. They sought to cure the evils by methods which did not seem to them to threaten many significant interests. It should be possible to achieve such reforms by sweet reason and popular enlightenment, without revolution or divisive class politics (Stretton, 1978: 21-22).

Such an orientation deeply influenced Canadian urban planning, at least in its early stages of development. It de-emphasized the conflicts of interest and the unequal distribution of wealth and power that formed a central part of urban structure.

Canadian Urban Planning

Although the emergence of urban planning as a bureaucratized activity and formal profession is a twentieth-century phenomenon, we must not ignore the historical roots of planning in Canada. Early eighteenth-century settlements reflected efforts to self-consciously incorporate clear spatial plans. The foundation of Louisburg in 1726 was carefully planned as a military base and town to accommodate several thousand inhabitants. As elsewhere, a gridiron plan was imposed on Halifax. Although it was never completed, in the late 1700s the first governor of Cape Breton envisioned a plan for Sydney that was remarkably similar to Howard's garden city—incorporating the notion of a centre, satellite communities, and preservation of open space (Gertler, 1968; see also Hugo-Brunt, 1972).

Despite these roots, planning, both social and physical, was at a rudimentary level throughout the nineteenth century. The rise of the commercial centre and the commercial-industrial city occurred without sustained efforts to regulate the changing physical and social structures. We find, for example,

during the first half of the 1800s, the continued failure of such communities as
Saint John, Halifax, and St. John's to develop a systematic employment policy
for the poor (Fingard, 1977). Nor were the structural causes of unemployment
directly attacked; instead poverty was interpreted as a moral, not an economic, problem. Individual character defects, such as intemperance, were of
greater concern than the sources of inequality. Such a bias continued well into
the present century.

The failure to institutionalize appropriate planning policies and procedures was reflected as well in the social conditions of the metropolitan community as it emerged in the late nineteenth century and the early decades of the
twentieth century. The years 1896-1921 represented a time of great economic
expansion in Canada, especially in its largest cities. The gross value of
manufacturing production in Toronto increased more than 500 percent between 1900 and 1921 (Piva, 1975). The number of highly skilled and white-
collar jobs grew rapidly. Yet the workforce expanded at an even faster rate,
causing severe unemployment, especially for blue-collar workers. In both
Montreal and Toronto during these years the working class benefited very little from industrial growth (Copp, 1974). For example, "real income" (that is,
wages measured against the cost of living) was more than 10 percent *lower* for
Toronto's construction and manufacturing workers in 1920 than it had been
eighteen years earlier (Piva, 1975). In the cities, few workers were able to rise
above the poverty line. At least two wage earners per family commonly were
necessary to do so. Women and children thus were encouraged to enter the
labour force, without adequate controls over their working conditions.

Despite the plight of the urban working class, little was done to improve
health, housing, educational, or economic conditions. Infant mortality in the
working class (especially among French-Canadian families) was Montreal's
greatest public health problem; yet, pasteurized milk was made widely
available to the less affluent only in the years after World War I (Copp, 1974).
The inadequacy of public health care systems was also reflected in the high
rate of tuberculosis evident at the time in working-class neighbourhoods. In
Toronto working mothers were blamed for the high death rate found among
their infants; the factors that forced them to enter the labour force during their
child-rearing years were ignored.

In each of the major industrial centres, the working class was unable to
significantly improve its economic and social position through political or
organized efforts. Although labour unrest was common during this period,
unionization did not advance the workers' interests. In 1920, for example,
Toronto experienced twenty-four strikes, of which only one-fifth successfully
achieved the employees' objectives. A number of union locals indeed disappeared that year (Piva, 1975). Workers were therefore dependent on the
reform activities of the wider community, which were extremely limited and
failed, as in earlier years, to deal with the direct causes of poverty.

What urban reform measures were implemented between 1880 and 1920
reflected the values and interests of the dominant middle class (Rutherford,

1974, 1977; Weaver, 1977, Van Nus, 1977). The architectural and planning achievements displayed at Chicago's 1893 World's Fair and the influence of the "city-beautiful movement" (Hines, 1974) stimulated the desire to construct civic monuments, promote a sense of civic grandeur, and in general create a more aesthetically appealing urban environment that might in itself, without changing the class structure, remedy some of the major social problems existing in the largest cities. As the inadequacies of this planning approach became more evident in the first decade of this century, emphasis was placed increasingly on "purifying" the city—that is, encouraging the internalization of middle-class values and mores among the less affluent. Reformers argued that relocating slum dwellers in new suburban residential areas, for example, would be an effective means to achieve this goal (Weaver, 1977). Housing codes were enforced and low-income housing destroyed in an effort to improve the physical environment, which was believed to breed vice and social disorganization, without equal attention being given to supplying adequate amounts of replacement housing for the poor.

The urban middle class also supported the move to municipal control of utility companies (Armstrong and Nelles, 1977). This was motivated by the desire to obtain cheap and reliable power and transport which would enhance real estate values and business profits, and make the city generally more attractive for industrial investment and expansion. Reflecting the influence of the American reform movement at the time, the urban municipality was increasingly viewed as a business corporation that must be managed efficiently and economically. Administration must be separated from politics, civic government bureaucratized and run by experts (Rutherford, 1977). City-wide boards and commissions and the separation of municipal legislative and executive functions were viewed as necessary instruments for a competent city government. They also served to insulate that government from political challenges to middle-class domination by the less affluent (Weaver, 1977).

As it began to emerge, modern city planning in Canada reflected a middle-class ethos. It also was influenced by American reform ideology as well as by the efforts in Britain to regulate urban life through legislation. One channel through which the British influence appeared was Thomas Adams, one of the founders of the British Town Planning Institute. In 1909 the Commission of Conservation was established, with Clifford Sifton as Chairman, to examine how Canada's natural resources might be better managed. One of their concerns was with the problems of town planning. Adams was invited to join the Commission in 1914, bringing with him experience in framing the British Town Planning Act of 1909. Adams subsequently aided in the writing of town planning laws and zoning by-laws in Canada before his work ended in 1921 (Gertler, 1968; Oberlander, 1976). Although he did not challenge the predominant middle-class ethos of planning, many of his ideas influenced and indeed anticipated the concerns of post-World War II urban planning. These included:

- The need for orderly, scientific planning of the city as a whole;
- The need to plan regionally—to co-ordinate town-country interdependence;
- The need to control land and development outside municipal boundaries;
- The need for a comprehensive, flexible city plan dealing with such prerequisites as efficient traffic circulation, adequate rapid transit, and parks;
- The need for advisory town planning commissions in each province, so that planning at the provincial level would parallel that done locally (Rutherford, 1977: 247f).

In summary, urban growth in the early years of this century demanded regulation—but in a form that would sustain the power and influence of the middle class. The "urban crisis" was one of inefficient municipal government, of moral and social departures from middle-class mores. Municipal and housing reforms were encouraged, but in ways that would not undermine the desirable "bourgeois character of the city" (Rutherford, 1977).

Contemporary efforts to regulate the urban system frequently reflect a continuation of this orientation, although not without challenge (Matthews, 1976). The continued growth of urban areas in the decades following World War II has created a variety of serious problems, ranging from the need for more efficient mass transit systems, to inadequate supplies of low-cost housing, to environmental decay (Science Council, 1971). That such problems require a more comprehensive understanding of the interrelation among the demographic, ecological, economic, social, and political aspects of urbanization and urbanism for their solution is increasingly recognized (Oberlander, 1976; Wiesman, 1976; Gertler, 1976). We shall briefly survey five critical issues in contemporary urban planning, emphasizing their social and ecological implications where appropriate. These include the following:

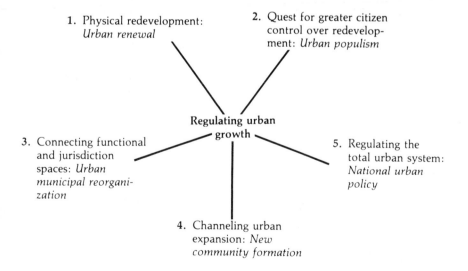

1. Physical redevelopment: *Urban renewal*

2. Quest for greater citizen control over redevelopment: *Urban populism*

Regulating urban growth

3. Connecting functional and jurisdiction spaces: *Urban municipal reorganization*

5. Regulating the total urban system: *National urban policy*

4. Channeling urban expansion: *New community formation*

These issues reveal at least some of the concerns of contemporary planning, ranging from attempts to renovate the physical and political structures of cities to the best means for redirecting urban growth at the national level.

Urban Renewal

During the last several decades in North American urban communities, an attempt to change especially the inner-city physical environment has been made through the development of urban renewal projects. These projects have varied greatly in scale and location, and include such cases as the total destruction of Africville, on the periphery of Halifax (Clairmont and Magill, 1971, 1973); the redevelopment of the Rose-Blanshard area of Victoria in the late 1960s (Robertson, 1973); and the rehabilitation of the Strathcona area in Vancouver (Wong, 1978). Urban renewal, in its simplest form, can be defined as "the process by which the various parts of an urban area are repaired or replaced as they become physically deteriorated, obsolete, or suitable for alternate use" (Bunge, 1967: 1). Increasing attention has been given to the social consequences of this process to determine how this instrument of planned urban change might be more beneficially utilized.

The development of urban renewal in Canada progressed through a series of legislative stages (Bunge, 1967; Report of the Task Force, 1969; Bettison, 1975). As in the United States, federal involvement in the housing industry was strengthened as a result of the Depression in the 1930s. In order to provide more adequate housing, the Dominion Housing Act was instituted in 1935. Through the federal Department of Finance loans were secured for residential mortgages. The scope of this assistance was increased in 1938. With the advent of World War II, however, the entire problem of housing in Canada became overshadowed by more pressing concerns. In 1941 it again became an important issue. The Curtis Subcommittee on Housing and Community Planning—part of the broader Committee on Post-War Reconstruction—predicted a serious shortage of adequate housing by 1946 and documented the existence of widespread slums in many communities. In order to remedy this bleak picture, the National Housing Act was passed in 1944. The act provided federal assistance to municipalities for slum clearance. The Central Mortgage and Housing Corporation was created to administer this program. Its lending role was enhanced through subsequent amendments in 1946 and 1947—which, as we noted earlier, laid the basis for the private house building industry's expansion (Lorimer, 1978).

Amendments to the National Housing Act were introduced in 1949; these established joint federal-provincial participation in public housing projects and federal involvement in land assembly schemes. Additional changes to the act seven years later were particularly critical in that they "made provision for urban renewal studies to be conducted to determine 'the condition of urban areas, means of improving housing and the need for additional housing or urban redevelopment.' The cost of these studies was to be shared 75% by Central Mortgage and Housing Corporation, and 25% by the municipality" (Bunge, 1967: 15). Areas designated in need of urban renewal were predominantly residential (Lowden, 1970: 1-1). This, however, was increasingly seen as too narrow a definition. In 1964 that restriction was removed. Urban renewal was broadened to include non-residential land use, and was taken now as involving more than merely "redevelopment"—that is, mass clearance and reconstruction of physically deteriorating areas. The need to pursue less drastic actions to preserve the physical structure of the inner city was also recognized. "Rehabilitation"—repair of existing structures—and "conservation"—maintenance of properties according to acceptable standards—were seen as equally important. The 1964 amendments systematized the procedures through which an urban renewal program was undertaken. Despite frequent difficulties in the co-ordination of different political levels, the 1964 legislation attempted to broaden urban renewal "from the provision of assistance for the clearance of slum housing and its replacement by low-income housing, into an attack on the physical problems affecting all parts of an urban area" (Bunge, 1967: 17). The 1967 amendment to the National Housing Act strengthened this "attack" by providing federal loans to those seeking to rehabilitate housing in any part of an urban community.

The effect of this governmental expansion in urban housing was revealed in the fact that by 1961 almost half of the total housing stock in Canada had been constructed during the post-World War II period. This represented, indeed, "the highest ratio of new housing additions in the entire Western world" (Report of the Task Force, 1969: 6). Between 1954 and 1968, almost three-fourths of the federal funding for urban renewal supported projects concentrated in Ontario and Quebec, reflecting their higher rates of urbanization and the greater ability of these provinces to provide matching funds. During that period, more than 200 urban renewal studies were initiated, with the majority completed (Lowden, 1970: 2-1f). Almost all of the federal assistance for urban renewal during these years was concentrated in cities with populations greater than 30,000. Because of the higher tax returns from commercial and industrial land uses, renewal programs were less concerned with improving the residential sector.

A number of weaknesses in the Canadian urban renewal program became increasingly evident. Its general objectives were not clearly defined, nor was there consensus among the different levels of government as to the nature of these goals. In many cases it was interpreted as a means for stimulating urban economic development, or as a means whereby a city could obtain improvements that it alone could not afford, or as an instrument for the physical redevelopment of the community. Paralleling this ambiguity in objectives was an underlying vagueness in the exact meaning of "blight," which appeared to be "whatever the municipality designated as blight" (Lowden, 1970: 1-10).

Instead of precise delimitation of the goals of the program, greater emphasis was given to the formulation of administrative procedures which all renewal projects were required to follow, regardless of local circumstances. As a result, smaller cities found it financially difficult to meet all the prerequisites —such as preparation of the urban renewal scheme according to the required format—for obtaining CMHC support. Physical deterioration within these communities tended to be less frequently clustered within definable areas. Yet, federal assistance was allocated to projects that had designated whole sections as in need of urban renewal. The federal guidelines, moreover, did not demand any regional planning considerations, despite the fact that this would have been especially advantageous for smaller cities.

Certainly a major problem with the urban renewal program derived from the difficulty of co-ordinating the three levels of government that were involved. As a result of the division of responsibilities and power established in the British North America Act, initiation of a project was restricted to the provinces and municipalities. Federal involvement occurred after the submission of applications for assistance, and was limited to the determination of whether they met the standardized guidelines. Such a system, indeed, produced a set of basic "anomalies":

> First, the municipalities have the necessary initiative but are ineffective because they haven't enough money. Second, the provinces have the necessary power but are ineffective because they see their role as a passive one, and do not offer leadership and direction, and have an anachronistic concept of their relationship to urban growth problems. Third, the national government has the necessary money but its range of participation in urban development is severely limited by both law and custom (Bunge, 1967: 35-36).

One important consequence was the difficulty of formulating a systematic and consistent approach to the solution of urban problems. Renewal tended to proceed in a more ad hoc fashion than was desirable. The need for approval from the three levels of government for each project encouraged unnecessary duplication and over-bureaucratized the entire administrative procedure. As a result, the time lag between initiation of a renewal study or scheme and actual implementation widened; five and a half years was not uncommon. This created additional problems:

> "The time lag caused by the extensive number of steps required to carry out a program often [resulted] in a change of the actual needs of the program from those originally proposed." Among these changes could have been the municipal council itself. A new council could decide on different priorities to those of its predecessors, resulting in only partial fulfillment of the renewal program . . . Another problem was the stigma created by a renewal designation on an area where no public action was taken, due to this extensive time lag. "Such designations create a semi-freeze of real estate transactions and tend to discourage maintenance and repairs." (Lowden, 1970: 3-49).

The most dramatic illustration of this is the case of Africville—a small black ghetto on the outskirts of Halifax (Clairmont and Magill, 1971, 1973). Although its actual final destruction began in the mid-1960s, the community had long experienced the threat of expropriation and the stigma of being defined as a slum. In the late 1800s Africville faced expropriation of some of its land for industrial use. Municipal authorities expected that eventually the entire community would be relocated to complete this process. As a result, little was done to improve basic services for its population. Facilities that were considered undesirable in the city proper, such as the dump and incinerator, were moved to an area near the community. In 1947 Halifax City Council formally approved the designation of Africville as industrial land; yet not until 1961 were details of the relocation project elaborated. During this period the community continued to experience physical deterioration and social disruption. The lengthy delay in implementing an effective renewal program that would respond more adequately to the needs of the residents facilitated the eventual total destruction of Africville.

A variety of other weaknesses in the renewal program were also increasingly recognized. These included overemphasis on the physical aspects of the urban environment, a general lack of concern for the dynamic processes in the urban real estate market, and inadequate attention to the problem of relocation (Carver, 1965; Prince, 1967; Rose, 1968)

RELOCATION FROM THE LORD SELKIRK PARK AREA

A repeated failure in such renewal projects as Africville, St. John's Blackhead Road (Williamson, 1971), and elsewhere (e.g., Robertson, 1973) occurred with respect to planning extensively for the social and economic adjustment required by those forced to relocate. A vivid illustration of this is the renewal scheme carried out in the Salter-Jarvis or Lord Selkirk Park area (as it was termed after completion of the project) in Winnipeg (Yauk, 1973). This was a section of the North End that continued to deteriorate physically during the 1950s. By 1961 most of its residents were relatively poor, many living in overcrowded and dilapidated housing. Indian and Metis families were replacing the Jewish residents who were moving out of the area.

Beginning in May of 1963, without widespread consultation with the residents (typical of many renewal projects) an expropriation and clearance program was initiated in the area. Proceeding through a series of stages, the renewal scheme was executed without adequate concern for those displaced (Yauk, 1973):

1. The project negatively affected the stability of other neighbourhoods nearby. That is, many of the relocatees sought accommodation in low-income housing available in other parts of the North End. Such an influx, in turn, encouraged out-migration of those who reacted negatively to this "invasion."

2. The project served to reduce the total supply of housing available to low-income families in the city by 640 units, which heightened competition for existing accommodation among the less affluent.

3. Most significantly, and again typical of what we find elsewhere, relocatees—both former tenants and homeowners—experienced substantial increases in their housing costs after the move. The quality of their new housing might have been improved in many cases, but this was counterbalanced by rental and mortgage increases. The compensation for homeowners was not enough to allow them to purchase comparable housing elsewhere. Nor was any responsibility taken for assisting tenants to find comparable housing; it was not uncommon for them to have experienced a 50 percent increase in rent after the move. Coupled with the disruption of local social ties, many could identify nothing that they had personally gained from expropriation.

4. Before urban renewal, the Lord Selkirk Park area had contained a number of small businesses with established clientele in the neighbourhood. Few of these businesses were successfully relocated. Many failed to re-open elsewhere, having lost their local market and not having received adequate compensation for the effects of expropriation on their business. Their establishments were closely linked to trade from the local area and in some cases, from surrounding rural Hutterite colonies. Expropriation destroyed these non-transportable ties.

This urban renewal project, in short, focused primarily on physical redevelopment, without equal concern for the consequences of such a project for the residents. The residents' lack of power and ability to articulate their interests in an effective way provided little basis for challenging the goals of this scheme.

In response to these problems and gaps, the federal government suspended the entire program in mid-1968, and initiated a careful evaluation by a housing task force of the most appropriate remedies. Its recommendations represented fundamental revisions in the whole process of urban planning and redevelopment—including, for example, the exercise of greater selectivity in demolition of existing housing and the avoidance of designating wide sectors as urban renewal areas. The task force emphasized the need to consider the social consequences of urban renewal programs. Any substantial clearance of housing has important social costs. It may, as in Boston's West End or Halifax's Africville, "destroy not only buildings, but also a functioning social system" (Social Planning Council of Hamilton and District, 1963: 25). Strong local social networks can be disrupted without meaningful replacements. As we saw in chapter 10, residents of inner-city areas slated for urban renewal are often satisfied with many aspects of their neighbourhood, and express a relatively strong sense of identification with it (Jense, Mezoff, and Richmond, 1970: 32f.). Forced relocation can have disruptive effects (Lipman, 1968; Robertson, 1973).

During the early 1970s amendments to the National Housing Act created two new programs, with greater attention given to preservation and improvement of existing neighbourhoods—the Neighbourhood Improvement Program and the Residential Rehabilitation Assistance Program (Wong, 1978). Yet, these programs fail to deal with that heterogeneity typically found in Canada's inner cities. Such programs are more oriented to protecting "stable areas" such as working-class neighbourhoods (McLemore, Aass, and Keilhofer, 1975), and fail to deal effectively with, for example, "declining areas" whose residents may be too poor to participate in rehabilitation and which may require more intense economic revitalization. A "diverse, multi-functional inner city" requires a selectively applied combination of programs that respect the varying interests and values of the different categories of residents—from the affluent in luxury highrises to the less advantaged in low-cost housing (McLemore, Aass, and Keilhofer, 1975). A central planning problem in the past has been to assume that the inner city represents a homogeneous ecological unit, for which a single set of programs is most appropriate to improve its physical and social environment.

Urban Populism

One important reaction to the urban renewal process and the dominance of the property industry is the generation of mounting demands by urbanites for greater control over the whole planning institution and wider participation in the political structures of their communities. Inner-city residents increasingly believe that redevelopment programs give insufficient attention to their needs, patterns of social life, and economic and cultural investments. "Urban populism" has emerged in recent years as a movement for greater local control —particularly in the inner city (Lotz, 1970; Head, 1971; Kotler, 1969). Countering the traditional manner in which cities have been governed, it proposes two fundamental principles: "(1) that people should have a say in decisions that affect them, and (2) that those decisions will be more closely in tune with the interests of the ordinary citizens" (Axworthy and Epstein, 1974: 2). The primary emphasis is on improved planning, more responsive municipal government, and meaningful local participation in the entire decision-making process. A basic premise of this movement, therefore, is that urban residents should not be powerless victims of governmental actions such as renewal schemes but rather full participants in the process determining the goals and contents of these actions (Axworthy, n.d.).

Trefann Court: An Illustration of Urban Populism

In recent years there has been an increasing number of examples of urban populism and citizen-organized self-help activities (e.g., Nowlan and Nowlan, 1970; Granatstein, 1971; Lorimer, 1970). These have most frequently occurred in response to proposed redevelopment projects for the inner city. One of the clearest illustrations of this movement, and perhaps one of the better known in Canada, is that which occurred in Trefann Court in Toronto (Fraser, 1972; Sewell, 1972).

Trefann Court is a small five-block area, located about a mile from City Hall and just south of a public housing project, Regent Park South. In the very centre of the area known as "Cabbagetown," its population consists of predominantly Anglo-Saxon working-class residents, many of whom are homeowners. The area has become a place of settlement for other ethnic groups as well, but is experiencing a decline in total population. Consistent with its location, it contains a significant mixture of residential housing, industry, and commercial establishments.

The lieutenant-governor's special committee which had investigated the state of housing in Toronto in 1934 reported that almost half the dwellings in all of Cabbagetown fell below minimum health standards. The Bruce Report also documented the inadequacy of the planning process in the city at the time and the absence of an integrated set of zoning by-laws. Various official plans were subsequently developed in Toronto to remedy these problems (Fraser, 1972: Ch. 3).

In 1944 the City of Toronto Planning Board examined the current state of seventy-eight neighbourhoods and evaluated them in terms of whether they were "sound," "vulnerable," "declining," "blighted," or fully "slums." The first category was least commonly applied to Toronto's older inner-city neighbourhoods. Hence, "the assumption grew during the 1950s that downtown Toronto would naturally stop being an area of residential neighbourhoods, its existing residential neighbourhoods would be demolished either for massive public housing projects or for industrial parks" (Fraser, 1972: 57). The construction of the Regent Park project was consistent with this assumption (Rose, 1958). The City of Toronto Planning Board repeated that view of downtown in its 1956 report, Urban Renewal: A Study of the City of Toronto. *Identifying a number of areas as pockets of "blight" which had to be removed, it recommended bulldozing that section of downtown between Queen, Dundas, River and Church Streets, and the construction of a number of public housing units. These plans were not immediately executed, but the effects of designating an area such as Trefann Court for urban renewal were still quite serious:*

"After that designation, people in the district found things cast into an

*uncertain state and when they asked the City whether or not to pro-
ceed with some contemplated renovation, the City discouraged them,
claiming that within a few years the area would be expropriated and
demolished. Thus, for nine years before a plan was actually introduced, the City had so panicked the people that the area was left to
atrophy. The normal process of 'unslumming' was discouraged, and
property values fell as the dark cloud hung over the area" (Sewell,
1972: 20-21).*

In 1963 city planners outlined the changes which were to occur in the
area and established the Trefann Court Redevelopment Area. Two years
later City Council passed the "Improvement Programme for Residential
Areas," which recommended three areas for clearance and construction
of public housing. These were Don Mount, Trefann Court, and Don
Vale. In February 1966, the planning board presented to City Council
more specific points regarding the fate of Trefann Court. It called for the
demolition of the whole area. In the spring of that year City Council formally designated the area for urban renewal, having accepted the
scheme. All of these steps were taken without full consultation with the
local residents themselves (Fraser, 1972).

Their initial reaction was one of confusion and fear. This was stimulated by what they saw to be the fate of homeowners in nearby Don
Mount, many of whom they believed had not obtained adequate compensation for the expropriation of their dwellings, and who were thus
unable to achieve comparable housing elsewhere. The Trefann Court
residents believed that they too would experience this. That they had not
been permitted to provide meaningful input to the proposed scheme for
this area intensified their anxiety and opposition. As one resident observed:

"Since when has the city come to the people and asked them any
questions, listened to their ideas, or consulted them as to what is
needed or desired in the area slated for redevelopment? The answer is:
never once. All the redevelopment areas in Toronto, Alexandra Park,
Don Mount Village, and now Trefann Court were ready-made pack-
ages handed down to us, and we are then told to put up or shut up.
When are our 'highly qualified' and 'professional' city planners going
to realize that we are fellow human beings, that we have families and
children whom we care for, that we have a way of life that we value,
that the majority of us like the area and would have wanted to see it
improved rather than torn down?" (Fraser, 1972: 79-80).

Such sentiments led to formation of the Trefann Court Residents' Association, organized to resist the renewal scheme. In its early stages the
association concentrated on attempting to obtain higher compensation
for the homeowners' expropriation. But in time the entire renewal plan
was attacked.

The municipal reorganization of Metropolitan Toronto on January 1, 1967 required that all bills and schemes which had not been formally approved by the Ontario Municipal Board by the last day of the previous year be referred back to City Council for approval. The plan for Trefann Court did not meet this deadline, but Toronto's City Council "refused either to approve the old plan a second time, or formally withdraw it for another two years, leaving it to hang in a strange, threatening state of semi-existence" (Fraser, 1972: 91). With this delay property values in the area continued to decline. The association was, however, able to convince the city to undertake a second survey on the condition of Trefann Court housing in 1967. Significantly, whereas the 1966 scheme had classified 148 dwellings as in poor condition, this later investigation was able to identify only 52 such houses. This discrepancy reinforced the association's opposition to the total destruction of the area.

As has occurred elsewhere too, one important pattern was the emergence of more than one interest group among the residents. The Trefann Neighbours and Tenants Association was established to represent the views of those segments of the local population who were actually in favour of urban renewal in the area. These were absentee owners, property owners anxious to sell their homes to the city, tenants, and an assorted array of persons from "caretaking" professions. The split between this organization and the Residents' Association was important in that it suggested to external political agencies that the community did not possess a clearly articulated and consistent attitude toward urban renewal. Each group attacked the other. Each felt the other did not take its interests fully into consideration: "the Residents' Association felt threatened by the tenants' demands for urban renewal, and made no efforts to meet the tenants in their approaches: the TNT [the Trefann Neighbours and Tenants Association] felt that tenants were being endangered by the TCRA [Trefann Court Residents' Association] demand that the City get out and impose the full housing standards" (Fraser, 1972: 140). If that demand were met, the tenants' rents would have been raised, forcing many of them to seek housing elsewhere. Citizen input into the renewal proposal became deadlocked until 1970.

In February of that year the federal government announced that Toronto would receive no more than $4 million for urban renewal over the next five years. The city had to decide the priority of those schemes which could be undertaken. Public meetings were held to tap the opinions of the local citizens in five possible renewal areas, including Trefann Court. Municipal interest in and support for citizen participation in the planning process had been strengthened by the election to City Council of those more sympathetic to urban populism. The result of the first public meeting in Trefann, at which representatives of both associations were present, was encouraging. It suggested an acceptable compromise could be reached, with residents having some control over the redevelopment project.

In March 1970, City Council designated Trefann Court as a priority area for the preparation of an urban renewal scheme. A working committee was established, providing both municipal and local input into the planning process. It included "a representative from the Planning Board and from the Development Department, the two ward aldermen, three members of the City Renewal Committee, five representatives each from the TCRA and TNT and two representatives of the business community" (Fraser, 1972: 181). A series of meetings was held beginning in June, with a final plan adopted in January 1972. Among the issues debated was the Residents' Association's emphasis on the need to consult continually with the local citizenry before a decision was reached, and the Neighbours and Tenants Association's concern that "something concrete" be achieved. The business representatives tended to serve a mediating function in this "process-versus-product" debate.

The final scheme gave emphasis to the rehabilitation of the area rather than to total demolition of all housing. The particular character of Trefann Court was to be maintained. Most of the existing housing was to be retained and the mix of owner-occupied and rented dwellings along with compatible industries was to continue. In addition, the working committee sought control over the choice of the planning staff assigned to help implement the plan. This control was partially granted when the final scheme was approved in March 1972. That this type of local participation was seen by the residents as necessary in areas other than urban renewal was clearly evident in their call for the establishment of a more permanent community council or form of neighbourhood government which would deal with a variety of issues of vital concern to the local community.

The Trefann Court renewal issue illustrates the emergence of urban populism. Citizen participation in the planning process over time was achieved and local control over the renewal scheme substantially enhanced. Trefann Court represented more than a case simply of citizen protest. Local involvement, as can be seen, was not achieved without numerous difficulties. Many of the residents did become weary and in time apathetic during the long period while the renewal scheme was opposed and redefined. The working committee itself, moreover, did not always sustain the interest and support of the local residents. Yet, this case of the formation of a renewal scheme did demonstrate "that conflicting interest groups in a community can reach a consensus on planning goals, that ordinary people can contribute usefully to replanning their neighbourhoods and can work extremely hard on points of incredible detail to achieve a solution which will, in fact, be better than one reached by any planner, no matter how sophisticated working alone"

(Fraser, 1972: 263). Citizen participation in inner-city political and administrative processes is, in short, feasible.

City politicians and appointed municipal officials have in the past resisted efforts to decentralize the process of decision making on the local level (Dixon, 1972; Rigby, 1975; Bureau of Municipal Research, 1970). In more recent years working committees or local planning groups have been established in cities such as Toronto (Bureau of Municipal Research, 1975) and Vancouver (Horsman and Raynor, 1978) to allow citizens an opportunity to provide input into the planning of their neighbourhoods. The amount of control they can exercise is, however, questionable. Efforts to institutionalize citizen participation in Winnipeg through establishment of resident advisory groups have not been especially successful (Repo, 1972; Axworthy and Cassidy, 1974; Bureau of Municipal Research, 1975; Higgins, 1977). Their role within Winnipeg's new municipal structure has not been carefully defined, nor have they gained the necessary support from City Council members who are fearful of political activism and challenge by these groups. In short, structural reform within an "inhospitable" political climate does not insure "meaningful" (in the sense of power-sharing) citizen participation.

The urban citizen participation movement also lacks internal cohesion (Bureau of Municipal Research, 1975; Rigby, 1975; Bystydzienski, 1974). Residents of working-class or low-status areas, because of their educational and economic disadvantages, are less likely to organize groups opposing some development project or renewal scheme. When these groups do emerge, their interests and objectives may not coincide with those found in middle-class groups. The former, for example, may place greater value on low-income housing and tenant rights than do the latter (Bureau of Municipal Research, 1975). The extent to which any particular community association adequately represents the range of interests in its neighbourhood is frequently a contentious issue. A group's leadership may be drawn from a highly select segment of the local population, and, as a result, fail to obtain widespread legitimacy or support in the neighbourhood (Rigby, 1975). As yet, the fate of urban "participatory democracy" is unclear.

Urban Municipal Reorganization

One characteristic of urbanization understood ecologically, as the spread of a more comprehensive and intricate territorial division of labour, is the increasing irrelevance of urban municipal boundaries. The "jurisdictional space" of a municipality does not parallel the functional integration of an area or region (Kaplan, 1965; Diemer, 1975). The scope of such problems as the need to control environmental pollution, curb urban sprawl, and provide improved transportation systems extends beyond municipal boundaries. Municipal fragmentation results in inefficient and costly duplication of services in the region, inequities in tax revenues and service expenditures among adjacent municipalities, and in inadequate planning generally. The absence of municipal coordination can have particularly important consequences for the distribution of land uses on the periphery. For example, post-war urban expansion in Southern Ontario has threatened the amount of farmland in the region. Between 1950 and 1970 land there was converted into urban uses at the rate of 61 square miles or 39,000 acres per year (Howard, 1972). With the continued disappearance of 150 acres of improved farm land per 1,000 population increase, this region could lose more than 250,000 acres by 1991, assuming the present growth rate is sustained. The amount of farmland within the entire Windsor-Quebec City urban region declined by 4,148 square miles during 1966-71 (Yeates, 1975). A good part of this loss was not directly due to urban expansion; its effects, however, cannot be ignored. For example, between 1951 and 1966 approximately 430 acres per year of valuable land in the Niagara peninsula fruit belt were withdrawn from agricultural use (Yeates, 1975). Urban sprawl involves not only the creation, without adequate planning, of new housing and developments on the periphery. It also affects the rural landscape through extension of highways, power lines, and other facilities. The "urban shadow" (Gertler, 1976) represents an extensive area around the city that is directly or indirectly affected by actual or potential expansion; agricultural land is eroded or held for speculative purposes in anticipation of future development. Private companies, as we observed earlier, seek to assemble large tracts of land on the periphery. Such rural-to-urban conversion, without adequate public controls, is marked by environmental imbalances (such as unsystematic placement of open spaces for public use) and rising land prices.

Only a very small proportion of British Columbia's total land area can produce appropriate levels of food crops. Much of this, however, is on the Lower Mainland where urban expansion is rapidly occurring (Evenden, 1978). The need to curb such urban sprawl and protect valuable agricultural land led to the establishment in 1973 of the B.C. Land Commission (Rawson, 1976). The functions of this body are to co-ordinate a system of zoning for agricultural use and to regulate urban intrusions (such as power lines and highways) on agricultural land.

Efforts have been made to reorganize urban municipalities in such a way that regional co-ordination and planning might be improved, and political fragmentation reduced:

1. *Creation of special-purpose agencies:* These have emerged in various metropolitan areas as ways of providing necessary services (such as transit systems) to residents in different jurisdictions. Throughout urban North America such agencies have become increasingly numerous; Metro Toronto alone contains ninety-four (Del Guidice and Zacks, 1976). Although they may provide a particular service with relative efficiency, they add to the prolifera-

tion and fragmentation of municipal authorities within one area. In addition, citizens' access to and influence on the decision-making process within these agencies are limited.

2. *Creation of two-tiered or federation-type municipal governments:* Metro Toronto, created in the early 1950s and modified in 1967, is the best example of this type of reorganization (Kaplan, 1967; Rose, 1972). Prior to this reorganization the Toronto region contained a total of thirteen independent, but economically and socially interdependent, municipalities. In such a two-tiered system, certain functions are shifted to the Metro level—such as public financing and provision of necessary service facilities—without disturbing existing municipal boundaries. A Metro council is created, with proportionate representation from the member municipalities. This system was weakened in Metro Toronto's early years by the continued stronger support which officials gave to the interests of their own municipalities than to those of Metro Toronto as a whole (Kaplan, 1967). Such issues as the need for greater public housing units were avoided, partly because of a lack of consensus in council as to their location. Metro Toronto dealt far more with physical planning and provision of services necessary for the opening up of peripheral areas for development than it did with social planning. This enabled private companies to meet the increased demand for single-family houses. During these years the City of Toronto's position within Metro Toronto eroded, as it experienced "a declining share of the total population and of total assessed valuation" in the region (Rose, 1972: 177-78). Less emphasis has been placed on the city's own redevelopment needs. This is a common problem in metropolitan government —an imbalance in the relative importance attached to centre city and suburban interests.

Increasingly, however, it has been recognized that regional planning must extend even beyond the limits of this metropolitan area. In 1970 the concept of the Toronto-centred region was introduced as a basis for restricting excessive growth within Toronto, decentralizing population, and regulating development within the entire region (Design For Development, 1970). In addition, the formation of regional governments, with regional councils responsible for planning and provision of a variety of services, is viewed as a useful means of insuring implementation of a development scheme that reflects the varied needs of an area. Following the lead of Alberta, which pioneered the establishment of "district planning regions to reflect the interdependence of town and country" (Gertler, 1976: 90), a large proportion of Ontario's population now live within such a two-tiered system (Higgins, 1977). British Columbia likewise has developed regional districts, such as the Greater Vancouver Regional District instituted in 1967 as an attempt to co-ordinate the planning activities of seventeen different municipalities in the area (Lioy, 1975). This does not represent, however, a metropolitan form of government as found in Toronto, in which a higher degree of political and functional integration is sought.

3. *Extension of urban municipal boundaries:* An alternative method of reducing municipal fragmentation is by extending the boundaries of the urban municipality—creating a single-tiered form of government in a region. *Amalgamation* is "the legal process by which a political unification occurs of two or more incorporated urban jurisdictions"; *annexation,* the other means through which urban expansion jurisdictionally occurs, represents "the legal process by which an incorporated area is added to a corporate city" (Diemer, 1975: 58). Amalgamation is not a common process in urban Canada. One example is the creation of Thunder Bay, Ontario in 1970 by integrating Fort William and Port Arthur (Kosny, 1978). The results of this amalgamation have been mixed. It allows for a more efficient provision of basic services and facilities to area residents. Nevertheless, because of its greater scale, this new governmental form does not allow for significant citizen input into local decision making. Administrative centralization which seeks to reduce duplication of services impedes public accountability (Kosny, 1978).

Perhaps the most striking illustration in recent years of the single-tiered form of municipal government is the creation of Unicity Winnipeg in 1972. Twelve municipalities were merged into one city, organized in terms of wards, community committees, and, as we noted earlier, resident advisory groups (Axworthy and Cassidy, 1974; Higgins, 1977). This system was introduced to achieve greater efficiency in the provision of services, and at the same time institutionalize citizen participation. The difficulties of the latter were matched by other problems. Members of the new expanded council had previously served on municipal councils where administration, not development of policies, was stressed. They continued to manifest this bias, and balked at dealing with complex policy issues, especially in the absence of a strong executive and municipal party system. Similarly, the influence of suburban interests on council has meant that development projects are strongly supported with less attention paid to the need, for example, for low-income housing or resolution of other inner-city problems (Axworthy and Cassidy, 1977).

Annexation is a tactic employed by Calgary to gain control over "contiguous metropolitan development" (Diemer, 1975: 139). Although this meets the need for additional land, it is not feasible in areas such as Edmonton where economically stable communities on the periphery resist the loss of any part of their jurisdiction—especially if it reduces their tax revenues and autonomy. Similar opposition exists to amalgamation; the fear of increased taxes and regulations encourages peripheral communities to resist extension of urban boundaries.

Attempts to adjust municipal boundaries to the planning and administrative needs of the urban system frequently reflect a greater emphasis on economy and efficiency in the provision of services than on citizen participation in local decision making. A fundamental issue is whether the two are inherently incompatible (Higgins, 1977; Lorimer, 1978).

New Community Formation

Beginning in the years after World War II, a number of new towns have been built in Britain in an attempt to regulate the spatial distribution of the population within the urban system (Bourne, 1975). The goal of this program is to create a series of viable communities, linked to regional development policies, offering employment opportunities to residents, and encouraging decentralization of the population. Similarly, in Sweden construction of new towns is viewed as an important strategy for creating a better-integrated social and physical environment. Less emphasis is placed on attaining relative self-sufficiency in terms of jobs; the new communities around Stockholm, for example, are economically closely tied to the centre city (Pressman, 1975).

New community formation has a long heritage in North America. During the nineteenth century and even earlier a number of utopian communities were founded in reaction against the perceived disharmony of the wider society (Kanter, 1972). They sought to implement in a new, more controlled environment religious values and a communal lifestyle. Few of these experiments survived for more than two or three years. Contemporary communes are more concerned with the personal fulfilment of their members through close relationships and emphasis on collectivism than with extensive social reform.

As in Europe, non-utopian new communities have become increasingly visible in North America. New towns have emerged, however, in the United States chiefly through private enterprise (Gertler, 1976). Unlike the Scandinavian and British examples, they are characterized by a less diverse mixture of residents from different social classes (Popenoe, 1977). American new towns are more oriented to the affluent, and in addition rely less on a system of public ownership of the land.

Over the past several decades a wide variety of types of new communities have been constructed in Canada (Pressman, 1975). These include:

1. *Resource-based single enterprise communities* (Lucas, 1971): This is the most common type of new community. Usually developed by a private company, they house and serve the needs of employees and their families. Closely tied to a single economic function, such communities are less stable than more diversified cities. Changes in the demand for that resource, for example, or competition from other locales in its exploitation, strongly influence employment conditions in this type of community. Settlements planned around communications (such as Gander) or administrative functions (such as Oromocto) experience a similar degree of vulnerability.

2. *Satellite towns:* These communities (for example, Don Mills and Kanata) are created to provide additional housing in a metropolitan area. They are frequently financed and constructed by private companies. These are similar to dormitory suburbs in that they offer few employment opportunities for their own residents, who must commute elsewhere in the region to their jobs.

3. *Satellite cities:* These seek to accommodate a larger population having greater self-sufficiency in employment. Established either through private enterprise or governmental sponsorship, such communities as Bramalea, Meadowvale, Erin Mills and North Pickering in Ontario are increasingly viewed as valuable channels for structuring regional growth and attaining a more balanced population distribution in an area.

A central question in planning is whether satellite towns and cities can be developed more extensively as a strategy for curbing excessive urban concentration and regulating more fully urban expansion. Several critical issues have emerged in the attempt to adopt this strategy (Pressman, 1976):

• To what extent can new communities become more than satellite subdivisions—that is, offer not only housing but employment opportunities to their residents? If they are to be "free-standing" or relatively independent communities, it is essential that a comprehensive socioeconomic environment be developed.

• New towns may not be integrated political and administrative units. Rather, they may be subject to the control and jurisdiciton of larger municipalities. The extent to which this inhibits the provision of necessary services and stifles housing and environmental innovations in a new community is unclear.

• The construction of new communities on a large scale requires an alliance between the public and private sectors to bear the costs of financing, land acquisition, and development of the necessary services or infrastructure. Reliance on the private sector alone for new community building is not realistic. Public land assembly projects, subsidized by CMHC, are seen as possible vehicles for developing new communities, as reflected in the 1973 amendments to the National Housing Act that made provision for a new communities program in Canada and provided loans to municipalities for land acquisition. Experience with this strategy is still rudimentary. We should note also the "phasing problem" that exists in the financing of new communities—new towns must supply the necessary services and have in place major facilities (such as water and sewerage systems), the costs of which must be borne before substantial revenues from the sale of houses and land are generated. Without adequate public control and regulations, developers may build poorly designed projects quickly; similarly, the price of housing rises as a way of subsidizing these costs, thus restricting the community to the upper middle class.

• Public participation in the planning of new communities and their development is necessary. The manner in which this can be most effectively achieved is unclear, especially at the beginning of a development project when there is no resident population in the community. In North Pickering, as development proceeded the hope was that as people arrived they would contribute to environmental management through a local citizens' environmental advisory committee.

• Attention must be given to the relationship between the building of new communities and the expansion of existing towns as alternate or complementary ways of deflecting urban growth. In addition, the new community must not be developed without adequate concern for its economic and spatial ties to other communities and cities in the region. In short, it must be integrated with the surrounding urban system. The Toronto-centred region scheme seeks to create a set of new communities above the lakeshore that would create a single labour market (Pressman, 1975).

• On a more theoretical level, it is critical to examine the varying social structures found in these new communities—whether some of the generalizations we have explored in earlier chapters (for example, regarding the nature of urban and suburban locality-based relationships) are applicable in these contexts. There are important planning implications here too. The extent to which a new community should contain a socially heterogeneous or homogeneous population—a compelling issue—cannot be adequately addressed until such an analysis is completed.

It is increasingly clear that the development of new communities is only one possible instrument for regulating the urban system. Its usefulness in the long run is dependent on how it is integrated within a more general national urban policy that addresses as well, for example, redevelopment of existing centres.

National Urban Policy

The goal of a national urban policy is to regulate on a national level the rate of growth and spatial distribution of urban development. The formulation of such a policy is more difficult to achieve in Canada than in countries such as Britain or Sweden where the political system is centralized, where there is greater public acceptance of government involvement in local affairs, and where a greater homogeneity of the population exists such that a consensus on policy goals is more feasible (Bourne, 1975). Even these societies have not yet fully attained their objectives in this matter. In Sweden, for example, the growth of regional centres has been encouraged as a way to control excessive concentration of population in the major metropolitan areas. Yet economic imbalances (measured in such terms as employment opportunities) among the regions continue to exist.

The term "national urban policy," it has been pointed out, is indeed a misleading one (Boothroyd and Marilyn, 1972). It suggests a uniform set of strategies in directing urban development, applicable regardless of local circumstances. Such an approach is undesirable in a country like Canada which contains significant regional differences. If we do wish to better regulate urban evolution, the strategies adopted must reflect the following:

1. The demographic and ecological meanings of urbanization or urban growth must be distinguished. Concern must be not only with the increase in population of individual centres such as Toronto, Montreal, and Vancouver,

but also with *structural* growth—that is, the evolution of a more comprehensive and intricate territorial division of labour as exists in a metropolitan region. Strategies for regulating each dimension of urbanization, although interrelated, may emphasize different problems. Whereas the demographic dimension might call, for example, for greater control over the destination of immigrants, the ecological directs us to more efficient mass transit systems that help to better integrate functionally the different communities in an area.

2. If Canada's entire set of urban areas should be conceptualized as a national system of cities, as we have argued in chapter 3, efforts to regulate it must treat that system holistically. The economic links among the different levels must be recognized. Such interdependence implies that attempts to curb or redirect growth within, for example, the Windsor-Quebec City sub-system, will have significant consequences for other regions and sectors of the national system. At the same time, it must be recognized that the different levels of that hierarchy may present different demographic, ecological, and economic problems that require diverse solutions.

3. A fundamental issue particularly relevant to Canada because of its political system is to better articulate the relative responsibilities of the different levels of government in regulating urbanization (Bourne, 1975). Federal and provincial policies dealing with urban development must be adequately co-ordinated. Political fragmentation impedes long-range planning.

4. Urban and regional planning must be closely linked. The use of urban growth centres as a strategy for regional economic development must be tied to a more complete understanding of the functional connections among different levels of settlement within the area (Guerette, 1970). The social and economic consequences of the creation of such centres for the other segments of this territorial system must be carefully analyzed beforehand (Matthews, 1976).

5. The question of seeking to impose greater limits to urban growth must be examined more explicitly in terms of which groups would or would not benefit from this (Bourne, 1975-76). Rigidly limiting suburban expansion, for example, may create serious costs, especially with respect to the availability of needed housing and jobs.

6. Similarly, the quest for regulating urban growth at times appears to be a panacea for resolving a number of social ills. In chapter 3 we saw that in Canada city size and rate of growth are not necessarily correlated with social, economic, and environmental problems. These must be directly attacked through social policies. Physical planning, in short, in itself cannot achieve such goals as equitable distribution of wealth and power.

7. Finally, it is increasingly recognized that efforts to regulate the urban system must be closely tied to other policy issues, such as control over the flow and distribution of immigration (recall from chapter 6 the clustering of immigrants in the larger urban communities), the need for a comprehensive land policy (to prevent excessive speculative gain by private developers, control

land prices, and facilitate public land assemblies), and control over foreign ownership (Bourne, 1975; Gertler, 1976; Spurr, 1976). A "package" of policies must be elaborated that reflects the interdependence of the social, ecological, economic, and political dimensions of Canadian urban society. Similarly, it is critical that policies and programs dealing with urban renewal, urban populism, urban municipal reorganization, and the development of new communities be closely co-ordinated within such a package, and at the same time incorporate the above planning prerequisites.

SUMMARY

1. Although this is not emphasized in classical urban theory, the spatial and social form of the urban system, we must recognize, are influenced by the way in which power is distributed and exercised.

2. There are three general approaches to the study of community power, influence, power structure, and decision-making structure: the positional or structural approach (which focuses on who occupies the central positions in community organizations); the reputational approach (which stresses perceptions of power); and the decisional approach (which analyzes how influence is exercised with respect to selected issues).

3. Since adoption of only one of these approaches may lead to a highly selective view of community power and decision-making structures, it is more fruitful to employ a combination of the three. In addition, an important task is to determine how these structures vary according to the size, rate of growth, and functions of a city, as well as their consequences, in such areas as the types of policies or programs pursued by a community and their level of implementation.

4. Our knowledge of the nature and variation of community power and decision-making structures in Canada is still limited. One pattern that has emerged is that community influentials are able to exercise power and leadership because they, more commonly than other residents, hold executive positions in a number of local organizations whose resources they can tap.

5. Although the municipal structure of formal decision making varies greatly across urban Canada, consistently we find that those of low socioeconomic status, women, and members of minority ethnic status groups are underrepresented on city councils. The process of local political recruitment is a relatively selective one, permitting, as in urban Alberta, the continued dominance of the more affluent, the better-educated, and those supportive of business interests.

6. A strong ideology of non-partisanship has existed in urban Canada. The introduction of parties into the urban political system was discouraged because of the fear that they would foster patronage and corruption. Non-partisanship in many cities helped to sustain the power and influence of middle-class business and professional groups; those desirous of advancing other sets of interests could not gain support through a formally organized local party.

7. This tradition of non-partisanship has eroded in recent years. As urban areas have continued to expand and municipal governments have become involved in more controversial issues such as development projects, local civic parties have increased in number. They may provide the means for more efficient urban policy making and implementation. The national parties also have become more directly involved in the urban political system. The consequences of this trend are as yet unclear.

8. In examining the patterns of power and influence in the urban community it is useful to conceive of the city as a political economy. Urban space and land are structured according to the distribution of wealth and power. Politics at the local level is one of apportioning valuable resources—such as land—for which various groups compete. Coalitions are formed to advance common interests.

9. One such coalition is that of the property industry. Since World War II the urban development industry has experienced rapid growth and increasing corporate concentration. Such economic dominance, it is contended, is matched by its political power and influence at the local level. The property industry, which consists of a coalition of all the businesses and professions that either own, manage, service, or supply urban property and accommodation, seek control over the city councils and municipal governments such that their interests are adequately protected and politically advanced. Although this thesis is a compelling one, it may underestimate the clash of interests within the property industry. There is a need, employing a combination of the three approaches to the study of community power, to examine how, for example, the proposed influence of the property industry over municipal government varies according to the size and functional structure of a city.

10. Urban planning is the formal and institutional attempt to regulate urbanization and urbanism. We consider it in this chapter because it frequently reflects and sustains the distribution of urban power and influence systems.

11. The history of Canadian urban planning illustrates this point. The period between 1896 and 1921 was one of significant economic expansion in Canada, yet the urban working class in communities such as Toronto and Montreal gained few benefits. Little was done to improve their health, housing, educational, or economic conditions. What urban reform measures were implemented reflected the values and interests of the middle class. Greater emphasis was placed on purifying the city environment or on making city government more efficient than on restructuring the manner in which wealth and power were redistributed. Modern city planning as it emerged thus assumed a middle-class ethos.

12. Such an orientation is reflected in contemporary efforts to regulate the urban system. For example, aside from ambiguities in policy objectives and administrative difficulties in their implementation, urban renewal projects failed to consider adequately the social costs of destroying existing communities and neighbourhoods and the social disruption caused by forced relocation among low-income groups.

13. The demand for greater local control and increased citizen participation in

the urban political system has emerged as a reaction to the manner in which both public and private development schemes have been implemented. City politicians and officials have resisted efforts to decentralize decision making. Attempts to institutionalize citizen participation, for example, in Winnipeg, have not been uniformly successful. This movement itself lacks internal cohesion: the interests of those in working-class or low-status areas do not necessarily coincide with the objectives of middle-class groups.

14. One serious problem in the continued process of urbanization is the increasing irrelevance of existing urban municipal boundaries in dealing with such issues as pollution, sprawl, and transportation. The coexistence of a number of distinct jurisdictions in an area impedes efficient planning and creates costly duplication of services. Attempts to reorganize urban municipalities include the creation of special-purpose agencies, of a two-tiered or federation type of municipal government (such as Metro Toronto), and of a single-tiered unit through extending the boundaries of a city by amalgamation or annexation. Such reorganization frequently places greater emphasis on the need for efficiency in the provision of services than on heightening citizen participation in decision making. This parallels to some extent an orientation to urban reform found earlier in this century.

15. Aside from municipal reorganization, an additional strategy that has been proposed to better regulate urbanization is the development of new communities. These might encourage decentralization of population and create on a regional scale a more fully integrated social and physical environment. A number of issues remain unresolved here, however—including, for example, whether the employment base of such communities can be strengthened so that they are more than large-scale housing subdivisions. Again, the role of citizen participation in their planning and development is unclear.

16. Urban renewal, urban populism, urban municipal reorganization, and the development of new communities must all be linked more explicitly to a set of policies which seek to regulate the urban system in a more systematic manner than has occurred in the past. This is not easily achieved in a nation as politically and regionally fragmented as Canada. It demands that the urban system be treated holistically—with sensitivity to the economic and ecological links and differences among its various levels. Efforts to physically limit urban growth must not supplant, as many urban reformers of the early 1900s failed to see, the formulation of social policies dealing directly with urban unemployment, poverty, and other economic and social problems in the city.

Conclusion

Evolving beyond its classical foundations, contemporary urban sociology is a highly diffuse and eclectic field. As has been noted, its concerns range from the process of entrance to the urban system, to the varying significance of the local community, to the manner in which social and spatial structures are interrelated. Our understanding of these issues within the Canadian context is still incomplete. The exciting and demanding task in the years ahead is the extension of that understanding and the determination of how the theories, concepts, and empirical generalizations pertaining to these issues apply within the Canadian urban scene.

PREREQUISITES FOR ADEQUATE URBAN RESEARCH

In the pursuit of that task, an understanding of urbanization and urban structure will more readily occur if research on the city meets several important prerequisites:

Historical. Urban sociologists must give full attention to the historical dimensions of the city if we are to avoid hasty and imprecise generalizing. Urban sociology must not be merely the study of the contemporary city. Michael Frisch (1972:3) criticizes the early work in American urban sociology:

> . . . most of such American sociological theory has been seriously time and culture bound, which is another way of saying that sociologists have often been careless about cause and effect. While observing and generalizing perceptively about social structure and traits, they have been less successful in examining how the city's characteristics developed, where they came from, and hence what they really represent. To raise such questions, to deal with the relations of development to context, of general to specific, of cause to process—to consider all these is to deal with questions in potentially historical terms, and to suggest the general value of the historical perspective.

Comparative. Manheim (1960: 229) has observed: "To become a true discipline, urban sociology will have to broaden its area of inquiry to articulate the whole range of conditions under which cities form and expand." In short, it must incorporate a comparative perspective. What this implies is that the relationships among the components of one social context—for example, between the industrial base of a community and its stratification system—cannot be

341

fully understood without examining those relationships in other contexts. The comparative perspective, cross-cultural or not, allows for the discovery of significant variables and a verification of hypotheses.

Societal. The urban community must be seen as a unit in a larger social system. Human ecologists have long held this perspective, but it is only recently that such a focus has become so widely and clearly emphasized. Much of what is occurring within the city is due to wider societal trends. For example, residential segregation patterns within a city reflect the level of modernization in the wider society (Timms, 1971). Given this general orientation, attention must focus on how the various levels of analysis can be theoretically articulated.

Processual. This attribute emphasizes the need for examining the dynamic forces occurring in the city. While a static structural analysis of urban institutions is necessary, it must be balanced by attempts to grasp the changes that occur over time in these institutions. In addition, the research methods selected will reflect these efforts. While cross-sectional analyses are useful, variations of panel studies are of particular relevance. Survey analysis must be supplemented by longitudinal case studies, within a comparative perspective if possible. A clearer understanding of the changes occurring in specific elements and the factors responsible for such development may thereby ultimately emerge.

Openness. In his book *Cities In Evolution* (1968 ed.), Patrick Geddes criticized the sociologists of his time—the early 1900s—for not demonstrating sufficient analytical interest in cities. They had, in his view, been too concerned with abstract society or with primitive communities. While we may no longer accept this criticism, the recommendation he proposed still has merit:

> For each and every city we need a systematic survey, of its development and origins, its history and its present. This survey is required not merely for material buildings, but also for the city's life and its institutions, for of these the builded city is but the external shell (Geddes, 1968 ed.: 225).

What is important here is his belief that for such a "survey" to achieve its aim fully, it must be interdisciplinary: "This survey must be in all aspects, contemporary as well as historic. It may be geographic and economic, anthropological and historical, demographic and eugenic, and so on . . ." (266).

One discipline can only attain a limited perspective of the whole. Urban sociology must incorporate knowledge gained from related disciplines; it must establish a "dialogue" with urban geography, urban political science, and urban economics. For example, a complete grasp of lifestyle variations in spatial distribution requires some attention to transportation facilities—their distribution, efficiency, and cost. The intricacy of the causal web characterizing urban structure forbids too parochial an approach. The findings of other disciplines must be combined with the unique perspectives of urban sociology.

The above constitutes a brief sketch of what are increasingly seen as prerequisites for an adequate urban sociology. They are complementary, and even at times overlapping. Both urban theory and research will continue to advance to the extent that they are able to comply with these requirements. Any specific focus of interest within this area—whether it be urban stratification systems, urban political structures, or urban social networks—must likewise meet these prerequisites as closely as possible. Indeed, they serve as standards by which we can judge whether actual research has fulfilled the ambitions first advanced by the classical urban theorists.

THE URBAN SYSTEM AND URBAN RESEARCH

This text has made frequent reference to the notion of an "urban system." This system must be conceptualized *as a set of interrelated levels*:

1. The urban family;
2. The urban neighbourhood;
3. The urban community as a whole—its population, institutional and functional structures;
4. The urban community and its hinterland;
5. The urban community as a unit within a regional and national system of cities.

The task of the urban sociologists in Canada, as elsewhere, is to specify the social and ecological processes operating at each of these levels and to identify and explain systematically the factors affecting those processes. As should be evident, much work remains to be done before we can fully grasp the complexity of the urban system.

On the most immediate level—that of the urban family—we must still systematically identify, for example, variations in the structure of kinship ties. While contemporary research challenges the isolated nuclear family thesis, we must develop more refined alternative conceptualizations. We must articulate more clearly how class, stage of the family life cycle, and ethnicity influence kinship patterns. We cannot assume that generalizations derived from other national and cultural contexts are directly applicable to the Canadian urban scene; their applicability must be demonstrated empirically. Most important, we cannot overlook the nature of kinship patterns at different historical stages of urban growth. We must examine the functions, norms, and ideologies of kinship involvement not only in the contemporary industrial-metropolitan community, but also in the early industrial city. Such a comparison will provide a deeper understanding of the role of kinship ties in enabling new entrants to adapt and in contributing to the attainment of urban social order.

With respect to the urban neighbourhood, it is necessary to rely on both social and ecological schemes for grasping its structure. An important issue is the process through which distinct "natural areas" form—in short, how spatial structure reflects social structure. As discussed briefly in Part Four of this book, patterns of residential segregation respond to the level of modernization and technological advancement in the wider society. The "sifting and sorting" of urban populations reflect the importance of class, lifestyle, life cycle, and ethnicity in determining housing and locational choices. We require much more detailed documentation of this process and of how neighbourhoods as natural areas emerge within Canadian cities.

An equally important research imperative, as noted in Part Five, is the determination of the social structure of the urban neighbourhood. Discarding the over-generalized myth of the demise of the local community, a central concern of contemporary urban sociologists is to determine how the significance of the neighbourhood as a social fact varies within the urban population. In exploring the nature of locality relationships, much further study is needed of the manner in which the neighbour role is conceptualized, of the functions and levels of involvement in neighbour relationships, and of the subjective spatial organization of the neighbourhood. The role of the neighbourhood as a status symbol and as a mechanism for sustaining class and ethnic identites has only been tentatively explored. Further study on all of these issues promises a more complete grasp of the place of the local community within the city.

At this level of the urban system, an important focus of attention is the nature of community life in the inner city—where the less affluent and culturally dissimilar segements of the urban population tend to concentrate. Not accepting the assumption of classical urban theory that inner-city life is disorganized, contemporary researchers seek to document how social order exists in the working-class neighbourhood and in the slum, and the frequent socially destructive effects of urban renewal programs. The increase of public housing projects and highrise apartments in the inner city and elsewhere since World War II has presented the important task of determining whether particular social and physical conditions of these new types of environment actually hinder the attainment of social order on the local level.

Beyond the structures of the urban family and urban neighbourhood, analysis of the urban system also requires consideration of the city as a whole —its population, institutional, and functional structures. From a demographic perspective, we must consider the city in terms of its size, density, heterogeneity, and age and sex distributions. Most important, the city as a locus of destination for internal migrants and immigrants must be recognized and the implications of this explored. An important concern of contemporary urban sociology, as we have seen, is the process of entrance to the urban system. We have emphasized the necessity of understanding the social dimensions of this process because of the critical role which migration and immigration have played in the evolution of Canada as an urban nation. The meaning of, and the stages in, the entrance process, the factors responsible for variations in adjustment, and the comparison of different categories of entrants—ranging from native peoples to immigrants—in terms of their patterns and relative levels of assimilation are all intriguing questions to which further research must be dedicated. It will be particularly fruitful to extend comparisons between Canadian urbanization and the dynamics of the entrance process as manifested in other contexts, such as in African cities. Much can be gained by examining the encapsulation and retribalization processes in African cities for understanding the possible fate of ethnic identities, and the impact of pre-existing ethnic communities on urban entrants.

Analysis of the urban system at this level also implies concern for the institutional and functional structures of the city. With respect to the first, urban sociologists are concerned with the political structure of the urban community, with the manner in which formal and informal decision making occurs, and how patterns of interest group formation and conflict influence and reflect the changing structure of the city. Aside from the political sector, it is necessary that the educational and religious institutions be examined not as isolated entities, but in terms of their connection to the class, ethnic, and ecological structures of the city. How, for example, does the urban school system influence the process of assimilation of new entrants? What function does the local educational institution perform in fostering neighbourhood cohesion? Similarly, in terms of the religious sector, to what extent is a local church, parish, or congregation successful in resisting residential succession by a different ethnic or income group? Complementing political, education, and religious institutions, voluntary associations also not infrequently perform vital functions for urban residents, and contribute to the attainment of social order. Urban sociologists have examined how such organizations relate to the process of entrance, how involvement in them varies by class, and how they compare with other forms of social involvement. But, again, more systematic analysis of their place within Canadian urban social organization is needed.

With respect to the functional structure of the city as a whole, we have noted in preceding pages that the central concern here is with the development of the industrial and commercial bases of the city and their implications for urban growth. As a city assumes metropolitan status, its economic functions become more complex and diversified. A central need in Canadian urban studies is for additional historical analyses of this process, such as those completed of the evolution of Toronto and Winnipeg. It is particularly important that these analyses be explicitly set within the ecological framework. This will allow us to see more clearly whether the variety of generalizations developed within that framework are applicable to the Canadian setting. A city's functional structure determines both its basic and non-basic employment patterns. Further research must concentrate on determining how each influences the stratification system of a city and its patterns of social mobility, and how the level of assimilation varies according to changes in, and vitality of, the functional structure.

The last two levels of analysis of the urban system underline the obvious fact that a city does not exist in isolation. Of key interest in urban ecology are the functional connections between an urban community and the surrounding hinterland, for which it provides vital services. It is essential to explore how these linkages change over time as the city grows in size and economic complexity. The urban community and its hinterland, viewed ecologically, represent an integrated unit in which the exchange of people, goods, and services occurs in an orderly and predictable fashion. An important research task is to trace how this unit evolves. Ecological theory gives particular emphasis to the impact of improved transportation and communication facilities in widening the scope of interdependence. The metropolitan community represents the product of this expanded organization.

One central feature of this process is the diffusion outward of the urban population—suburbanization. Initially, it was assumed that suburban residence in itself had profound implications for the structure of social life. As we have seen, however, this assumption has increasingly been challenged. An important task of contemporary urban sociology in Canada—aside from documenting more thoroughly the ecological factors responsible for suburbanization—is to clarify whether indeed relocation in a suburban residential setting does have any implications for how social organization is evolved, in contrast, for example, to how social order is achieved in the inner city.

Finally, a particularly demanding task facing urban sociologists is the examination of the urban community as a unit within a regional and national system of cities. This is the most comprehensive level of ecological organization—one that is characteristic of a highly urbanized society such as Canada. We can conceptualize this society as an integrated network of urban "nodes" —each of varying size, function, and relative dominance. Such heightened interdependence means that the economic, social, and ecological changes occurring in any city must be examined in terms of how they reflect the linkages that community has externally. Patterns of growth and change in the entire system may filter through and effect particular modifications in the structure of a specific node. Our grasp of this process in the Canadian setting is still relatively incomplete. The need to evolve a more comprehensive ecological theory to clearly articulate this process is evident.

Certainly, it is also apparent when examining these five levels of analysis of the "urban system" that urban sociologists must rely on a diversity of methodologies and research techniques in acquiring the relevant information. The use of participant observation and ethnographic approaches in the study of neighbourhood social life are as valid and necessary as the use of historical documents, survey analyses, and census materials in the investigation of urban growth and its correlates. The nature of the city is too complex to permit restriction to a limited number of data-gathering instruments. Our study of the fruits of these instruments and methodologies must be equally receptive to insights regardless of the manner in which they are gained.

As early as 1911, J. S. Woodsworth (1972 ed.: 30) pointed to the need in Canada for a "comprehensive city plan." Six decades later, Lithwick (1970) emphasized the continued failure to fill this need and to design a sophisticated and enlightened public policy for the cities of this country. Such major urban problems as poverty, escalating housing costs, and transportation congestion are a product of our inability to conceptualize and regulate the urban process as a whole. Urban sociology, while not dealing directly with the solution of these specific problems, can contribute to the formation of national urban policies by providing through its research a greater theoretical understanding of that process. A central goal of this field is a more complete analysis of the dynamic forces operating at each level of the urban system. It seeks to dispel our myths about city living, to reveal the complexity of urban structure. If knowledge is a necessary prerequisite for reform, the further development of urban sociology with adequate funding (King, 1976) can be viewed as one important step in achieving a more humane urban environment in Canada.

Bibliography

Ablon, Joan. "Relocated American Indians in the San Francisco Bay Area: Social Interaction and Indian Identity." *Human Organization* 23 (1964): 296-304.

Abramson, Jane A. *Barriers to Population Mobility: Four Economically Lagging Areas in Atlantic Provinces and Quebec.* Saskatoon: Canadian Centre for Community Studies, 1968a.

————. *Rural to Urban Adjustment.* Saskatoon: Canadian Centre for Community Studies, 1968b.

Abu-Laban, S. M. *Social Bonds in the Urban Industrial Setting: A Metasociological Analysis.* Ph.D. dissertation, University of Alberta, 1974.

Abu-Lughod, Janet. "Migrant Adjustment to City Life: The Egyptian Case." *American Journal of Sociology* 67 (1961): 22-32.

————. "The City is Dead—Long Live the City: Some Thoughts on Urbanity." In *Urbanism in World Perspective,* edited by Sylvia Fleis Fava. New York: Thomas Y. Crowell Co., 1968, pp. 154-65.

————. "Testing the Theory of Social Area Analysis: The Ecology of Cairo, Egypt." *American Sociological Review* 34 (1969): 198-212.

Adams, Bert N. *Kinship in an Urban Setting.* Chicago: Markham Co., 1968.

————. "Ugandan Asians in Exile: Household and Kinship in the Resettlement Crisis." *Journal of Comparative Family Studies* 8 (1977): 167-78.

Aiello, John R., and Andrew Baum. *Residential Crowding and Design.* New York: Plenum Press, 1979.

Aiken, Michael, and David Goldberg. "Social Mobility and Kinship: A Reexamination of the Hypothesis." *American Anthropologist* 71 (1969): 261-70.

Aldous, Joan. "An Exchange Between Durkheim and Toennies on the Nature of Social Relations." *American Journal of Sociology* 77 (1970): 1191-1200.

Alexander, John W. "The Basic-Non-Basic Concept of Urban Economic Functions." In *Readings in Urban Geography,* edited by Harold M. Mayer and Clyde E. Kohn. Chicago: University of Chicago Press, 1959, pp. 87-100.

Alihan, Milla Aissa. *Social Ecology.* New York: Columbia University Press, 1938.

Allen, Robert Thomas. "Portrait of Little Italy." *Macleans* (March 1964), 17-19, 43-46.

Ames, Herbert Brown. *The City Below the Hill*. Toronto: University of Toronto Press, 1972 ed. First published in 1898.

Amyot, Michael and M. V. George. *Intraprovincial Migration Streams in Quebec and Ontario 1956-1961*. Analytical and Technical Memorandum No. 8. Ottawa: Statistics Canada, 1973.

Anderson, Grace M. *Networks of Contact: The Portuguese and Toronto*. Waterloo: Wilfred Laurier University, 1974.

Anderson, J. D. "Non-Partisan Urban Politics in Canadian Cities." In *Emerging Party Politics in Urban Canada*, edited by Jack K. Masson and James D. Anderson. Toronto: McClelland and Stewart, 1972, pp. 5-21.

Anderson, Michael. *Family Structure in Nineteenth-Century Lancashire*. Cambridge: At the University Press, 1971.

Armstrong, Christopher, and H. V. Nelles. *The Revenge of the Methodist Bicycle Company: Sunday Streetcars and Municipal Reform, 1888-1897*. Toronto: Peter Martin Associates, 1977.

Armstrong, Frederick H. "Metropolitanism and Toronto Reexamined, 1825-1850." In *The Canadian City: Essays in Urban History*, edited by Gilbert A. Stelter and Alan F. J. Artibise. Toronto: McClelland and Stewart, 1977, pp. 37-50.

Armstrong, Frederick H., and Daniel J. Brock. "The Rise of London: A Study of Urban Evolution in Nineteenth-Century Southwestern Ontario." In *Aspects of Nineteenth-Century Ontario*, edited by F. H. Armstrong, H. A. Stevenson, and J. D. Wilson. Toronto: University of Toronto Press, 1974, pp. 80-100.

Artibise, Alan F. J. *An Urban Environment: The Process of Growth in Winnipeg. 1874-1914*. Paper presented at the Canadian Historical Association meetings, Montreal, 1972a.

_____. *An Urban Environment: The Process of Growth in Winnipeg. 1874-1914*. Historical Papers, 1972. Toronto: The Canadian Historical Association, 1972b.

_____. *Winnipeg: A Social History of Urban Growth. 1874-1914*. Montreal and London: McGill-Queen's University Press, 1975.

Atwell, Phyllis H. *Kinship and Migration Among Calgarian Residents of Indian Origin*. M.A. thesis, University of Calgary, 1969.

Aubin, Henry. *City for Sale*. Toronto: James Lorimer and Company, 1977.

Axelrod, Morris. "Urban Structure and Social Participation." *American Sociological Review* 21 (1956): 13-18.

Axworthy, Lloyd. *The Citizen and Neighborhood Renewal*. Future City Series No. 3. University of Winnipeg: Institute for Urban Studies, n.d.

Axworthy, Lloyd, and Jim Cassidy. *Unicity: The Transition*. Future City Series No. 4. Winnipeg: The Institute for Urban Studies, University of Winnipeg, 1974.

Axworthy, Lloyd, and Donald Epstein. *A Discussion Paper on Urban*

Populism and Urban Policy-Making. Paper presented at the Conference on the Canadian Urban Experience, Toronto, May 30, 1974.

Bailey, Dickson H. R. *Electoral Cleavages in Metropolitan Hamilton: An Ecological Analysis of the Federal and Provincial Elections, 1962-1972*. M.A. thesis, McMaster University, 1973.

Baine, Richard P. *Calgary: An Urban Study*. Toronto: Clarke, Irwin and Company Limited, 1973.

Balakrishnan, T. R. "Ethnic Residential Segregation in the Metropolitan Areas of Canada." *Canadian Journal of Sociology* 1 (1975): 481-98.

Balakrishnan, T. R. and George K. Jarvis. "Socioeconomic Differentiation in Urban Canada." *Canadian Review of Sociology and Anthropology* 13 (1976): 204-16.

_____. "Changing Patterns of Spatial Differentiation in Urban Canada, 1961-1971." *Canadian Review of Sociology and Anthropology* 16 (1979): 218-27.

Banfield, Edward. *The Moral Basis of a Backward Society*. New York: Free Press, 1958.

Banks, J. A. "The Contagion of Numbers." In *The Victorian City: Images and Realities*, edited by H. J. Dyos and Michael Wolff. Vol. 1. London: Routledge and Kegan Paul, 1973, pp. 105-22.

Banton, Michael. *West African City: A Study of Tribal Life in Freetown*. London: Oxford University Press, 1957.

_____. "Social Alignment and Identity in a West African City." In *Urbanization and Migration in West Africa*, edited by Hilda Kuper. Berkeley and Los Angeles: University of California Press, 1965, pp. 131-47.

Barker, Graham, Jennifer Penney, and Wally Seccombe. *Highrise and Superprofits: An Analysis of the Development Industry in Canada*. Kitchener: Dumont Press Graphix, 1973.

Barnes, J. A. "Networks and Political Process." In *Social Networks in Urban Situations*, edited by J. Clyde Mitchell. Manchester: Manchester University Press, 1969, pp. 51-76.

_____. *Social Networks*. Don Mills: Addison-Wesley, 1972.

Barrow, Graham T. *A Factorial Ecology of Three Cities: Edmonton, Regina and Winnipeg, 1961*. M.A. thesis, University of Calgary, 1972.

Barth, Fredrik. *Ethnic Groups and Boundaries*. London: George Allen and Unwin, 1969.

Baskett, Harold Kenneth. *Concepts of Neighbourhood: Perspectives of Planners and Downtown High-Rise Dwellers in the City of Calgary*. M.A. thesis, University of Calgary, 1970.

Beals, Ralph L. "Urbanism, Urbanization, and Acculturation." *American Anthropologist* 53 (1951a): 1-10.

_____. "Life in a Mexican Village: Tepoztlan Restudied by Oscar Lewis." *American Sociological Review* 16 (1951b): 895-96.

Becker, Howard. "Sacred and Secular Societies." *Social Forces* 28 (1950): 361-76.

Bedarida, Francois, and Anthony Sutcliffe. "The Street in the Structure and Life of the City: Reflections on Nineteenth-Century London and Paris." *Journal of Urban History* 6 (1980): 379-96.

Bell, Wendell. "Economic, Family, and Ethnic Status: An Empirical Test." *American Sociological Review* 20 (1955): 45-52.

_____. "The Utility of the Shevky Typology for the Design of Urban Sub-Area Field Studies." In *Studies in Human Ecology*, edited by George A. Theodorson. New York: Harper & Row, 1961, pp. 244-52.

_____. "The City, the Suburb, and a Theory of Social Choice." In *The New Urbanization*, edited by Scott Greer *et al.* New York: St. Martin's Press, 1968, pp. 132-68.

Bell, Wendell, and Marion D. Boat. "Urban Neighborhoods and Informal Social Relations." *American Journal of Sociology* 62 (1957): 391-98.

Bell, Wendell, and Charles C. Moskos. "A Comment on Udry's 'Increasing Scale and Spatial Differentiation'." *Social Forces* 42 (1964): 414-17.

Berger, Bennett. *Working-Class Suburb*. Berkeley: University of California Press, 1960.

Bernard, Jessie. *The Sociology of Community*. Glenview, Illinois: Scott, Foresman and Co., 1973.

Berry, Brian J. "Cities as Systems Within Systems of Cities." In *Regional Development and Planning: A Reader*, edited by John Friedmann and William Alonso. Cambridge: MIT Press, 1964, pp. 116-37.

_____. "Introduction: The Logic and Limitations of Comparative Factorial Ecology." *Economic Geography* 47 (1971): 209-19.

_____. *The Human Consequences of Urbanization*. New York: St. Martin's Press, 1973.

Berry, Brian J., and Philip H. Rees. "The Factorial Ecology of Calcutta." *American Journal of Sociology* 74 (1969): 445-91.

Bettison, David G. *The Politics of Canadian Urban Development*. Edmonton: University of Alberta Press, 1975.

Binzen, Peter. *Whitetown USA*. New York: Random House, 1970.

Birch, David. "From Suburb to Urban Place." *The Annals* 422 (1975): 25-35.

Blau, Peter. "Structural Effects." *American Sociological Review* 25 (1960): 178-93.

Blumberg, Leonard, and Robert E. Bell. "Urban Migration and Kinship Ties." *Social Problems* 6 (1959): 328-33.

Blumin, Stuart M. *The Urban Threshold: Growth and Change in a Nineteenth-Century American Community*. Chicago: University of Chicago Press, 1976.

Boek, W. E., and J. K. Boek. *The People of Indian Ancestry in Manitoba: A Social and Economic Study. Volume II. The People of Indian Ancestry in*

Greater Winnipeg. Winnipeg: Department of Agriculture and Immigration, 1959.

Boissevain, Jeremy. *The Italians of Montreal: Social Adjustment in a Plural Society*. Ottawa: Studies of the Royal Commission on Bilingualism and Biculturalism, 1970.

Bonjean, Charles M., and Michael D. Grimes. "Community Power: Issues and Findings." In *Social Stratification: A Reader*, edited by Joseph Lopreato and Lionel S. Lewis. New York: Harper and Row, 1974, pp. 377-99.

Booth, Alan. *Urban Crowding and its Consequences*. New York: Praeger Publishers, 1976.

Booth, Charles. *Life and Labour of the People in London*. 17 volumes. New York: AMS Press edition, 1970.

Boothroyd, Peter, and Frank Marilyn. "National Urban Policy: A Phrase in Search of a Meaning." *Plan Canada* 12 (1972): 4-11.

Borgfjord, Marvin R. *Central Area Planning for Small Urban Centres*. Master of City Planning thesis, University of Manitoba, 1973.

Borhek, J. T. "Ethnic-Group Cohesion." *American Journal of Sociology* 76 (1970): 33-46.

Boswell, D. M. "Personal Crises and the Mobilization of the Social Network." In *Social Networks in Urban Situations*, edited by J. Clyde Mitchell. Manchester: Manchester University Press, 1969, pp. 245-96.

Bott, Elizabeth. *Family and Social Network*. London: Tavistock Publications, 1957.

Bourne, L. S. *Urban Systems: Strategies for Regulation*. Oxford: Clarendon Press, 1975.

———. "Limits to Urban Growth: Who Benefits? Who Pays? Who Decides? A Commentary On The Current Planning Climate In Canadian Cities." *Urban Forum* 1 (1975-1976), 36-46.

Bourne, L. S., and Gerald M. Barber. "Ecological Patterns of Small Urban Centers in Canada." *Economic Geography* 47 (1971): 258-65.

Bourne, L. S., and R. D. MacKinnon. *Urban Systems Development in Central Canada: Selected Papers*. Toronto: University of Toronto Press, 1972.

Bourne, L. S., Ross D. MacKinnon, Jay Siegel, and James W. Simmons. *Urban Futures for Central Canada: Perspectives on Forecasting Urban Growth and Form*. Toronto: University of Toronto Press, 1974.

Bourne, L. S., and R. A. Murdie. "Interrelationship of Social and Physical Space in the City: A Multivariate Analysis of Metropolitan Toronto." *The Canadian Geographer* 16 (1972): 211-29.

Bowles, Roy T., and Prudence Craib. "Canada: Economy, Opportunity and Class." In *Economy, Class and Social Reality: Issues in Contemporary Canadian Society*, edited by John Allan Fry. Toronto: Butterworths, 1979, pp. 51-77.

Bracey, H. E. *Neighbours: Subdivision Life in England and the United States*. Baton Rouge: Louisiana State University Press, 1964.

Breton, Raymond. *Ethnic Communities and the Personal Relations of Immigrants*. Montreal: The Social Research Group, 1961.

_____. "Institutional Completeness of Ethnic Communities and the Personal Relations of Immigrants." *American Journal of Sociology* 70 (1964): 193-205.

_____. "The Structure of Relationships Between Ethnic Collectivities." In *The Canadian Ethnic Mosaic: A Quest for Identity*, edited by Leo Driedger. Toronto: McClelland and Stewart, 1978, pp. 55-73.

Breton, Raymond, and Maurice Pinard. "Group Formation Among Immigrants: Criteria and Processes." In *Canadian Society*, edited by B. Blishen *et al.* Toronto: Macmillan, 1965, pp. 74-88.

Breton, Raymond, and Howard Roseborough. "Ethnic Differences in Status." In *Canadian Society*, edited by B. Blishen *et al.* Toronto: Macmillan, 1968, pp. 683-701.

Briggs, Asa. *Victorian Cities*. London: Odhams Press Limited, 1963.

Brody, Hugh. *Indians on Skid Row*. Ottawa: Information Canada, 1971.

Brown, Roger Craig, and Ramsay Cook. *Canada: 1896-1921*. Toronto: McClelland and Stewart, 1974.

Browning, Harley L., and Waltraut Freindt. "The Social and Economic Context of Migration to Monterrey, Mexico." In *Latin American Urban Research*, edited by Francine P. Rabinovitz and Felicity M. Trueblood. Beverly Hills: Sage Publications, 1971, pp. 45-70.

Bruner, Edward M. "Medan: The Role of Kinship in an Indonesian City." In *Peasants in Cities: Readings in the Anthropology of Urbanization*. Boston: Houghton Mifflin Co., 1970, pp. 122-34.

Brunet, Michel. "The British Conquest: Canadian Social Scientists and the Fate of the 'Canadians'." *Canadian Historical Review* 40 (1957): 93-107.

Bunge, John C. *Urban Renewal in Canada: An Assessment of Current Practice*. M.Sc. thesis, University of British Columbia, 1967.

Bureau of Municipal Research. *Neighbourhood Participation in Local Government: A Study of the City of Toronto*. Toronto: Civic Affairs, 1970.

_____. *Citizen Participation in Metro Toronto: Climate for Cooperation?* Toronto: Civic Affairs, 1975.

Burgess, Ernest W. "The Growth of the City: An Introduction to a Research Report." In *The City*, edited by Robert Park and Ernest W. Burgess. Chicago: University of Chicago Press, 1967 ed., pp. 47-62.

Butler, Peter M. *Migrants and Settlers: The Influence of Geographical Mobility on the Retention of Extended Kinship Ties*. M.A. thesis, University of New Brunswick, 1967.

Bystydzienski, J. M. J. *A Case Study of Housing Rehabilitation in a Low-Income Area of Montreal: A Sociological Analysis of Purposive Intervention at the Community Level*. M.A. thesis, McGill University, 1974.

Canada Year Book 1973. Ottawa: Queen's Printer, 1973.

Caplow, Theodore. "The Social Ecology of Guatemala City." In *Studies in*

Human Ecology, edited by George A. Theodorson. New York: Harper and Row, 1961, pp. 331-48.

Caplow, Theodore, Sheldon Stryker, and Samuel E. Wallace. *The Urban Ambience*. Totowa, N.J.: The Bedminster Press, 1964.

Careless, J. M. S. "Frontierism, Metropolitanism, and Canadian History." In *Approaches to Canadian History*, edited by Ramsay Cook *et al.* Toronto: University of Toronto Press, 1967, pp. 63-83.

_____. "Some Aspects of Urbanization in Nineteenth-Century Ontario." In *Aspects of Nineteenth-Century Ontario*, edited by F. H. Armstrong, H. A. Stevenson, and J. D. Wilson. Toronto: University of Toronto Press, 1974a, pp. 65-79.

_____. "Urban Development in Canada." *Urban History Review* (1974b): 9-14.

_____. "Aspects of Urban Life in the West, 1870-1914." In *The Canadian City: Essays in Urban History*, edited by Gilbert A. Stelter and Alan F. J. Artibise. Toronto: McClelland and Stewart, 1977, pp. 125-41.

_____. *The Rise of Cities in Canada Before 1914*. Canadian Historical Association Booklet No. 32. Ottawa: Canadian Historical Association, 1978.

Carns, Donald E., Sheldon Goldenberg, and Scott Greer. "Some Neglected Considerations on the American Urban Family." In *Cities in Change: Studies on the Urban Condition*, edited by John Walton and Donald E. Carns. Boston: Allyn and Bacon, Inc., 1973, pp. 226-37.

Carrier, Roch. *They Won't Demolish Me!* Translated by Sheila Fischman. Toronto: House of Anansi Press, 1973.

Carver, Humphrey. *Cities in the Suburbs*. Toronto: University of Toronto Press, 1962.

_____. "Community Renewal Programming." *Habitat* 8 (1965): 6-10.

Castells, Manuel. "Theory and Ideology in Urban Sociology." In *Urban Sociology: Critical Essays*, edited by C. G. Pickvance. London: Tavistock, 1976, pp. 60-84.

_____. *The Urban Question: A Marxist Approach*. Cambridge: MIT Press, 1977.

Caulfield, Jon. *The Tiny Perfect Mayor*. Toronto: James Lorimer and Company, 1974.

Census of Canada. 1961. Vol. 1, Part 2 (Bulletin 1.2-5).
1971. Vol. 1, Part 1 (Bulletin 1.1-9).
1971. Vol. 1, Part 3 (Bulletin 1.3-6).
1973. Vol. 1, Part 3 (Bulletin 1.3-2).

Chan, Kang C. *A Factorial Ecology of Singapore, 1970*. M.A. thesis, University of Windsor, 1975.

Chandler, David. *The Residential Location of Occupational and Ethnic Groups in Hamilton*. M.A. thesis, McMaster University, 1965.

Checkland, S. G. *The Rise of Industrial Society in England, 1815-1885*. London: Longmans, 1964.

Childe, V. Gordon. *Man Makes Himself*. New York and Toronto: Mentor Books, 1951.

Chimbos, Peter D. "A Comparison of the Social Adaptation of Dutch, Greek and Slovak Immigrants in a Canadian Community." *International Migration Review* 6 (1972): 230-44.

Cho, George, and Roger Leigh. "Patterns of Residence of the Chinese in Vancouver." In *Peoples of the Living Land: Geography of Cultural Diversity in British Columbia*, edited by Julian V. Minghi. Vancouver: Tantalus Research Limited, 1972, pp. 67-84.

Christie, H. A. *The Function of the Tavern in Toronto, 1834 to 1875, with Special Reference to Sport*. Master of Physical Education thesis, University of Windsor, 1973.

Clairmont, Donald H., and Dennis W. Magill. *Africville Relocation Report*. Halifax: The Institute of Public Affairs, 1971.

_____. *Africville Relocation Report Supplement*. Halifax: The Institute of Public Affairs, 1973.

Clark, S. D. *The Suburban Society*. Toronto: University of Toronto Press, 1966.

_____. "Canadian Urban Development." *Urban History Review* (1974): 14-19.

_____. *The New Urban Poor*. Toronto: McGraw-Hill Ryerson, 1978.

Clark, Terry N. *Community Structure and Decision-Making: Comparative Analyses*. San Francisco: Chandler Publishing Co., 1968.

Clignet, Remi and Joyce Sween. "Accra and Abidjan: A Comparative Examination of the Theory of Increase in Scale." *Urban Affairs Quarterly* 4 (1969): 297-324.

Cohen, Abner. *Custom and Politics in Urban Africa*. London: Routledge and Kegan Paul, 1969.

Coleman, B. I. *The Idea of the City in Nineteenth-Century Britain*. London: Routledge and Kegan Paul, 1973.

Collier, Robert W. "Downtown: Metropolitan Focus." In *Vancouver: Western Metropolis*, edited by L. J. Evenden. Western Geographical Series, Vol. 16. University of Victoria: Department of Geography, 1978, pp. 159-77.

Cooley, Charles Horton. "The Theory of Transportation." In *Sociological Theory and Social Research*, edited by Robert Cooley Angell. New York: Augustus M. Kelley, 1969, pp. 17-118; first published in 1898.

Cooper, J. L. "The Social Structure of Montreal in the 1850's." *The Canadian Historical Association Report* (1956): 63-73.

Copp, Terry. *The Anatomy of Poverty: The Condition of the Working Class in Montreal, 1897-1929*. Toronto: McClelland and Stewart, 1974.

Coult, Alan D., and Robert W. Habenstein. "The Study of Extended Kinship in Urban Society." *Sociological Quarterly* 3 (1962): 141-45.

Cowan, Elaine M. *The Effect of Ethnicity on Class Position and Upward Mobility in St. Boniface.* M.A. thesis, University of Manitoba, 1971.

Cowley, Stan. *Kinship Knowledge: An Empirical Study.* M.A. thesis, University of Alberta, 1972.

Cox, Kevin R. *Urbanization and Conflict in Market Societies.* Chicago: Maaroufa Press, Inc., 1978.

Craig, Gordon A. "The City and the Historian." *Canadian Journal of History.* 5 (1970): 47-55.

Craven, Paul, and Barry Wellman. *The Network City.* Toronto: University of Toronto Centre for Urban and Community Studies Research Paper No. 59, 1973.

Creighton, Donald. *The Empire of the St. Lawrence.* Toronto: The Macmillan Company of Canada Limited, 1956.

Cromwell, James. "Perceptual Differences Between Established and New Residents in the Rural-Urban Fringe: Surrey, British Columbia." In *Peoples of the Living Land: Geography of Cultural Diversity in British Columbia,* edited by Julian V. Minghi. Vancouver: Tantalus Research Limited, 1972, pp. 229-42.

Crowley, Ronald W. "Reflections and Further Evidence on Population Size and Industrial Diversification." *Urban Studies* 10 (1973): 91-94.

Crysdale, Stewart. *Occupational and Social Mobility in Riverdale: A Blue Collar Community.* Ph.D. dissertation, University of Toronto, 1968.

Dahir, James. *The Neighborhood Unit Plan: Its Spread and Acceptance.* New York: Russell Sage Foundation, 1947.

Danziger, Kurt. *The Socialization of Immigrant Children. Part I.* York University: Ethnic Research Programme, Institute for Behavioural Research, 1971.

Darroch, A. Gordon, and Wilfred G. Marston. "Ethnic Differentiation: Ecological Aspects of a Multidimensional Concept." *International Migration Review* 4 (1969): 71-95.

_____. "The Social Class Basis of Ethnic Residential Segregation: The Canadian Case." *American Journal of Sociology* 77 (1971): 491-510.

Davey, Ian, and Michael Doucet. "The Social Geography of a Commercial City, Ca. 1853." In *The People of Hamilton, Canada West,* edited by Michael Katz. Cambridge: Harvard University Press, 1975, pp. 319-42.

Davie, Maurice R. "The Pattern of Urban Growth." In *Studies in Human Ecology,* edited by George A. Theodorson. New York: Harper and Row, 1961, pp. 77-92.

Davies, Wayne K. D. "A Multivariate Description of Calgary's Community Areas." In *Calgary: Metropolitan Structure and Influence,* edited by Brenton M. Barr. Western Geographical Series, Vol. II. Victoria: University of Victoria, Department of Geography, 1975, pp. 231-68.

Davies, W. K. D., and G. T. Barrow. "A Comparative Factorial Ecology of

Three Canadian Prairie Cities." *The Canadian Geographer* 17 (1973): 327-53.

Davies, Wayne K. D., and T. T. Gyuse. "Changes in the Central Place System Around Calgary: 1951-1971." In *Calgary: Metropolitan Structure and Influence,* edited by Brenton M. Barr. Western Geographical Series, Vol. II. Victoria: University of Victoria, Department of Geography, 1975, pp. 123-54.

Davis, Arthur K. *Edging into Mainstream: Urban Indians in Saskatchewan.* Vol. II. Calgary: A Northern Dilemma. Reference Papers, 1965.

Davis, Kingsley. "The Origin and Growth of Urbanization in the World." *American Journal of Sociology* 60 (1955): 429-37.

_____. *World Urbanization 1950-1970. Volume I. Basic Data for Cities and Regions.* Population Monograph Series, No. 4. Berkeley: University of California Institute of International Studies, 1969.

_____. *World Urbanization 1950-1970. Volume II. Analysis of Trends, Relationships and Development.* Berkeley: University of California Institute of International Studies, 1972.

Dawley, David. *A Nation of Lords: The Autobiography of the Vice Lords.* Garden City, N.Y.: Anchor Press, 1973.

Dawson, C. A. *The City as an Organism.* Montreal: McGill University Publications, Series XIII, No. 10, 1926.

De Coulanges, Fustel. *The Ancient City: A Study on the Religion, Laws, and Institutions of Greece and Rome.* Boston: Lee and Shepard, 1901.

Delegan, W. R. "Life in the Heights." In *The Underside of Toronto,* edited by W. E. Mann. Toronto: McClelland and Stewart, 1970, pp. 75-94.

Del Guidice, Dominic, and Stephen M. Zacks. "The 101 Governments of Metro Toronto." In *Politics and Government of Urban Canada,* edited by Lionel D. Feldman and Michael D. Goldrick. 3d ed. Toronto: Methuen, 1976, pp. 285-95.

Dennis, Norman. "The Popularity of the Neighbourhood Community Idea." In *Readings in Urban Sociology,* edited by R. E. Pahl. Toronto: Pergamon Press, 1968, pp. 74-92.

Denton, Trevor. "Migration from a Canadian Indian Reserve." *Journal of Canadian Studies* 7 (1972): 54-62.

_____. "Canadian Indian Migrants and Impression Management of Ethnic Stigma." *Canadian Review of Sociology and Anthropology* 12 (1975): 65-71.

De Ruyter, Barbara. "Ethnic Differentials in Age at First Marriage, Canada 1971." *Journal of Comparative Family Studies* 7 (1976): 159-66.

Dewey, Richard. "The Rural-Urban Continuum: Real but Relatively Unimportant." *American Journal of Sociology* 66 (1960): 60-66.

Diemer, Henrikus L. *Annexation and Amalgamation in the Territorial Expansion of Edmonton and Calgary.* M.A. thesis, University of Alberta, 1975.

Dixon, Patrick. *Neighbourhood Groups and Urban Planning.* M.A. thesis, University of Calgary, 1972.

Dobriner, William M. *Class in Suburbia.* Englewood Cliffs, N.J.: Prentice-Hall, 1963.

Domhoff, G. William. *Who Really Rules? New Haven and Community Power Reexamined.* Santa Monica: Goodyear Publishing Co., 1978.

Donaldson, Scott. *The Suburban Myth.* New York: Columbia University Press, 1969.

Donnelly, M. S. "Ethnic Participation in Municipal Government: Winnipeg, St. Boniface and the Metropolitan Corporation of Winnipeg." In *Politics and Government of Urban Canada: Selected Readings,* edited by L. D. Feldman and M. D. Goldrick. 3d ed. Toronto: Methuen, 1976, pp. 118-28.

Dosman, Edgar J. *Indians: The Urban Dilemma.* Toronto: McClelland and Stewart, 1972.

Downey, Glanville. "Aristotle on the Greek Polis: A Study of Problems and Methods." *Urbanism Past and Present* 3 (1976-1977): 21-25.

Doxiadis, C. A. "Historic Approaches to New Towns. The Ancient Greek City and the City of the Present." *Ekistics and Science of Human Settlement* 18 (1964): 345-64.

Doyle, Don H. "The Social Functions of Voluntary Associations in a Nineteenth-Century Town." *Social Science History* 1 (1977): 333-53.

Driedger, Leo. "Toward a Perspective on Canadian Pluralism: Ethnic Identity in Winnipeg." *Canadian Journal of Sociology* 2 (1977): 77-95.

_____. "Ethnic Identity in the Canadian Mosaic." In *The Canadian Ethnic Mosaic: A Quest for Identity.* Toronto: McClelland and Stewart, 1978a, pp. 9-22.

_____. "Ethnic Boundaries: A Comparison of Two Urban Neighborhoods." *Sociology and Social Research* 62 (1978b): 193-211.

Dreidger, Leo, and Glenn Church. "Residential Segregation and Institutional Completeness: A Comparison of Ethnic Minorities." *Canadian Review of Sociology and Anthropology* 11 (1974): 30-52.

Duncan, Kenneth. "Irish Famine Immigration and the Social Structure of Canada West." *Canadian Review of Sociology and Anthropology* 2 (1965): 19-40.

Duncan, Otis Dudley. "Review of *Social Area Analysis.*" *American Journal of Sociology* 61 (1955): 84-85.

_____. "Community Size and the Rural-Urban Continuum." In *Cities and Society,* edited by Paul K. Hatt and Albert J. Reiss. New York: Free Press, 1957, pp. 35-45.

Duncan, Otis Dudley, and Beverly Duncan. *The Negro Population of Chicago: A Study of Residential Succession.* Chicago: University of Chicago Press, 1957.

_____. "Residential Distribution and Occupational Stratification." In *Studies in Human Ecology*, edited by George A. Theodorson. New York: Harper and Row, 1961, pp. 155-65.

Duncan, Otis Dudley, and Albert J. Reiss. "Suburbs and Urban Fringe." In *The Suburban Community*, edited by William M. Dobriner. New York: G. P. Putnam's Sons, 1958, pp. 45-66.

Duncan, Otis Dudley, and Leo F. Schnore. "Cultural, Behavioral, and Ecological Perspectives on the Study of Social Organization." *American Journal of Sociology* 65 (1959): 132-46.

Durkheim, Emile. *Professional Ethics and Civic Morals*. Translated by Cornelia Brookfield. Glencoe, Ill.: Free Press, 1958.

_____. *The Division of Labor*. Translated by George Simpson. New York: Free Press, 1964.

Economic Council of Canada. "From the 1960's to the 1970's: Urban Growth." In *Politics and Government of Urban Canada: Selected Readings*, edited by Lionel D. Feldman and Michael D. Doldrick. Toronto: Methuen, 1972, pp. 5-8.

Eisenstadt, S. N. "The Process of Absorption of New Immigrants in Israel." *Human Relations* 5 (1952): 222-35.

Ellis, Maureen C. *Local Migration in East Central Alberta*. M.A. thesis, University of Alberta, 1972.

Engels, Friederich. *The Condition of the Working Class in England*. Translated and edited by W. O. Henderson and W. H. Chaloner. Stanford: Stanford University Press, 1968.

Epstein, A. L. *Politics in an Urban African Community*. Manchester: Manchester University Press, 1958.

_____. "Urbanization and Social Change in Africa." *Current Anthropology* 8 (1967): 275-95.

_____. "The Network and Urban Social Organization." In *Social Networks in Urban Situations*, edited by J. Clyde Mitchell. Manchester: Manchester University Press, 1969, pp. 77-116.

Evenden, L. J. "Shaping the Vancouver Suburbs." In *Vancouver: Western Metropolis*, edited by L. J. Evenden. Western Geographical Series, Vol. 16. Victoria: University of Victoria, Department of Geography, 1978, pp. 179-99.

Fairbairn, Kenneth J. "Locational Changes of Edmonton's High Status Residents, 1937-1972." In *Edmonton: The Emerging Metropolitan Pattern*, edited by P. J. Smith. Western Geographical Series, Vol. 15. Victoria: University of Victoria, Department of Geography, 1978, pp. 199-231.

Fathi, Asghar. "Mass Media and a Moslem Immigrant Community in Canada." *Anthropologica* 15 (1973): 201-30.

Fava, Sylvia Fleis. "Suburbanism as a Way of Life." *American Sociological Review* 21 (1956): 34-38.

_____. "Contrasts in Neighboring: New York City and a Suburban County."

In *The Suburban Community,* edited by William M. Dobriner. New York: G. P. Putnam's Sons, 1958, pp. 122-29.

_____. "Beyond Suburbia." *The Annals* 422 (1975): 10-24.

Fellin, Phillip, and Eugene Litwak. "Neighborhood Cohesion Under Conditions of Mobility." *American Sociological Review* 28 (1963): 364-77.

Fennario, David. *Without a Parachute.* Toronto: McClelland and Stewart, 1974.

Fenton, C. Stephen. *Assimilation Processes Among Immigrants: A Study of German and Italian Immigrants to Hamilton.* M.A. thesis, McMaster University, 1968.

Festinger, Leon, Stanley Schachter, and Kurt Black. *Social Pressures in Informal Groups.* Stanford: Stanford University Press, 1950.

Fingard, Judith. "The Relief of the Unemployed: The Poor in Saint John, Halifax, and St. John's, 1815-1860." In *The Canadian City: Essays in Urban History,* edited by Gilbert A. Stelter and Alan F. J. Artibise. Toronto: McClelland and Stewart, 1977, pp. 341-67.

Finley, A. Gregg. "The Morans of St. Martins, N.B., 1850-1880: Toward an Understanding of Family Participation in Maritime Enterprise." In *The Enterprising Canadians: Entrepreneurs and Economic Development in Eastern Canada, 1820-1914,* edited by Lewis R. Fischer and Eric W. Sager. St. John's: Memorial University Maritime History Group, 1979, pp. 37-54.

Firey, Walter. "Sentiment and Symbolism as Ecological Variables." *American Journal of Sociology* 10 (1945): 140-48.

Firth, Raymond, Jane Hubert, and Anthony Forge. *Families and Their Relatives: Kinship in a Middle-Class Sector of London.* New York: Humanities Press, 1970.

Firth, Sophia. *The Urbanization of Sophia Firth.* Toronto: Peter Martin Associaties Ltd., 1974.

Fischer, Claude S. " 'Urbanism as a Way of Life': A Review and an Agenda." *Sociological Methods And Research* 1 (1972): 187-242.

_____. "On Urban Alienation and Anomie: Powerlessness and Social Isolation." *American Sociological Review* 38 (1973): 311-28.

_____. "Toward a Subcultural Theory of Urbanism." *American Journal of Sociology* 80 (1975): 1319-41.

_____. *The Urban Experience.* New York: Harcourt Brace Jovanovich, 1976.

_____. *Networks and Places: Social Relations in the Urban Setting.* New York: The Free Press, 1977.

Foran, Max. "Early Calgary, 1875-1895: The Controversy Surrounding the Townsite Location and the Direction of Town Expansion." In *Cities in the West: Papers of the Western Canada Urban History Conference,* edited by A. R. McCormack and Ian MacPherson. Ottawa: National Museum of Man, 1975, pp. 26-45.

Foster, George M. "What Is Folk Sociology?" *American Anthropologist* 55 (1953): 159-73.

Fowler, Edmund P., and Robert L. Lineberry. "The Comparative Analysis of Urban Policy: Canada and the United States." In *People and Politics in Urban Society Vol. 6*, edited by Harlan Hahn. Beverly Hills: Sage Publications, 1972, pp. 345-68.

Fraser, Graham. *Fighting Back: Urban Renewal in Trefann Court*. Toronto: Hakkert, 1972.

Freeman, Linton, and Robert Winch. "Societal Complexity: An Empirical Test of a Typology of Societies." *American Journal of Sociology* 62 (1957): 461-66.

Fried, Marc. "Grieving for a Lost Home." In *The Urban Condition*, edited by Leonard J. Duhl. New York: Basic Books, 1963, pp. 151-57.

_____. "Transitional Functions of Working-Class Communities: Implications for Forced Relocation." In *Mobility and Mental Health*, edited by Mildred B. Kantor. Springfield, Ill.: Charles C. Thomas, 1965, pp. 123-65.

_____. *The World of the Urban Working Class*. Cambridge: Harvard University Press, 1973.

Fried, Marc, and Peggy Gleicher. "Some Sources of Residential Satisfaction in an Urban Slum." In *Urban Renewal: People, Politics, and Planning*, edited by Jewel Bellush and Murray Hausknecht. New York: Doubleday, 1967, pp. 120-36.

Frideres, J. S. *Canada's Indians: Contemporary Conflicts*. Scarborough: Prentice-Hall of Canada, 1974.

Friedman, John. "Cities in Social Transformation." *Comparative Studies in Society and History* 4 (1961): 86-103.

Frisch, Michael H. *Town into City: Springfield, Massachusetts and the Meaning of Community, 1840-1880*. Cambridge: Harvard University Press, 1972.

Fromson, Ronald D. *Acculturation or Assimilation: A Geographic Analysis of Residential Segregation of Selected Ethnic Groups: Metropolitan Winnipeg. 1951-1961*. M.A. thesis, University of Manitoba, 1965.

Gale, Donald. "The Impact of Canadian Italians on Retail Functions and Facades in Vancouver, 1921-1961." In *Peoples of the Living Land: Geography of Cultural Diversity in British Columbia*, edited by Julian V. Minghi. Vancouver: Tantalus Research Limited, 1972, pp. 107-24.

Gans, Herbert J. "Urbanism and Suburbanism as Ways of Life: A Re-Evaluation of Definitions." In *Human Behavior and Social Processes*, edited by Arnold Rose. Boston: Houghton Mifflin, 1962a, pp. 625-48.

_____. *The Urban Villagers*. New York: Free Press, 1962b.

_____. *The Levittowners*. New York: Pantheon Books, 1967.

_____. "Planning And Social Life: Friendship and Neighbor Relations in Suburban Communities." In *People and Plans*. New York: Basic Books, 1968, pp. 152-65.

Garbarino, Merwyn. "Life in the City: Chicago." In *The American Indians in Urban Society,* edited by Jack O. Waddell and O. Michael Watson. Boston: Little, Brown and Company, 1971, pp. 169-205.

Garigue, Philip. "French Canadian Kinship and Urban Life." *American Anthropologist* 58 (1956): 1090-1101.

Garner, Hugh. *Cabbagetown.* Toronto: Ryerson Press, 1968 ed.

Gates, Albert S., Harvey Stevens, and Barry Wellman. *What Makes a 'Good Neighbor'?: A Multivariate Analysis of Neighboring in Toronto.* Paper presented at the annual meeting of the American Sociological Association, New York City, 1973.

Geddes, Patrick. *Cities in Evolution.* New York: Harper and Row, 1968 ed.

Germani, Gino. "Migration And Acculturation." In *Handbook for Social Research in Urban Areas,* edited by Philip M. Hauser. Paris: UNESCO, 1965, pp. 159-78.

Gertler, L. O. *Planning the Canadian Environment.* Montreal: Harvest, 1968.

———. *Making Man's Environment: Urban Issues.* Toronto: Van Nostrand Reinhold Ltd., 1976.

Gertler, L. O., and Ron Crowley. *Changing Canadian Cities: The Next 25 Years.* Toronto: McClelland and Stewart, 1977.

Gettys, Warner E. "Human Ecology and Social Theory." In *Studies in Human Ecology,* edited by George A. Theodorson. New York: Harper and Row, 1961, pp. 98-103.

Gibbs, Jack P., and Walter T. Martin. "Toward a Theoretical System of Human Ecology." *Pacific Sociological Review* 2 (1959): 29-36.

Gibson, Edward. *The Urbanization of the Strait of Georgia Region: A Study of the Impact of Urbanization on the Natural Resources of Southwestern British Columbia.* Geographical Paper No. 57. Ottawa: Lands Directorate, Environment Canada, 1976.

Gibson, Geoffrey. "Kin Family Network: Overheralded Structure in Past Conceptualizations of Family Functioning." *Journal of Marriage and the Family,* 34 (1972): 13-23.

Gist, Noel P. "The Urban Community." In *Review of Sociology,* edited by Joseph B. Gittler. New York: John Wiley and Sons, 1957, pp. 159-85.

Glazebrook, G. P. de T. *A History of Transportation in Canada.* Toronto: McClelland and Stewart, 1964.

Glazer, Nathan, and Daniel Patrick Moynihan. *Beyond the Melting Pot.* Cambridge: MIT Press, 1963.

Gluckman, M. "Anthropological Problems Arising from the African Industrial Revolution." In *Social Change in Modern Africa,* edited by Aidan Southall. London: Oxford University Press, 1961, pp. 67-82.

Glynn, Thomas, and John Wang, "Chinatown." *Neighborhood: The Journal for City Preservation* 1 (1978): 9-23.

Goheen, Peter G. *Victorian Toronto: 1850-1900.* Research Paper No. 117. Chicago: University of Chicago, Department of Geography, 1970.

Goldenberg, Sheldon. "Kinship and Ethnicity Viewed as Adaptive Responses to Location in the Opportunity Structure." *Journal of Comparative Family Studies* 8 (1977): 149-65.

Goldkind, Victor. "Sociocultural Contrasts in Rural and Urban Settlement Types in Costa Rica." *Rural Sociology* 26 (1961): 365-80.

Goldlust, John, and Anthony H. Richmond. "A Multivariate Model of Immigrant Adaptation." *International Migration Review* 8 (1974): 193-225.

Gordon, Milton M. *Assimilation in American Life.* New York: Oxford University Press, 1964.

Gottschalk, Shimon S. *Communities and Alternatives: An Exploration of the Limits of Planning.* Toronto: Schenkman Publishing Co., 1975.

Granatstein, J. L. *Marlborough Marathon: One Street Against a Developer.* Toronto: Hakkert, 1971.

Granovetter, Mark S. "The Strength of Weak Ties." *American Journal of Sociology* 78 (1973): 1360-80.

Graves, Theodore D. "Alternative Models for the Study of Urban Migration." *Human Organization* 25 (1966): 295-99.

Graves, Theodore D., and Minor Van Arsdale. "Values, Expectations and Relocation: The Navaho Migrant to Denver." *Human Organization* 25 (1966): 300-307.

Gray, James. *Red Lights on the Prairies.* Toronto: Macmillan of Canada, 1971.

Grayson, J. Paul. *Neighbourhood and Voting: The Social Basis of Conservative Support in Broadview.* Ph.D. dissertation, University of Toronto, 1972.

Green Paper on Immigration and Population. *Volume 1. Immigration Policy Perspectives. A Report of the Canadian Immigration and Population Study.* Ottawa: Information Canada, 1974.

_____. *Volume 2. The Immigration Program. Canadian Immigration and Population.* Ottawa: Information Canada, 1974.

_____. *Volume 3. Immigration and Population Statistics.* Ottawa: Information Canada, 1974.

_____. *Volume 4. Three Years in Canada. First Report of the Longitudinal Survey on the Economic and Social Adaptation of Immigrants.* Ottawa: Information Canada, 1974.

Greer, Scott. "Urbanism Reconsidered: A Comparative Study of Local Areas in a Metropolis." *American Sociological Review* 21 (1956): 19-25.

_____. *The Emerging City.* New York: Free Press, 1962.

_____. "Postscript: Communication and Community." In *The Community Press in an Urban Setting,* by Morris Janowitz. Chicago: University of Chicago Press, 1967 ed., pp. 245-70.

_____. *The Urbane View: Life and Politics in Metropolitan America.* New York: Oxford University Press, 1972.

Greer, Scott, and Ella Kube. "Urbanism And Social Structure: A Los Angeles

Study." In *Community Structure and Analysis,* edited by M. B. Sussman. New York: Thomas Y. Crowell Co., 1959, pp. 93-115.

Greer, Scott, and Peter Orleans. "The Mass Structure and the Parapolitical Structure." In *The New Urbanization,* edited by Scott Greer, *et al.* New York: St. Martin's Press, 1968, pp. 201-21.

Grenke, Arthur. *The Formation and Early Development of an Urban Ethnic Community: A Case Study of the Germans in Winnipeg, 1872-1919.* Ph.D. dissertation, University of Manitoba, 1975.

Griffen, Sally, and Clyde Griffen. "Family and Business in a Small City: Poughkeepsie." *Journal of Urban History* 1 (1975): 316-38.

Gross, Neal. "Cultural Variables in Rural Communities." *American Journal of Sociology* 53 (1948): 344-50.

Guerette, Gilles. *Urbanism in a Regional Context, with Special Reference to Northwestern New Brunswick.* Master of City Planning thesis, University of Manitoba, 1970.

Guest, Avery. "The Applicability of the Burgess Zonal Hypothesis to Urban Canada." *Demography* 6 (1969): 271-77.

Guindon, Hubert. "The Social Evolution of Quebec Reconsidered." *Canadian Journal of Economics and Political Science* 29 (1960): 533-51.

Gusfield, Joseph R. *Community: A Critical Response.* Oxford: Basil Blackwell, 1975.

Gutman, Robert, and David Popenoe. "The Field of Urban Sociology: A Review and Assessment." In *Neighborhood, City, And Metropolis.* New York: Random House, 1970, pp. 3-23.

Gutstein, Donald. *Vancouver Ltd.* Toronto: James Lorimer and Company, 1975.

Gyuse, Timothy. *Service Centre Change in Metropolitan Hinterlands: A Case Study of Calgary and Saskatoon, 1951-1971.* M.A. thesis, University of Calgary, 1974.

Handlin, Oscar. *The Uprooted.* Boston: Little, Brown and Company, 1951.

Hannerz, Ulf. "Ethnicity and Opportunity in Urban America." In *Urban Ethnicity,* edited by Abner Cohen. London: Tavistock Publications, 1974, pp. 37-76.

Hardwick, Walter G. "The Georgia Strait Urban Region." In *Studies in Canadian Geography: British Columbia,* edited by J. Lewis Robinson. Toronto: University of Toronto Press, 1972, pp. 119-33.

_____. *Vancouver.* Don Mills: Collier-Macmillan Canada, 1974.

Hareven, Tamara K. "Family Time and Industrial Time: Family Work in a Planned Corporation Town, 1900-1924." *Journal of Urban History* 1 (1975): 365-89.

_____. "Introduction." In *Family and Kin in Urban Communities, 1700-1930,* edited by Tamara K. Hareven. New York: New Viewpoints, 1977, pp. 1-15.

Hareven, Tamara K., and Randolph Langenbach. *Amoskeag: Life and Work in an American Factory-City*. New York: Pantheon Books, 1978.

Harney, Robert F. "Boarding And Belonging." *Urban History Review* 2-78 (1978): 8-37.

Harney, Robert F., and Harold Troper. *Immigrants: A Portrait of the Urban Experience, 1890-1930*. Toronto: Van Nostrand Reinhold Ltd., 1975.

_____. "Introduction." *Urban History Review* 2-78 (1978): 3-7.

Harris, Chauncy, and Edward Ullman. "The Nature Of Cities." In *Cities and Society*, edited by Paul K. Hatt and Albert J. Reiss, Jr. New York: Free Press, 1957, pp. 237-47.

Harrison, J. F. C. *The Early Victorians: 1832-51*. St. Albans: Panther Books, 1973.

Harrison, Peter. *The Retailing Structure of Canadian Metropolitan Areas*. Victoria: University of Victoria, Department of Geography, 1970.

Harvey, David. *Social Justice and the City*. London: Edward Arnold, 1973.

_____. "Labor, Capital, and Class Struggle Around the Built Environment in Advanced Capitalist Societies." In *Urbanization and Conflict in Market Societies*, edited by Kevin R. Cox. Chicago: Maaroufa Press, Inc., 1978, pp. 9-37.

Hauser, Philip M. "World and Asian Urbanization in Relation to Economic Development and Social Change." In *Urbanization in Asia and the Far East*. Calcutta: Research Centre on the Social Implications of Industrialization in Southern Asia, 1957, pp. 53-94.

_____. "Observations on the Urban-Folk and Urban-Rural Dichotomies as Forms of Western Ethnocentrism." In *The Study of Urbanization*, edited by Philip M. Hauser and Leo F. Schnore. New York: John Wiley and Sons, 1965, pp. 503-14.

Hawkins, Freda. "Canadian Immigration Policy and Management." *International Migration Review* 8 (1974): 141-53.

Hawley, Amos. *Human Ecology: A Theory of Community Structure*. New York: The Ronald Press, 1950.

_____. *The Changing Shape of Metropolitan America: Deconcentration Since 1920*. Glencoe: Free Press, 1956.

_____. "Introduction". In *Roderick McKenzie: On Human Ecology*. Chicago: University of Chicago Press, 1968a, pp. vii-xxii.

_____. "Ecology: Human Ecology." In *International Encyclopedia of the Social Sciences* Vol. 4, edited by David Sills. New York: The Macmillan Company, 1968b, pp. 328-36.

_____. "Community Power and Urban Renewal Success." *American Journal of Sociology* 68 (1968c): 422-31.

_____. *Urban Society: An Ecological Approach*. New York: The Ronald Press, 1971.

Hawley, Amos, and Otis Dudley Duncan. "Social Area Analysis: A Critical Appraisal." *Land Economics* 33 (1957): 337-45.

Hawley, Willis D., and James H. Svara. *The Study of Community Power: A Bibliographic Review.* Oxford and Santa Barbara: ABC-CL1O, 1972.

Haynes, Kingsley E. "Spatial Changes in Urban Structure: Alternative Approaches to Ecological Dynamics." *Economic Geography* 47 (1971): 324-35.

Hayter, Jacqueline Green. *Residential Mobility and the Function of Seven Selected High-Rises in Central Edmonton.* M.A. thesis, University of Alberta, 1973.

Head, Wilson A. "The Ideology and Practice of Citizen Participation." In *Citizen Participation: Canada,* edited by James Draper. Toronto: New Press, 1971, pp. 14-29.

Helling, Rudolf A. *A Comparison of the Acculturation of Immigrants in Toronto, Ontario and Detroit, Michigan.* Ph.D. dissertation, Wayne State University, 1962.

———. *The Position of Negroes, Chinese, and Italians in the Social Structure of Windsor, Ontario.* Toronto: Ontario Human Rights Commission, 1965.

Henripin, Jacques. *Trends and Factors of Fertility in Canada.* 1961 Census Monograph. Ottawa: Statistics Canada, 1972.

Hershberg, Theodore. "The New Urban History: Towards an Inter-disciplinary History of the City." *Journal of Urban History* 5 (1978): 3-40.

Higgins, Donald J. H. *Urban Canada: Its Government and Politics.* Toronto: The Macmillan Company of Canada, 1977.

Hill, Frederick. *Migration in the Toronto-Centered (MTARTS) Region.* Research Paper No. 48. Toronto: University of Toronto, Centre for Urban and Community Studies, 1971.

Hill, Frederick I. *Canadian Urban Trends. Volume 2. Metropolitan Perspective.* Toronto: Copp Clark, 1976.

Hines, Thomas S. *Burnham of Chicago: Architect and Planner.* New York: Oxford University Press, 1974.

Hobsbawm, E. J. *The Age of Capital, 1848-1875.* New York: Charles Scribner's Sons, 1975.

Hodge, William H. "Navajo Urban Migration: An Analysis from the Perspective of the Family." In *The American Indian in Urban Society,* edited by Jack O. Waddell and O. Michael Watson. Boston: Little, Brown and Company, 1971, pp. 347-91.

Horsman, A., and P. Raynor. "Citizen Participation in Local Area Planning: Two Vancouver Cases." In *Vancouver: Western Metropolis,* edited by L. J. Evenden. Western Geographical Series, Vol. 16. Victoria: University of Victoria, Department of Geography, 1978, pp. 239-53.

Howard, John F. *The Impact of Urbanization on the Prime Agricultural Land of Southern Ontario.* M.A. report, University of Waterloo, 1972.

Howell, Janet E. *Sources of Differential Leisure Participation Among Halifax Housewives.* M.A. thesis, Dalhousie University, 1970.

Howton, F. William. "City, Slums, and Acculturative Process in the Developing Countries." In *Urbanism, Urbanization, and Change,* edited by Paul Meadows and Ephraim H. Mizruchi. 2d ed. Don Mills: Addison-Wesley, 1976, pp. 407-23.

Hoyt, Homer. *The Structure and Growth of Residential Neighborhoods in American Cities.* Washington: Federal Housing Administration, 1939.

_____. "Recent Distortions of the Classical Models of Urban Structure." *Land Economics* 40 (1964): 199-212.

Hughes, Everett C. *French Canada in Transition.* Chicago: Phoenix Books, 1963.

Hugo-Brunt, Michael. *The History of City Planning.* Montreal: Harvest House, 1972.

Hull, Richard W. *African Cities and Towns Before the European Conquest.* New York: W. W. Norton and Company, 1976.

Hunter, A. A., and A. H. Latif. "Stability and Change in the Ecological Structure of Winnipeg: A Multi-Method Approach." *Canadian Review of Sociology and Anthropology* 10 (1973): 308-33.

Hunter, Albert. *Symbolic Communities: The Persistence and Change of Chicago's Local Communities.* Chicago: University of Chicago Press, 1974.

_____. "The Loss of Community: An Empirical Test Through Replication." *American Sociological Review* 40 (1975): 537-52.

Hunter, David R. *The Slums: Challenge and Response.* New York: Free Press, 1968.

Hutchison, Ray. *The Process of Community Attachment: Cross-Cultural Perspectives.* Paper presented at the annual meeting of the Canadian Sociological and Anthropological Association, London, 1978.

Information Canada. *Internal Migration and Immigrant Settlement.* Ottawa: 1975.

Irving, Howard H. *The Family Myth.* Toronto: Copp Clark, 1972.

Isaacs, Reginald R. "Are Urban Neighborhoods Possible?" *Journal of Housing* (July 1948): 177-80.

Jacobs, Jane. *The Economy of Cities.* New York: Vintage Books, 1970.

Jancewicz, Walter. *Socio-Political Factors in Urban Transportation Planning.* Master of Engineering Report, Sir George Williams University, 1972.

Janowitz, Morris. *The Community Press in an Urban Setting.* Chicago: University of Chicago Press, 1967 ed.

Jansen, Clifford J. "Leadership in the Toronto Italian Ethnic Group." *International Migration Review* 4 (1969): 25-43.

_____. "Assimilation in Theory and Practice: A Case Study of Italians in Toronto." In *Social Process and Institution: The Canadian Case,* edited by James E. Gallagher and Ronald D. Lambert. Toronto: Holt, Rinehart and Winston, 1971, pp. 466-74.

_____. "Community Organization of Italians in Toronto." In *The Canadian Ethnic Mosaic: A Quest for Identity,* edited by Leo Driedger. Toronto: McClelland and Stewart, 1978, pp. 310-26.

Jenness, R. A. "Canadian Migration and Immigration Patterns and Government Policy." *International Migration Review* 8 (1974): 5-22.

Jensen, Brigitte, Richard Mozoff, and Anthony H. Richmond. *Sociological Aspects of Urban Renewal in Toronto.* Toronto: York University, Institute for Behavioural Research, 1970.

Johnson, Leo A. *History of the County of Ontario, 1615-1875.* Whitby, Ont.: The Corporation of the County of Ontario, 1973.

Johnson, Valerie. "Our Isolated Immigrants." *Saturday Night* (February 1971): 16-20.

Johnston, R. J. "Some Limitations of Factorial Ecologies and Social Area Analysis." *Economic Geography* 47 (1971): 314-23.

Jones, Kenneth H. *The Intra-Urban Mobility of the Elderly: A Study of a Suburban Silver Threads Centre, Victoria, B.C.* M.A. thesis, University of Victoria, 1975.

Joy, Richard J. *Languages in Conflict.* Ottawa: Published by the author, 1967.

Joyce, J. G., and H. A. Hossé. *Civic Parties in Canada.* Montreal: Canadian Federation of Mayors and Municipalities, 1970.

Kalbach, Warren. *The Impact of Immigration on Canada's Population.* Ottawa: Dominion Bureau of Statistics, 1970.

_____. *The Effect of Immigration on Population.* Ottawa: Information Canada, 1974.

Kalbach, Warren, and Wayne W. McVey. *The Demographic Bases of Canadian Society.* Toronto: McGraw-Hill, 1971.

Kanter, Rosabeth Moss. *Commitment and Community: Communes and Utopias in Sociological Perspective.* Cambridge: Harvard University Press, 1972.

Kaplan, Harold. *The Regional City: Politics and Planning in Metropolitan Areas.* Ottawa: Canadian Broadcasting Corporation, 1965.

_____. *Urban Political Systems: A Functional Analysis of Metro Toronto.* New York: Columbia University Press, 1967.

Kasahara, Yoshiko. "A Profile of Canada's Metropolitan Centers." *Queen's Quarterly* 70 (1963): 303-13.

Kasarda, John D., and Morris Janowitz. "Community Attachment in Mass Society." *American Sociological Review* 39 (1974): 328-39.

Katz, Michael B. *The People of Hamilton, Canada West: Family and Class in a Mid-Nineteenth-Century City.* Cambridge: Harvard University Press, 1975.

Katz, Michael B., Michael J. Doucet, and Mark J. Stearn. "Migration and the Social Order in Eric County, New York: 1855." *Journal of Interdisciplinary History* 7 (1978): 669-701.

Kay, Barry J. "Voting Patterns in a Non-Partisan Legislature. A Study of Toronto City Council." *Canadian Journal of Political Science* 4 (1971): 224-42.

Keith, Margaret P. *Testing the Theory of Increasing Societal Scale: The Ecology of Toronto, 1951-1961.* M.A. thesis, University of Manitoba, 1973.

Kelebay, Yarema Gregory. *The Ukrainian Community in Montreal.* M.A. thesis, Concordia University, 1975.

Keller, Suzanne. *The Urban Neighborhood: A Sociological Perspective.* New York: Random House, 1968.

Kelner, Merrijoy. "Ethnic Penetration into Toronto's Elite Structure." In Social Stratification: Canada, edited by James E. Curtis and William G. Scott. Scarborough: Prentice-Hall, 1973, pp. 98-104.

Kerr, Donald. "Metropolitan Dominance in Canada." In *Canada: A Geographical Interpretation,* edited by John Warkenton. Toronto: Methuen, 1968, pp. 531-55.

Kerr, Donald, and Jacob Spelt. *The Changing Face of Toronto.* Ottawa: Department of Energy, Mines and Resources, 1965.

Kerr, Madeline. *The People of Ship Street.* London: Routledge and Kegan Paul, 1958.

Keyfitz, Nathan. "Some Demographic Aspects of French-English Relations in Canada." In *Canadian Dualism: Studies of French-English Relations,* edited by Mason Wade. Toronto: University of Toronto Press, 1960, pp. 129-48.

_____. "The Changing Canadian Population." In *Canadian Society: Sociological Perspectives,* edited by B. Blishen *et al.* Toronto: Macmillan, 1965, pp. 23-37.

King, Leslie J. "Cross-Sectional Analysis of Canadian Urban Dimensions: 1951 and 1961." *The Canadian Geographer* 10 (1966): 205-24.

_____. *The Funding of Urban Research in Canada.* Social Science Research Council of Canada, 1976.

Kiser, Clyde V. *Sea Island to City.* New York: Columbia University Press, 1967 ed.; first published in 1932.

Klein, Maury, and Harvey A. Kantor. *Prisoners of Progress: American Industrial Cities, 1850-1920.* New York: Macmillan, 1976.

Koch, Agnes, and Sanford Labovitz. "Interorganizational Power in a Canadian Community: A Replication." *Sociological Quarterly* 17 (1976): 3-15.

Kokich, George J. V. *The 1971 Canadian Census Tract Program.* Proceedings of the Social Statistics Section, American Statistical Association, 1970, 296-99.

Konig, Rene. *The Community.* London: Routledge and Kegan Paul, 1968.

Kornblum, William. *Blue Collar Community.* Chicago: University of Chicago Press, 1974.

Kosny, Mitchell. *A Tale of Two Cities: An Evaluation of Local Government*

Organization Theory and Its Implications for Municipal Reorganization in Thunder Bay, Ontario. Ph.D. dissertation, University of Waterloo, 1978.

Kotler, M. *Neighborhood Government.* Indianapolis: Bobbs-Merrill, 1969.

Kralt, John. *1971 Census of Canada. Profile Studies. The Urban and Rural Composition of Canada's Population.* Catalogue 99-702. Vol. 1 Part 1, Bulletin 5.1-2. Ottawa: 1976.

Krause, Corinne A. "Urbanization Without Breakdown: Italian, Jewish and Slavic Immigrant Women in Pittsburgh, 1900 to 1945." *Journal of Urban History* 4 (1978): 291-305.

Kubat, Daniel, and David Thornton. *A Statistical Profile of Canadian Society.* Toronto: McGraw-Hill Ryerson, 1974.

Kumove, Leon. *The Social Structure of Metropolitan Toronto.* Toronto: Municipality of Metropolitan Toronto Planning Department, 1975.

Kuper, Hilda. *Urbanization and Migration in West Africa.* Berkeley: University of California Press, 1965.

Kuper, Leo. *Living in Towns.* London: The Cresset Press, 1953.

Lambrou, Yianna. *The Greek Community of Vancouver: Social Organization and Adaptation.* M.A. thesis, University of British Columbia, 1974.

Lamontagne, Maurice, and J. C. Falardeau. "The Life Cycle of French-Canadian Urban Families." *Canadian Journal of Economics and Political Science* 13 (1947): 233-47.

Lanctot, Jean B. *The Impact of Urbanization on Rural Areas.* Paper delivered at the International Conference on Social Work, Washington, D.C., Sept. 6, 1966.

Langlois, Claude. "Problems of Urban Growth in Greater Montreal." *Canadian Geographer* 5 (1961): 1-11.

Lansbury, Coral. "Engels in Manchester." *The Yale Review* 64 (1974): 106-109.

Larsen, Karen. "Review of Oscar Handlin's *The Uprooted.*" *American Historical Review* 57 (1952): 703-704.

Laslett, Peter. "Introduction: The History of the Family." In *Household and Family in Past Time,* edited by Peter Laslett and Richard Wall. Cambridge: At the University Press, 1972a, pp. 1-89.

_____. "Mean Household Size in England Since the Sixteenth Century." In *Household and Family in Past Time,* edited by Peter Laslett and Richard Wall. Cambridge: At the University Press, 1972b, pp. 125-58.

Lee, Everett S. "A Theory of Migration." In *Migration,* edited by J. A. Jackson. Cambridge: At the University Press, 1969, pp. 282-97.

Lee, Nancy Howell. *The Search for an Abortionist.* Chicago: University of Chicago Press, 1969.

Lee, Terence. "Urban Neighborhood as a Socio-Spatial Scheme." *Human Relations* 21 (1968): 241-68.

Lees, Lynn H. "Patterns of Lower-Class Life: Irish Slum Communities in the Nineteenth-Century London." In *Nineteenth-Century Cities; Essays in the*

New Urban History, edited by Stephan Thernstrom and Richard Sennett. New Haven: Yale University Press, 1969, pp. 359-85.

Lemelin, Roger. *The Town Below.* Toronto: McClelland and Stewart, 1965 ed.

Lenski, Gerhard. *The Religious Factor.* New York: Doubleday, 1963.

Lewis, Oscar. "Urbanization Without Breakdown: A Case Study." *Scientific Monthly* 75 (1952): 31-41.

_____. *Life in a Mexican Village: Tepoztlan Restudied.* Urbana: University of Illinois Press, 1963 ed.

_____. *A Death in the Sanchez Family.* New York: Random House, 1969.

Lieberson, Stanley. *Ethnic Patterns in American Cities.* New York: Free Press, 1963.

_____. "Bilingualism in Montreal: A Demographic Analysis." *American Journal of Sociology* 71 (1965): 10-25.

_____. *Language and Ethnic Relations in Canada.* Toronto: John Wiley and Sons, 1970.

Liell, John T. *Levittown: A Study in Community Planning and Development.* Ph.D. dissertation, Yale University, Department of Sociology, 1952.

Light, Ivan. "From Vice District to Tourist Attraction: The Moral Career of American Chinatowns, 1880-1940." *Pacific Historical Review* 43 (1973): 367-94.

Lightbody, James. "The Rise of Party Politics in Canadian Local Elections." *Journal of Canadian Studies* 6 (1971): 39-44.

Lincoln, James R. "Power and Mobilization in the Urban Community: Reconsidering the Ecological Approach." *American Sociological Review* 41 (1976): 1-15.

Lines, Kenneth. *A Bit of Old England: The Selling of Tourist Victoria.* M.A. thesis, University of Victoria, 1972.

Linton, Ralph. "The Natural History of the Family." In *The Family: Its Function and Destiny,* edited by Ruth Nanda Anshen. New York: Harper and Row, 1959, pp. 30-52.

Lioy, Michele. *Social Trends in Greater Vancouver.* Vancouver: Gordon Soules Economic and Marketing Research, 1975.

Lipman, Marvin Harold. *Relocation and Family Life: A Study of the Social and Psychological Consequences of Urban Renewal.* D.S.W. thesis, University of Toronto, 1968.

Lithwick, N. H. *Urban Canada: Problems and Prospects.* Ottawa: Central Mortgage and Housing Corp., 1970.

Little, Kenneth. *West African Urbanization: A Study of Voluntary Associations in Social Change.* London: Cambridge University Press, 1965.

_____. *Urbanization as a Social Process.* London: Routledge and Kegan Paul, 1974.

Litwak, Eugene. "Occupational Mobility and Extended Family Cohesion." *American Sociological Review* 25 (1960a): 9-21.

————. "Geographic Mobility and Extended Family Cohesion." *American Sociological Review* 25 (1960b): 385-94.

Lofland, Lyn. *A World of Strangers: Order and Action in Urban Public Space.* New York: Basic Books, 1973.

Loomis, Charles P., and J. Allan Beegle. *Rural Social Systems.* New York: Prentice-Hall, 1950.

Lorimer, James. *The Real World of City Politics.* Toronto: James Lewis and Samuel, 1970.

————. *A Citizen's Guide to City Politics.* Toronto: James Lewis and Samuel, 1972.

————. *The Developers.* Toronto: James Lorimer and Company, 1978.

————. "Introduction: The Post-Developer Era for Canada's Cities Begins." *City Magazine Annual 1981.* Vol. 5, 1, pp. 6-11.

Lorimer, James, and Myfanwy Phillips. *Working People: Life in a Downtown City Neighbourhood.* Toronto: James Lewis and Samuel, 1971.

Lorimer, James, and Evelyn Ross. *The City Book: The Politics and Planning of Canada's Cities.* Toronto: James Lorimer and Company, 1976.

Lotz, Jim. "Citizen Participation." *Habitat* 13 (1970): 16-23.

Lowden, James D. *Urban Renewal in Canada—A Postmortem.* M.A. thesis, University of British Columbia, 1970.

Lucas, Rex A. *Minetown, Milltown, and Railtown.* Toronto: University of Toronto Press, 1971.

Lukomskyj, Oleh. *The Relationship Between Change in Household Structure and Intra-Urban Mobility.* M.A. thesis, University of Alberta, 1974.

Lynch, Kevin. *The Image of the City.* Cambridge: Technology Press, 1960.

Lynch, Kevin, and Malcolm Rivlin. "A Walk Around the Block." In *Environmental Psychology,* edited by Harold M. Proshansky *et al.* New York: Holt, Rinehart and Winston, 1970, pp. 631-42.

Macdonald, John S., and Leatrice D. Macdonald. "Chain Migration, Ethnic Neighborhood Formation, and Social Networks." *Milbank Memorial Fund Quarterly* 42 (1964): 82-97.

MacDonald, Norbert. "Seattle, Vancouver and the Klondike." *Canadian Historical Review* 49 (1968): 234-46.

————. "Population Growth and Change in Seattle and Vancouver, 1880-1960." *Pacific Historical Review* 39 (1970): 297-321.

————. "A Critical Growth Cycle for Vancouver, 1900-1914." *BC Studies* 17 (1973): 26-42.

Mackintosh, W. A. "Economic Factors in Canadian History." In *Approaches to Canadian Economic History,* edited by W. T. Easterbrook and M. H. Watkins. Toronto: McClelland and Stewart Limited, 1967, pp. 1-15.

MacLennan, Hugh. *Two Solitudes.* Toronto: Macmillan, 1945.

————. *Barometer Rising.* Toronto: Macmillan, 1969 ed.

Manheim, Ernest. "Theoretical Prospects of Urban Sociology in an Urbanized Society." *American Journal of Sociology* 66 (1960): 226-29.

Mann, W. E. *Sect, Cult, and Church in Alberta.* Toronto: University of Toronto Press, 1955.

_____. "Sect and Cult in Western Canada." In *Canadian Society: Sociological Perspectives,* edited by B. Blishen *et al.,* Toronto: Macmillan, 1965, pp. 347-77.

_____. *The Underside of Toronto.* Toronto: McClelland and Stewart, 1970.

Marcus, Steven. *Engels, Manchester, and the Working Class.* New York: Random House, 1974.

Marr, William L., and Donald G. Paterson. *Canada: An Economic History.* Toronto: Macmillan of Canada, 1980.

Marshall, Harvey. "Suburban Life Styles: A Contribution to the Debate." In *The Urbanization of the Suburbs,* edited by Louis Massottia and Jeffrey K. Hadden. Beverly Hills: Sage Publications, 1973, pp. 123-48.

Martin, Walter T. "The Structuring of Social Relationships Engendered by Suburban Residence." *American Sociological Review* 21 (1956): 446-53.

Masters, D. C. *The Rise of Toronto: 1850-1890.* Toronto: University of Toronto Press, 1947.

_____. *The Winnipeg General Strike.* Toronto: University of Toronto Press, 1950.

Matthews, Ralph. *"There's No Better Than Here": Social Change in Three Newfoundland Communities.* Toronto: Peter Mann Associates, 1976.

Matthiasson, Carolyn J. "Coping in a New Environment: Mexican Americans in Milwaukee, Wisconsin." *Urban Anthropology* 3 (1974): 262-77.

Matwijiw, Peter. *Ethnic Space in the Urban Region.* M.A. thesis, University of Western Ontario, 1975.

Maunula, Francis A. *Demographic Characteristics of Urban Indians.* M.A. thesis, University of Calgary, 1973.

Mayer, Adrian C. "The Significance of Quasi-Groups in the Study of Complex Societies." In *The Social Anthropology of Complex Societies,* edited by Michael Banton. London: Tavistock Publications, 1966, pp. 97-122.

Mayer, Gustav. *Friedrich Engels: A Biography.* New York: Howard Fertig, 1969.

Mayer, Philip. *Townsmen or Tribalism.* Cape Town: Oxford University Press, 1961.

_____. "Migrancy and the Study of Africans in Towns." In *Readings in Urban Sociology,* edited by R. E. Pahl. Toronto: Pergamon Press, 1968, pp. 306-30.

Maxwell, J. W. "The Functional Structure of Canadian Cities: A Classification of Cities." *Geographical Bulletin* 7 (1965): 79-104.

Mayhew. Henry. *London Labour and the London Poor.* 4 vols. New York: Dover, 1968 ed.

McAfee, Ann. "Evolving Inner-City Residential Environments: The Case of Vancouver's West End." In *Peoples of the Living Land: Geography of Cultural Diversity in British Columbia,* edited by Julian V. Minghi. Vancouver: Tantalus Research Limited, 1972, pp. 163-81.

McCalla, Douglas. *The Upper Canada Trade 1834-1872: A Study of the Buchanans' Business.* Toronto: University of Toronto Press, 1979.

McCann, L. D. "Urban Growth in Western Canada, 1881-1961." *The Albertan Geographer* 5 (1968-69): 65-74.

McCaskill, Donald N. *Migration, Adjustment, and Integration of the Indian into the Urban Environment.* M.A. thesis, Carleton University, 1970.

McClenahan, B. "The Social Causes of the Decline of Neighbourhoods." *Social Forces* 20 (1942): 471-76.

McCormack, Thelma. *Maritime Migrants to Toronto: Selected Cases.* Saskatoon: Canadian Centre for Community Studies, 1968.

McCracken, Kevin W. J. *Patterns of Intra-Urban Migration in Edmonton and the Residential Relocation Process.* Ph.D. dissertation, University of Alberta, 1973.

McElrath, Dennis. "Societal Scale and Social Differentiation." In *The New Urbanization,* edited by Scott Greer *et al.* New York: St. Martin's Press, 1968, pp. 33-52.

McGahan, Peter. "The Neighbor Role and Neighboring in a Highly Urban Area." *Sociological Quarterly* 13 (1972a): 397-408.

_____. *Maritime City: A Study in the Sociology of Neighbor Relations.* Unpublished manuscript, 1972b.

_____. *Urban Neighboring and the Hypothesis of Alternative Social Structures.* Paper presented at the 68th annual meetings of the American Sociological Association, New York City, 1973.

_____. "Review of *Residential Crowding and Design.*" *Canadian Police College Journal* 4 (1980): 286-88.

McGee, T. G. *The Urbanization Process in the Third World.* London: G. Bell and Sons Ltd., 1971.

McGillivray, C. Louise. "Mental Maps of a Canadian City: Edmonton, Alberta." *The Albertan Geographer* 10 (1974): 30-42.

McGinley, Phyllis. *The Province of the Heart.* New York: Viking Press, 1959.

McInnis, Marvin. "Provincial Migration and Differential Economic Opportunity." In *Migration in Canada: Some Regional Aspects,* edited by Leroy Stone. Ottawa: Dominion Bureau of Statistics, 1969, pp. 131-202.

McKenzie, Roderick. *The Metropolitan Community.* New York: McGraw-Hill, 1933.

_____. "The Ecological Approach to the Study of the Human Community." In *Roderick McKenzie: On Human Ecology,* edited by Amos Hawley. Chicago: University of Chicago Press, 1968a, pp. 3-18.

_____. "The Scope of Human Ecology." In *Roderick McKenzie: On Human Ecology,* edited by Amos Hawley. Chicago: University of Chicago Press, 1968b, pp. 19-32.

_____. "Demography, Human Geography, and Human Ecology." In *Roderick McKenzie: On Human Ecology,* edited by Amos Hawley. Chicago: University of Chicago Press, 1968c, pp. 33-48.

_____. "The Rise of Metropolitan Communities." In *Roderick McKenzie: On*

Human Ecology, edited by Amos Hawley, Chicago: University of Chicago Press, 1968d, pp. 244-305.

_____. "The Neighborhood: A Study of Local Life in the City of Columbus, Ohio." In *Roderick McKenzie: On Human Ecology,* edited by Amos Hawley. Chicago: University of Chicago Press, 1968e, pp. 51-94.

McLemore, Reg, Carl Aass, and Peter Keilhofer. *The Changing Canadian Inner City,* Ministry of State for Urban Affairs. Ottawa: Information Canada, 1975.

Mercer, Warwick M. *The Windsor French: Study of an Urban Community.* M.A. thesis, University of Windsor, 1974.

Merton, Robert, "The Social Psychology of Housing." In *Current Trends in Social Psychology,* edited by Wayne Dennis. Pittsburgh: U.P., 1948, pp. 163-217.

Michelson, William. *Man and His Urban Environment: A Sociological Approach.* Don Mills: Addison-Wesley, 1970.

_____. *Environmental Change.* Research Paper No. 60. Toronto: University of Toronto, Centre for Urban and Community Studies, 1973a.

_____. *The Place of Time in the Longitudinal Evaluation of Spatial Structures by Women.* Toronto: University of Toronto, Centre for Urban and Community Studies, 1973b.

_____. *Environmental Choice, Human Behavior, and Residential Satisfaction.* New York: Oxford University Press, 1977.

Miner, Horace. *The Primitive City of Timbuctoo.* Princeton: Princeton University Press, 1953.

_____. "The Folk-Urban Continuum." In *Cities and Society,* edited by Paul K. Hatt and Albert J. Reiss, Jr. Glencoe: Free Press, 1957, pp. 22-34.

_____. *St. Denis: A French-Canadian Parish.* Chicago: Phoenix Books, 1966 ed.

Mitchell, J. Clyde. *The Kalela Dance.* Manchester: Manchester University Press, 1956.

_____. "Theoretical Orientation in African Urban Studies." In *The Social Anthropology of Complex Societies,* edited by Michael Banton. London: Tavistock Publications, 1966, pp. 37-68.

_____. "The Concept and Use of Social Networks." In *Social Networks in Urban Situations.* Manchester: Manchester University Press, 1969a, pp. 1-50.

_____. "Urbanization, Detribalization, Stabilization, and Urban Commitment in Southern Africa: A Problem of Definition and Measurement." In *Urbanism, Urbanization, and Change: Comparative Perspectives,* edited by Paul Meadows and Ephraim H. Mizruchi. Don Mills: Addison-Wesley, 1969b, pp. 470-93.

Molotch, Harvey. "The City as a Growth Machine: Toward a Political Economy of Place." *American Journal of Sociology* 82 (1976): 309-32.

Montero, Gloria. *The Immigrants.* Toronto: James Lorimer and Company, 1977.

Monu, Erasmus D. *Rural Migrants in an Urban Community: A Study of Migrants from the Interlake Region of Manitoba in Winnipeg and Brandon.* M.A. thesis, University of Manitoba, 1969.

Moore, William. *The Vertical Ghetto.* New York: Random House, 1969.

Morah, Benson C. *The Assimilation of Ugandan Asians in Calgary.* M.A. thesis, University of Calgary, 1974.

Morehouse III, Ward. " 'New Gentry' Drama on Urban Stage." *The Christian Science Monitor* (February 7, 1979): 6.

Morris, R. N. *Urban Sociology.* London: George Allen and Unwin, 1968.

Morton, W. L. *Manitoba: A History.* Toronto: University of Toronto Press, 1957.

Mumford, Lewis. *The City in History.* New York: Harcourt, Brace and World, 1961.

––––––. "Neighborhood and Neighborhood Unit." In *The Urban Prospect.* New York: Harcourt, Brace and World, 1968, pp. 56-78.

––––––. "Suburbia: The End of a Dream." In *The End of Innocence: A Suburban Reader,* edited by Charles M. Haar. Glenview: Scott Foresman and Co., 1972, pp. 5-8.

Munson, Byron. "Attitudes Toward Urban and Suburban Residence in Indianapolis." *Social Forces* 35 (1956): 76-80.

Murdie, R. A. *Factorial Ecology of Metropolitan Toronto.* Research Paper, No. 116. Chicago: University of Chicago, Department of Geography, 1969.

Nader, George A. *Cities of Canada. Volume One: Theoretical, Historical and Planning Perspectives.* Toronto: Macmillan of Canada, 1975.

Nagata, Judith A. "Adaptation and Integration of Greek Working Class Immigrants in the City of Toronto, Canada: A Situational Approach." *International Migration Review* 4 (1969): 44-70.

Nagler, Mark. *Indians in the City: A Study of the Urbanization of Indians in Toronto.* Ottawa: Canadian Research Centre for Anthropology, 1970.

Nann, Richard. "Relocation of Vancouver's Chinatown Residents Under Urban Renewal." *Journal of Sociology and Social Welfare* 3 (1975): 125-30.

Nease, Barbara J. S. *An Ecological Approach to the Measurement of Juvenile Delinquency in Hamilton.* M.S.W. thesis, University of Toronto, 1965.

Newman, William M. *American Pluralism: A Study of Minority Groups and Social Theory.* New York: Harper and Row, 1973.

Nicholson, T. G., and M. H. Yeates. "The Ecological and Spatial Structure of the Socio-Economic Characteristics of Winnipeg, 1961." *Canadian Review of Sociology and Anthropology* 6 (1969): 172-78.

Nisbet, Robert A. *The Sociological Tradition.* New York: Basic Books, 1966.

Noble, E. J. "Entrepreneurship and Nineteenth Century Urban Growth: A Case Study of Orillia, Ontario, 1867-1898. *Urban History Review* 9 (1980): 64-89.

Nohara, Shigeo. "Social Context and Neighborliness: The Negro in St. Louis."

In *The New Urbanization*, edited by Scott Greer *et al.* New York: St. Martin's Press, 1968, pp. 179-88.

Nowlan, David, and Nadine Nowlan. *The Bad Trip: The Untold Story of the Spadina Expressway.* Toronto: New Press, 1970.

Oberlander, H. Peter. *Canada: An Urban Agenda. A Collection of Papers.* Ottawa: Community Planning Press, 1976.

Obright, Douglas C. *The Residential Location Decision: A Study of Four Operationally Defined Residential Areas Within Ten Miles of Downtown Kingston.* M.A. thesis, Queen's University, 1973.

Odum, Howard W. "Folk Sociology as a Subject Field for the Historical Study of Total Human Society and the Empirical Study of Group Behavior." *Social Forces* 31 (1953): 193-223.

Orleans, Peter. "Robert Park and Social Area Analysis: A Convergence of Traditions in Urban Sociology." *Urban Affairs Quarterly* 1 (1966): 5-19.

Ossenberg, Richard T. "The Social Integration and Adjustment of Post-War Immigrants in Montreal and Toronto." In *Canada: A Sociological Profile*, edited by W. E. Mann. 2d ed. Toronto: Copp Clark, 1971, pp. 49-58.

Osterreich, Helgi. "Geographical Mobility and Kinship: A Canadian Example." In *The Canadian Family*, edited by K. Ishwaran. Toronto: Holt, Rinehart and Winston, 1971, 434-47.

Pahl, R. E. "A Perspective on Urban Sociology." In *Readings in Urban Sociology.* Toronto: Pergamon Press, 1960, pp. 3-44.

_____. *Patterns in Urban Life.* New York: Humanities Press, 1970.

Park, Robert. "Human Migration and The Marginal Man." *American Journal of Sociology* 33 (1928): 881-93.

_____. *Human Communities.* New York: Free Press, 1952, pp. 178-209.

_____. "Human Ecology." In *Studies in Human Ecology*, edited by George A. Theodorson. New York: Harper and Row, 1961, pp. 22-29.

_____. "The City: Suggestions for the Investigation of Human Behavior in the Urban Environment." In *The City*, edited by Robert Park and Ernest W. Burgess. Chicago: University of Chicago Press, 1967 ed., pp. 1-46.

Park, Robert, and Ernest W. Burgess. *Introduction to the Science of Sociology*, abridged by Morris Janowitz. Chicago: University of Chicago Press, 1970 ed.

Parsons, Talcott. "The Social Structure of the Family." In *The Family: Its Function and Destiny*, edited by Ruth Nanda Ansha. New York: Harper and Row, 1959, pp. 241-74.

_____. "Age and Sex in the Social Structure of the United States." In *Essays in Sociological Papers.* New York: Free Press, 1964a, pp. 89-103.

_____. "The Kinship System of the Contemporary United States." In *Essays in Sociological Theory.* New York: Free Press, 1964b, pp. 177-96.

Passin, Herbert, and John Bennett. "Changing Agricultural Magic in Southern Illinois: A Systematic Analysis of Folk-Urban Transition." *Social Forces* 22 (1943): 98-106.

Perry, Clarence Arthur. *The Neighborhood Unit*. New York: Regional Plan of New York, Vol. 7, 1929, pp. 22-140.

Petersen, William. *Planned Migration: The Social Determinants of the Dutch-Canadian Movement*. Berkeley: University of California Press, 1955.

_____. "A General Typology of Migration." *American Sociological Review* 23 (1958): 256-66.

_____. "The Ideological Background to Canada's Immigration." In *Canadian Society*, edited by B. Blishen *et al*. Toronto: Macmillan, 1965, pp. 38-52.

Petroff, Lillian. "Macedonians in Toronto: From Encampment to Settlement." *Urban History Review* 2-78 (1978): 58-73.

Peucker, Thomas K., and Wolf D. Rase, "A Factorial Ecology of Greater Vancouver." In *Contemporary Geography: Western Perspectives*, edited by Roger Leigh. B.C. Geographical Series, No. 12, Occasional Papers in Geography. Vancouver: Tantalus Research Limited, 1971, pp. 81-96.

Pfautz, Harold. "Charles Booth: Sociologist of the City." In *Charles Booth on the City: Physical Pattern and Social Structure. Selected Writings*. Chicago: University of Chicago Press, 1967, pp. 3-170.

Philpott, Stuart B. "Remittance Obligations, Social Network and Choice Among Montserratian Migrants in Britain." *Man* 3 (1968): 465-76.

Pickvance, C. G. *Urban Sociology: Critical Essays*. London: Tavistock, 1976.

Piddington, Ralph. "The Kinship Network Among French Canadians." *International Journal of Comparative Sociology* 6 (1965): 145-65.

Pineo, Judith A. *Residential Mobility and Migration*. M.A. thesis, University of Toronto, 1968.

Pineo, Peter. "The Extended Family in a Working-Class Area of Hamilton." In *Canadian Society*, edited by B. Blishen *et al*. Toronto: Macmillan, 1965, pp. 135-45.

_____. *Basic Characteristics of a Neighbourhood: Preliminary Report. North End Study*. Unpublished report, 1966.

Piva, Michael J. *The Condition of the Working Class in Toronto 1900-1921*. Ph.D. dissertation, Concordia University, 1975.

Popenoe, David. *The Suburban Environment: Sweden and the United States*. Chicago: University of Chicago Press, 1977.

Poplin, Dennis E. *Communities*. New York: Macmillan, 1972.

Porter, John. *The Vertical Mosaic*. Toronto: University of Toronto Press, 1965.

Pressman, Norman E. P. *Planning New Communities in Canada*. Ottawa: Ministry of State for Urban Affairs, 1975.

_____. *Exploring Planned Environments. Contact* 8 (1976).

Price, John A. "U.S. and Canadian Indian Urban Ethnic Institutions." *Urban Anthropology* 4 (1975): 25-52.

Prince, Raymond. "Urban Renewal: The Modern Juggernaut." *Canada's Mental Health* 15 (1967): 14-20.

Purcell, John W. *English Sport and Canadian Culture in Toronto 1867-1911.* Master of Physical Education thesis, University of Windsor, 1974.

Radecki, Henry. *Ethnic Organizational Dynamics: A Study of the Polish Group in Canada.* Ph.D. dissertation, York University, 1975.

Rainwater, Lee. *Behind Ghetto Walls: Black Families in a Federal Slum.* Chicago: Aldine Publishing Co., 1970.

Rawson, Mary. *Ill Fares the Land.* Ottawa: Ministry of State for Urban Affairs, 1976.

Ray, D. Michael. "From Factorial to Canonical Ecology: The Spatial Inter-relationships of Economic and Cultural Differences in Canada." *Economic Geography* 47 (1971): 344-55.

_____. *Canadian Urban Trends. Volume 1. National Perspective.* Toronto: Copp Clark, 1976.

Ray, D. Michael, and Robert A. Murdie. "Canadian and American Urban Dimensions." In *City Classification Handbook: Methods and Applications,* edited by Brian J. L. Berry. Toronto: John Wiley and Sons, 1972, pp. 181-210.

Ray, Michael, and Roger Roberge. "The Pattern of Post-War Urban Growth: Multinationals as City and Regional Planners." *City Magazine Annual 1981.* Vol. 5, 1, pp. 14-24.

Redfield, Robert. *Tepoztlan: A Mexican Village.* Chicago: University of Chicago Press, 1930.

_____. *The Folk Culture of Yucatan.* Chicago: University of Chicago Press, 1941.

_____. "The Folk Society." *American Journal of Sociology* 52 (1947): 293-308.

_____. "The Natural History of the Folk Society." *Social Forces* 31 (1953): 224-28.

Reed, Paul. "Situated Interaction: Normative and Non-Normative Bases of Social Behavior in Two Urban Residential Settings." *Urban Life and Culture* 2 (1974): 460-87.

Rees, Philip H. "Concepts of Social Space: Toward an Urban Social Geography." In *Geographic Perspectives on Urban Systems,* edited by Brian J. Berry and Frank E. Horton. Englewood Cliffs, N.J.: Prentice-Hall, 1970, pp. 307-94.

_____. "Factorial Ecology: An Extended Definition, Survey, and Critique of the Field." *Economic Geography* 47 (1971): 220-33.

Rees-Powell, Alan. "Differentials in the Integration Process of Dutch and Italian Immigrants in Edmonton, Canada." *International Migration* 4 (1966): 100-113.

Rego, Assumpta B. *Some Aspects of the Migration of Young Working Adults in Southwestern Ontario with Special Reference to London.* M.A. thesis, University of Western Ontario, 1969.

Reid, Frederick L. *The Supply of Immigrants to Canadian Cities: 1921-1961.* M.A. thesis, Queen's University, 1973.

Reisman, David. "The Suburban Dislocation." In *Abundance for What?* New York: Doubleday, 1964, pp. 226-57.

Reiss, Albert, Jr. "An Analysis of Urban Phenomena." In *The Metropolis in Modern Life,* edited by Robert M. Fisher. New York: Russell and Russell, 1955, pp. 41-51.

Repo, Marjaleena. "The Fallacy of 'Community Control'." In *Making It: The Canadian Dream,* edited by Bryan Finnigan and Cy Gonick. Toronto: McClelland and Stewart, 1972, pp. 524-44.

Report of the Royal Commission on Bilingualism and Biculturalism. Ottawa: Queen's Printer, 1967.

Report of the Federal Task Force on Housing and Urban Development. Ottawa: Queen's Printer, 1969.

Richler, Mordecai. *Son of a Smaller Hero.* London: Andre Deutsch, 1955.

_____. *The Street: A Memoir.* London: Weidenfeld and Nicolson, 1969.

Richmond, Anthony H. "The Standard of Living of Post-War Immigrants in Canada." *Canadian Review of Sociology and Anthropology,* 2 (1965): 41-51.

_____. *Post-War Immigrants in Canada.* Toronto: University of Toronto Press, 1967a.

_____. *Immigrants and Ethnic Groups in Metropolitan Toronto.* Toronto: York University, Institute for Behavioural Research, 1967b.

_____. "Immigration and Pluralism in Canada." *International Migration Review* 4 (1969): 5-24.

_____. *Ethnic Residential Segregation in Metropolitan Toronto.* Toronto: York University, Institute for Behavioural Research, 1972.

Richmond, Anthony H., and John Goldlust. *Family and Social Integration of Immigrants in Toronto.* Toronto: York University, Ethnic Research Programme, 1977.

Rigby, Douglas W. *Citizen Participation in Urban Renewal Planning: A Case Study of an Inner City Residents' Association.* Ph.D. dissertation, University of Waterloo, 1975.

Rioux, Marcel. *Kinship Recognition and Urbanization in French Canada.* Bulletin No. 173. Ottawa: National Museum of Canada, 1961, pp. 1-11.

Robertson, R. W. "Anatomy of a Renewal Scheme." In *Residential and Neighbourhood Studies in Victoria,* edited by C. N. Forward. Western Geographical Series, Vol. 5. Victoria: University of Victoria, Department of Geography, 1973, pp. 40-100.

Robineault, Gilles. *Social Area Analysis of Metropolitan Ottawa.* M.A. thesis, Carleton University, 1970.

Robinson, J. Lewis, and Walter G. Hardwick. *British Columbia: One Hundred Years of Geographical Change.* Vancouver: Talonbooks, 1973.

Roper, Marion Wesley. "The City and the Primary Group." In *Contributions to Urban Sociology*, edited by E. W. Burgess and D. J. Bogue. Chicago: University of Chicago Press, 1964, pp. 231-45.

Rose, Albert. *Regent Park: A Study in Slum Clearance.* Toronto: University of Toronto Press, 1958.

————. "Crisis in Urban Renewal." *Habitat* 11 (1968): 2-8.

————. *Governing Metropolitan Toronto: A Social and Political Analysis, 1953-1971.* Berkeley: University of California Press, 1972.

Rosenberg, George S., and Donald F. Anspach. *Working Class Kinship.* Lexington, Mass.: Lexington Books, 1973.

Ross, John H. *Urban Vacation Hinterlands: Four British Columbia Cities as Examples.* M.A. thesis, University of Victoria, 1969.

Rossi, Peter H. *Why Families Move.* Glencoe: Free Press, 1955.

Rowley, Gwyn. " 'Plus Ca Change . . .': A Canadian Skid Row." *Canadian Geographer* 22 (1978): 211-24.

Roy, Gabrielle. *The Tin Flute.* Toronto: McClelland and Stewart, 1969 ed.

Rush, G. B., and J. H. Mansfield. *Apprenticeship for Adulthood: Growing Up in Shore City.* Unpublished manuscript, 1973.

Rutherford, Paul. *Saving the Canadian City: The First Phase 1880-1920.* Toronto: University of Toronto Press, 1974.

————. "Tomorrow's Metropolis: The Urban Reform Movement in Canada, 1880-1920." In *The Canadian City: Essays in Urban History*, edited by Gilbert A. Stelter and Alan F. J. Artibise. Toronto: McClelland and Stewart, 1977, pp. 368-92.

Ruzicka, Stanley E. *The Decline of Victoria as the Metropolitan Centre of British Columbia, 1885-1901.* M.A. thesis, University of Victoria, 1973.

Safa, Helen Icken. "Puerto Ricans' Adaptations to the Urban Milieu." In *Race, Change, and Urban Society*, edited by Peter Orleans and William Russell Ellis, Jr. Beverly Hills: Sage, 1971, pp. 153-90.

Salins, Peter D. "Household Location Patterns in American Metropolitan Areas." *Economic Geography* 47 (1971): 234-47.

Saunders, Robert E. "What Was the Family Compact?" *Ontario History* 49 (1957): 165-78.

Schellenberg, Arnold. *A Study of Acculturation Proneness of an Ethnic Subculture Within an Urban Community: Mennonite Musicians in Winnipeg.* M.A. thesis, University of Manitoba, 1968.

Scheu, William J. *The Effects of Residential Opportunity Structures on Participation Patterns in Voluntary Organizations.* Ph.D. dissertation, University of British Columbia, 1975.

Schmid, Calvin F., Earle H. MacCannell, and Maurice D. Van Arsdol, Jr. "The Ecology of the American City: Further Comparison and Validation of Generalizations." *American Sociological Review* 23 (1958): 392-401.

Schmidt, Martin. *Residential Differentiation and Life Styles.* M.A. thesis, University of British Columbia: Department of Geography, 1975.

Schneider, David M., and George C. Homans. "Kinship Terminology and the American Kinship System." *American Anthropologist* 57 (1955): 1194-1208.

Schnore, Leo F. *The Urban Scene: Human Ecology and Demography.* New York: Free Press, 1965a.

_____. "On the Spatial Structure of Cities in the Two Americas." In *The Study of Urbanization*, edited by Philip M. Hauser and Leo F. Schnore. New York: John Wiley and Sons, 1965b, pp. 347-98.

_____. *Class and Race in Cities and Suburbs.* Chicago: Markham, 1972.

Schnore, Leo F., and Gene B. Petersen. "Urban and Metropolitan Development in the United States and Canada." *The Annals* 316 (1958): 60-68.

Schwartz, Toni. *Acculturation and Integration: Indian Students and Winnipeg.* M.A. thesis, University of Manitoba, 1973.

Schwirian. Kent P. "Analytical Convergence in Economical Research: Factorial Research, Gradient and Sector Models." In *Models of Urban Structure*, edited by David C. Sweet. Lexington: Lexington Books, 1972, pp. 135-58.

Science Council of Canada. *Cities for Tomorrow: Some Applications of Science and Technology to Urban Development.* Report No. 14. Ottawa: Information Canada, 1971.

Scobie, James R. *Buenos Aires: Plaza to Suburb, 1870-1910.* New York: Oxford University Press, 1974.

Seabrook, Thomas G. *The Nature of Attachments of Residents to Their Neighbourhood.* M.A. thesis, McGill University, 1964.

Seeley, John. "The Slum: Its Nature, Use, and Users." *Journal of the American Institute of Planners* 25 (1969): 7-14.

Seeley, John, A. Alexander Sim, and E. W. Loosley. *Crestwood Heights.* Toronto: University of Toronto Press, 1956.

Seifried, N. "The Expanding Urban Economy of a Spontaneous Growth Centre: Edmonton, Alberta." *The Albertan Geographer* 14 (1978): 105-16.

Sennett, Richard. *Families Against the City: Middle Class Families of Industrial Chicago: 1872-1890.* Cambridge: Harvard University Press, 1970.

Sesay, Chernoh M. *The Role of Private Land Developers in the Decision-Making Process in the Regional Municipality of Ottawa-Carleton: A Test of Lorimer's Hypothesis That Private Land Developers Run City Hall.* Ph.D. dissertation, Carleton University, 1978.

Sewell, John. *Up Against City Hall.* Toronto: James Lewis and Samuel, 1972.

Shannon, Lyle W., and Magdaline Shannon. "The Assimilation of Migrants to Cities." In *Social Science and the City: A Survey of Urban Research*, edited by Leo F. Schnore. New York: Praeger Publishers, 1968, pp. 49-75.

Sharp, Harry, and Morris Axelrod. "Mutual Aid Among Relatives in an Urban Population." In *Principles of Sociology*, edited by Ronald Freedman *et al.* New York: Henry Holt and Co., 1956.

Shevky, Eshref, and Marilyn Williams. *The Social Areas of Los Angeles.* Berkeley: University of California, 1949.

Shevky, Eshref, and Wendell Bell. *Social Area Analysis.* Stanford: Stanford University Press, 1955.

Shils, Edward A. "The Study of the Primary Group." In *The Policy Sciences,* edited by Daniel Lerner and Harold Lasswell. Stanford: Stanford University Press, 1951, pp. 44-69.

_____. "Primordial, Personal, Sacred, and Civil Ties." *British Journal of Sociology* 8 (1957): 130-45.

Shorter, Edward. *The Making of the Modern Family.* New York: Basic Books, 1975.

Shrimpton, Mark. *Urban Ecological Differentiation and Patterns of Social Visiting: A Case Study of St. John's, Newfoundland.* M.A. thesis, Memorial University, 1975.

Shulman, Norman. *Mutual Aid and Neighboring Patterns: The Lower Town Study,* 1967.

_____. *Urban Social Networks: An Investigation of Personal Networks in an Urban Setting.* Ph.D. dissertation, University of Toronto, 1972.

_____. "Life Cycle Variations in Patterns of Close Relationships." *Journal of Marriage and the Family* (1975), 813-21.

_____. "Role Differentiation in Urban Networks." *Sociological Focus* 9 (1976): 149-58.

Shuval, Judith Tannenbaum. *Class and Ethnicity: A Study in Community Structure and Interpersonal Relations.* Ph.D. dissertation, Radcliffe College, 1955.

_____. "Class and Ethnic Correlates of Casual Neighboring." *American Sociological Review* 21 (1956): 453-58.

Sidel, Ruth. *Families of Fengsheng: Urban Life in China.* London: Penguin Books, 1974.

Sidlofsky, Samuel. *Post-War Immigrants in the Changing Metropolis with Special Reference to Toronto's Italian Population.* Ph.D. dissertation, University of Toronto, 1969.

Simic, Andrei. *The Peasant Urbanites: A Study of Rural-Urban Mobility.* New York: Seminar Press, 1973.

Simmel, Georg. "The Metropolis and Mental Life." In *The Sociology of Georg Simmel,* edited by Kurt H. Wolff. New York: Free Press, 1950a ed., pp. 409-24.

_____. "On the Significance of Numbers for Social Life." In *The Sociology of Georg Simmel,* edited by Kurt H. Wolff. New York: Free Press, 1950b ed., pp. 87-104.

Simmons, James W. "Changing Residence in the City: A Review of Intra-Urban Mobility." *Geographical Review* 58 (1968): 622-51.

_____. *Canada as an Urban System: A Conceptual Framework.* Toronto: University of Toronto, Centre for Urban and Community Studies, Research Paper No. 62, 1974a.

_____. *Patterns of Residential Movement in Metropolitan Toronto.* Toronto: University of Toronto, Department of Geography, 1974b.

Sjoberg, Gideon. "Folk and 'Feudal' Societies." *American Journal of Sociology* 58 (1952): 231-39.

_____. *The Preindustrial City: Past and Present.* New York: Free Press, 1960.

_____. "The Rural-Urban Dimension in Preindustrial, Transitional, and Industrial Societies." In *Handbook of Modern Society,* edited by Robert E. L. Faris. Chicago: Rand McNally, 1964, pp. 127-59.

_____. "The Origin and Evolution of Cities." In *Cities: Their Origin, Growth and Human Impact.* San Francisco: W. H. Freeman, 1973, pp. 19-26.

Slemko, Brian J. *The Recruitment of Local Decision-Makers in Five Canadian Cities: Some Preliminary Findings.* M.A. thesis, Queen's University, 1974.

Smith, Joel, William H. Form, and Gregory P. Stone. "Local Intimacy in a Middle-Sized City." *American Journal of Sociology* 60 (1954): 276-84.

Smith, P. J., and Denis B. Johnson. *The Edmonton-Calgary Corridor.* Calgary: University of Alberta, Department of Geography, 1978.

Snider, Earle, and George Kupfer. "Urbanization In Alberta: A Sociological Perspective." In *Urbanization and Urban Life in Alberta,* edited by R. Gordon McIntosh and Ian E. Housego. Edmonton: Programme Development Unit, Alberta Human Resources Research Council, 1970, pp. 46-60.

Snyder, Peter Z. "The Social Environment of the Urban Indian." In *The American Indian in Urban Society,* edited by Jack O. Waddell and O. Michael Watson. Boston: Little, Brown and Company, 1971, pp. 207-43.

Social Planning Council of Hamilton. *The Social Costs of Urban Renewal.* Hamilton: 1963.

Sorokin, Pitirim, and Carle G. Zimmerman. *Principles of Rural-Urban Sociology.* New York: Kraus Reprint Co., 1969 ed.

Southall, Aidan W. "Introductory Summary." In *Social Change in Modern Africa.* London: Oxford University Press, 1961, pp. 1-66.

Spaulding, J. A. "Serendipity and the Rural-Urban Continuum." *Rural Sociology* 16 (1951): 29-36.

Spectorsky, A. C. *The Exurbanites.* Philadelphia: J. B. Lippincott, 1955.

Spelt, Jacob. *Urban Development in South-Central Ontario.* Toronto: McClelland and Stewart, 1972.

Spurr, Peter. *Land and Urban Development: A Preliminary Study.* Toronto: James Lorimer and Company, 1976.

Srinias, M. N., and Andre Bereille. "Networks in Indian Social Structure." *Man* 64 (1964): 165-68.

Stack, Carol B. *All Our Kin: Strategies for Survival in a Black Community.* New York: Harper and Row, 1974.

Stamp, Robert. "The Response to Urban Growth: The Bureaucratization of Public Education in Calgary, 1884-1914." In *The Canadian City: Essays in*

Urban History, edited by Gilbert A. Stelter and Alan F. J. Artibise. Toronto: McClelland and Stewart, 1977, pp. 282-99.

Stanbury, W. T. *Success and Failure: Indians in Urban Society*. Vancouver: University of British Columbia Press, 1975.

Statistics Canada. *Perspective Canada II. A Compendium of Social Statistics 1977*. Ottawa: Minister of Supply and Services Canada, 1977.

————. *Canada's Cities*. Ottawa: 1980.

Stein, Maurice. *The Eclipse of Community*. New York: Harper, 1965.

Stelter, Gilbert A. "The Urban Frontier in Canadian History." In *Cities in the West*, edited by A. R. McCormack and Ian MacPherson. Ottawa: National Museum of Man, 1975, pp. 270-86.

Stelter, Gilbert A., and Alan F. J. Artibise. *The Canadian City: Essays in Urban History*. Toronto: McClelland and Stewart, 1977.

Stevenson, A., E. Martin, and J. O'Neill. *High Living: A Study of Family Life in Flats*. Melbourne: Melbourne University Press, 1967.

Stewart, John N. *et al. Urban Indicators: Quality of Life Comparisons for Canadian Cities*. Ministry of State for Urban Affairs. Ottawa: Information Canada, 1976.

Stone, Gregory P. "City Shoppers and Urban Identification: Observations of the Social Psychology of City Life." *American Journal of Sociology* 60 (1954): 36-45.

Stone, Leroy O. *Urban Development in Canada*. Ottawa: Queen's Printer, 1967.

————. *Migration in Canada: Some Regional Aspects*. Ottawa: Dominion Bureau of Statistics, 1969.

————. "What We Know About Migration Within Canada—A Selective Review and Agenda for Future Research." *International Migration Review* (1974): 267-81.

Stone, Leroy O., and Andrew J. Siggner. *The Population of Canada: A Review of the Recent Patterns and Trends*. Ottawa: Statistics Canada, CICRED Series, 1974.

Storrie, Kathleen. *The Integration of Rural Male Migrants Into an Urban Community*. M.A. thesis, Dalhousie University, 1968.

Strauss, Anselm L. "Strategies for Discovering Urban Theory." In *Urban Research and Policy Planning*, edited by Leo F. Schnore and Henry Fagin. Beverly Hills: Sage Publications, 1967, 74-99.

Stretton, Hugh. *Urban Planning in Rich and Poor Countries*. Oxford: Oxford University Press, 1978.

Sturino, Franc. "A Case Study of a South Italian Family in Toronto, 1935-60." *Urban History Review* 2-78 (1978): 38-57.

Stymeist, David H. *Ethnics and Indians: Social Relations in a Northwestern Ontario Town*. Toronto: Peter Martin Associates, 1975.

Sussman, Marvin B. "The Help Pattern in the Middle Class Family." *American Sociological Review* 18 (1953): 22-28.

_____. "The Isolated Nuclear Family: Fact or Fiction." *Social Forces* 6 (1959): 333-40.

Sussman, Marvin B., and Lee Burchinal. "Kin Family Network." In *Marriage and Family in the Modern World*, edited by Ruth S. Cavan. New York: Thomas Y. Crowell, 1969, pp. 353-65.

Sutter, Ruth E. *The Next Place You Come To: A Historical Introduction to Communities in North America*. Englewood Cliffs: Prentice-Hall, 1973.

Suttles, Gerald D. *The Social Order of the Slum*. Chicago: University of Chicago Press, 1968.

_____. *The Social Construction of Communities*. Chicago: University of Chicago Press, 1972.

Taeuber, Karl, and Alma F. Taeuber. *Negroes in Cities: Residential Segregation and Neighborhood Change*. Chicago: Aldine Publishing Co., 1965.

Taraska, Elizabeth A. *The Calgary Craft Union Movement, 1900-1920*. M.A. thesis, University of Calgary, 1975.

Tarasoff, Koozma J. *A Study of Russian Organizations in the Greater Vancouver Area*. M.A. thesis, University of British Columbia, 1963.

Tax, Sol. "Culture and Civilization in Guatemalan Society." *Scientific Monthly* 48 (1939): 463-67.

_____. "World View and Social Relations in Guatemala." *American Anthropologist* 43 (1941): 27- 42.

Thomas, William I., and Florian Znaniecki. *The Polish Peasant in Europe and America*. New York: Dover, 1958 ed.

Thomas, William I., Robert Park, and Herbert A. Miller. *Old World Traits Transplanted*. Montclair: Patterson Smith, 1971 ed.

Thomlinson, Ralph. *Urban Structure: The Social and Spatial Character of Cities*. New York: Random House, 1969.

Thompson, E. P. *The Making of the English Working Class*. London: Victor Gollancz, 1964.

Thrasher, Frederick M. *The Gang*. Chicago: University of Chicago Press, 1963 ed.

Tilly, Charles, and C. Harold Brown. "On Uprooting, Kinship, and the Auspices of Migration." *International Journal of Comparative Sociology* 8 (1967): 139-64.

Timms, Duncan. *The Urban Mosaic: Toward a Theory of Residential Differentiation*. Cambridge: At the University Press, 1971.

Tisdale, Hope. "The Process of Urbanization." *Social Forces* 20 (1942): 311-21.

Toennies, Ferdinand. *Community and Society*, translated and edited by Charles P. Loomis. New York: Harper, 1963 ed.

Tomasi, Lydio F. "The Italian Community in Toronto: A Demographic Profile." *International Migration Review* 11 (1977): 486-513.

Tomeh, Aida K. "Informal Group Participation and Residential Patterns." *American Journal of Sociology* 70 (1964): 28-35.

_____. "Informal Participation in a Metropolitan Community." *Sociological Quarterly* 8 (1967): 85-102.

Tuan, Yi-Fu. *Topophilia*. Englewood Cliffs: Prentice-Hall, 1974.

Turrittin, Jane Sawyer. "Networks and Mobility: The Case of West Indian Domestics from Montserrat." *Canadian Review of Sociology and Anthropology* 13 (1976) 305-20.

Udry, J. Richard. "Increasing Scale and Spatial Differentiation: New Tests of Two Theories from Shevky and Bell." *Social Forces* 42 (1964): 403-13.

Useem, Ruth Hill, John Useem, and Duane L. Gibson. "The Function of Neighboring for the Middle-Class Male." *Human Organization* 19 (1960): 68-76.

Vallee, Frank G., Mildred Schwartz, and Frank Darknell. "Ethnic Assimilation and Differentiation in Canada." In *Canadian Society*, edited by B. Blishen *et al.* Toronto: Macmillan, 1965, pp. 63-73.

Van Arsdol, Maurice, Santo Camilleri, and Calvin F. Schmid. "The Generality of Urban Social Area Indexes." *American Sociological Review* 23 (1958): 277-84.

Van Nus, Walter. "The Fate of City Beautiful Thought in Canada, 1893-1930." In *The Canadian City: Essays in Urban History*, edited by Gilbert A. Stelter and Alan F. J. Artibise. Toronto: McClelland and Stewart, 1977, pp. 162-85.

Villeneuve, P. Y. "Changes Over Time in the Residential and Occupational Structures of an Urban Ethnic Minority." In *Contemporary Geography: Western Viewpoints*. B.C. Geographical Series, No. 12. Occasional Papers in Geography, edited by Roger Leigh. Vancouver: Tantalus Research Limited, 1971, pp. 115-28.

Vogel, Ezra F. *Japan's New Middle Class: The Salary Man and His Family in a Tokyo Suburb*. Berkeley: University of California Press, 1971.

Voget, Fred W. "The Folk Society—An Anthropological Application." *Social Forces* 33 (1954): 105-13.

Voisey, Paul L. "Two Chinese Communities in Alberta: An Historical Perspective." *Canadian Ethnic Studies* 2 (1970): 15-30.

Walhouse, Freda. *The Influence of Minority Ethnic Groups on the Cultural Geography of Vancouver*. M.A. thesis, University of British Columbia, 1961.

Ward, David. *Cities and Immigrants: A Geography of Change in Nineteenth-Century America*. New York: Oxford University Press, 1971.

Warner, Sam Bass. *Streetcar Suburbs*. Cambridge: Harvard University Press, 1962.

_____. *The Private City*. Philadelphia: University of Pennsylvania Press, 1968.

Watkins, M. H. "A Staple Theory of Economic Growth." In *Approaches to Canadian Economic History*, edited by W. T. Easterbrook and M. H. Watkins. Toronto: McClelland and Stewart, 1967, pp. 49-73.

Wayne, Jack. *Networks of Informal Participation in a Suburban Context.* Ph.D. dissertation, University of Toronto, 1971.

_____. "The Case of the Friendless Urbanite." In *The City: Attacking Modern Myths,* edited by Alan Powell. Toronto: McClelland and Stewart, 1972, pp. 80-92.

Weaver, John C. "Tomorrow's Metropolis: The Urban Reform Movement in Canada, 1880-1920." In *The Canadian City: Essays in Urban History,* edited by Gilbert A. Stelter and Alan F. J. Artibise. Toronto: McClelland and Stewart, 1977, pp. 393-418.

_____. "From Land Assembly to Social Maturity. The Suburban Life of Westdale (Hamilton), Ontario, 1911-1951." *Social History* 22 (1978): 411-40.

Webber, Melvin M. "The Post-City Age." *Daedalus* 97 (1968): 1091-1110.

_____. "Order in Diversity: Community Without Propinquity." In *Environmental Psychology,* edited by Harold M. Proshansky *et al.* New York: Holt, Rinehart and Winston, 1970, pp. 533-49.

Weber, Adna. *The Growth of Cities in the Nineteenth-Century.* Ithaca: Cornell University Press, 1963 ed.

Weber, Max. *The City,* translated and edited by Don Martindale and Gertrud Neuwirth. New York: Free Press, 1958.

Weir, Thomas R. *Atlas of Winnipeg.* Toronto: University of Toronto Press, 1978.

Wellman, Barry. *The Network Nature of Future Communities: A Predictive Synthesis.* University of Toronto: Centre for Urban and Community Studies, Research Paper No. 58, 1973.

_____. *The Community Question: The Intimate Networks of East Yorkers.* Toronto: University of Toronto, Centre for Urban and Community Studies and Department of Sociology, 1978. (See also *American Journal of Sociology* 84 (1979): 1201-31.)

Wellman, Barry *et al. The Uses of Community: Community Ties and Support Systems.* University of Toronto: Centre for Urban and Community Studies, 1971.

Whyte, Donald R. "Rural Canada in Transition." In *Rural Canada in Transition,* edited by Marc-Adelard Tremblay and Walton J. Anderson. Ottawa: Agricultural Economics Research Council of Canada, 1966, pp. 1-113.

_____. "Social Determinants of Inter-Community Mobility." *Canadian Review of Sociology and Anthropology* 4 (1967): 1-23.

Whyte, William H. *The Organization Man.* New York: Doubleday, 1957.

_____. "Urban Sprawl." In *The Exploding Metropolis,* edited by *Fortune.* New York: Doubleday, 1958, pp. 115-39.

Wiesman, Brahm. "A New Agenda for Our Cities." In *Canada: An Urban Agenda. A Collection of Papers,* edited by H. Peter Oberlander. Ottawa: Community Planning Press, 1976, pp. 11-43.

Willhelm, Sidney M. "The Concept of the 'Ecological Complex': A Critique." In *Urbanism, Urbanization, and Change: Comparative Perspectives*, edited by Paul Meadows and Ephraim H. Mizruchi. Don Mills: Addison-Wesley, 1969, pp. 106-12.

Williamson, T. Morgan. *Blackhead Road: A Community Study in Urban Renewal*. M.A. thesis, Memorial University, 1971.

Willmott, Peter, and Michael Young. *Family and Class in a London Suburb*. London: Routledge and Kegan Paul, 1960.

Wirth, Louis. Urbanism as a Way of Life." *American Journal of Sociology* 44 (1938): 1-24.

―――. "Human Ecology." *American Journal of Sociology* 50 (1945): 483-88.

―――. *Louis Wirth: On Cities and Social Life*, edited by Albert J. Reiss, Jr. Chicago: University of Chicago Press, 1964.

Wiseman, Adele. *The Sacrifice*. New York: Viking Press, 1956.

Wong, S.T. "Urban Redevelopment and Rehabilitation in the Strathcona Area: A Case Study of an East Vancouver Community. In *Vancouver: Western Metropolis*, edited by L. J. Evenden. Western Geographical Series, Vol. 16. Victoria: University of Victoria, Department of Geography, 1978, pp. 255-69.

Woodsworth, J. S. *My Neighbor*. Toronto: University of Toronto Press, 1972 ed.

Wynn, Graeme. "Industrialism, Entrepreneurship, and Opportunity in the New Brunswick Timber Trade." In *The Enterprising Canadians: Entrepreneurs and Economic Development in Eastern Canada, 1820-1914*, edited by Lewis R. Fischer and Eric W. Sager. St. John's: Memorial University of Newfoundland: Maritime History Group, 1979, pp. 7-22.

Yam, Joseph. "The Size and Geographic Distribution of Canada's Jewish Population (Preliminary Observation)." *Canadian Jewish Population Studies* 3 (1974): 1-31.

Yancey, William L., Eugene P. Ericksen, and Richard N. Juliani. "Emergent Ethnicity: A Review and Reformulation." *American Sociological Review* 41 (1976): 391-403.

Yauk, Thomas B. *Residential and Business Relocation from Urban Renewal Areas: A Case Study, the Lord Selkirk Park Experience*. Master of City Planning Thesis, University of Manitoba, 1973.

Yeates, Maurice. *Main Street: Windsor to Quebec City*. Ottawa: Information Canada, 1975.

Yeo, Eileen, and E. P. Thompson. *The Unknown Mayhew*. New York: Pantheon Books, 1971.

Young, E. *Street of T'ongs: Planning in Vancouver's Chinatown*. M.A. thesis, University of British Columbia, 1975.

Young, Frank W., and Ruth Young. "Occupational Role Perceptions in Rural Mexico." *Rural Sociology* 27 (1962): 42-52.

_____. "Individual Commitment to Industrialization in Rural Mexico." *American Journal of Sociology* 71 (1966): 373-83.

Young, Michael, and Peter Willmott. *Family and Kinship in East London.* London: Routledge and Kegan Paul, 1957.

_____. *The Symmetrical Family.* New York: Pantheon Books, 1973.

Yuan, D. Y. "The Rural-Urban Continuum: A Case Study of Taiwan." *Rural Sociology* 29 (1964): 247-60.

Yusuf, Ahmed Beitallah. "A Reconsideration of Urban Conceptions: Hausa Urbanization and the Hausa Rural-Urban Continuum." *Urban Anthropology* 3 (1974): 200-21.

Zelan, Joseph. "Does Suburbia Make a Difference? An Exercise in Secondary Analysis." In *Urbanism in World Perspective: A Reader,* edited by Sylvia Fleis Fava. New York: Thomas Y. Crowell, 1968, pp. 401-8.

Zieber, G. H. "The Dispersed City Hypothesis with Reference to Calgary and Edmonton." *The Albertan Geographer* 9 (1973): 4-13.

_____. "Calgary as an Administrative and Oil Operations Centre." In *Calgary: Metropolitan Structure and Influence,* edited by Brenton M. Barr. Western Geographical Series, Vol. II. Victoria: University of Victoria, Department of Geography, 1975, pp. 77-121.

Ziegler, Suzanna G. *The Adaptation of Italian Immigrants to Toronto: An Analysis.* Ph.D. dissertation, University of Colorado, 1971.

_____. *Characteristics of Italian Householders in Metropolitan Toronto.* Toronto: York University, Institute for Behavioural Research, 1972.

Zinman, Rosaling. *Lachute, Quebec: French-English Frontier: A Case Study in Language and Community.* M.A. thesis, Concordia University, 1975.

Zito, Jacqueline M. "Anonymity and Neighboring in an Urban High-Rise Complex." *Urban Life and Culture* 3 (1974): 243-63.

Zorbaugh, Harvey Warren. *The Gold Coast and the Slum.* Chicago: University of Chicago Press, 1929.

Index